John Matusik

1,4,5,9

SUBURBAN SPRAWL

SUBURBAN SPRAWL

Culture, Theory, and Politics

Edited by
Matthew J. Lindstrom
and
Hugh Bartling

ROWMAN & LITTLEFIELD PUBLISHERS, INC.
Lanham • Boulder • New York • Oxford

ROWMAN & LITTLEFIELD PUBLISHERS, INC.

Published in the United States of America
by Rowman & Littlefield Publishers, Inc.
A Member of the Rowman & Littlefield Publishing Group
4501 Forbes Boulevard, Suite 200, Lanham, Maryland 20706
www.rowmanlittlefield.com

PO Box 317
Oxford
OX2 9RU, UK

Copyright © 2003 by Rowman & Littlefield Publishers, Inc.

All rights reserved. No part of this publication may be reproduced, stored in a retrieval system, or transmitted in any form or by any means, electronic, mechanical, photocopying, recording, or otherwise, without the prior permission of the publisher.

British Library Cataloguing in Publication Information Available

Library of Congress Cataloging-in-Publication Data

Suburban Sprawl : culture, theory, and politics / edited by Matthew J. Lindstrom and Hugh Bartling.
p. cm.
Includes bibliographical references and index.
ISBN 0-7425-2580-5 (alk. paper)—ISBN 0-7425-2581-3 (pbk. : alk. paper)
1. Suburbs—United States. 2. Cities and towns—United States—Growth. 3. Cities and towns—Growth—Environmental aspects—United States. 4. Regional planning—United States. I. Lindstrom, Matthew J., 1969– II. Bartling, Hugh, 1969–
HT352.U5S83 2003
307.74'0973—dc21 2002155820

Printed in the United States of America

∞™ The paper used in this publication meets the minimum requirements of American National Standard for Information Sciences—Permanence of Paper for Printed Library Materials, ANSI/NISO Z39.48-1992.

For Anna and Isaac

—Matt Lindstrom

For Marianne

—Hugh Bartling

Contents

Acknowledgments

Certainly there are many people who contributed to the completion of this anthology. We greatly appreciate the support of our two employers, Siena College and the University of Central Florida. In particular, Matt received research support from the Siena College Program for Sustainable Land Use. Rob Messia and Liz Virga were helpful undergraduate research assistants doing everything from tracking down articles and addresses to reviewing chapters and transcribing interviews. John Lindstrom, Matt's dad, provided frequent clippings and steady encouragement. Hugh thanks Howard Sanborn and David Williamson for their assistance with the interviews. We also greatly appreciate the interest, flexibility, and participation of our excellent contributors and interviewees. Thanks also to Brian Romer, our Rowman & Littlefield editor, for his enthusiastic support of the project, his top-notch professional standards, and his cooperative helpful actions. Finally, we thank our families for their patience, insight, and inspiration. To all listed and to those who are not, we appreciate your support.

Introduction

On November 1, 2002, in an unincorporated section of northern Los Angeles County, John Quigley, an environmental educator from Pacific Palisades, climbed atop an old California oak tree called "Old Glory" by residents of nearby Santa Clarita. Old Glory is situated on property owned by John Laing Homes, who has plans to cut down the 400-year-old tree in order to widen Pico Canyon Road, which would accommodate the traffic generated by their 270-home Stevenson Ranch subdivision and the future development of Newhall Ranch, a neighboring 21,000-home master-planned community. Quigley is critical of municipal governmental decisions to widen the road and, in the process, destroy a magnificent tree, and he is vowing to continue to sit in Old Glory until its preservation is ensured. The effort to save Old Glory, however, is not merely about protecting this one tree. For activists such as Quigley, the destruction of Old Glory would represent the triumph of uncharted development, ecological despoilment, and the general denigration of the quality of life affecting metropolitan communities throughout the country. In the words of one of Quigley's supporters, "It's not just about the tree. It's about all things wild. Every day we lose more and more, especially in the metropolitan area."[1]

Quigley's supporter is right. Fifty-plus years of suburban development characterized by restrictive zoning, automobile-centered transportation, a preponderance of single-family residences on large lots, and government subsidies has resulted in a social, ecological, and economic environment that many people are starting to vigorously question. Massive, extensive land development—more familiarly called "sprawl"—has had dramatic consequences in a number of important cultural and political areas. The title of a recent book, *The Bulldozer and the Countryside,* elicits visions of woods, farms, and meadows being cleared and leveled to make room for paved streets, identical homes, and new subdivisions named after the natural landscapes that were destroyed.

The result of sprawled development has been dramatic on a number of levels. Sprawl is often thought of as a wave of development occurring at the fringes of metropolitan areas. As such, it is a process of shifting the boundary between the urban and the rural outward from established metropolitan areas. The funding of suburban growth and the disinvestment of cities continue to inflict serious social and financial costs on urban residents and governments.

Sprawl also has particular consequences not only for wilderness areas but also for farmland. The American Farmland Trust has found that between 1982 and 1997, the population of the United States increased by 17 percent while the amount of urbanized land grew by 47 percent. Much of the land being urbanized has been and remains agriculturally productive. The American Farmland Trust predicts that if the trend of sprawling expansion continues, much of the country's dairy, fruit, and vegetable production could be in jeopardy.[2] As sprawl continues, farmers find themselves unable to meet their increasing tax burden and adapt to changes in microclimates and ecologies that occur as contiguous development disrupts wildlife habitats, drainage patterns, and the health of aquifers.

Sprawl is also targeted as being a variable in the denigration of "quality of life" in many metropolitan areas. Many critics of sprawl have forcefully argued that the ways we have been developing our suburbs contribute to social isolation. The fact that much of the suburban development over the past fifty years has marginalized pedestrian traffic, public transportation, and spaces of spontaneous civic interaction is often cited as contributing to a general social malaise whereby Americans rarely get to know their neighbors, join civic organizations, or participate in the political process.

While it is important to recognize that these larger trends of social isolation have occurred within the context of globalizing markets, the consolidation of corporate media, and rising income inequalities, our patterns of suburbanization often exacerbate the effects of these larger trends. In introducing his Blue Ribbon Panel to develop solutions for the region's endemic traffic problems, Richard Crotty, chairman of the Orange County, Florida, Board of Commissioners, described traffic gridlock as "a quality of life issue as much as anything else.... When you spend more time in your car than with your kids, it's a crisis."[3] This "crisis" in the way we move throughout metropolitan areas is a major symptom of sprawl. As transportation and land use planners developed systems of mobility based solely on one form of transportation and as restrictive zoning made mixed-use development difficult, traffic congestion has emerged as a major problem in North American metropolitan areas.

Census figures indicate that the national percentage of the population driving to work is expanding while the percentage of the population commuting by public transportation is declining. The 1960 census reported that 12.1 percent used public transportation for commuting and that 64 percent drove an automobile. For 1970, the figures were 8.9 percent for public transportation and 77.7 percent for automobile; in 1980, the respective percentages were 6.4 and 84.1; in 1990, 5.3 and 86.5; and in 2000, 4.7 and 87.9. These figures—particularly when population growth is considered—suggest that there are more single-occupancy vehicles on the road while public transportation use is languishing. One result is more time stuck in traffic for many metropolitan residents and less time engaging in other, socially productive activities.

Sprawled development has other components that pose challenges for policymakers, activists, and citizens concerned about the changing dynamics in their communities. Ecologically, sprawl poses problems for municipal water supplies. Excessive paving and construction reduces groundwater recharge capabilities and contributes to excessive runoff, which can result in persistent flooding. More extensive development brings with it various hazardous materials and compounds that get introduced into water supplies, such as gasoline and oil runoff. More vehicle miles traveled, coupled with congestion, results in undesirable air pollution levels stemming from automobile emissions. Simultaneously, when our suburbs are built to accommodate only motorized vehicles, pedestrian mobility suffers. Lack of walking opportunities contributes to the growing rates of obesity seen in the United States.

The synergy of these trajectories of sprawl contributes to the "crisis" described by County Chairman Crotty. In 2002, Orange County and the Orlando, Florida, metropolitan area were given a grade of "F" by the American Lung Association for its air quality. The region's leaders seriously discussed the idea, popular in the world's desert regions such as the Persian Gulf, of developing desalination plants to supply the area water even though they receive fifty-three inches of rainfall per year and are situated more than fifty miles from the ocean. In addition, the region was rated by the Surface Transportation Policy Project as being the most likely place to be killed as a pedestrian nationwide.[4] To top it off, Crotty's own response to the "crisis" he proclaimed was his purchase of a 2003 Ford Expedition sport utility vehicle nine days after his election victory while simultaneously approving the local public transit system's plan to cut bus routes in underserved parts of the county.[5]

These examples illuminate the seemingly intractable and complex situation that has emerged in a half century of metropolitan development. Suburban sprawl has emerged as a result of conscious political choices whose impacts were either not anticipated or not fully revealed. With the issue of sprawl receiving nationwide attention, effective models of urban in-fill development being devised and implemented, and theories of regionalism being revisited, many believe that we are currently on the cusp of major reform and rethinking of how our metropolitan areas can be rendered more livable. In November 2002, many municipalities and states voted on ballot initiatives to earmark public investment toward growth management and multimodal transportation options. From Bismarck to Miami, from Charlotte to Las Vegas, citizens supported changes to their metropolitan development strategies that could have the potential to transform the dominant sprawl dynamic.

While public sentiment and the rhetoric of political leadership may be changing, it is important to recognize that suburban sprawl did not just emerge "out of the blue." It was the product of conscious decisions, political contestation, and the assertion of social, political, and economic relations of power. In the remainder of this introduction, we will highlight the emergence of sprawl by investigating the historical and cultural context of suburbanization in the twentieth century. This will set the stage for the chapters that make up the rest of this volume. Each author, while having disparate interpretations and explanations for the various ways sprawl manifests itself, nevertheless understands the complexity of our current metropolitan condition and illuminates the challenges for interpreting future metropolitan change.

Exploring the Roots of Sprawl

During the last decade of the nineteenth century, Frederick Jackson Turner made his famous proclamation that the American frontier was closed. The ethic of expansionism, Turner argued, was an essential component in the development of the "American character." Rising above the challenges presented by a hostile environment, the European settler cultivated the individual initiative and ability to pacify nature that contributed to the economic and democratic prosperity of the United States. With the official "closing" of the frontier indicated by the 1890 census, Turner foresaw an uncertain future for the American character and the health of its democracy.

If the nineteenth century was dominated by the myth of the frontier, it could be argued that the twentieth century saw the rise of the "myth of the metropolis." The closing of the frontier was concomitant with the rise of the industrial city, whose exponential growth was accompanied by a host of social, political, economic, and ecological challenges. The city became the symbol and host both of great wealth and great poverty. As the contradictions of the industrial city became more intense, a variety of approaches toward negotiating the emergent complex, urban metropolis were offered from various quarters. Rational planning, cooperative housing, and worker-owned production, among other initiatives, were indicative of the responses presented by critics, academics, and policymakers.

While these initiatives varied in their success and failure, perhaps the most prevalent practical response to the emergent urban challenges of the industrial city was the sustained trend toward suburbanization. Just as Turner argued that the expansion offered by the American frontier set the stage for the development of American social and political culture during the nineteenth century, the expansion of the metropolis in the peculiar form of suburbanization provides the contours of twentieth-century social, political, and, increasingly, ecological development. Thus, the issue of "sprawl" is the function of a variety of fundamental changes to the prevailing social structures of the twentieth century.

Controlling Nature, Mechanization, and Sprawl

For Lewis Mumford, suburbanization in the form of the megalopolization of the metropolis constituted a fundamental shift in the nature of urban habitation and, consequently, had portentous implications for society and the human condition. Technological innovations in transportation, construction, and communication changed the nature of urbanism. This rendered "the removal of quantitative limits . . . [and] marks the change from an organic system to a mechanical system, from purposeful growth to purposeless expansion."[6] Because of the triumph of the machine in the twentieth century, metropolitan development takes on unique and powerful forms that contribute to the emergence of our contemporary sprawling landscape. This "technological triumph" is manifested in a number of ways.

First, the changes in dominant modes of transportation and substantial government subsidies engender "the age of the automobile," allowing the ascendancy of private, individualized transport. The interstate highway system (financed by the federal government under the guise of ensuring national defense), the affordability of the automobile, and the dismantling of metropolitan mass transit systems made the sprawling landscape possible. Transportation—best understood as a series of processes by which people circulate through space in the course of their daily lives—has a dramatic influence on urban possibilities. The industrialized city necessitated intensive use of land that made mass transportation cost effective. Lack of private automobile ownership ensured that demand for public transportation would be significant. However, as automobiles became less expensive and limited-access highways were built to accommodate increasing traffic, the metropolitan fringes became reasonable places to develop residential settlement. Today, of course, the sprawled environment is overwhelmingly the purview of the automobile—residential subdivisions lack sidewalks, municipal zoning codes require substantial parking spaces for new commercial and business development, and road construction and widening receives considerably more public funds than pedestrian and bicycle paths and metropolitan public transportation.[7]

A second mechanistic change has been explored by Adam Rome in his book *The Bulldozer and the Countryside.* As immigration and birthrates increased in the United States during the first half of the twentieth century, the need to adequately shelter a growing populace became a pressing public policy issue. Unsightly and insalubrious tenements dominated the nineteenth-century city, and the incendiary quality of many tenements exacerbated the devastation experienced by many cities as they faced fires, floods, earthquakes, and epidemics. Population pressure, coupled with poor housing conditions, made the development of new housing an urgent task. As Rome points out, innovators such as William Levitt began to wed the mechanistic processes that animated industrial mass production with housing construction. The Levittown developments were characterized by housing built with interchangeable components on land that had been flattened and cleared of much of the existing vegetation. The power of earthmoving machinery, along with the efficiency of mass production, prefigured a whole wave of suburban development that featured homogeneous architectural styles and the relative disregard for the contours of existing landscapes and ecosystems.[8]

The mechanistic impulse of twentieth-century suburbanization can also be thought of in the context of the rise of urban planning and civil engineering as institutionalized scientific endeavors. While both disciplines trace their modern origins to the nineteenth century, their development as definable fields of expertise proliferated as industrialization became more important in the United States. Schools, institutes, professional organizations, and credentialing bodies helped construct urban planning and civil engineering as specialized domains that made planning a scientific, professional endeavor. As with much of modern science, mechanistic metaphors and epistemologies were employed in these new disciplines, and with the imprimatur of expert knowledge, specialists in these fields were able to institute changes to the urbanizing landscape with a degree of authority unmatched by the mass citizenry.

Seeking to impose order on the chaotic elements of the industrial city, the new class of planners, architects, and engineers used the model of the machine, with its elegance, predictability, and symmetry, as the template for a new urbanism. Ebenezer Howard, while not trained as a planner, nevertheless exemplified this new approach in his seminal work *Garden Cities of To-morrow.*[9] For Howard, the garden city was to be a perfectly ordered place where the functions of social life—living, working, consuming, producing, and engaging in civic activity—were to be given their specific place, spatially separated from each other. Significantly, Howard considered himself an "inventor" who had developed plans for a new urban "machine."

This separation of function (housing, business, recreation, industry, education, and government), which was so elegantly presented by Howard, became the template for planning practices that contributed to our contemporary sprawling suburbia. In the United States, municipal zoning laws were developed as a specific response to the chaos of the city, seeking to separate function in the name of order. While New York City's law of 1916 is often cited as the first comprehensive attempt at zoning, it was in suburban areas that zoning restrictions were most aggressively applied.[10] Because the urban fabric of the industrial city had arisen over decades of inhabitance, radical efforts toward separation were unrealistic. Suburban areas, as newly developed enclaves on the edge of industrial cities, were much more amenable to employing restrictive zoning as they were "clean slates." As independent municipal entities, suburbs undertook restrictive zoning, particularly keeping housing from commerce, to ensure health and safety in their towns. The experience of industrial urbanism had taught the new residents of suburbs that the intermingling of functions had deleterious consequences. In suburbia, therefore, planning and control should be imposed at the outset of development. This sentiment is reinforced in the U.S. Supreme Court decision of *The Village of Euclid v. Ambler Realty.*[11] In this decision, which upheld the constitutionality of restricting private property use through zoning, the court favorably quoted an Illinois Supreme Court case that justified zoning as the

> promotion of the health and security from injury of children and others by separating dwelling houses from territory devoted to trade and industry; suppression and prevention of disorder; facilitating the extinguishment of fires, and the enforcement of street traffic regulations and other general welfare ordinances; aiding the health and safety of the community by excluding from residential areas the confusion and danger of fire, contagion and disorder which in greater or less degree attach to the location of stores, shops and factories.

Following this argument, zoning is justified as a method of civic betterment by bringing order through separation. In this logic of separation, a selective component of Howard's vision is institutionalized in the pursuit of supplanting urban chaos with rational planning.

While the rationalization of urban planning was predicated on order, the substantial rate of suburban growth indicative of the post–World War II period brought forth challenges to the wisdom of restrictive zoning. In practice, restrictive zoning in suburbia created the potential for great domains of large-scale development based on a singular function. Because of the widespread use of the private automobile, the development of federally subsidized restricted-access highways, and low land prices on the urban fringe, suburban development became extremely discontinuous. Suburban zoning maps set aside large parcels of land for single-family residential development. Commercial and office areas would generally require less land but would be situated contiguously to large arterial roads that connect commercial land with scattered residential developments.

This rationalization by zoning is a central component of sprawl. Because all the elements of life that a human needs to survive in a wage-based economy are separated and lacking in spatial propinquity, mechanized transportation becomes an essential component of suburban mobility. The North American cities that formed in the pre-automobile era, where mobility was characterized by pedestrian traffic and horse-drawn omnibus, were more prone to have urban conveniences relatively close together since moving across vast expanses of space was impractical. Postwar suburbia was characterized by the opposite: expansive use of space that could be traversed in a practical manner through individual mechanized forms of transportation. Expansive land development had the corollary effect of spreading out functions, making mass transportation impractical. Thus, the separated functionality of the sprawling suburb requires intensive mechanization in transportation. This condition of contemporary suburbia, in turn, requires a host of other inputs that have dramatic effects on ecology, economy, and, one could argue, the foreign policy of the United States.

Culture and Sprawl: Suburban Culture versus Suburban Reality

Most often, sprawl is considered a land use problem; it is a matter of developing land in a particular way that is distinct from an "urban" landscape. While explaining and defining sprawl in relation to land use patterns is useful and even indispensable, it cannot be fully understood without examining the cultural context of its prominence as a metropolitan form. Patterns of human spatial development do not take place within a vacuum. They emerge from and influence the ways in which humans relate socially and culturally. Sprawl, because of its national ubiquity, not only has come to describe changes in the metropolitan landscape but is also situated within larger debates about American identity.

After a half century of metropolitan development, sprawl represents the apotheosis of contradictory tendencies in American culture. On the one hand, postwar suburbia and its concomitant sprawl can be thought of as an effect of individualism's prominence as the dominant ideology in the United States. The American mythos of the rugged, persevering individual was cultivated in the nineteenth century as European settlement "conquered" the frontier and as industrial capitalism became the dominant economic form. In the twentieth century, with the frontier conquered and industrial capitalism firmly entrenched, the individualist ideal moved to the suburbs. This was prefigured by technological changes discussed previously—in particular, the development of the widespread use of the automobile.

Technology allowed the creation of a set of utopian ideals whose sites of realization were, either explicitly or implicitly, suburban. This impulse was most clearly evident in the rise of a culture of mass consumption. Stuart Ewen charts the emergence of the modern advertising industry dedicated to the production of consumers to the 1920s but notes the strong postwar economy and substantial state intervention whereby "government loans to G.I. families and others helped to erect suburban communities which would prove to be the fertile soil for the cultivation of a consumer Eden."[12] The rise in the number of new homes being built and the extensive land use patterns characteristic of suburbanization provided the opportunity for a consumer identity to gain prominence. Owning a house required purchasing a variety of accoutrements: appliances, furnishings, tools, and so on. The absence of public transportation and the substantial distances between residential, commercial, and occupational locations made private automobile ownership mandatory.

With the circumstances for new and widespread forms of consumption being facilitated by government subsidies for suburbanization, corporate interests carefully cultivated a consumerist identity that drew inspiration from and reinforced the suburban landscape. Media representations of American life began to be inundated with images of suburban families inhabiting domiciles equipped with a plethora of consumer items. Television sitcoms such as *Leave It to Beaver, Father Knows Best,* and *The Dick Van Dyke Show* not only provided normalized visions of the American family but also contributed to the production of patterns of consumption whereby the production sets of network studios became templates for nationwide styles.

The emergent culture of consumption that glorified the suburb was concomitant with the decline of inner cities as the primary centers of commodity display. Retailers, taking advantage of inexpensive land prices and seeking to be closer to their consumer base, began to establish operations in suburban areas. Malls supplanted many central-city business districts as spaces for consumption and corporate investment. Because of the primacy of automobile transportation in suburban planning, large malls, smaller strip malls, and "big box" retail establishments saturated the landscape. Restrictive, single-use zoning guaranteed that a sprawling environment ensued where pedestrian access to retail was rendered ineffectual and traffic congestion flourished. As automobile-centric retail design became normalized and suburban retail development became driven by the demands of large corporate chains, retailers often demanded large parking lots, wide access roads, and a homogeneous architecture to accommodate their centrally planned stores and restaurants. The production of a society of mass consumers created an accompanying physical infrastructure for its sustenance.

While the culture of consumption propelled the consumptive subject served by the sprawled suburban landscape to the forefront of an "American" identity, it simultaneously had unintended effects. Nearly as important to American culture as individualism and the twentieth century's morphing of the "individual" into the "consumer" has been the concept of what Leo Marx called the "pastoral ideal."[13] The pastoral ideal refers to the notion of North America as a space of uncharted settlement that serves as the antidote to the corrupting nature of urbanized civilization; it is a space not only of escape but also of renewal. In the nineteenth century, the pastoral ideal was evident in such sociocultural articulations as government policies of Manifest Destiny and the Romantic literary tradition of authors such as Thoreau and Emerson. With the closing of the frontier in the 1890s, the pastoral ideal did not vanish; rather, it was reenvisioned in suburbia.

Howard's garden city concept—while developed in the British context—embodies the pastoral ideal in its emphasis on the healing and rejuvenating capacity of nature. In advocating his "invention," Howard argues that the "key to the problem [of] how to restore the people to the land—that beautiful land of ours, with its canopy of sky, the air that blows upon it, the sun that warms it, the rain and dew that moisten it—the very embodiment of Divine love for man is indeed a Master Key."[14] Thus, the Master Key, according to Howard, is reinstating humans' connection to nature—which had been debased through industrial urbanism. Designers of nascent suburbs such as Clarence Stein made a disciplined natural environment central to their new town plans. It is in its relationship to nature that suburbia represented what Peter Rowe calls the "middle landscape."[15] Suburbia stands between two extremes. The industrial city is the embodiment of civilization's mastery over nature with its imposing physical structures and pollution; the city is also representative of civilization hyperextended to the point of cultural and social depravity where crime, immorality, and vice are rampant. Wilderness is situated in opposition to the city. It is the pristine, unadulterated, authentic representation of the majesty of creation. But it is also the realm of the unknown, the savage, and the unrelenting. Suburbia, as an ideal, rectifies the tension between city and wilderness by combining the civilizing forces of urbanity with the purifying capacity of the carefully manicured natural world.

Rome discusses how the appeal to the pastoral ideal has been employed by developers of postwar suburbia to justify the absence of open park space. Since new home owners are getting their own "private parks" in the form of a lawns or yards, the provision of large public open space is unneeded. Similarly, developers of residential suburban subdivisions emphasize the pastoral in the naming and marketing of properties, a process that strikes Duany, Plater-Zyberk, and Speck as ironic in that "subdivisions can be identified . . . by their contrived names which tend toward the romantic—Pheasant Mill Crossing—and often pay tribute to the natural or historic resource they have displaced."[16] Lewis Mumford attributes this aspect of suburbanization to a newfound romanticism: "At the beginning the suburb was the expression of a new way of life, less effortful, less regimented, less sterile, less formalized in every way than that of the production-minded urban centers."[17]

While the pastoral ideal was astutely mobilized to define and market suburbia, the gulf between the ideal and suburban reality widened, and through rampant development, discontinuity ensued. The pastoral ideal soon became invoked for critiques of the sprawling suburban environment. Mumford cites the ensuing dominance of the motorcar and the accompanying high levels of automobile traffic in suburbia as evidence of an offense to this romantic sensibility. Necessitated by the sprawl of low-density development, automobiles became prominent, and "the pedestrian scale of the suburb disappeared, and with it, most of its individuality and charm. . . . The suburb needed its very smallness, as it needed its rural background, to achieve its own kind of semi-rural perfection. Once that limit was over-passed, the suburb ceased to be a refuge from the city and became part of the inescapable metropolis."[18] As the metropolis engulfed the suburb, efforts to stave off sprawl have been justified using variants of pastoralism. William H. Whyte, for instance, in his early critiques of sprawl, stresses the legitimacy of preserving open space on the urban fringe purely for aesthetic reasons. While addressing the ecological, economic, and social context of sprawl, he asserts the sustenance of a cultural aestheticism as essential in changing land use patterns. Recognizing the important work of conservationists in promoting the protection of sensitive habitats for wildlife, he questions their sufficiency for swaying the masses behind preservation: "People of the urban region are more concerned with the 'man' part of the equation; specifically, what's in it for him? Plenty, of course, but the most elemental appeal is the aesthetic, and we should make the most of it."[19]

The pastoral ideal continues to animate discussion and critique of sprawl. Since the late 1960s and early 1970s with the establishment of federal environmental legislation—itself an outcome informed by decades of changing American cultural values—public concern about the ecological consequences of human behavior has become exceedingly widespread.[20] With this mainstreaming of environmentalist values, connections between sprawled suburban development and the destruction of a "way of life" informed by the pastoral have been made by local and national activists and critics of sprawl. Richard Moe and Carter Wilkie discuss the controversy in the 1990s involving the Walt Disney Company's now abandoned plans to develop an amusement park in northern Virginia around the theme of American history. The site of the proposed project—on the fringe of the Washington, D.C., metropolitan area and in the shadow of important Civil War battlefields and other historical sites—prompted community activists to decry the destruction of such a unique and sensitive landscape. While Disney's proposal to "theme" American history elicited a large degree of reasonable skepticism, perhaps a more important motivating factor for opposition to the project stemmed from the region's experience with the effects of sprawl and the recognition that a development on the scale of what Disney was proposing would fundamentally change the character of this bucolic setting.[21] The experience in Virginia is not unique. National organizations, such as the Sierra Club, have dedicated substantial resources to addressing the ways sprawl affects the quality of life in suburban areas and emphasizing how stronger land use controls will enhance both the ecology of regions and social conditions.

Society and Sprawl

Increasingly, sprawl is having an impact on social and political relations in a myriad of ways. The fragmented nature of metropolitan governance has long been a theme of urban studies. Because municipal governments receive much of their revenue from property taxes, impact fees, sales taxes, and other place-based activity, they are often in competition with one another for attracting profitable ventures. This is especially the case in metropolitan areas where the concentration of large numbers of autonomous municipalities can cause these processes of competition to intensify. Municipalities situated in the same metropolitan region can have vast differences in wealth, creating incentives for poorer municipalities to relax restrictions on land use. Sprawl is likely to occur in these conditions because municipalities see themselves in direct competition with their neighbors and recognize that a lucrative development could easily locate themselves in a neighboring community.[22]

On a metropolitan level, the stratification that ensues from fragmentation can exacerbate latent social tensions. As Mike Davis has demonstrated in his work on southern California and Robert Bullard et. al. in their work on Atlanta, resentment against ethnic minorities and other "marginalized" peoples contributes to the ways in which the contemporary metropolis is governed and planned. Policies such as "redlining," the designation of selected areas as unsuited for public and private investment, directly served as catalysts for suburban growth. This was coupled with other federal disinvestments in urban centers, resulting in vast divergences in property values, school quality, criminal activity, and indicators of public health. Because these conditions have historically adversely affected low-income communities and communities of color disproportionately, it is important to recognize that the land use policies usually associated with metropolitan development influence other social relations.[23]

The sprawled landscape requires a set of behaviors and capacities that entail a large degree of individual investment, creating challenges for the poor. The circulation of people through space is perhaps an essential condition for human sustenance. People require mobility to work, consume, produce, and socialize. Sprawl, with its low-density automotive focus and decenteredness, coupled with little support for public transportation, make the individual bear many of the costs of mobility. While the roads and highways, public safety coverage, and environmental costs associated with automotive-driven development are highly subsidized through general sources of revenue, an individual, in order to take advantage of this subsidy, must own and operate a motor vehicle. The American Automobile Association estimates that the cost of operating a vehicle during 2001 was $7,000.[24] This is a substantial investment, particularly for people of modest means.

Without owning an automobile, individuals living in sprawled environments are at the mercy of underfunded public transportation systems (primarily employing buses) that were introduced as an afterthought and hence ill equipped for providing efficient and safe service. Passengers have to contend with schedule delays, drop-off spots located far from destination points, multiple transfers, infrequent service, and unsafe street crossings. For the working poor, transportation challenges can impact job opportunities, familial responsibilities, and social advancement. These experiences are the direct results of land use and transportation systems that highly subsidize a form of automotive mobility with a substantive entrance fee.

Sprawl has also been implicated as a culprit in the larger social malaise of civic disengagement. Although quantifying civic disengagement and tracing its causes is a formidable task, there is a large degree of scholarship and commentary that suggests that American society over the past thirty years has become more individualistic and less concerned with notions of community. The sprawling suburb is often cited as a manifestation of this transformation. The absence of public space, the dispersion of public buildings, the homogeneity of housing and retail, forms of mobility that are essentially private, and the perceived absence of local history are all thought of as oppositional to community. Robert Putnam, in his highly acclaimed book *Bowling Alone,* charts the decline of social capital in the United States over the past century by discussing suburban sprawl within the context of decreasing levels of membership in service organizations and decreasing levels of political participation. Edward Blakely and Mary Gail Snyder point to the increasing prominence of gated communities in suburban areas as an indication of a growing social insularity prominent in American political and social life.[25]

Whether sprawl is a symptom of social malaise or a cause is impossible to determine. It is safe to say, however, that the sprawled landscape simultaneously is constitutive of and provides the setting for a large part of contemporary social interactions in the United States today.

Volume Overview

The chapters and edited interviews in this volume are designed to provide a multifaceted exploration into the ways that suburban sprawl is being defined, experienced, interpreted, promoted, resisted, and transformed in our contemporary era. We have brought together scholars and practitioners from a variety of disciplinary backgrounds to explore the complexity of the issue and to suggest the various ways that our metropolitan futures are being envisioned.

In part I, "Culture and Society: Contested Visions and Values," Lydia Savage and Mark Lapping provide a discussion of the ways sprawl destabilizes and often annihilates the physical, social, and economic character of rural areas at the "exurban" edge. Michele Byers provides a theoretical chapter that interrogates the metaphor of the "gate" and shows how much of suburban sprawl can be thought of as constituting literal and virtual separations. Wende Vyborney Feller shows how history is politicized, imagined, rewritten, and marketed in housing developments and neighborhoods in two seemingly incongruous settings. Finally, Robert Messia examines the multifaceted roles of the lawn in suburban development.

This part also contains interviews with a variety of practitioners involved in metropolitan development in very different ways. Bill Carpenter is the town supervisor of Pittsford, New York, and has successfully protected family farms and Pittsford's budget from sprawl. Mike Watkins is a member of the Congress for the New Urbanism and the head of Andres Duany and Elizabeth Plater-Zyberk's Kentlands, Maryland, office. Kentlands was designed by the Duany, Plater-Zyberk firm and is one of the most successful New Urbanist developments in the country. Don Chen directs the Smart Growth Network, an advocacy group based in Washington, D.C., for urban reform, and Elizabeth Humphrey directs the Growth Management Leadership Alliance. The final interview is with the former governor of Maryland, Parris Glendening, who oversaw some of the strongest antisprawl legislation in the country and is the former head of the National Governors Association.

Part II, "Contesting Theories of Sprawl: Race, Class, and Culture," features a critical discussion of the New Urbanism phenomena by Amanda Rees. Milton Curry's chapter shows how the current embrace of New Urbanist techniques by the U.S. Department of Housing and Urban Development perpetuates racial discontinuities and inequities. Ronald Hayduk discusses the ways in which the public policies of suburbanization have affected racial inequalities. Josh Protas looks at how identity, landscape, and ecological protection intersect in his discussion of Camelback Mountain, outside of Phoenix. These chapters are accompanied by interviews with Alex Morton, Geoffrey Anderson, Mel Martinez and Richard Moe.

Alex Morton is a resident of Celebration, Florida—the New Urbanist planned community developed by the Disney Company in metropolitan Orlando. In 1998, he started publishing the *Celebration Independent* to give residents of the town a voice to express concerns within this new suburban community. Richard Moe is the president of the National Trust for Historical Preservation and the author, with Carter Wilkie, of *Changing Places: Rebuilding Community in the Age of Sprawl* (Henry Holt, 1997). His work with the National Trust and the subject of his book has shown how historical preservation is an effective strategy at mitigating sprawl. Mel Martinez is the current secretary of Housing and Urban Development for the Bush administration. Prior to his appointment in 2001, Martinez was the chairman of the County Commission in Orange County, Florida. As county chairman, Martinez instituted growth management reforms and was appointed by Florida's governor to lead a statewide growth management taskforce. Geoffrey Anderson works with the U.S. Environmental Protection Administration's Development, Community and Environment division, which assists states and municipalities in developing smart-growth strategies.

Part III, "Development, Equity, and Policy Options: Theory and Cases," explores ways in which public policy has contributed to sprawl and also ways that it can be refashioned to impart a changing suburban dynamic. Patricia Salkin offers a detailed discussion of the legal ramifications of recent smart-growth initiatives in the United States. William Batt provides a generalized economic argument for addressing sprawl. The chapter by Mark Edward Braun is a case study of the Milwaukee, Wisconsin, metropolitan region and discusses the ways in which particular policy decisions have dramatically changed the region's physical and social landscape. Ulf Zimmerman, Göktuğ Morçöl, and Bethany Stich, in their case study of Atlanta, show how the region exacerbated the sprawl that seems endemic to the area by adopting policy and initially rejecting regionalist approaches for urban development until recently.

This part includes interviews with a variety of political officeholders. U.S. Congressman Earl Blumenauer from Portland is the chairman of the House Bicycle Caucus and a strong proponent of federal smart-growth legislation. Ted Mondale is chairman of the Metropolitan Council of the Twin Cities, a regional government authority battling over the issue of sprawl. Greg LeRoy, the executive director of Good Jobs First, emphasizes the ways in which sprawl undermines worker security and advocates for the labor movement to address metropolitan development.

As we worked on this volume, we came to realize that, while the surface appearance of sprawl may appear homogeneous and tied to what James Kunstler calls a "geography of nowhere," in reality the phenomena of suburban sprawl takes place in localities with distinctive ecologies, histories, and cultures. Perhaps the reassertion of locality within the context of the homogenizing tendencies apparent in our culture and economy of creeping globalism can serve as a foundation for recognizing new metropolitan forms for the twenty-first century. Each of our authors and interviewees, in various ways, contributes to variations on this goal.

Notes

1. Naush Boghossian, "Locals Showing Support for Oak," *The Daily News of Los Angeles* (Santa Clarita Edition), November 19, 2002, SC1.
2. William Presecky, "State's Best Farmland in Danger, Study Finds: Illinois Ranks 5th Loss in U.S.," *Chicago Tribune,* October 8, 2002, 1. See also American Farmland Trust, *Farming on the Edge: Sprawling Development Threatens American Farmland* (Washington, D.C.: American Farmland Trust, 2002).
3. Richard T. Crotty, Introductory Address, Chairman's Transportation Commission, Orlando, September 25, 2002.
4. Susan Lundine and Noelle Haner-Dorr, "The Air Out There: Not As Clean As You May Think," *Orlando Business Journal,* May 10, 2002, 1; Debbie Salamone, "Florida's Water Crisis: Salt and Rain," *Orlando Sentinel,* August 11, 2002, 1; Surface Transportation Policy Project, *Mean Streets 2002* (Washington, D.C.: Surface Transportation Policy Project, 2002).
5. Jon Steinman, "Crotty Sports Win in New Ride," *Orlando Sentinel,* November 8, 2002.
6. Lewis Mumford, *The City in History* (San Diego: Harcourt, Brace, 1961), 540.
7. On transportation and suburban sprawl, see Andres Duany, Elizabeth Plater-Zyberk, and Jeff Speck, *Suburban Nation: The Rise of Sprawl and the Decline of the American Dream* (New York: North Point Press, 2000), and Jane Holtz Kay, *Asphalt Nation: How the Automobile Took Over America and How We Can Take It Back* (Berkeley: University of California Press, 1999).

8. Adam Rome, *The Bulldozer and the Countryside* (Cambridge, U.K.: Cambridge University Press, 2001).

9. Ebenezer Howard, *Garden Cities of To-Morrow* (Cambridge, Mass.: MIT Press, 1965).

10. See Seymour Toll, *Zoned American* (New York: Grossman, 1969), and William Fischel, "An Economic History of Zoning and a Cure for Its Exclusionary Effects," Dartmouth College Working Paper 2-03 (Hanover, N.H.: Dartmouth College, 2001).

11. *Euclid v. Ambler Realty*, 272 U.S. 365 (1926).

12. Stuart Ewen, *Captains of Consciousness: Advertising and the Social Roots of the Consumer Culture* (New York: McGraw-Hill, 1976), 206.

13. Leo Marx, *The Machine in the Garden* (London: Oxford University Press, 1964).

14. Howard, *Garden Cities of To-Morrow*, 44.

15. Peter G. Rowe, *Making a Middle Landscape* (Cambridge, Mass.: MIT Press, 1991).

16. Duany et al., *Suburban Nation*, 5.

17. Mumford, *The City in History*, 493.

18. Mumford, *The City in History*, 505.

19. William H. Whyte, *The Last Landscape* (Garden City, N.Y.: Doubleday, 1968), 353.

20. See Rome, *The Bulldozer and the Countryside*, and Matthew J. Lindstrom and Zachary A. Smith, *The National Environmental Policy Act* (College Station: Texas A&M University Press, 2001).

21. Richard Moe and Carter Wilkie, *Changing Places: Rebuilding Community in the Age of Sprawl* (New York: Henry Holt, 1997). For a discussion of the region's experience with sprawl, see Joel Garreau, *Edge City: Life on the New Frontier* (New York: Anchor Books, 1991).

22. See, for instance, John R. Logan and Harvey L. Molotch, *Urban Fortunes: The Political Economy of Place* (Berkeley: University of California Press, 1987).

23. Mike Davis, *Ecology of Fear* (New York: Metropolitan Books, 1998).

24. American Automobile Association, *Your Driving Costs 2002* (Heathrow, Fla.: AAA Association Communication, 2002).

25. Edward Blakely and Mary Gail Snyder, *Fortress America* (Washington, D.C.: Brookings Institution Press, 1997); Robert Putnam, *Bowling Alone.* (New York: Simon & Schuster, 2000).

I

Culture and Society: Contested Visions and Values

FORMER SPEAKER OF THE HOUSE Tip O'Neal's famous proclamation that "all politics is local" could perhaps be embellished for our purposes to read, "All politics is spatial." People relate to each other and come to understand their experience through social interaction in material environments. The ways in which these material environments are constructed and defined are subject to political contestation because of their importance in our daily lives.

Suburbanization and sprawl have not occurred in a vacuum. Racial segregation, ecological deterioration, the transformation of rural economies, and other factors both impact and influence sprawl. Some of these more unsettling aspects of suburban development have been highly controversial, and the ways in which changes to the suburban fringe are interpreted, described, and reacted to provide insight into larger structures animating society and culture. In this part, the various contributors and interviewees address the ways in which sprawl intersects with society and culture and some of the specific ways social conflict emerges and is defined in debates surrounding suburban reform.

In chapter 1, Lydia Savage and Mark Lapping highlight the important—and often overlooked—consequences of sprawl for rural communities. While it is often publicized by advocacy organizations such as the Sierra Club and American Farmland Trust that yearly substantial agricultural acreage is "lost" to sprawl, Savage and Lapping probe further, examining the larger social context of suburban sprawl for the rural United States. Farmers on the metropolitan fringe are often forced to give up farming because of rising tax rates that make agriculture unprofitable. Additionally, Savage and Lapping argue that many farmers see fringe development as being "inevitable" and consequently fail to make the requisite investment in their agricultural operations to remain competitive. They argue that this resignation, in turn, is a self-fulfilling prophecy, as farmers often feel discouraged from taking creative action to continue farming and are put in a financial situation where they need to sell quickly, causing prices to fall, which fails to contribute adequately to farmers' financial health and encourages continued suburbanization. On a social level, Savage and Lapping argue, changing demographics on the rural fringe seriously disrupt existing social networks as farming related businesses close, affordable housing for agricultural laborers dissipates, and residents with a distaste for farming's externalities (such as smell) transform the local political climate.

In chapter 2, Michele Byers looks at the concept of the "gate" and relates it to postmodern interrogations into the importance of spatial politics in culture and society. For Byers, the gate is the predominant symbol of postmodern suburban sprawl. Gates are literally evident as required accoutrements in the many exclusive residential communities that dot the sprawled landscape; but for Byers, gates work on a more symbolic level, connoting general separation and privatization. Byers also examines how the boundary construction associated with processes of "gating" achieves newfound prominence as a result of the dominant technoculture of our postmodern age. She argues that there is a significant connection between the concomitant rise of the Internet and gated communities of suburbia. Both purport to offer "community" but fail to come to terms with the obstacles to access that are their defining attributes.

In chapter 3, Wende Vyborney Feller, in her discussion of the historical development of Modesto, California, and Rochester, New York, discusses the ways in which an appeal to a nonexistent past is being employed in efforts to promote New Urbanist housing developments in these very different cities. As each community experienced challenges of incorporating new residents from different ethnic and cultural backgrounds into their rapidly growing cities, developers and community groups developed selective understandings of the past in an effort to extract accommodation on the part of new residents. Feller defines these selective deployments of history as evidence of acts of *impostures*—associating these new communities with a set of historical references that are essentially unrelated to actual historical conditions of the communities. Like Byers, Feller shows us the power of metaphor and euphemisms in occluding existing social inequalities in Rochester and Modesto and offers a healthy skepticism for assessing New Urbanist attempts to mitigate sprawl.

Robert Messia's concluding chapter in this part provides a historical analysis of the symbolic, social, and ecological functions and consequences of the ubiquitous suburban lawn. Messia's chapter on the lawn's evolution clearly articulates how it is deeply embedded in humanity's struggle to domesticate nature as a means to creating an ordered, privatized space at the top of nature's hierarchy. Again, the lawn is at the center of the suburban paradox. It represents a sculptured sense of natural beauty, while at the same time the sixty-seven million plus pounds of chemical additives dumped on the grass to "improve" nature contribute to polluted air and waters and a deleterious environment for human and animal health.

The interviews interspersed between each chapter give a variety of perspectives from practitioners who are working at various policymaking levels. This diverse group of elected politicians, civil servants, town planners, and interest group advocates share the challenge of rethinking common notions about suburbia, growth, and sprawl, and all the interviews offer new and innovative approaches to remaking our suburban future.

1

Sprawl and Its Discontents: The Rural Dimension

Lydia Savage and Mark Lapping

SPRAWL HAS SIGNIFICANT SPATIAL and social dimensions. Largely a rural–urban fringe phenomenon, far too many policy analysts, students of the problem, and others mistakenly see sprawl occurring on a landscape largely devoid of established communities, existing resource utilization patterns, and social and political arrangements. Indeed, sprawl impacts rural communities in many and significant ways. It is a process and a force that alters in permanent ways how rural people live and work, how they sustain their families and social and cultural networks, how they construct their communities and decision-making processes, and how they define their spatial and cognitive realities. Sprawl occurs not on a tabula rasa landscape but rather on a peopled and working rural landscape.[1] Sprawl is an amazingly disruptive force that triggers conflict and rearranges the rural and village geography, economy, and society in the most profound ways.[2]

By its very nature, sprawl is difficult to define but far easier to describe. One recognizes sprawl when one is in its midst. The territorial dimensions of sprawl can best be understood as those semirural lands and communities beyond the boundaries of traditional suburbs but still within the urban shadow or commutershed of metropolitan centers. As Daniels writes, such places are "hybrid regions no longer remote and yet with a lower density of population and development than a city or suburb."[3] Sprawl has followed the introduction and diffusion of transportation systems—especially the private automobile on publicly funded and maintained roads—and the changing economics of land, housing subsidies, tax policies, and development costs across the American metropolitan landscape. It is a fragmented, piecemeal, uncoordinated, unplanned, and inefficient land use process that very much follows the path of least resistance when confronting the land use regulatory system.

The Working Rural Landscape

While increasing numbers of rural residents earn their living in the service-based economy—specifically the rapidly growing tourism sector as well as in manufacturing—and through the cycling of transfer payments in the local economy, these activities have not totally replaced agriculture, small-scale forestry, gravel extraction and mining, and fisheries in all rural–urban fringe areas. Because of their reliance on the rural land base, agriculture and forestry are particularly susceptible to disruption by sprawl.

Agriculture in the rural–urban fringe tends to be defined by the production of perishables that have been developed to meet markets in nearby metropolitan areas. As suburban sprawl spills out into the countryside, some extraordinary pressures are exerted on agriculture. Perhaps the most obvious of these is that farmers are consistently outbid for land by developers and others who seek to take advantage of the land economics of sprawl. This makes it nearly impossible for farmers to maintain, much less expand, their operations on contiguous or near-contiguous pieces of land. If they seek to expand their operations or to diversify them, then farmers must attempt to purchase lands farther from their farmstead and/or to rent lands. The latter is not an uncommon practice, but in an area where the local land market is "hot"—an area witnessing substantial residential and commercial development—it is often difficult for farmers to obtain long-term rental agreements, thereby introducing greater risk and uncertainty into their operations. When a farmer's operation is spread over the countryside rather than on a centralized farmstead, issues of transportation, the safety of equipment, and the security of crops and animals becomes yet another threat to the continuation of an efficient agriculture in areas witnessing sprawl and development. Of course, there is a flip side to this: With land becoming more valuable and development pressure growing, additional pressures are applied to farmers because increased land value translates itself into a greater property tax burden for those who own substantial amounts of land. The great difficulty for farmers, especially those working on small and medium-size farms, has been and remains that the yield from farming too rarely creates the kinds of incomes and returns that permit farmers to deal with rapidly escalating land values and tax burdens. To address this problem, all states have opted for some form of preferential or differential tax policies that allow farmers to receive a "use-value" assessment rather than a market value according to the "highest-and-best" yield formula applied under contemporary land assessment principles.[4] Some states offering such protection require land to stay in active agricultural use for a set number of years. If a farmer converts land before the contract period is reached, then a "rollback" of taxes forgiven and/or a penalty is applied to the farmer. In other cases, the definition of a "bona fide" farmer is lacking, thus making it possible for this form of protection to be given to banks, corporations, and even developers who meet the minimal criteria for what constitutes "agricultural land" as well as to farmers.

Farms produce additional fiscal benefits for the communities in which they exist. A growing number of studies, some of which have been conducted by the American Farmland Trust, indicate that farms generate local tax revenues in excess of what they require, while housing, as an example, tends to be just the very opposite—requiring far more in the way of services than they generate in tax revenues.[5] Or, as Daniels and Bowers put it so succinctly, "Residential development does not pay its own way. This finding is really not surprising because educating children makes up the largest segment of most local budgets. So the more residential housing, the higher property taxes must be raised to pay for education costs."[6]

Finally, among this cascade of issues emanating from sprawl-induced changes in the local land market, any number of farmers will assume that they will be the beneficiaries of the demand created by developers. They sense an imminent sale of their land. This leads to a phenomena known as the "impermanence syndrome," wherein farmers who believe that their land will soon be purchased begin to wind down their operations as well as fail to make or postpone making necessary investments in their farms to keep them viable in an already difficult environment.[7] What results is something of a self-fulfilling prophecy: Farmers neglect making investments crucial for efficient operation; farms then deteriorate, making it less likely to provide a living and thus pushing farmers to sell their lands merely to survive.

Yet still another land-related problem emerges from sprawl in the case of the decline in farm "critical mass."[8] Like any business, agriculture depends on a multitude of off-farm inputs for efficient operation. Depending on what is grown and raised, these inputs take the form of equipment sales and repair services, seed sales, milling and related services, large animal veterinary services, and so on. If enough farms cease to operate, then the critical mass necessary to maintain these relevant business services also declines, and with the withdrawal of business services, the difficulty for those farmers remaining in production becomes that much greater. Farmers find it more difficult and more expensive to access these necessary support systems, and in time they too will decline and leave production. Agriculture in the rural–urban fringe is subject to many of the same pressures as small businesses in general and some that are unique to it.

A host of other problems accompany sprawl for farmers. These tend to reflect some of the tensions and pressures inherent in the mix of agriculture and residential land uses. Many people are attracted to a community on the rural–urban fringe because of the open-space amenities such places provide. It is inherent in the very nature of sprawl that such development seeks to take advantage of open-space resources for the market demand it seeks to satisfy. Those who are attracted by the suburbanizing landscape often have a desire to enjoy such open-space amenities, country lifestyles, and the provision of certain amenities and services, such as the perception of better schools or personal safety or cheaper and larger building sites. In any case, farms often provide much of the land and space that sprawl both requires and devours to maintain itself. Indeed, it is the bucolic nature of the landscape that so many who are part of the sprawl really seek. But in doing so, they often create a new set of paradoxical conflicts. This results from the fact that too few seem to understand that farmland is created by farmers and that farming is an active form of land use that often generates noise, odors, and other externalities that can deeply annoy and offend adjoining and nearby nonfarming neighbors. Such nonfarming local interests have sought to enjoin certain farm practices through the manipulation of the local community planning process, nuisance lawsuits, and other interventions. With growing complaints from farmers, many states and several Canadian provinces have passed "right-to-farm" laws that seek to establish a "first in time, first in right" principle wherein farms established prior to sprawl development are protected from such questionable attacks.[9] But what if a farmer him- or herself creates the problem by selling land adjoining the farm or near it while still attempting to stay in production on the core farmstead? Only Washington State has responded to this problem by making sure that its right-to-farm law does not provide legal protection to farmers who create their own problems. The larger point is this: Farms constitute a most important type of wealth-creating enterprise and a key component of a working rural landscape, and as such they create certain spillover effects that are not always compatible with the type of land uses fostered by the sprawl economy.

As sprawl makes farming ever more difficult, so too with forest-based businesses and wood products firms. Sprawl tends to lead to the fragmentation of the forest through the process of the subdivision of "contiguous blocks of forest land by roads, development, and other non-forest forces."[10] Along with this usually comes the "parcelization" of forestlands into many individual ownerships and more "terminal harvests" wherein the land is cleared of all standing timber in anticipation of land subdivision and development. A recently published U.S. Forest Service study on sprawl in the southern forest indicates that it "will have the most direct, immediate and permanent effects on the extent, condition and health of forests."[11] In an immediate sense, forestland fragmentation tends to intensify forest fire threats and makes it more difficult to fight disease and pest outbreaks.[12] Likewise, fragmentation increases the operating costs of forest harvesting as road construction, land and equipment moving, and landowner communications all rise, thus making it especially difficult for small, independent jobbers (contractors) and woodcutters to survive in an already highly competitive market. In terms of overall sound forest management, fragmentation and parcelization lead to lower prices for landowners, higher per acre operating costs, fewer harvests carried out under the supervision of a forester, and a smaller opportunity to practice sustainable forest investment and management.[13] Moreover, because the future of the wood base is in some jeopardy as less land is managed and harvests are less predictable, mill operators are concerned about the general availability of timber in the coming years. One study of New Hampshire mill operators (the forest products industry accounts for 12 percent of the state's gross state product) indicates that 68 percent are "very concerned" about the availability of future forest resources. All this breeds insecurity in the sector, and as it does, the likelihood that necessary investments will be made in labor and equipment is put in question. While a number of imaginative and creative state-level programs have been established to address the problem of forest fragmentation, it must be said that this is an issue that only recently has caught the attention of the policy community.[14]

Finally, local communities attempting to control sprawl and to manage growth often do so by implementing large-lot zoning approaches. This tends to drive up the price of housing, intensifies affordable housing problems, and may actually take greater amounts of productive farm- and forestland out of production by preventing development on smaller lots that will utilize land for development more efficiently. Responses to this include a host of emerging smart-growth development practices that are now being promulgated across the country by such groups as the Smart Growth America and Maryland's Smart Growth Institute.[15]

Urban Meets Rural: Sprawl and Its Social Impacts

Aside from clashes over land use in rural areas created by sprawl in regard to agriculture and forestry, there are many less visible, though no less important, changes in rural and semirural areas arising from sprawl. As communities grow, it is almost inevitable that the people moving in ("newcomers" for lack of a better term) bring their own expectations, ideas, and cultural values with them to an already existing community. Newcomers tend to be employed in the service sector, commute to work, and have the discretionary income to purchase the rural landscape that is being commodified, advertised, and sold by developers.[16] Even as they locate in rural and fringe areas to escape urban problems and/or to avail themselves of the advantages of rural living, they bring sets of expectations about things such as public and private services that should be available, desirable land uses, appropriate forms of governance and political organizations, and educational values.

Without romanticizing the political structures and processes in rural and rural–urban fringe areas, they are very different from city governments where a paid, professional workforce manages day-to-day business. Town councils and school boards are two of the fundamental political structures in rural settlements. These elected entities typically operate in the evenings, allowing for direct participation by residents if they so choose. As towns experience growth and problems and issues seemingly become more complex, there is often a move to "professionalize" town governance by hiring town managers and town planners who ostensibly carry out the wishes of the elected town council and planning boards. This creates a managerial class in the countryside working on behalf of residents during the day, and this may result in a minimization of direct participation by local residents.

The rural political agenda becomes contested as newcomers push for a service-based suburban political agenda and the collision of values becomes clear. The list of desired services to be provided by local government is well known by now: the extension of public services such as water and sewers to new housing developments, better roads (blacktop often replacing dirt roads), bigger schools, different school programs, and so on. Study after study shows that property taxes generated by new developments seldom are enough to pay for the increased expenditures required to meet the desires of new residents. Johnson et al. found that fiscal burdens in the rural areas are lowest in areas with slow population growth but greater in areas with a population change of 10 percent or more over five years.[17]

For example, residents who commute to and from the rural community on a daily basis see good roads—well paved and wide—as an important investment, though such improvements tend to place additional burdens on already strained budgets. Aside from the initial investment, building new roads or improving existing ones increases the funds required for road maintenance, and in some regions of the country they may easily double or triple moneys required for seasonal services, such as snowplowing. As roads are built, the new transportation arteries often trigger additional changes. Wider, faster roads facilitate movement between rural and urban areas and the growth in commercial establishments along these arteries. This leads to the almost inevitable decline of town and village downtowns and commercial cores. If population growth is substantial enough to produce the required consumer market, "big-box" commercial development often takes place. Seeking larger lots for stores, ample parking, easy access for multiple communities, and heavy commuting traffic, big-box developments locate on the outskirts rather than in the existing town commercial centers. Residents then have to make a decision about their local shopping—to do so in the traditional downtown or on the outskirts of town. Even in shopping habits, differences seem to emerge between newer and long-term residents. The newer residents are likely to already commute to work (after all, they are the ones requiring improvements in roads) and make shopping a secondary stop on their commute; they are less apt to shop in village and town centers than are longer-term residents.[18]

One of the most consistent complaints about sprawl is its impact on existing metropolitan central business districts and the commercial areas of older suburban communities. It should be recognized that sprawl also erodes the vitality of small-town and village commercial districts where many of the business establishments are locally and independently owned, often with roots in the community going back several generations. From the 1950s until the present day, retail sales have migrated from traditional downtowns, both urban and small community, to suburban and sprawl locations. One recent study of retail trade in Vermont, for example, has documented a steady decline in the share of such sales for the state's six major population centers while growth has occurred in communities on the rural–urban fringe.[19] Developers in rural and small towns seek out lower land costs, less restrictive zoning and permitting regimes, cheaper site preparation and construction costs for larger buildings (which more closely conform to the needs of the national merchandisers they serve), and ample parking and access to several communities. The consequences of the destruction of small-town commercial districts for their communities are almost impossible to reverse: Assets leave the community, sources of local support for entrepreneurial risk and community institution building become ever fewer, and some of the organizational leadership within the community is narrowed or, worse, lost. Added to this is a decline in revenues, increased dependence on commuting to shopping and services, and a change in the overall texture in community life as once-multifaceted communities are turned into bedroom communities.

Growing populations in rural areas also lead to the need for school expansion. In Maine, for example, school spending has increased rapidly despite an overall decline in the statewide population of school-age children. Between 1975 and 1995, Maine state government alone spent $727 million on new school construction and additions. Forty-six percent of the amount was spent on building school capacity in towns that were experiencing rapid growth.[20] In effect, a large amount of money was spent on relocating school capacity that already existed in urban areas. Schools are funded largely by property taxes and rural residents who are already earning less than the newcomers and may not be able to afford the increases in property taxes that are required for new schools, personnel, services, programs, and so on.

Local zoning boards become important mechanisms through which to implement ideas about appropriate landscape amenities in the cultural clash between newer and long-term residents. Seats on these bodies become contested as residents try to further their own political and social agendas. Newer residents tend to see open space for its aesthetic and recreational value. As a result, many argue that newer residents are more likely to perceive strict zoning as a way to preserve their property values, while longer-term residents are just as likely to see zoning as an infringement on their property rights. For example, the creation of historical preservation districts or the passage of antiweed ordinances can be used to preserve a desired rural character. Alternatively, sludge spreading and the keeping of farm animals can be restricted, as they are seen not as part of a desirable working landscape but as nuisances. Large-lot strategies do reduce the population density in a given area, but this approach consumes more land and makes affordable housing difficult to develop, as do ordinances that attempt to restrict and limit mobile homes.[21] While affordable housing may not be an issue for newer residents who can afford to "buy into" the quaint rural landscape and escalating land market, longer-term residents worry that their own children will be priced out of the housing market and forced to relocate from the communities of their heritage.

A less tangible but equally important aspect of how sprawl affects rural areas lies in the phrase "sense of place." Rural residents often have identities that emphasize their differences from urbanites and vice versa.[22] Rural people see themselves as different from "city folks" in the same manner that urban residents distinguish themselves from "country folks." Rural residents speak of "a way of life," a "sense of community," and the presence of their family as things that distinguish them from city dwellers. Often rural residents have a strong "sense of place" fostered by the continuity of community created through kinship ties to an area where they have chosen to remain, perhaps for multiple generations. The social capital, interactions, and networks existing between residents generated in rural communities often are greater than those in urban areas, as people are less mobile residentially and weave themselves more deeply into the social fabric of the community.

Beggs, Hurlbert, and Haines examined the strength of social ties and community participation in rural parishes of Louisiana.[23] It is perhaps not surprising that they found that the length of time one resides in an area has a significant and positive relationship with the number of local social ties. Residents with lower levels of education have stronger social ties than do those with higher education attainment. Interestingly, length of residence has no relationship to participation in local groups, although education does; the more education a resident has, the more likely he or she is to belong to a community, school, church, or interest group. Beggs et al. also found that residents with higher incomes are less satisfied with the community, and the authors propose that high-income residents have greater expectations for services and/or amenities that the community fails to provide.

The authors examined a rural area and did not address the issues of population growth or sprawl. Nonetheless, their findings have implications for rural and rural–urban fringe communities experiencing sprawl since their variables tend to address differences between long-term and newer residents in rapidly growing communities. For example, rural residents also tend to have lower levels of education and income than do newcomers. Newer residents also tend to rely on their automobiles more so than longer-term residents since they commute to urban areas for work. Freeman found that the strength of neighborhood social ties was unrelated to residential density but significantly related to the reliance on automobiles by residents.[24]

As rural areas are transformed into commuter-based communities, local social capital is transformed. In turn, the traditionally participatory components of rural life become difficult to sustain and become mechanisms for cultural transformation. For example, volunteer fire departments become overextended, as they must provide services to the newly developed and scattered housing settlements of newcomers. Likewise, crucial response time becomes longer, thus imperiling people and property. Fire departments become responsible for the new residents' homes even while the newer residents volunteer at lesser rates than do longer-term residents.

In many ways, volunteer fire departments are symbols of rural communities. The need for volunteer fire departments arises from the fact that a paid fire department force is financially impractical for most rural communities. Volunteer units also are indicative of the strong local ties and social capital in communities where residents need to rely on one another for something as fundamental as the protection of life and property. Eighty percent of all firefighters in the United States are volunteers, and they protect approximately 75 percent of the land area of the nation.[25]

The commitment made by a volunteer firefighter is significantly different in several ways from many of the other community-based groups one can choose to join. Being a volunteer firefighter not only entails time and effort but also includes the potential for personal danger and constitutes an open-ended commitment to the provision of a vital public service that is not scheduled. Volunteers are expected to commit to training, regular meetings, and responding to a certain percentage of calls each month no matter the time of day. In other words, the on-call nature of being a volunteer firefighter is unique among most voluntary civic activities. In addition, many volunteer firefighters spend time raising funds for equipment and supplies and participating in community events, such as parades, fairs, and educational programs.[26]

Simpson argues that newer residents in rural communities are more likely to join interest groups, such as historic preservation committees, than fraternal or socially inclusive groups, such as volunteer fire departments.[27] This can be explained, in part, by the preferences of the newcomer, but Simpson also argues that volunteer fire departments are akin to fraternal organizations in which membership hinges on family and social ties and that these may preclude the involvement of those newcomers who might ordinarily seek to join. In his study of a fire department in Clinton County, New York, that moved from being a rural department to one providing coverage to middle-class subdivisions, he finds that it is the working class, longer-term resident who chooses to serve as a volunteer. Middle-class residents, he contends,

> found civic organizations and revived historical associations to extend their cultural influence over their new localities, and to protect their property values. They supported zoning controls, historic districting, and anti-junk car ordinances. Their image of locality emphasized scenic amenities rather than existing social fabric. Unlike the former middle class workers in older extractive industries and paper processing, the new middle class has supported environmental lobbies and tight land-use restrictions on private land in the region's state park. They consume the land with a recreational passion and a tourist's gaze.[28]

Working-class residents are more residentially stable and have ties to the area that create a moral obligation to participate in the provision of services to the community. Moreover, they often work shifts, leaving them time during the day to answer calls when the middle-class service workers are in the office, most usually outside the local community. Indeed, many of the newcomers to a sprawl community do not work in the same place they live. This serves as yet another barrier to their participation in demanding voluntary organizations, such as the local fire department.

Conclusions

When sprawl takes place, it unleashes many forces that generate environmental, cultural, economic, social, and political change. Where sprawl takes place in the rural–urban fringe almost always implies that these changes will be profound. Though sprawl takes place over a period of time and in increments—

sometimes it feels like a community is being "nickeled and dimed" to death—it is nevertheless a watershed process in the life and economy of the community. How a place looks, feels, operates, decides, works, and lives during and after sprawl will undoubtedly be very different from life prior to the changes that sprawl produces. It is well to remember that sprawl does not occur in a landscape devoid of the realities, artifacts, and conceits of life in an era of globalization and contest and conflict.

Notes

1. Mark B. Lapping, "Toward a Working Rural Landscape," in *New England Prospects and Choices,* ed. C. Reidel (Hanover, N.H.: University Press of New England, 1982).

2. See Owen J. Furuseth and Mark B. Lapping, *Contested Countryside: The Rural Urban Fringe in North America* (Brookfield, Vt.: Ashgate, 1999).

3. Thomas Daniels, *When City and Country Collide: Managing Growth in the Metropolitan Fringe* (Washington, D.C.: Island Press, 1999), 9.

4. Current land assessment principles require that land be assessed on its market value use. This may mean that a farm is assessed as if it were a housing development and the farmer has to pay property tax that reflects this "market" value. This is known as the "highest and best" yield formula. To alleviate these pressures and burdens, especially in rapidly changing areas such as those communities experiencing sprawl, states provide that farms be assessed for property taxes on a "current" use, as a farm, rather than at a market use, in some other more intense urban use. This lowers the tax burden on farmers and usually secures a commitment from the farmer to keep the land in active agriculture for a specified period of time. See Raleigh Barlowe, *Land Resource Economics: The Economics of Real Estate* (Englewood Cliffs, N.J.: Prentice Hall, 1985).

5. American Farmland Trust, *Fiscal Impacts of Major Land Uses in the Town of Hebron, Connecticut* (Washington, D.C.: American Farmland Trust, 1986); *Duchess County: Cost of Community Services Survey* (Washington, D.C.: American Farmland Trust, 1989); *Does Farmland Protection Pay: The Costs of Services in Three Massachusetts Towns* (Washington, D.C.: American Farmland Trust, 1992); *Alternatives for Future Urban Growth in California's Central Valley: The Bottom Line for Agriculture and Taxpayers* (Washington, D.C.: American Farmland Trust, 1995).

6. Thomas Daniels and Deborah Bowers, *Holding Our Ground: Protecting America's Farms and Farmland* (Washington, D.C.: Island Press, 1997), 55.

7. Gerald Vaughan, *Land Use Planning in the Rural-Urban Fringe,* Extension Bulletin No. 157 (Newark: University of Delaware, 1994); Thomas Daniels and Deborah Bowers, *Holding Our Ground: Protecting America's Farms and Farmland* (Washington, D.C.: Island Press, 1997).

8. P. S. Dillon and D. A. Derr, "Critical Mass of Agriculture and the Maintenance of Productive Open Space," *Journal of Northeastern Agricultural Economics Council* 3

(1974): 23–24; Mark B. Lapping, "Underpinnings for an Agricultural Land Retention Strategy," *Journal of Soil and Water Conservation* 34 (1979): 124–26.

9. Mark B. Lapping, G. Penfold, and S. MacPherson, "Right-to-Farm Laws: Do They Resolve Land Use Conflicts?" *Journal of Soil and Water Conservation* 38 (1993): 465–67.

10. Sarah Thorne, *New Hampshire's Forest Land Base: Conversion, Fragmentation and Parcelization* (Concord, N.H.: Society for the Protection of the New Hampshire Forest, 2000).

11. Katherine Q. Seelye, "Sprawl Seen to Hurt South's Forests," *New York Times,* November 27, 2001, A10.

12. D. J. Mansius, "Fragmentation and Urban Sprawl: Effects on Forests," in *Forest Fragmentation and Urban Sprawl: Effects on Forests* (Portsmouth, N.H.: Urban Forestry Center, U.S. Forest Service, 2000).

13. Sarah Thorne, *New Hampshire's Forest Land Base: Conversion, Fragmentation and Parcelization* (Concord, N.H.: Society for the Protection of the New Hampshire Forest, 2000).

14. U.S. Forest Service, *Forest Fragmentation and Urban Sprawl: Effects on Forests* (Portsmouth, N.H.: Urban Forestry Center, 2000).

15. See www.smartgrowthamerica.com and www.op.state.md.us/smartgrowth.

16. Mark B. Lapping, Thomas L. Daniels, and John W. Keller, *Rural Planning and Development in the United States* (New York: Guilford, 1989); Greg Halseth, "Disentangling Policy, Governance, and Local Contention over Change in Vancouver's Rural Urban Fringe," and Gerald Walker, "Contesting the Countryside and Changing Social Composition in the Greater Toronto Area," in *Contested Countryside: The Rural Urban Fringe in North America,* ed. Owen J. Furuseth and Mark B. Lapping (Brookfield, Vt.: Ashgate, 1999).

17. Kenneth M. Johnson, John P. Pelissero, David B. Holian, and Michael T. Maly, "Local Government Fiscal Burden in Nonmetropolitan America," *Rural Sociology* 60 (1995): 381–98.

18. James R. Pinkerton, Edward W. Hassinger, and David J. O'Brien, "Inshopping by Residents of Small Communities," *Rural Sociology* 60 (1995): 467–80.

19. Vermont Forum on Sprawl, *Economic, Social, and Land Use Trends Related to Sprawl in Vermont,* Exploring Sprawl series, no. 6 (Burlington: Vermont Forum on Sprawl, 1999).

20. Maine State Planning Office, *The Cost of Sprawl* (Augusta: State of Maine, 1997), 10.

21. Mark B. Lapping, "Changing Rural Housing Policies: Vermont's Mobile Home Zoning Law," *Small Town* 12 (1982): 24–27.

22. Michael M. Bell, "The Fruit of Difference: The Rural-Urban Continuum as a System of Identity," *Rural Sociology* 57 (1992): 65–82; David M. Hummon, *Commonplaces: Community Ideology and Identity in American Culture* (Albany: State University of New York Press, 1990).

23. John J. Beggs, Jeanne S. Hurlbert, and Valeria A. Haines, "Community Attachment in a Rural Setting: A Refinement and Empirical Test of the Systematic Model," *Rural Sociology* 61 (1996): 407–26.

24. Lance Freeman, "The Effects of Sprawl on Neighborhood Social Ties: An Explanatory Analysis," *Journal of the American Planning Association* 67 (2001): 69–77.

25. Kenneth B. Perkins, "Volunteer Fire Departments: Community Integration, Autonomy, and Survival," *Human Organization* 46 (1987): 432–48.

26. Perkins, "Volunteer Fire Departments"; Charles R. Simpson, "A Fraternity of Danger: Volunteer Fire Companies and the Contradictions of Modernization," *American Journal of Economics and Sociology* 55 (1996): 17–35.

27. Simpson, "A Fraternity of Danger."

28. Simpson, "A Fraternity of Danger."

A Conversation with Bill Carpenter

The suburban town of Pittsford, near Rochester, New York, made history in the late 1990s by overwhelmingly passing a $9.9 million bond issue to purchase the development rights of six of the town's remaining seven farms—1,200 acres of farmland. What is behind this stunning vote was a brilliant consensus-building process involving all sectors of the town and, apparently, most of the population! The campaign to gain approval for this initially divisive measure was spearheaded by Town Supervisor Bill Carpenter, a self-described "very conservative Republican." He persuaded all interest groups in the community that the cost to taxpayers would be significantly lower if all future development was prevented on much of the town's remaining open space.

Would you tell us how you became involved in the Open Space and Resource Protection Plan of Pittsford, New York?

Carpenter: The Town of Pittsford is about twenty-four square miles in size; population, 27,000. The town had been looking for ways to save the open spaces in the community. We are mainly a residential community with the largest land use being single-family homes. Residents work for Kodak, Xerox, and Bausch and Laumb here in the Rochester area. The second land use is agricultural. Two percent of our land is commercial–industrial, 4 percent is not-for-profit colleges.

In 1986, we adopted "50-50 Zoning," which means that whenever a parcel was developed, 50 percent of the land went to open space. It was nice in thought but not very good for farmers. The farmers and developers were looking to utilize the exact same space—the open lands, the flatlands, the non-environmentally-sensitive lands—so you really can't develop half a farm and have a farm left.

In 1993, I decided to run for town supervisor (prior to that I was the commissioner for public works) to bring the community to consensus on this issue. I began office in 1994 and set right on into a comprehensive plan that we adopted in the spring of 1995. One component called for resource protection and for the preservation of 2,000 acres of the 3,600 acres of open space remaining in our community.

A committee was formed to identify what resources were to be preserved and to develop methodologies of how to make the decision. Three resources were to be protected as open space: 1) agriculture, 2) ecological lands (wetlands and woodlots), and 3) greenways, historic areas, and cultural areas.

There was really no good way of rating land, so this group had to develop the rating system. They field walked the acreage and developed a prioritized system for what had the highest and best rating of the resources left. We took those highest-rated properties from each of the three categories and laid them on an 1,800-acre map that would take us over and above the 2,000 acres; we felt we had done the job. We felt we had developed a perfect greenprint for this community.

The problem was that of the 1,800 acres, 1,200 were farmlands. How were we going to save seven farms on these 1,200 acres? We developed the purchase of development rights. The town was successful on one farm and defeated [by voters] on four others. The difficulty was the voters were in a sense paying high value (90 to 95 percent of the property value) but not allowed to walk on the property. Farmers did not want the government to buy the land and then become feudal serfs to us.

We developed two financial areas of value in the town [60 percent tax incentives and 40 percent borrowing]. We had to borrow $9.9 million to buy those 1,200 acres of development rights. We were able to show the community that it was a "pay me now or pay me later" question. If those lands were developed with houses, we projected it would cost an average of *$250 per year forever* to pay for those services required by those parcels. Buying the development rights, it would cost *$67 per year for twenty years* for $1,300 fixed cost that would end after twenty years.

So we felt we demonstrated to the community from a financial sense that it made a lot more sense to buy the development rights rather than not buy them. I am really a very conservative Republican, and when you start to talk about borrowing $9.9 million, it doesn't seem so smart, but when you really do the math, it really does make sense from a financial long-term standpoint. We have purchased six of the seven farms, and we have picked up a grant for the seventh farm, so by the end of this year we are hoping to finish the protection of the seven farms we set out to.

How was the community involved in the Resource Advisory Committee and in the process at large? Does the policy have a legal or regulatory impact?

Carpenter: From January 1994 through 1998, when we finished up the greenprint and the financial packages, we held over one hundred community meetings. We met with property owners. We did focus groups with engineers, farmers, developers, and environmentalists. The Resource Protection Group was made up of seventeen people representative of every stakeholder interest on the issue. They had six months to do their jobs. There was no law adopted to make it happen. No property owner has to sell it to us, but everyone knows it is a win-win plan. It is really based on policy. I am not a believer that laws always effectuate the best government. I believe building consensus among diverse groups is the best way of getting people to agree to a plan.

The results we came up with are necessary for the community of Pittsford. Each community has to decide what resources are important. Many communities have so much resource they do not feel any urgency to [preserve open space]. It saddens me because we got down to the point that we had only 3,600 acres left, partly because we did not have the tools that are available now.

Essentially our plan was nailed down to getting the details of how we were going to pull it off. Most of our peers around us scoffed at me. They thought I was a little wacky. There are now nine communities around us trying to do what we did five years ago. It is a trend. I think we found the right way. The secret is blood, sweat, and tears. There has got to be leadership somewhere in the community. Someone has to commit a tremendous amount of time to the education and selling of the plan and building consensus.

Note

This interview, conducted by Matt Lindstrom and Nikii Pezzulo, originally appeared in *New Connections*, the quarterly newsletter of the Regional Farm and Food Project, Albany New York (www.farmfood.org).

2

Waiting at the Gate: The New, Postmodern Promised Lands

Michele Byers

> Self-invention and self-location are interdependent, but developing a coherent sense of how either one can be achieved is possible only by recognizing the mutability of both the cultural geography and cultural memory, the endlessly reconfigurable landscapes and histories which are made to serve, nonetheless, as immutable points of reference within specific maps, envisionings and narratives.[1]

THE GATE IS AN IMPORTANT METAPHOR in the study of sprawl. Like the door of the family home, the gate suggests a boundary marker of community, albeit one that it is permeable (it is, after all, a gate, not a wall or a moat). The urban enclave is rooted in the towering high-rise with its dead bolts and doorpeople and intercoms. Gated space is a defining characteristic of contemporary suburbia, designed to "enhance and harden the suburbanness of the suburbs."[2] The gate *is* the boundary marker of contemporary sprawl. It makes manifest the function of suburban domestic space, separated from work and commerce (though not necessarily leisure and consumption). The gate is, literally, the end of the road, the arterials linking that which is within the boundary to that which lies outside its sphere. Blakely and Snyder suggest that gates make those within them feel safe. Borders are seen to be defensible in ways that open communities (especially ones that are not bounded by function, commerce, for instance, as in urban centers) are not. But the boundary/gate is not only about defense; it is also meant to elicit desire and envy in those who are barred from access, those who can only ever be waiting at the gate.

In the pages that follow, I will be talking about gated communities, but I will also be discussing virtual ones. I argue that it is increasingly important to theorize these two types of communities in conjunction with rather than in exclusion of each other. The reason for this is twofold, both of which are discussed by Davis. First, the gated community is hardwired into a "virtual scanscape" characterized by the presence of "electronic guardian angels" and "intelligent buildings."[3] Second, there is an even more simulative impulse of the gated community that is seen in its relationship to the World Wide Web. Especially in relation to the relative affluence of the sprawlscape, the Internet and the gated community can be seen as having overlapping borders of power and privilege. Far from being open to any and all comers, the Internet replicates many of the power relationships that structure sprawl communities. Though these two impulses may seem at first quite separate, they are actually indicative of a larger process that has been active during the last two decades of suburbanization. Drawing on Burgess's dartboard of spatial hierarchy (of 1920s Chicago), Davis has created what he calls the "ecology of fear."[4] His dartboard is characterized by blue-collar suburbs that rely on community surveillance techniques (neighborhood watch and drug-free parks) and privatized communities of the gate. But much of this discussion eclipses the virtual realm that links many (if not most) of the residents of the outer rim. The impulse to simulation that the surveillance of the gated community evidences (as opposed to the human surveillance of the inner suburban rims and urban centers) is not the only type of simulation that gets played out there. The movements toward heightened levels of surveillance (video camera, retinal and fingerprint scans, pass cards) and the parallel surveillance conducted in the simulated world of the Internet, including all the data collected about the individual: financial information, employment history, parking tickets are both noted by Sorkin in the introductory chapter of his anthology *Variations on a Theme Park*. He writes, "It is no longer merely physical—a matter of egregious densities or metastasizing reach—the new city also occupies a vast, unseen, conceptual space. This invisible Cyburbia . . . takes form as necessary, sprouting like sudden mushrooms at capital's promiscuous nodes."[5] I too want to try to reclaim these simuspaces and suggest that these ideas are linked.

Sprawl is a postmodern process of expansion: rooted in the material and the virtual, green space and screen space, the past (memory) and the future (projection). Postmodernism, unlike sprawl, sends ripples of anxiety through many of my students. But sprawl is a useful illuminator of postmodern catchwords—fragmentation, multiplicity, simulation. Even though I work in a relatively small city and many of my students come from small towns, they understand exopolis (see Soja) intrinsically: exit ramps, strip malls, cul-de-sacs, subdivisions of identical row houses, mega–chain stores, and mainstream movie houses. Even if they have not lived it, the aesthetics of sprawl are already known and disseminated by the mass media (today in the books of Douglas Copeland, the movies of Kevin Smith—not to mention the suburban angst, ranging from the merely uncomfortable to the truly dark, of *The Ice Storm, Welcome to the Dollhouse, Suburbia, The River's Edge, American Beauty,* and *Happiness*—and television shows from *Buffy the Vampire Slayer* to *Roseanne.*[6] Sometimes a little theory can get in the way of a good thing known intrinsically from experiences of selfhood and space daily lived and screened. To get through the gate, I think we have to get out of our heads a little and come to theory from the body, the screen, or the "city." Like Baudrillard, maybe we have to drive across America; or (and maybe even more postmodernly) we can do it without leaving home at all by looking to screenic simulation, hyperreality, and (eventually) virtuality.[7] Douglas Copeland, in one of his books, *Life after God,* references a ubiquitous suburban sign that reads, "If you lived here, you'd be home by now." In the sprawl of the exopolis (both real and virtual), you are always already there; perhaps you never even left.

The main problem with—and maybe the main difference between—these two orders of gates (material and virtual) is tactility; that is, in the material world, the ability to touch, taste, and smell are taken for granted by large portions of the population. Bogard talks about this in terms of the current limits of virtual reality, as does Barlow in relation to the limits (or absences) of the virtual community.[8] This is relatively straightforward; even if you can get to (and through) the virtual gate, there are limitations (technological ones mostly that will likely be overcome in the future) to what can be felt there. Life beyond the virtual gate is flat; there is nothing to smell or taste or feel, there is no connection and diversity, and difference is illusory (a simulation). But wait! Is that so unlike life at the gate of the real? True, we can touch and taste and smell, and our identities are constructed by more complex (and often visible) markers than words selected and typed on screen. But connection may be fragmented here, and diversity, difference in sprawl, is also often illusory. What is the point of the gate if not to keep someone out (and others in)? If there was no fear that the stranger, the Other who embodies difference, might intrude on pristine, homogeneous spaces, than might we not do away with gates all together? Gates in both spaces seem to be about access and choice (Where do you want to live? How do you want to spend your leisure time?) and do much to elide the structural inhibitors (particularly things such as availability and affordability of housing and/or technology) and how these are embedded in historical relations of power that have at their core issues of difference in terms of race, ethnicity, religion, ability, gender, age, sexual orientation, nationality, class, and location.

This list is not exhaustive, and some might find it unnecessary, mundane, politically correct, indulgent, or whatever. But identity politics certainly have not ceased to exist despite the claim made by some postmodernists, so we cannot simply leave these things behind (again, at the gate as it were). This is especially so in terms of the subject being discussed here where questions of identity and diversity are so often hidden from view. The previously mentioned list both is and is not important. That is, its importance lies in the intersection of these "selves" and how these intersections create fertile grounds for the development and performance of identity. To keep postmodern about it, however, I would also suggest that these fertile grounds are in constant motion so that identity is not static but fluid. That does not mean that we pick and choose our identities randomly or completely at will but that certain constellations of identity become more important in certain contexts. If this is the case, then our identities are constantly in motion. This is not new. It may be, however, that with the increasing complexity of daily life, we are forced to be more aware of this process as it becomes necessary to attend to our shifting constellations of identity in daily life. At the same time, and likely in response to this uncanny recognition, people increasingly cultivate a nostalgic impulse to contain a sense of personal and spatial unity, attempting to maintain a unified sense of "I" and to control the space in which this "I" exists.[9] This impulse is characterized by two expressions toward social control: first, the desire to construct "safe" social spaces where everything can be controlled and, second, by exploring new possibilities of control in the creation of virtual communities, identities, and identifications. Both of these—the virtual and material worlds—hold out promises based on the unacknowledged issues of homogeneity and the exclusion of the Other whose presence is always necessary to make life inside the gate seem better, richer, fuller, and safer.

The first impulse toward social control finds its best expression in the current proliferation of gated communities in North America. These communities are actively constructed around three things: notions of safety, control, and homogeneity. Often, they germinate and prey on fears of difference, change, and cultural hybridity that are seen as the hallmark of social spaces that are allowed to develop "naturally," without control, what Barlow refers to as the production of the "nonintentional community."[10] Unlike the nonintentional community, the gated community is excessively intentional (every aspect down to color scheme and favorite leisure activities of residents may be selected prior to construction). Part of this intentionality is demonstrated in a central concern with the construction of borders in an age when borders (especially transnational) are increasingly understood as abstract and permeable. For many, this is simply another gate at which to wait for entry into the new, postmodern promised lands. Those who wait are mired in identity politics that suggest that, today, it is the norm to have and engage in constant and unrestricted movement across borders (see, for example, Iyer).[11] One of the effects of transnational borders is to take focus away from border problems much more in the immediate vicinity (in our communities themselves). If things (people, goods, and capital) can move freely and at will from place to place across the globe, it seems ludicrous to suggest that average North Americans, for example, are restricted from moving through such simple spaces as borderland communities, suburban malls, and modem connections. But these communitarian border maintainers—security gates, armed guards, call boxes, and cul-de-sacs—are often more concrete than those we understand as transnational—passports, airport lounges, and travel agencies.[12] But they are also ideological in the sense that they recuperate notions of appropriate community based primarily on class and leisure privilege (but also on racial segregation) or the privileging of (most often) whiteness and/or racial and ethnic homogeneity. Calhoun suggests that with the move toward a more "telematically linked society . . . each of us [will be able] to pursue isolation from everything different, or unfamiliar, or threatening, [and] removing the occasions for contact across lines of class, race and culture."[13] But essentially, the gated community already does this by underwriting itself on the materiality of the bodies it privileges through inclusion—literally, who is allowed to enter and who is left waiting at the gate. That privilege is also indebted to the idea that the community has the right of "choice," that is, to choose which bodies are appropriate to its inclusion, who is allowed across its carefully constructed and maintained borders.

It is pretty straightforward in a way. Blakely and Snyder suggest that "setting up boundaries is a political act," and most people seem to understand that gated communities make inherently political statements, using the mask of merit and achievement to hide growing fears about coming into contact with anything that is Other.[14] Increasingly, it seems, North Americans feel that gates are their only recourse (estimates are at about three million and quickly rising) to create boundaries separating people "by race and income."[15] As Mike Davis points out, this kind of spatial organization reverberates not only through suburban sanctuaries but through urban spaces as well (more on this later).[16] If gated communities are proliferating at this historical moment—and opening up to include not only the "superrich" but middle-income North Americans as well—then this suggests that they offer a "lifestyle paradigm" that reflects the ideological positions (belief systems) and moral anxieties of growing numbers of (particularly white, middle- and upper-class) North Americans. As Graham suggests, "Suburbanites are increasingly paranoid about crime and the incursions of different social groups, leading to physical gates and electronic surveillance systems being installed, which further their isolation and fear. And so the cycle continues."[17] If there is such a cycle of escalating fear and paranoia that encourages the creation and proliferation of borders (gates), then the specific politics involved in the construction of gated communities must be attended to.

Let us take the next step. Many gated communities are newly built suburban tracts that are literally hardwired. I mean that in two ways. First, that their spaces are controlled through technological mediation—security cameras, infrared, pass cards, and alarms linked to law enforcement. Second, that they may possess highly sophisticated computer and media technologies within. The technologies inside the home *seem* to fragment (not to obliterate but to reorganize) the borders that the gated community so actively constructs. The abundance of media products available within the home seem to offer the potential for identification across the very borders (physical and locational) the gated community attempts to shore up.[18] This is, of course, one of the great mythologies of cyberculture/space: that it will provide a forum within which all constellation of identity will enjoy the possibility of equal airtime and existence. Of course, this is not really how virtual cultures have developed, but it seems to have, for some time, provided a comfortingly liberal–egalitarian perspective on the utopian possibilities of cyberspace.[19] The idea that access to a diversity of media and media products will allow people to develop empathic, communitarian relations with "Others" persists.

More intriguing is what goes on within technological proliferation, especially in the supposedly "ungated" world of the Internet. The virtual realm at first seems antithetical to the project of suburbanization, whose aims are surveillance/vision or visibility and restriction of movement/access and bodily control. It is suggested that virtual identity is much more problematically grounded in the materiality of the body than it is in the gated community (or in more traditional information media forms such as print, television, and film). Like gated communities, virtual communities are growing in number. And one of the pleasures (dangers) associated with on-line communities is that they "appear" to offer the ability to transgress the borders of the flesh and blood body, with its markers of gender, race, class, and ability. But this is an illusion, a reflection of the markers that "players" choose to put on and perform within the flat surfaces of the Internet. And given that the "performers" or "players" are (in an incredible majority) white, middle-class, American and European men, the choices they make as they don masks of different ages, races, ethnic groups, genders, sexual orientations, and so on reflect their positions of knowledge, power, and privilege vis-à-vis these groups.[20] Questions of privilege, as raised earlier, are largely absent from critical writing about Internet communities, though they have begun to be taken up by writers such as Nakamura.[21] They are of particular importance in that they provide a discourse of counterclaims to that which suggests that diverse identities (in terms of both players and characters played) are proliferating on the Internet. They insist that attention be paid to who "plays" these parts (what material bodies don what masks) and to what versions of identities (whether they are, for example, built on racist and/or stereotyped versions of particular racial or cultural groups) are at play.[22]

You may have noted that the word that most obviously links the gated and the virtual is "community." Blakely and Snyder explain very clearly how this vague term is "loaded with history, moral connotations, nostalgia, and romanticism."[23] Communities are imagined as groups of people to whom we are connected primarily through physical proximity or some kind of shared interest or aspect of identity. Not all communities can be imagined with any completeness, and in this way virtual communities are, like the nation as described by Anderson, imagined communities. The fact that a community cannot be seen (or felt, touched, or interacted with) in its entirety means that it is constantly evolving within the imagination and can be fully understood only there.[24] The virtual, like the gated community, hides behind a scrim of access and diversity, acting as if there were no gate or as if the gate were of little importance (a mere structural detail). If anything, the virtual seems more compelling, more real, more meaningful than what lies outside it,[25] trading, as it does, "equally, on notions of radical difference and sameness": "We are all different" (but equal and thus the same), "we are all the same" (but we can be different in any way that we choose).[26] But it is all an illusion—a lie—and a paper thin one at that. McBeath and Webb are right about the issue of radical difference and sameness, though, and how these act as mechanisms of trade. Virtual communities offer the radical possibility (though not the real possibility, not a real offer) that difference and sameness might merge into each other, might be one and the same, might become irrelevant. But this possibility is annihilated by the fact that difference always already exists and that it cannot simply be changed into sameness (and why should we want it to, really) any more than sameness can simply become difference. There are bodies controlling those virtual identities and their constitution is overdetermined on the basis of race, class, and gender. This sameness, by contrast, cannot simply become a field of users with a diversity of constellations of identity.

The more I read about virtual and gated communities, the more similarities I see between them. The privilege inherent in life in the gated community means that it is a space from which many people make the leap into cyberspace, suggesting that there is a large overlap in the populations of these two communities—a very important connection. The way both of these communities are socially constructed suggests that they share many characteristics. For one thing, they are both simulated. The virtual community is more obviously so—literally simulated—but the gated community (think of something like Celebration, Florida)[27] is a simulation, mediated by fantasies of safety and homogeneity that are based on media memories that themselves belong not to the order of the real but to the hyperreal (see, again, the last footnote as it relates to Celebration, Florida).[28] They are, literally as well as figuratively, constructed (intentional) communities. That is, their emergence is strategized and controlled to maximize profit. Soja has called Orange County "the last frontier of the American Dream," but is it?[29] Instead of moving ever forward, out toward the vast expanses of, for example, the West (think, go west young "man," go west), we are moving deeper and deeper inside (the country, the home, the self). Both gated and virtual communities may offer new, if increasingly more exclusive (and thus exclusionary), "American dream" frontiers for the new millennium. But a great many more (and more diverse types of) people made it to California (even if they found only hopelessness and poverty there, even if their fate was only to "burn out and fade away") than will today make it any further than queuing up and waiting at the gate.

Davis has referred to gated communities as eutopic (or non-) spaces, spaces that exist (or that are at least birthed, brought into being) in the (collective, corporate?) imagination.[30] This is an excellent way to think through the development of suburban sprawl and, especially, gated communities. It is also connected to the ubiquitous production of other mundane spaces that dot the North American landscape: the fast-food restaurant, the interstate rest stop, the chain store (Blockbuster, Wal-Mart, Kinkos, The Gap, Famous Player's multiplexes). What all these spaces share is that they are reproduced almost exactly in every location and are thus everywhere and nowhere at once: They are like pieces of "ageographical cities."[31] The idea of a creatively (or corporately) emerging nonspace is even more appropriate when applied to the way we think about virtual communities. Just as the gated community seems to be(come) unanchored from the social and cultural landscape (sprawl) that it is built into (but not really a part of), so the virtual community seems to be delinked from the material bodies that make up its populations. Neither evolves in any "natural" (unintentional) way but are, rather, the fully formed products of a hyperreal/hypermediated postmodern imaginary (perhaps something akin to what was once thought of as a collective unconscious) that we (whoever that is) are supposed to share but that definitely privileges certain (dominant) constellations of identity: whiteness, heterosexuality, masculinity. This is exacerbated by the overlap between the populations of gated and virtual communities. Graham makes this connection explicit by looking at how "social polarization," brought on by "telematics-based in shifts in work, social interaction and urban culture," moves into "the emergence of a paranoid and 'fortressed' home-based culture . . . based on spiraling fears of the 'Other.'"[32] Thus, these two emerging community types develop out of similar ideological spaces, structures, and patterns of belief about social organization and hierarchy (and are often built and lived in by the very same people), and it is the particular way they articulate these things that is different and sometimes appears oppositional. That is, the gated community expresses itself in terms of exclusivity (exclusion), materiality, privilege, power, and unified, static identity. The virtual community expresses itself in terms of inclusivity (inclusion), simulation, equality/egalitarianism, knowledge, and fragmented, fluid identities of choice. But both of these are just articulations and do not fully or accurately reflect the "realities" of either type of community or the populations who dwell there.

The overlap between virtual and gated communities is also evidenced in their excessive concern with security (physical in the material world and identificatory in the protection of the anonymity in the virtual). This concern is more obvious in the gated community—but think of how careful people are about putting their credit card numbers or other secure information on the Internet; think of the words we use (lurkers, hackers) for those who seem to slip through cybersecurity. The gated community imposes material security systems—measures that are central to the way the gated community imagines itself—which helps alleviate the anxiety created by the possibility that those who are "Other" might find their way inside.[33] Likewise, cybercommunities assume that everyone within a specific site is the same (whether physically or ideologically), not merely role playing or indulging in voyeurism. But, at least at present, cybersecurity measures are minimal, and communities can do little to police their populations or to rid themselves of those they feel do not belong. The moral outrage in the discovery that the sympathetic woman with whom you have been talking about your divorce is actually a well spoken (written) fifteen-year-old boy cannot really go much further than moral outrage. There is no one to call and complain to, no one to escort the "poser" (passer) to the nearest exit, no laws being broken, no obvious physical trespass. The best the cybercommunity can do is socially sanction the transgressor by ostracization and by spreading their "true" identity around the Internet (and the relationship between trying to pass and being outed, in the virtual or "real," cannot go unnoticed here), although in some virtual communities there can be attempts at retribution.[34]

In the "real" world, security exists in a different order. This is true not only of the gated community but also of contemporary city–states (New York, Los Angeles, or Toronto).[35] As Davis has pointed out, the millennial city is itself becoming a security fortress where all buildings and transport systems are interconnected and all points of entry are protected by private security forces.[36] New inner-city buildings function like their suburban (gated) counterparts. That is, they come complete with private security forces, but with the additional (urban) incentives of internal connections to transport, leisure, necessities, and entertainment.[37] Davis suggests that high-tech urban environments continue to be the most highly gated and virtualized because the computer industries—and thus the capital they generate—are located there (of course, there are also strongholds of the high-tech industry that are more distinctly suburban). But the gated community in its increasingly familiar suburban form must also be attended to even if it seems more obvious (perhaps because of its location, so spread out, as can occur only outside the urban and its tendency toward homogeneity that makes anything that deviates even remotely from the "norm" stand out).[38] Security is the primary concern of gated communities and their residents. One of the greatest selling points of the gated community tends to be its "exclusion, or separation and protection from the outside," especially dangerous "Others" who do not belong inside (usually based on their racial or class positions).[39] The most exclusive gated communities are laden with all the bells and whistles that reassure residents that they will always be alerted (or, better, that they will never need to be alerted) to the presence of anyone or thing who should not be allowed through the gate. This is done by means of infrared cameras, pass cards, walls and fences, electronic or guarded gates, twenty-four-hour surveillance, and private law enforcement.

But are they kidding themselves? The gated community can never really keep itself as pure and free of Otherness as it insidiously (and usually only implicitly) suggests (you have earned the right to live within borders that allow you to regulate action, behavior, and especially access). The increasing fortress mentality merely pretends to stave off the inevitable "return of the repressed" that, it is suggested, along with media-induced moral panics, leads to everything from dropping property values to teenaged pregnancy.[40] In fact, the gated community has moved so far into its own hyperreality that it has become as much a fictional space as a cyberworld. The virtual community, by contrast, only plays at diversity, at the erosion or eradication of borders (or perhaps more accurately, the pretense that they have never been) and the surveillance/security of those borders. Sardar links cyberia and the notion of return explicitly to the panopticon, writing, "Underneath the fabricated tranquility of cyberspace lies the possibility of surveillance by the all-knowing, all-seeing, central network system operator."[41] Sardar also draws on the trope of empire/colonialism in discussing the virtual community:

> We are [thus] set to move from the physical colonization of the Other to virtual colonization of everything by virtual capitalism.[42]
>
> These, whether it be "discovery" of the New World, the spice empires, settling the American West or cyberspace, are all the same, white supremacism, the West as the yardstick of civilization. . . . The supposed democracy of cyberspace only hands more control more effectively back to a centralized elite, the ideology of the free citizen making everyone oblivious to the more enduring deep structures of control.[43]

Virtuality plays on the idea that cyberspace is open to any and all comers and that its most radical potential may lie in its rendering obsolete traditional categories of materiality.[44] But even if there is plenty of room for role playing on the Internet (whose body will I try on in the MUD today?), virtual identities are still tied to material bodies that are gendered, racialized, and classed and that enter into cyberspace from very specific locations (and many of whom do not or cannot enter at all).

I would like, rather briefly and before moving on, to touch on another facet of social reality that has been mediated by both the gated and the virtual community, that is, the question of civics and social values. According to Blakely and Snyder, "Civic space is more than a political or jurisdictional construct. It is a manifestation of society, culture, and the shared polity."[45] They are speaking here directly to the question of civic responsibility and its relation to the proliferation of gated communities in today's society. I, however, have been surprised at how much information on this subject resonated with what I had been reading about virtual communities. It seemed, as I was thinking about the topics that I wanted to write about in this chapter, that subjects such as homogeneity, borders, and geographies of opportunity were much more likely to demonstrate kinship between gated and virtual communities than something as practical (and old-fashioned sounding) as civics. But the fact is that despite the (potentially) great diversity in experiences of gated and virtual life, the way both are theorized in relation to civics and social values/responsibilities has yielded strangely similar results, what Morley calls "community at zero cost."[46] What this means is that, within both of these terrains, community is forged primarily as pretense, transient connection, and opportunism. Each member takes a certain "arm's-length" approach to community where "you can shut people off at the click of a mouse and go elsewhere"—to a new site or the next gate.[47] Similarly, Turkle suggests that the potential for virtual utopias may discourage people from focusing on problems manifest in the "real" world. The same could be argued in relation to the gated community.[48]

In a very interesting study undertaken in Manhattan in 1995, Bayne and Freeman attempted to answer the question raised in the previous paragraph in relation to the civic concerns of citizens of gated versus non-gated communities (or what they call residential social enclaves). They found that

> an individual is attracted to enclave living in order to avoid the problems and tensions of a deeply troubled mass society; living in an enclave, in turn, heightens the individual's inclination to withdraw from the kind of civic involvements that would lend support to those beyond the enclaves who seek to cope with prevailing social problems.[49]

Morley refers to the way in which homogeneity seems to inevitably lead toward intolerance and reactionary politics in suburbia as "anticivics."[50] Later, he goes on to talk about the relationship between this suburban (or enclaval) anticivics and its parallel development within the virtual landscape. He makes this link explicit in a very interesting way, and I will be coming back to him several times in what follows. Morley suggests that new technologies

> entice us to withdraw from the noisy physical world of social division, conflict and difference . . . potentially troublesome others are screened out [of cyberspace] by the expense of the entry costs to its (effectively) gated communities . . . on the whole, global on-line culture has largely become the international public sphere of the globally privileged, increasingly divorced from disadvantaged members of their own society, communicating mainly with each other.[51]

Thus, it is suggested, virtual, like gated communities, are very homogeneous. Where they differ is as follows: In virtual communities, we can pretend that there are people out there who are "different" (in that role-playing way that the media often takes up as one of the boundary-breaking mechanisms of virtual reality). The idea is that "we" are passing among "them" just as "they" are passing among "us." Though this would never be allowed in the "real" world of gates and guards, we pretend that it is in the virtual arena. What this pretense does not point to clearly is the fact that virtual populations are as homogeneously drawn as materially gated ones.

What about the homogeneity of gated and virtual communities? Again, the former seems much more self-evident than the latter. Blakely and Snyder write that homogeneity, along with stability and predictability, are among the four primary social values sought out by gated community dwellers.[52] The authors elaborate by demonstrating that this desire for homogeneity extends not only to race (though this is a crucial issue, especially in the United States, where despite the rise in suburbanization of diverse racial groups, the integration of racial and ethnic groups in the suburbs has remained virtually unchanged for years) but to "income, interests and lifestyle" as well.[53] Davis, looking at developments in deurbanization (suburbanization), draws on a modified version of Burgess' dartboard of spatial hierarchy "into which the struggle for the survival of the urban fittest supposedly sorts social classes" through "concentration, centralization, segregation, invasion, and succession."[54] What these authors suggest is that suburbanization (which, it could be argued, finds both its beginning and its end in the production of the gated community) is intrinsically linked to homogeneity and segregation. Although the virtual community may not be articulated in this way exactly, it remains tied to the material bodies of users with varying relationships to technology, relationships that cannot be completely delinked from questions of access, which are themselves inextricably linked to Otherness and marginalized constellations of identity. Exclusion from virtual communities is effected on the basis of access to technology (which is mediated by race and class, just as access to gated communities is). When Morley asks, "What (or who) is missing from cyberspace?" he attempts to answer his own question by suggesting that part of the success of the Internet has been due to its hyperhomogeneity, the fact that the populace has already been "selected by ethnicity, nationality, class and gender."[55] He suggests that "ironically, for a technology which has been lauded for its capacity to transcend geography, the Internet turns out to have a very real geography which replicates and reinforces existing patterns of social, economic and cultural division."[56] Thus, the pretense of diversity of virtual communities turns out to be just that: pretense. And, as I will show in the final section of this chapter, it relies on hiding the very real differences between populations and very real differences in access to technology of very real bodies existing in the material world.

Barlow makes lists of all the things absent from the virtual community that can be found in what he calls "meat space." He lists as being poorly represented "women, children, old people, poor people, and the genuinely blind . . . the illiterate and most of the continent of Africa."[57] Barlow is making an interesting point, though in his taxonomy he replicates the omission of many groups based, for instance, on race and class. Earlier in the same paragraph, he also lists things like weather, sex, and violence, which he suggests are entirely absent from cyberspace, something that authors such as Turkle, who writes about sex and violence in cyberspace, and Beckles, who writes about "racial terrorism" there, would probably like to argue with him about.[58] These authors make a similar argument to that made by Bayne and Freeman in that they suggest that virtual communities, like material "intentional" (or enclaval) communities in the "real world," are built on the premise of self-interest and seem to reject any notion of civic or social responsibility.[59] Rather than allowing for the emergence of difference and diversity and fostering an egalitarian existence for all, homogeneity and harmony are made primary in order to hide anything that might prove disruptive to the community. This may, for instance, force "cyberplayers" to take up only certain identity markers, those reinforcing existing stereotypes and forms of privilege. Nakamura suggests that asserting race in these spaces is policed by the desire of the players to leave "real-world" issues at the virtual gate. She elaborates,

> While the textual conditions of self-definition and self-performance would seem to permit players total freedom . . . this choice is an illusion. This is because the choice not to mention race does in fact constitute a choice—in the absence of racial description, all players are assumed to be white. . . . This system

> of regulation does permit racial role-playing when it fits within familiar discourses of racial stereotyping.[60]

Beckles takes this even further, arguing as a specific example that there are vast structural barriers to Internet access to the African American community. These are not restricted to issues of class and location; they also stem from, first, "reconcentration of power along class and race lines" and, second, that the Internet is "being readily utilized by historically violent white racist individuals and organizations for the preservation of white power."[61] Finally, Turkle asks how we understand the conventions that govern virtual worlds and how we can (or even should) raise questions about accountability for behavior that is sanctionable in "real life." For instance, Turkle lists such actions as rape and other forms of sexual violence and degradation, murder and assault, destruction of (virtual) property, and cruelty to animals.[62] But in the end, she also cautions that we should not be so distracted by "coding" civil responsibilities into virtual communities that we relinquish ever more responsibility for those that occur in the "real world."

What Davis calls the "mythography of the city" I believe can be a useful concept in the study of the intentional communities of sprawl culture.[63] I take its meaning at face value: that our ideas about spaces are mediated by the myths through which they have become anchored to our social reality. In the case of actively constructed communities (those behind virtual and material gates), these mythographies become excessive, built as they are not only into every strand of the community's fabric but also into its ideological underpinnings (the reasons behind which it was constructed in the first place and what exactly went into that construction). These myths are intimately tied up with ideas about security and demography, and myths about both types of communities seem to start off in much the same spaces. (Who knows best the myths that have grown up around virtual reality or gated communities but the people who have the most likelihood of achieving access to them?) The idea of myth is recurrent in the literatures of urban and virtual sprawl.[64] Benedikt, for example, suggests that our fascination with virtuality is simply an extension of the human desire to live in a world of fiction, fantasy, and myth.[65] This suggests that a "new" or "better" world is out there (as it was for the colonials) for the taking; only this time it will be built exactly to the specifications of our desires. Others argue that the greatest and most dangerous myths are those that suggest that virtuality is a space of equality and free access.[66] This myth is very like the one that underpins the gated community, the myth of equal opportunity in America—that through nothing more than hard work, everyone has an equal chance of getting through the gate. On the flip side of this is, of course, the preoccupying myth that the gate provides safety from all that (those who) threatens to overflow the borders of all the nonintentional spaces that lie outside the safety of the gate.

Wilson argues that a "key figure in urban life is the stranger," and Morley expands this thought by arguing that "each kind of society produces its own kind of stranger."[67] Gated communities create strangers by rendering (or trying to) hypervisible all those who are allowed within their hypervigilant spaces. Virtual communities also create a fear of strangers who "lurk" and "pass," who purport to be "like" and yet cannot ever be proven to be. Both of these spaces depend on the stranger for their articulation, although their needs are quite different (maybe even oppositional). The gated community needs the stranger in order to define clearly who its members are (and what they are) and who they are not. Without the stranger kept waiting at the gate, how would anyone ever know it was desirable to get inside? The virtual community plays at being strangerless; its pretense (myth) is that everyone is welcome and that access is always available. The gated community pretends that it is totally safe because no one could possibly get through the gate, which is, of course, ridiculous because all systems can be undermined. The virtual community pretends it has nothing to fear because it is without the possibility of strangers. This is equally ridiculous as incidents of theft, stalking, and sexual abuse (especially pedophilia) surface from the Internet. The irony here is that, in all likelihood, the transgressive "cyberstranger" is more a mental specter than a reality. The gated community can pretend that by keeping "Others" out, it can keep those within its borders safe. However, the homogeneity of the virtual community suggests that those who perpetrate crimes there, those to fear, are not strangers at all.

I think it is important to clarify that the "Other" around which the gates of sprawl erect themselves is not monolithic or even necessarily concrete. The other can be "Other" on the basis of class, age, geography, nationality, religion, occupation, sexuality, race or any number of more elusive traits that are imagined to be undesirable. According to Singer, writing for the Brookings Institution about the 2000 U.S. census, attempts to define diversity are very complicated.[68] Frey provides a very interesting analysis of the census data, which indicate increasing racial and ethnic diversity in the suburbs in the past decade.[69] This trend might seem to contradict some of the suggestions I have made here. However, Frey himself points to the problematic nature of the statistics he analyzes. For one thing, the suburbs are not monolithic but are characterized by differences in age, affluence, and so on. For another, while statistics indicate that some suburbs have experienced growth among minority groups, others have experienced a decline in white populations. In some ways, these statistics just raise more questions for me: What does it really mean to say that in some areas "minorities and whites are similarly distributed between cities and suburbs"? When whites leave the suburbs, where do they go, and why do they leave? What does it mean to suggest that "economic factors are more important than immigration and race in accounting for most of this movement"?[70] It also raises questions about the increasing expense of living in major metropolitan cities, even as there seems to be a move toward reurbanization. Frey himself ends his conclusion with some excellent questions:

> Does the suburban experience for today's minorities represent the same upward mobility transition as it did for whites in earlier decades? Are minorities re-segregated in separate communities within the suburbs? Is the economic and social status selectivity associated with suburban movers more diluted than in the past?[71]

I would also be interested in knowing more about who the increasing suburban diversity represents. Is it primarily new immigrants, the urban poor, a growing minority middle class? Answering these question will take us closer to an understanding of how the "face" of the suburban community is actually changing. Part of what makes me wonder about this is the question of patterns of Internet use that I have referred to in this chapter. People quickly jumped on the idea of a diverse community living together harmoniously on the Internet. However, studies so far have tended to refute these claims. It is not clear that the increasing numerical count of minority groups in the American suburbs actually tells us whether suburban communities are integrated in any meaningful way. Imagine, for example, six gated communities existing side by side with one another, each being homogeneous unto itself but, taken as whole, diverse (say, culturally or racially or classed). What does this actually tell us about sprawl and gates? What does it elide? Does it tell us that suburbia is more diverse? Yes. But it does not tell us that more fundamental changes have taken place. It does not tell us whether people are ready to give up their gates and embrace diversity or that they are ready to embrace the "Other," literal or virtual.

The ideas I have been talking about suggest a proliferating fascination with borders, their rigid maintenance, and a desire to transgress them. Both are problematic. The gated community is an extreme example of a cultural desire to create and maintain a vision of sameness that is grounded in the materiality and lived experience of the body. It needs the body as a marker, a measure of what is desirable and what is not, what should be included and what should remain waiting at the gate. This seems like a nostalgic impulse, a desire to locate the "I" (the body, the self) by grounding it on the bodies of all those who are not "I" as "Other." At the same time, the virtual community unleashes (or seems to) the possibility that the "I" does not have to be grounded in materiality. In the virtual arena, more ludic and fluid identities appear to be made possible because of the illusion that a self can be constructed that crosses all possible thresholds (another word for gate, I guess) in the creation of a constellation of identity. What both of these types of community point to in very different ways is the problematic relationship between borders and bodies in the contemporary cultural/technological context. In response to the anxiety created by the fragmentation, multiplicity and simulation of the postmodern is an attempt to shore up something that can be controlled: social space or sprawl. But it is necessary to continually expose the fallacy in the mythologies of gated and virtual communities. This will encourage the critique of, especially, the way access to these communities is restricted on the basis of fluctuating constellations of identity, depending of what aspects are privileged in a particular time and space. This will, further, allow for the recognition that certain identities are routinely and systematically excluded from both gated and virtual communities. Finally, the dangers (physical, political, and ideological) in the creation and maintenance of these communities must also be scrutinized.

Notes

1. Jim Collins, "Home, Home on the Array," in *Architectures of Excess: Cultural Life in the Information Age* (New York: Routledge, 1995), 88.

2. Edward J. Blakely and Mary Gail Snyder, *Fortress America: Gated Communities in the United States* (Washington, D.C.: Brookings Institution Press; Cambridge, Mass.: Lincoln Institute of Land Policy, 1997), 11.

3. Mike Davis, *Ecology of Fear: Los Angeles and the Imagination of Disaster* (New York: Metropolitan Books, 1998), 366–68.

4. Mike Davis, *City of Quartz* (New York: Vintage, 1992), 365.

5. Michael Sorkin, "Introduction: Variations on a Theme Park," in *Variations on a Theme Park: The New American City and the End of Space* (New York: Hill & Wang and Farrar, Strauss & Giroux, 1992), xii.

6. It is interesting to note how many of these, especially the films, take place in the 1970s and early 1980s, and thus the suburban u/dys/topias depicted there are, in some sense, presprawl, at least as it is "lived" today. I speculate that this is because these texts are produced by people who (like me) came of age in these eras and thus write to (re)create the sprawl of their own youths, when many suburbs had not yet grown into the fullness of sprawl. It will be interesting, however, to see how sprawl is depicted as new generations (especially those raised there) come to the age where they can be nostalgic for the suburbias/sprawls in their youths.

7. Jean Baudrillard, *America* (London: Verso, 1988).

8. William Bogard, *The Simulation of Surveillance: Hypercontrol in Telematic Societies* (Cambridge, U.K.: Cambridge University Press, 1996); John Perry Barlow, "Cyberhood

vs. Neighborhood," in *Common Culture: Reading and Writing about American Popular Culture* (3rd ed.), ed. Michael Petracca and Madeleine Sorapure (Englewood Cliffs, N.J.: Prentice Hall, 2001), 359–65.

9. I use "uncanny" here in the Freudian sense of something familiar being made strange and frightening. What could me more familiar than "I"? The recognition that "I" am multiple and shifting (and at times contradictory) rather than unified and static forces the "I" into uncanny territory.

10. Barlow, "Cyberhood vs. Neighborhood," 360.

11. Pico Iyer, *The Global Soul* (New York: Knopf, 2000).

12. The idea that all people simply have the freedom to "get up and go" virtually anywhere in the world is an effect of discourse. This is not merely a question of money but also of imperialism and the shifting space and ground of identity. The question is, For whom are transnational (or communitarian or virtual) borders permeable?

13. In Stephen Graham, "Imagining the Real-Time City," in *Imagining Cities: Scripts, Signs, Memory,* ed. Sallie Westwood and John Williams (New York: Routledge, 1997), 41.

14. Blakely and Snyder, *Fortress America,* 1997, 1.

15. Blakely and Snyder, *Fortress America,* 1997, 145.

16. Davis, *Ecology of Fear,* chap. 7.

17. Graham, "Imagining the Real-Time City," 41.

18. Television shows, movies, video games, educational (and other) software, and Internet sites seem to let users see, "meet," and get to know and identify with people and places very different from themselves.

19. Graham, "Imagining the Real-Time City," 41.

20. Ziauddin Sardar, "Alt.Civilization.Faq: Cyberspace as the Darker Side of the West," in *The Cybercultures Reader,* ed. David Bell and Barbara M. Kennedy (New York: Routledge, 2000), 732–52; Barlow, "Cyberhood vs. Neighborhood."

21. Lisa Nakamura, "Race in/for Cyberspace: Identity Tourism and Racial Passing on the Internet," in *The Cybercultures Reader,* ed. David Bell and Barbara M. Kennedy (New York: Routledge, 2000), 712–20.

22. This is important if, for instance, a researcher studies characters on a site and takes at face value the roles adopted by the "players." The roles or characterizations may represent considerable diversity, but the players themselves may belong to the very homogeneous groups described earlier. The diverse characterizations may be completely anchored to negative stereotypes of minority groups.

23. Blakely and Snyder, *Fortress America,* 30.

24. Benedict Anderson, *Imagined Communities: Reflections of the Origin and Spread of Nationalism* (New York: Verso, 1991). Gated and virtual communities are both, in a sense, imagined. First, there is the myth of the gate itself. Second, there is the myth of virtuality, which embraces diversity and anonymity. Finally, there is the enclaval community, which provides the mythology of isolation (safety) from others. These themes and the idea of the myths behind them will be taken up at more length later.

25. Sherry Turkle, "Virtuality and Its Discontents," in *Common Culture: Reading and Writing about American Popular Culture* (3rd ed.), ed. Michael Petracca and Madeleine Sorapure (Englewood Cliffs, N.J.: Prentice Hall, 2001), 366–78.

26. Graham B. McBeath and Stephen A. Webb, "Cities, Subjectivity and Cyberspace," in *Imagining Cities: Scripts, Signs, Memory,* ed. Sallie Westwood and John Williams (New York: Routledge, 1997), 250.

27. Located in Osceola County, Florida, just south of Disney World, Celebration is an "intentional" community developed under the auspices of the Disney Corporation. The advertising campaign summed up the "Celebration experience" as follows:

> There is a place that takes you back to the time of innocence. A place where the biggest decision is whether to play Kick the Can or King of the Hill. A place of caramel apples and cotton candy, secret forts, and hopscotch on the streets. That place is here again, in a new town called Celebration. . . . A new American town of block parties and Fourth of July parades. Of spaghetti dinners and school bake sales, lollipops, and fireflies in a jar. And while we can't return to these times we can arrive at a place that embraces all of these things. Someday, 20,000 people will live in Celebration, and for each and every one of them, it will be home. (cited in Andrew Ross, *The Celebration Chronicles* [New York: Ballantine, 1999], 18)

28. That is, they are based on ideas of a past that never really existed. A past that is rendered in celluloid, brought to the public imagination through fiction (books, comics, film, and television).

29. Edward W. Soja, *Thirdspace: Journeys to Los Angeles and Other Real-and-Imagined Places* (Malden, Mass.: Blackwell, 1996), 238.

30. Davis, *Cities of Quartz,* 6.

31. Sorkin, "Introduction," xi.

32. Graham, "Imagining the Real-Time City," 41.

33. Blakely and Snyder, *Fortress America,* 71.

34. Turkle, "Virtuality and Its Discontents."

35. Witness the recent indie film *Way Down Town,* in which a bunch of office workers in downtown Toronto make a bet about who can go the longest without ever stepping outside. New developments in the core make the desirability of this arrangement explicit for the downtown office worker who can now be linked to home, work, services (supermarkets, dry cleaners, copy centers, liquor stores, shopping malls, medical centers, health clubs, beauty salons, and so on), and entertainment (movie theaters, video stores, restaurants, nightclubs, bars, hotels, party rooms, and so on) by underground walkways or the subway. And anything that cannot be obtained this way can always be tracked down through the Internet.

36. Davis, *Cities of Quartz;* see also George Rigakos, "Hyperpanoptics as Commodity: The Case of the Parapolice," *Canadian Journal of Sociology* 24, no. 31 (1999): 381–409.

37. Here you do not have to drive anywhere (a hallmark of sprawl)—you do not even need a car!

38. In the urban environment, gates are erected and exclusion is enacted primarily on the basis of class (people talk about New York, for example, as being populated by transnational or global wealth). Suburban gated communities are certainly also inclusive on the basis of class but seem more markedly homogeneous in relation to other constellations of identity, such as race, ethnicity, religion, and leisure activities.

39. Blakely and Snyder, *Fortress America,* 44.

40. Sardar, "Alt.Civilization.Faq," 746. One of the most telling (and rather funny) examples of this return (sneaking through the gate) is presented in the *New York Times Magazine*'s issue on suburbia. Randall Patterson ("The Serpent in the Garden," *New York Times Magazine,* April 9, 2000, 58–61) describes the infiltration of "serpents" into the pristine spaces of a middle-class gated community.

41. The panopticon is a prison system in which a central guard tower controls the multitude of cells that surround it through the "idea" of the all-seeing eye/"I." This eye/"I," however, needs to be present only as a suggestion; the threat of its presence is enough to keep people in line (like "big brother").

42. Sardar, "Alt.Civilization.Faq," 746.

43. Sardar, "Alt.Civilization.Faq," 751.

44. On the subject of gender/sexuality in cyberspace, see, for example, Bogard, *The Simulation of Surveillance.*

45. Blakely and Snyder, *Fortress America,* 1.

46. David Morley, *Home Territories: Media, Mobility and Identity* (London: Routledge, 2000), 190.

47. Morley, *Home Territories.*

48. Turkle, "Virtuality and Its Discontents."

49. Jason Ian Bayne and David M. Freeman, "The Effects of Residence in Enclaves on Civic, Concern: An Initial Exploration" *Social Science Journal* 32, no. 41 (1995): 420.

50. Morley, *Home Territories,* 129.

51. Morley, *Home Territories,* 189.

52. Blakely and Synder, *Fortress America,* 44.

53. Blakely and Snyder, *Fortress America,* 148, 129.

54. Davis, *Cities of Quartz,* 363.

55. Morley, *Home Territories,* 186, 187.

56. Morley, *Home Territories,* 187.

57. Barlow, "Cyberhood vs. Neighborhood," 362.

58. Turkle, "Virtuality and Its Discontents"; Colin Beckles, "Black Struggles in Cyberspace: Cyber Segregation and Cyber-Nazis," in *Common Culture: Reading and Writing about American Popular Culture* (3rd ed.), ed. Michael Petracca and Madeleine Sorapure (Englewood Cliffs, N.J.: Prentice Hall, 2001), 381.

59. Bayne and Freeman, "The Effects of Residence."

60. Nakamura, "Race in/for Cyberspace," 713.

61. Beckles, "Black Struggles in Cyberspace," 389.

62. Turkle, "Virtuality and Its Discontents."

63. Davis, *Cities of Quartz,* 392.

64. The gate itself acts as a mythological figure, as does the gatekeeper, a figure who deserves its own chapter and (re)reading.

65. Michael Benedikt, "Cyberspace: First Steps," in *The Cybercultures Reader,* ed. David Bell and Barbara M. Kennedy (New York: Routledge, 2000), 29–44.

66. Graham, "Imagining the Real-Time City," and Sandar, "Alt.Civilization.Faq."

67. Elizabeth Wilson, "Looking Backward, Nostalgia and the City," in *Imagining Cities: Scripts, Signs, Memory,* ed. Sallie Westwood and John Williams (New York: Routledge, 1997), 249; Morley, *Home Territories,* 34.

68. Audrey Singer, "America's Diversity at the Beginning of the 21st Century: Reflections from Census 2000," Brookings Institution, Washington, D.C., 2002, at http://111.brookings.edu/dybdocroot/es/urban/issues/demographics.htm (accessed April 20, 2002).

69. William H. Frey, "Melting Pot Suburbs: A Census 2000 Study of Suburban Diversity," Brookings Institution, Washington, D.C., 2001, at www.brookings.edu/dybdocroot/es/urban/issues/demographics/raceethnicity.htm (accessed April 20, 2002).

70. Frey, "Melting Pot Suburbs," 4, 5, 6.

71. Frey, "Melting Pot Suburbs," 13.

A Conversation with Mike Watkins

Mike Watkins is an architect and town planner for the architectural firm DPZ—the firm started by Andres Duany and Elizabeth Plater-Zyberk. He oversees DPZ's Kentlands, Maryland, office and is a charter member of the Congress for New Urbanism. Kentlands is one of DPZ's most successful New Urbanist developments.

Tell us a little about why you became interested in the issue of livable communities.

Watkins: Well, I grew up in the southern part of Ohio and went to school at the University of Cincinnati, where I got a bachelor of architecture in 1985. I went to a design firm in Baltimore, and it was then that I started nagging Andres and Liz about coming to work for them. Eventually they hired me after I worked for them during the Kentlands design charette. So I have been at Kentlands since 1988.

One of the important contributions of New Urbanism is its critique of dominant municipal zoning policies. What are the challenges you encounter when teaching policymakers about smart zoning decisions?

Watkins: Teaching the policymakers is a pleasure. Teaching the politicians, on the other hand, is very frustrating. I find the work we are doing grounded in common sense and good design principle. We are well received among policymakers because what we are doing is not some marketing gimmick or the latest fad. Once they understand what New Urbanism and smart growth is all about, then we have great allies. So that's a pleasure. The tough part is the politicians who are really interested in the votes and enhancing their career and status as a politician. They are not as understanding.

You mention that New Urbanist design is based on common sense. If this is such common sense, why do many folks choose to live in traditional suburban cul-de-sacs? Do they not have common sense? What are they lacking if it is common sense?

Watkins: First of all, let me say that some people, in spite of the fact that this is common sense in terms of responsible growth, still continue to choose a two-acre lot on a cul-de-sac. That's just what they prefer. We are concerned about offering the neighborhood as an option. For some the option of living in a new house in a neighborhood has not occurred to them.

How do you evaluate and measure success in a New Urbanist community, especially considering the goal of building community?

Watkins: For me, it is the quality of life of the people who live here. I immediately think of families who live here in Kentlands. There are a couple of kids across the street. Before they lived here, they rode the bus forty-five minutes to school each way every day, but once they were here, they could walk. It's about a ten-minute walk past the lake and the houses where their friends live. Immediately upon moving here, the lives of those kids change, and the whole experience growing up changes. We have another family about a block away whose grandparents live in the neighborhood, so the grandmother, who can't drive, and the grandchildren, who can't drive, will actually walk to see one another at their own choosing. And that's made a huge difference. The other thing is the relationships that are formed within the community. You see that when you walk into the coffee shop here or the diner or when you are out for a walk with your dog; those sort of chance meetings happen all the time. In fact, I have a coffee shop now outside the neighborhood that I go to, so when I have work I have to get done, I can actually finish it.

How do you respond to critiques of New Urbanist communities that take developers to task for not including enough affordable housing in their developments?

Watkins: I think it's an unfair criticism. The important thing, first of all, is the range of income levels that can be accommodated within the neighborhood. One has to understand that places like Kentlands, Celebration, or Seaside are actually located in areas that demand a certain price for the ground. So there's a financial as well as a physical context that exists. The more important answer to the question is that, absolutely, they should all include a range. It's actually easier to provide affordable housing but difficult to see that it remains affordable. The problem is that there is such a small supply of good inexpensive housing that the demand for it just drives prices up, and the only way I know to address that is to increase the supply.

One of the other criticisms of New Urbanist communities is that they are often on the suburban fringe. Residents still need the automobile to travel to work, to shop, and so on. What steps are being taken to integrate alternative transportation options in New Urbanist communities?

Watkins: You raise a number of issues. First of all, in-fill is by far the most responsible form of development since the infrastructure is already there. However, we have inadvertently made it extremely difficult to do that. Developers are driven by profit. It's not like it's more fun to build on green fields;

it's just easier. Now, thanks largely to environmentalists, that's getting more difficult, and developers are starting to look back into cities to find sites. As far as transit goes, decisions about transit are made at a regional level. What we can do, however, is make our neighborhoods transit ready. Some people would say we should only be developing on transit lines. But you know with California, for example, growing at the rate of Pasadena one every month, that's a lot of transit stops you would have to develop. There's just not enough transit out there to capture all the growth. So what we do need to do is design our neighborhoods so that they're transit ready.

You mentioned earlier that you have been involved with conducting design charettes. Could you describe how this process works?

Watkins: Essentially, we set up an office as close to or on the site where we are working and invite the public in to the design process. Most of the design team has never been to the site before, but we are very quick studies. We begin drawing immediately. Because we start drawing immediately, we get great reaction from the citizens. They respond very well to drawings, so it becomes a very interactive process with residents and politicians, officials, developers, and builders all engaging in this dialogue about the project that centers around design work. As the days go on, the drawings become more informed, and we eagerly discuss wetlands boundaries and tree-stand areas, and we start getting closer to the numbers the developers are after. The unique thing is that it includes public participation during the design process.

How important do you think the Congress for New Urbanism is today as an organization for new energy and new ideas about design?

Watkins: It is important for two main reasons. First of all because it brings together those of us who are practicing New Urbanists and gives us the opportunity to critique one another's work. That level of dialogue is really among the most valuable that we have. That's the way the early Congress, the first several Congresses, worked. They were great then. As the movement grew, we began to get a lot of people who were interested but not as familiar with all of the principles. So more of the fundamental principles began to be debated at the Congress and some of those who have been involved in this for some time found it less useful, less interesting, but still necessary. It's absolutely essential that we educate more people and also broaden the constituency—not just include architects and planners but also politicians and environmentalists, sociologists, and the medical profession, just the broadest range of people possible.

What are your strongest critiques of some of the projects out there today?

Watkins: Well, let me start with Kentlands. A great disappointment is the lack of a corner store. There's one neighborhood in particular that, because of its distance, suffers because the neighbors don't have a place they can walk to easily so they can get a cup of coffee or a newspaper or just sit waiting for a neighbor to walk by and enjoy a chance conversation. Frankly, the reason for that is the developer didn't listen. We told them to consider the group corner store as an amenity. When you have 352 acres, giving away a quarter of an acre for a corner store is nothing. You don't notice a quarter of an acre, so we instructed them to give away the land instead of building the extra tennis court. Tennis courts are $80,000 a pop. Instead, use that money to begin to build the corner store so that a structure could be offered to someone who would operate the corner store and not have the burden of a mortgage. Instead, what was done was that it was sold for below market rate to someone who wanted to do exactly what we were after. So we were excited about that. Regrettably, this person, because of life circumstances, moved out of the area, and because they got the ground-floor market prices, now they are seeing dollar signs, and they are now asking triple of what they paid for the property. There is no way we could find a successful person out there who can carry those payments. That's a big disappointment.

3

Urban Impostures: How Two Neighborhoods Reframed Suburban Sprawl as a New Urbanist Paradise without Changing a Thing

Wende Vyborney Feller

"URBAN BY CHOICE," proclaim banners along Thurston Road in the Nineteenth Ward neighborhood of Rochester, New York. "A community that brings you back to the early days," confides the brochure for Florsheim Homes' Rose Lane development in Modesto, California. Separated by almost 3,000 miles, Modesto, in the center of California's agricultural Central Valley, and Rochester, on New York's Niagara frontier, look to the urban past for salvation from community tensions about sprawl, identity, and change. Both claim connections to a New Urbanist response to sprawl that emphasizes "the reconfiguration of sprawling suburbs into communities of real neighborhoods."[1]

Rochester and Modesto belong to a tier of 170 midsize cities with populations of more than 100,000 but less than 250,000. In 1870, when fifty-year-old Rochester boasted about the same population as its current 219,773, it ranked twenty-first in the nation; now, the city itself, apart from its metropolitan area, places eightieth. Modesto, with a 2000 population of 188,856, is ranked 104th.[2] The two cities are also roughly comparable in area, giving both a fairly high population density at about 6,000 people per square mile, similar to Milwaukee, Wisconsin, and somewhat less dense than Detroit. In contrast, San Jose had a 1990 density of only 2,800 people per square mile.[3]

Although both cities were reshaped by growth spurts in the 1920s and suburbanization in the 1950s, Rochester and Modesto reached their present population and density from opposite directions. Rochester, which reached its peak at 300,000 in the 1920s, has been losing population to its suburbs since; Modesto, able to annex growth along its borders, tripled its population between

1960 and 1980, then grew another 23 percent between 1985 and 1990.[4] While concerns about sprawl in Rochester are linked to fear of decline, the same concerns in Modesto are motivated by fear of excessive growth. Opinion leaders in both communities seek a solution by hearkening back to a halcyon era between 1900 and 1930 by employing New Urbanist programs, which are openly inspired by urban planning tactics of the 1910s and 1920s.[5]

In Rochester, rehabilitation of an urban past started in the late 1960s with the Nineteenth Ward Community Association's enticements to new home owners to "come alive on the urban frontier" in their early twentieth-century neighborhood. In Modesto, developers such as Florsheim Homes market new subdivisions as representative of an "old Modesto" defined by early twentieth-century neighborhoods near downtown. As we will see here, the Nineteenth Ward and genuine older Modesto neighborhoods are similar in street layout, density, and architectural styles; but the Nineteenth Ward is not typical of historic urban Rochester, and the "new old Modesto" bears little resemblance to the original Modesto.

Rather than re-creating the historic urban fabric, these references to an urban past reframe existing patterns of suburban development as "urban." Unlike postmodern philosopher Jean Baudrillard's simulacrum, the copy with no original that elicits nostalgia for a past that never was,[6] the Nineteenth Ward and the Florsheim developments might be better defined as *impostures.* An imposture claims one original yet shows the characteristics of another. Like simulacra, effective impostures reshape our understanding of social realities. However, while a simulacrum invents a mythical tradition, an imposture substitutes one past for another.

Comfortable Neighborhoods between 1900 and 1930

Built between 1900 and 1930, Rochester's Nineteenth Ward and Modesto's Graceada neighborhood share patterns of street layout, house placement, and housing styles. Commercial and civic functions are restricted to major traffic arteries along the edges of the neighborhood. The interior streets are lined with what architectural historian Alan Gowans names the Comfortable House: a freestanding, single-family house set back from the street with a small yard, with side and back facades that gives a sense of openness by facing toward landscaping. The Comfortable House was rarely architect designed and was most often built from mail-order plans or kits.[7] In both neighborhoods, Colonial Revival, Prairie, and Tudor Revival are popular exterior styles; the Graceada neighborhood also includes Spanish Revival exteriors.

While Comfortable House interiors were similar in being more compact and informal than those of Victorian houses, mail-order builders such as Loiseaux promised that "architectural style determines interior arrangement," and the plan books seem to support this claim.[8] Prairie four-squares have large side entrance halls, with the living room set to one side and the dining room behind it; Colonials and similarly shaped Spanish Revivals have a center hall with the living room to one side and the dining room to the other; bungalows (the workingman's Comfortable House) enter directly into the living room, with the dining room behind it. This match between exterior and interior styles contrasts with new neotraditionalist neighborhoods such as Celebration, Florida, where single-story houses sport fake second-story dormer windows and interior layouts are similar in houses with different exterior architecture.[9]

Although both neighborhoods would now qualify as "sprawl," being comparatively low-density growth beyond the city's core, in 1900 such growth was seen as pragmatically and morally desirable. In a long-established settlement such as Rochester, the central city was associated with disorder and chaos. "Inner city," Gowans explains, "was now the place where immigrant laborers and lumpen proletariat lived—in aging row houses blackened and shaken by overhead trains, sunk in the shadow of grand office towers, whole families crowded into a few rooms."[10] Reformers and civic organizations launched well-intentioned efforts to improve Rochester's inner-city housing, with little perceived effect.[11]

In contrast, a 1902 brochure for the Hillcrest development, just inside the Nineteenth Ward, promised "freedom from dust, smoke, and city odors. Desirable neighbors owning their own homes. Pure country air. . . . Reasonable, desirable restrictions. No stores or factories can be built, or liquor sold."[12] A move to the Nineteenth Ward, however, meant more than escape from dirt and noise. Stories in popular magazines such as *Ladies Home Journal* contrasted the "restraint in character," "growth of self control," and "feelings of social debt [and] of community obligations" resulting from home ownership with the "nervousness, aggressiveness, overhaste, and excitement" of urban living.[13] Home ownership represented the critical defense of family life against the commercialization, sin, and alienation of the city.[14]

Modesto, then with a population of fewer than 10,000, promoted itself in 1916 as an entire settlement that provided escape from city ills:

> Since the development is of the community rather than of the city, the ideals of the citizen are expressed rather in the building of a home city with those charms which attract the lover of home. Modesto has no submerged tenth, no section in which the poor or impoverished live! There is no quarter given to the laboring class, which most cities deem necessary to a "live" town.[15]

Nothing in the geography of California suggests that the reader was fleeing any specific city. Founded in 1870, Modesto was itself a major market town platted by the Central Pacific Railroad in its march down the Central Valley; the fleshpots of San Francisco were ninety miles west, beyond the Coast Range. Isolated from the older big cities of the coast, Central Valley railroad towns such as Modesto, Merced, Fresno, and Visalia were growing into a new kind of city: an urban center with the scale and layout of a suburb.

To say that Modesto had no "submerged tenth" was, of course, to stretch the facts. The poorer neighborhoods on the southwest edge of town, between downtown and the Tuolumne River, might be unincorporated and thus technically not part of Modesto, but local leaders also bemoaned the "skid row" along Ninth Street (then U.S. Highway 99) into the 1920s.[16] In writings for the general public, however, poverty and immorality were absorbed into a seamy Wild West past now a generation gone. Local historian Sol Elias described an 1880s Modesto where Ninth Street "became the rendezvous of the most daring sports, gamblers, and saloon habitués that could be found in the state."[17] For a farm town that had perhaps 2,000 inhabitants, such a rollicking time can only be a simulacra; lending glamour to the low-slung valley town dozing beneath its trees, this myth also consigned dirt and danger safely to the past. The community of home lovers was the future.

Integrating the Invaders

Suburban growth alone did not trigger fear of sprawl. In the early 1970s, at a time when Modesto's population had increased by 70 percent in ten years, transforming it from a town of 36,000 to a rapidly growing small city of 61,000, growth was still reason for celebration. Local historian Jeannette Gould Maino speaks positively of the disappearance of provincialism as well as the "need for more houses, more schools, more recreation, more of everything." An aerial photo in the same book shows rows of single-story freestanding houses spreading into a haze beyond the edge of the picture.[18] Similarly, the migration of Rochester's population into its suburbs—by the mid-1960s, the suburban population equaled that of the city—apparently did not in itself cause alarm.

The catalyst for concern about sprawl was fear of pollution from outsiders moving into the community—not from many sources but from a single source that became a focus of hostility. In Rochester, the "other" was an African American population lured north by the false promise of economic opportunity; in Modesto, it was "people from the Bay Area" lured east by the hope of affordable housing. As anthropologist Mary Douglas explains, social constructions of purity and impurity include rules about what degree of contact carries pollution as well as methods of managing or erasing impurity. When these rules are challenged, Douglas continues, a community can ignore the challenge, condemn it, or try to reframe the social order so that the challenge fits into the new pattern.[19] The promotion of the Nineteenth Ward as "urban by choice" and of Modesto's new developments as the "new old Modesto" demonstrate efforts to reorganize the social understanding of "community" so that newcomers can be absorbed with minimal disruption. These efforts center around the meaning of home ownership, control of the landscape, and, as we will explore further, control of how the landscape is read.

The perceived ability to identify a single major source of outsiders was critical to identifying "the other" as a source of pollution. African Americans were not new to Rochester; by 1920, the number of African Americans in Rochester, settled mostly in the Third Ward, had reached 5 percent of the city's population. When the African American population of Rochester more than tripled in the 1950s, reaching 23,000, this still represented less than 10 percent of the total urban population and affected primarily the mixed-income Third Ward, located between downtown and the Nineteenth Ward, and the traditionally immigrant and impoverished Seventh Ward north of downtown.[20]

While uneasiness toward these new residents was attributed to their violence and poverty—jobs in Rochester's low-unemployment, high-tech economy usually required at least a high school education, which 54 percent of unemployed African Americans lacked[21]—an "influx of middle-class professionals and scientists" was also characterized as a problem because their interest in "equality" rather than "help" or "better treatment" complicated the deliberations of the National Association for the Advancement of Colored People. Despite a 1957 survey that found African Americans felt unwelcome in most neighborhoods, Rochester's community leaders expressed "a feeling of satisfaction that things were moving in the right direction."[22]

This satisfaction was shattered on July 24, 1964, when a minor disagreement at a Seventh Ward street dance escalated into two days of race riots throughout the Seventh and Third wards. The city report on the riots, issued in the spring of 1965, warned that Rochester was "tragically close to talking itself into another riot."[23] For residents in the Nineteenth Ward, a trickle of African American families into their neighborhood put a face to their fears. Although the Nineteenth Ward was still 99.7 percent white, its African American population had tripled in just the prior four years.[24] Numbers were likely to increase because of generous rezoning agreements, allowing single-family homes to be rezoned as duplexes, and real estate agents who capitalized on residents' fears by finding African American buyers for one house on a block and then urging neighbors to sell quickly before their property values plummeted.

In Modesto, the late 1970s and early 1980s brought more than 30,000 Hmong, Laotian, and Vietnamese immigrants—enough new residents to account for three-quarters of the population gain between 1975 and 1985. Yet public concern was more often expressed about people who moved to Modesto "to escape the San Francisco Bay Area's soaring housing prices and sprawl."[25] By 2000, 20 percent of employed people in Modesto and surrounding communities commuted to Bay Area jobs, the highest rate in the Central Valley.[26] While Modesto's obscurity and distance from the Bay Area had long been a favorite theme of *Modesto Bee* columnist Dave Cummerow, in November 1985 he announced, "Somehow or other, they found us. . . . These are the Bay Area commuters we're talking about. They're coming over the hills in increasing numbers and settling here."[27]

Like Rochester's African Americans, the Bay Area commuters were perceived as taking over and ruining entire neighborhoods through their lack of commitment to the community and their effect on housing prices—in this case, the ability to afford mortgages beyond the locals' means. Perhaps the favorite urban legend of the 1980s was that the city's highest burglary rate was in the expensive new developments, where houses sat empty all day because both spouses were away at jobs in Silicon Valley. One Bay Area commuter in nearby Patterson commented to the *Modesto Bee*, "We'd go out and meet people, and they'd always let you know how they felt about you being here."[28]

Modesto's political response focused on control of the landscape. The 1986 ballot was the first to include a major antigrowth initiative, Measure A, which attempted to decrease growth by requiring a more restrictive process for approving sewer extensions. In the late 1990s, Modesto created a Mello Roos district on its outskirts, allowing the city to levy special taxes on new development to support extension of public services. The most ambitious attempt to control the landscape—the one that would spawn the "new old Modesto"—was designation of an undeveloped area on the east side of the city as Village One, a planned community that would adhere to New Urbanist principles for mixed-income, mixed-use, neotraditional development. As originally conceived by San Francisco–based ROMA Design Group, Village One represented a shift from condemning Bay Area commuters to aggressively integrating them into the community's values of home ownership and connection to place.[29]

In the Nineteenth Ward, efforts to control the landscape were spearheaded by the grassroots Nineteenth Ward Community Association (NWCA), which was formed in the wake of the riots. Rather than trying to prevent racial integration, the association emphasized taming "the other" by integrating them into the suburban values of stability, home ownership, and neighborliness. Its objectives stated, "The overall goal is to preserve the 19th Ward as a desirable residential community, open to all who can afford to maintain a home. It is hoped that it could provide a model for the possibility of a racially integrated community within a stable residential area. When we speak of a stable community, we mean one in which property owners are largely resident on the premises, in which homes are largely one or two family residences."[30]

The NWCA used code enforcement, cease-and-desist orders against blockbusting real estate agents, political efforts to rezone duplexes to single-family use and to prevent new duplex or multiunit rezonings, and peer pressure to maintain the neighborhood's single-family suburban character. In 1968, the association took control of local home sales by forming the Real Estate Service. By 1973, the Real Estate Service was handling over $1.4 million in property transactions, and 650 real estate agents were forbidden from soliciting business in the Nineteenth Ward.[31]

Redefining the Urban Landscape

With efforts to control the landscape came complementary efforts to control how the landscape is read. What makes the response to sprawl an imposture is that the desired reading involves associating the landscape with a genuine original that is not the original on which it was actually based. In Rochester's Nineteenth Ward, these efforts centered on three slogans: "Come alive on the urban frontier," "Urban by choice," and "Variety is . . ."

"Come alive on the urban frontier" was the NWCA's first marketing slogan, used as the title of a 1968 Real Estate Service brochure. In defining the Nineteenth Ward as a frontier, the group associated it with two types of space. On the one hand, *frontier* implied that the neighborhood, now surrounded on all sides by development (and, on the side facing the Third Ward, by decay), had somehow retained its suburban character of distance from city problems. At the same time, a frontier is an edge, "a zone of conflicting and competing energies" where lifestyles are tested.[32] Anthropologist Victor Turner points out that edges, or liminal states, are ritually dangerous spaces in which cultures confront both the sacred and the impure and in which the sacred and the impure can switch places.[33] The Nineteenth Ward thus defined itself as an edge zone in which the redeeming power of suburban-style home life would be tested against the lure of urban lawlessness.

The *urban* frontier might be interpreted as the frontier where urban met suburban, thereby defining the Nineteenth Ward as a buffer zone between the high-density central city and the suburban developments beyond the city limits. The NWCA's slogan since 1994, "Urban by choice,"[34] explicitly identified the Nineteenth Ward with the central city. The tree-lined streets, comfortable single-family houses, and low-rise commercial fringe districts were now to be read as *urban*, or as affiliated with the bustling, high-density, mixed-use central city from which the Nineteenth Ward had once represented escape.

What made the Nineteenth Ward *urban*? Political scientist Wilhemina Leigh argues that simply having a substantial African American population causes a neighborhood to be seen as both more African American and more urban than it is.[35] By accepting African American home owners, the Nineteenth Ward may have literally become *urban by choice*. The slogan has, however, another dimension. The biennial neighborhood house tour, started in 1971, chose "Variety is . . ." as its first slogan, and subsequent coverage has emphasized the variety of the housing in the neighborhood.[36] Unlike Modesto's Graceada neighborhood, where individual builders' decisions mean that diverse housing styles sit side by side, the Nineteenth Ward was developed as a series of tracts of essentially identical homes. What gives these homes—with their appealing but mass-produced deep woodwork and leaded glass windows—a claim to variety is their contrast with the raw new houses being built beyond the city limits to meet increased demand that everyone should be able to afford a home. Even as these wildly popular housing tracts were increasingly being marketed with multiple features and options, they were being characterized by the intelligentsia as characterless, depersonalizing, and alienating.[37] To be *urban* and offer *variety* was to be ideologically positioned against suburbia and with a vibrant, intellectually stimulating city more characteristic of Manhattan's myth than Rochester's reality.

In controlling the reading of the landscape, developers in Modesto also looked back to neighborhoods of the 1920s, not to establish this landscape as urban but rather to redefine settlements of contemporary tract homes as conveying small-town character. The most aggressive and explicit attempts to naturalize new development through connections to the community's past were produced by Florsheim Homes in their Rose Lane, Rose Hollow, and Rose Circle developments as part of the Sacramento-based builder's efforts to dominate the San Joaquin Valley market. "Why do people just get nostalgic when they visit Modesto's newest housing gems?" asks the combined brochure for Rose Lane and Rose Hollow. The brochure asserts—and the design firm William Hezmalhalch Architects affirms—that the Rose developments were designed by studying the local vernacular, including the Graceada Park neighborhood, so as to "emulate the qualities that made these neighborhoods so solid and enduring."[38]

The names of the model homes echo local tradition: McHenry, for Modesto's wealthiest family in the 1880s; Graceada; Sycamore; and Coffee, for a prominent ranching family. At Rose Circle, twenty miles south in the smaller city of Turlock, the same models are renamed for old Turlock families: Ferreira, Donnelly, and Caswell. The decorative staging at the Rose models intensifies identification with the past by featuring late Victorian furniture and sepia-toned photos.

What the "new old Modesto" does not echo is the scale, layout, or architectural styles of the old Modesto, on which it is supposedly based. The Graceada neighborhood and other neighborhoods of the same era are based on an orthogonal street grid that rarely includes cul-de-sacs; streets in the Rose developments are a maze of curving lanes and cul-de-sacs with few outlets to the major thoroughfares. The mail-order and plan-book houses that sold best in Modesto were models that sit low beneath the sycamore trees; the Rose houses are tall and blocky. While Rose houses can be built with bungalow-style details, the same model can equally readily be obtained with New England clapboard siding and shutters or with country French details. Unlike the original Graceada houses, in which exterior architecture partly determined interior plan, Rose houses are a domesticated version of Robert Venturi's "decorated shed."[39]

By claiming New Urbanist aspirations, the Village One developments—as of mid-2002, Adrianna (a gated community), Center Court, Davante Villas, Impressions, Mill Brook, Nottingham, Palisades, and Windmere—also implicitly identify themselves with the local vernacular and traditional forms. But the Village One developments, the Rose subdivisions, and the other edge tracts are fundamentally indistinguishable.[40] The only New Urbanist feature that routinely appears in Modesto subdivisions is generous space for public parks; but no new ideology was needed to obtain this, as reserving space for parks has been a routine part of city growth since about 1910.[41] To be New Urbanist in the world of Village One—or "the new old Modesto"—is to be like the developments of the rapid-growth years: rows of garage-dominated "snout houses" set on mazelike streets, well separated from high-traffic commercial arteries and multifamily dwellings.

Replacing One Past with Another

If anything, Village One is less spatially connected to the community than the frankly sprawling development of the 1970s and 1980s. The acres of moderately sized tract homes built by developers such as Horn and Allan Grant, built for families with jobs in the local economy, were placed within walking distance of schools and shopping centers; not until the mid-1980s did Modesto gain its first gated subdivision. Non–Village One developments, such as Generations, Monterey Bay, Vizcaya, and Rose Lane, while priced for Bay Area budgets, are sited to take advantage of existing commercial areas. Village One, however, while planned to include industrial, commercial, and civic areas, has been built without these amenities. The city of Modesto recently concluded that, other than a new high school exclusively for Village One teenagers, the planned nonresidential areas would probably never be built; much of the land designated for industrial use is on land that cannot be zoned industrial or that has already been developed as housing.[42]

Far from being a small-town boondoggle, Village One, the Florsheim "Rose" developments, and their imitators are successful impostures that typify the face of New Urbanism in central California. The Peter Calthorpe–designed Laguna West development on the southern outskirts of Sacramento proved on a January 2001 visit to be a collection of "snout houses" with garage-dominated facades laid out in a tangle of cul-de-sacs served by high-speed feeder streets lined with blank walls.[43] The only nonresidential space is a community center building and a park fronting an artificial lake. No shopping or office area is within walking distance or even accessible by bus. Laguna West differs dramatically from the New Urbanist pattern of balanced use, an orthogonal street grid, streets fronted by properties, rear alleys giving access to rear garages, and diverse housing types.[44] Demographia, a self-proclaimed "pro-choice" development group that rates New Urbanist communities from 1 (not noticeably adhering to the principles of the movement) to 5 (exceptional example), gives a 1.5 rating to the development.[45]

These developments claim traditional local vernacular forms of the early twentieth century as their original, although they do not follow those forms. What makes them impostures rather than simulacra is that they do have a local vernacular original: the sprawl of the 1970s. By 1985, when concerns about sprawl became widely vocalized, 70 percent of Modesto's population was comprised of people who had arrived during the post-1960 boom. While Modesto was then in the midst of a building boom, even the 1985–1989 land rush would not equal the proportion of housing stock—over one-fifth of the city's total—built between 1970 and 1979. (In contrast, less than 5 percent of the city's housing stock, as of 1990, had been built before 1939.[46]) For most Modestans, sprawling subdivisions *are* the traditional regional vernacular.

The most recent participants in this tradition seem to be the most concerned about its impact: A 1999 survey found that people who had moved to the Central Valley within the past five years were more likely than longtime residents to be concerned about loss of farmland to development.[47] By identifying sprawling acres of snout houses with tradition, history, family, and progressive urban planning, developments such as Village One, the Roses, and Laguna West express an ideology that potentially allows the "old-timers" from the 1970s to accept the new developments as traditional while allowing the invaders to feel good about settling on former farmland located nearly two hours' drive from their Silicon Valley jobs.

The Nineteenth Ward, a genuine 1920s neighborhood, owes its status as imposture to its impact on Rochester's vision of *the urban.* Judged against its own goal of promoting integration through home ownership, the Nineteenth Ward is arguably a success. While the Rochester city limit elsewhere defines an economic and racial divide between suburban dwellers (as of 1990, 95 percent white, 75 percent home owners) and city dwellers (31 percent African American, 44 percent home owners), the Nineteenth Ward boasts a home ownership rate almost identical to that of the suburbs and unchanged since 1960 despite being 55 percent African American.

The Nineteenth Ward is also the city's only remaining example of a stable African American settlement. Although "nearly all" of the 250 businesses damaged in the riot had reopened within ten months,[48] historically African American commercial districts in the Seventh and Third Wards were later demolished and redeveloped as housing projects or not at all. The "thriving residential and commercial enclave"[49] on the Third Ward's Clarissa Street vanished for many years, to be replaced in the late 1990s by neo-Victorian townhouses and condominiums. The Jacksonian-era Third Ward, now calling itself Corn Hill, has been largely rebuilt as a Nineteenth Ward style of residential neighborhood with late Victorian Stick Style facades. Similarly, the neotraditional Anthony Square development that recently replaced the FIGHT Square housing project—one of the few triumphs of postriot African American activism—is a tiny enclave of Comfortable Houses. In the absence of a historic central city—much of downtown was replaced 1964 by an indoor shopping mall, now failed[50]—the Nineteenth Ward has become the benchmark for historic urban character. Its website further naturalizes its suburban flavor as Rochester's authentic historic urban fabric, claiming the neighborhood as "one of the earliest settlements in Rochester" based on the 1804 location of a tavern somewhere nearby.[51] Although the Nineteenth Ward's model was suburban sprawl, its claim to authentic *urban* form is such a successful imposture that it now defines the city's historic urban character.

Searching for Paradise in Urban Form

That suburban form is *urban* is, of course, implicitly the claim of New Urbanism, given that movement's loyalty to early twentieth-century forms. Architecture professor Michael Pyatok argues that New Urbanism's response to sprawl is less about restoring the urban than about using architecture and urban planning to promote a suburban middle-class ideal of home and family.[52] The Rochester experience, with its emphasis on neotraditional Comfortable Homes at the expense of commercial African American neighborhoods in Italianate rows, supports this contention.

If class is substituted for race, Modesto's history of sprawl tells the same story. A 1948 planning study used to justify aggressive and far-reaching annexation of northeastern suburbs labels settled areas to the south and west of downtown "Oklahoma" for their concentration of white laborers who came to California from Oklahoma, Texas, and Arkansas.[53] Some of these West Side neighborhoods remain unincorporated today, in the corner of town with the largest concentration of Hispanics (40 percent) and noncitizen immigrants (20 percent); the poverty rate in this area is 30 percent or more. Historic Modesto names from the West Side—Tuolumne, Paradise, Washington, Mellis, Marshall, and Burbank—are not used to name model homes sold to affluent Bay Area commuters.

Of Modesto's many rounds of visioning for smart growth, the one in 1987 prompted Dave Cummerow to write, "We can be anything we want to be. . . . The only problem is that now we aren't exactly sure what we want to be. Mainly because we aren't really us anymore."[54] The quest for a New Urbanist—or old urban—solution to "sprawl" may be less about controlling growth than about promoting nostalgia for an imagined time when we were really us, before the invasion of *them,* a time when, to borrow from the brochure for the neotraditional community of Celebration, Florida, "neighbors greeted neighbors in the quiet of summer twilight . . . and porch swings provided easy refuge from the cares of the day."[55]

The fundamental American philosophy about cities and growth may be best expressed by Wink van Ripple, Dave Cummerow's occasional mouthpiece for concerns about loss of local identity. Musing on the downtown preservation woes of a city that was founded when merchants abandoned older settlements in Paradise and Empire City, Wink comments, "Maybe . . . we should all move back to Paradise."[56]

Notes

1. "Charter for the New Urbanism," *CNU: Congress for the New Urbanism,* at www.cnu.org/cnu_reports/Charter.pdf (accessed May 26, 2002).

2. Sam Bass Warner Jr., *The Urban Wilderness: A History of the American City* (1972; reprint, with foreword by Charles Tilly, Berkeley: University of California Press, 1995), 70; "U.S. Cities with Population Over 100,000," *Learning Network,* at www.infoplease.com/ipa/A0108676.html (accessed May 24, 2002).

3. Campbell Gibson, "Population of the 100 Largest Cities and Other Urban Places in the United States: 1790–1990," Population Division, U.S. Bureau of the Census, Working Paper No. 27, June 1998, at www.census.gov/population/www/documentation/twps0027.html (accessed May 24, 2002).

4. Unless otherwise noted, population figures and characteristics are derived from U.S. Census data.

5. Bettina Drew, *Crossing the Expendable Landscape* (St. Paul, Minn.: Greywolf, 1998), 194.

6. Jean Baudrillard, "Simulacra and Simulations," in *Jean Baudrillard, Selected Writings*, ed. Mark Poster (Stanford, Calif.: Stanford University Press, 1988), 166–84.

7. Alan Gowans, *The Comfortable House: North American Suburban Architecture 1890–1930* (Cambridge, Mass.: MIT Press, 1986), 29–33, 41–63.

8. *Classic Houses of the Twenties*, reprint of *Loiseaux's Plan Book No. 7* (1927; Mineola, N.Y.: Dover, 1992), B. For interior plans, see also *117 House Designs of the Twenties*, reprint of *Gordon-Van Tine Homes* (1923; Mineola, N.Y.: Dover, 1992); *Sears, Roebuck Catalog of Houses, 1926*, reprint of *Honor Bilt Modern Homes* (1926; Mineola, N.Y.: Dover, 1991); and Henry L. Wilson, *California Bungalows of the Twenties*, reprint of *A Short Sketch of the Evolution of the Bungalow: From Its Primitive Crudeness to Its Present State of Artistic Beauty and Cozy Convenience* (n.d.; Mineola, N.Y.: Dover, 1993).

9. Douglas Frantz and Catherine Collins, *Celebration, U.S.A.: Living in Disney's Brave New Town* (New York: Henry Holt, 1999), 66, 20.

10. Gowans, *Comfortable House*, 17.

11. Blake McKelvey, *Rochester: The Quest for Quality, 1890–1925* (Cambridge, Mass.: Harvard University Press, 1956), 71–120.

12. Quoted in Doris M. Meadows, *Neighborhood in Community: The Nineteenth Ward in Rochester, New York* (Rochester, N.Y.: Neighborhood History Project, 1984), 12–13.

13. Maude Radford Warren, "A Young Married Couple in a Hotel," *Ladies Home Journal*, April 1909, 13ff.

14. Gowans, *Comfortable House*, 8.

15. Modesto Chamber of Commerce, *Modesto, California* (San Francisco: Mysell-Rollin Co., 1916).

16. Colleen Stanley Bare, *Modesto: Then and Now* (Modesto, Calif.: McHenry Museum Press, 1999), 84.

17. Quoted in Jeannette Gould Maino, *One Hundred Years: Modesto, California, 1870–1970* (Modesto, Calif.: Belt Printing, 1970), 19.

18. Maino, *One Hundred Years*, 14, 60.

19. Mary Douglas, *Purity and Danger: An Analysis of the Concepts of Pollution and Taboo* (London: Ark, 1984, 1988), 34–38.

20. Eugene E. Du Bois, *The City of Frederick Douglass: Rochester's African American People and Places* (Rochester, N.Y.: The Landmark Society of Western New York, 1994), 6, 17.

21. Lou Buttino and Mark Hare, *The Remaking of a City: Rochester, New York, 1964–1984* (Dubuque, Iowa: Kendall/Hunt, 1984), 3–4.

22. Blake McKelvey, "The Rochester Riots: A Crisis in Civil Rights, Juvenile Delinquency or 'Cityatrics'?" (pamphlet, ca. 1965), General Collection, Rochester Public Library, 5–10.

23. McKelvey, "Rochester Riots," 1.

24. U.S. Bureau of the Census, *Current Population Reports: Special Census of Monroe County, New York, April 1, 1964*, Series P-28, No. 1376, October 13, 1964.

25. Ellen Chrismer, "The 80's: Immigrants, Commuters and Computers Bring a New Way of Life," *Modesto Bee* Special Report, at www.modbee.com/reports/lookingback/9looking.html (accessed June 20, 2000); reprints can be obtained from the *Modesto Bee.*

26. Public Policy Institute of California, "Regional Perceptions," November 1999, at www.ppic.org/publications/CalSurvey7/survey7.ch3.html (accessed May 26, 2002).

27. Dave Cummerow, "Here They Come," in *Modesto on My Mind* (Modesto, Calif.: McHenry Museum Press, 1995), 20, reprint of column in the *Modesto Bee,* November 9, 1985.

28. Chrismer, "The 80's."

29. See Goodwin Consulting Group, "Infrastructure Financing Plan: Village One," (administrative draft), May 21, 2002, at www.modestogov.com/cmo/cfd/pdfs/villageonegoodwin/village_one_goodwin.pdf (accessed May 24, 2002).

30. Quoted in Mim Bush and Margaret Weiss, *A History of the 19th Ward Community Association, 1965–1979* (draft), Local History Collection, Rochester Public Library, 2.

31. Bush and Weiss, *History,* 9, 14–15.

32. Grady Clay, *Real Places: An Unconventional Guide to America's Generic Landscape* (Chicago: University of Chicago Press, 1994), 157–58, 163–65.

33. Victor W. Turner, "Liminality and Communitas," in *Readings in Ritual Studies,* ed. Ronald L. Grimes (Upper Saddle River, N.J.: Prentice Hall, 1996), 511–19.

34. Sherrie Negrea, "19th Ward Promotes City Life," *Rochester Times-Union,* June 3, 1994, 3B, reprint at www.19thward.org/art/Article3.jpg (accessed May 26, 2002).

35. Wilhemina A. Leigh, "Trend in the Housing Status of Black Americans across Selected Metropolitan Areas," in *The Housing Status of Black Americans,* ed. Wilhemina A. Leigh and James B. Stewart (New Brunswick, N.J.: Transaction, 1992), 43–64.

36. Bush and Weiss, *A History of the 19th Ward Community Association,* 25; "19th Ward Open House," *Democrat & Chronicle,* October 14, 1995, 1E, reprint at www.19thward.org/art/Article2.jpg (accessed May 26, 2002).

37. Typical of this genre is Richard E. Gordon, Katherine K. Gordon, and Max Gunther, *The Split-Level Trap* (New York: Bernard Geis Associates, 1960, 1961), a study of anomie and disintegration in Bergen County, New Jersey. Herbert J. Gans addresses and, to some extent, rebuts these concerns in *The Levittowners* (New York: Vintage Books, 1967).

38. "Features" (brochure for Rose Lane and Rose Hollow by Florsheim Homes, ca. 1998); "Implementing a Design Vision in Residential Communities," *Builders Digest,* December 1999, at www.whainc.com/news/12.99.html (accessed May 26, 2002).

39. Robert Venturi, Denise Scott Brown, and Steven Izenour, *Learning from Las Vegas* (rev. ed.) (Cambridge, Mass.: MIT Press, 1972, 1977, 1988).

40. This conclusion is based on reviewing the brochures for the developments and, in most cases, visiting the models in person. The first date in parentheses is the approximate date of the brochure; the second is the date of a visit. Village One developments include Adrianna (ca. 2000, July 2000); Center Court at Charleston Place by J. C.

Williams Co. (ca. 1996, July 2000); Davante Villas by NOVA Development Group (ca. 2001, June 2001); Impressions at the Village by Kaufman Broad (ca. 1999, July 2000); Mill Brook by Bright Homes (ca. 1999, July 2000); Nottingham by Lew-Garcia-Davis, Kaufman-Meeks + Partners, SKW & Associates, and Dahlin Group (ca. 1996; July 2000); The Palisades at the Village (ca. 2000, July 2000); and Windmere by Heritage Homes (ca. 1997, July 2000). Developments in Modesto and neighboring smaller towns, outside Village One, include Autumn Brook by Bright Homes (ca. 2001), Celebration Series at Creekwood by Oakwood Builders (ca. 1997, July 2000), Generations by Florsheim Homes (2001, June 2001), Monterey Bay (2001, June 2001), Summer Creek by Bright Homes (ca. 1999, January 2001), Vizcaya by SCM (2001, July 2001), and Yosemite Meadows by Lowe Development (ca. 1996).

41. Bare, *Modesto,* 50.

42. Goodwin Consulting Group, "Infrastructure Financing Plan."

43. Tracts being sold and constructed at the time included Laguna Park by JMC and West Lake Island by Kaufman and Broad.

44. Andres Duany, Elizabeth Plater-Zybeck, and Jeff Speck, *Suburban Nation: The Rise of Sprawl and the Decline of the American Dream* (New York: North Point, 2000), 245–52.

45. Demographia, "Laguna West: New Urbanist Snout Houses," *Neo-Traditional Community Reviews,* May 21, 2000, at www.demographia.com/db-nu-calgw.htm (accessed May 26, 2002).

46. *Demographic and Economic Profile of Stanislaus County* (Modesto, Calif.: Stanislaus County Economic Development Corporation, 1993), 62.

47. Public Policy Institute of California, "Regional Perceptions."

48. McKelvey, "The Rochester Riots," 9.

49. DuBois, *City of Frederick Douglass,* 18–21.

50. Midtown Plaza was the nation's first indoor shopping mall, according to Bernard J. Frieden and Lynne B. Sagalyn, *Downtown, Inc.: How America Rebuilds Cities* (Cambridge, Mass.: MIT Press, 1989), 84. The failure of Midtown Plaza and surrounding similar developments is documented in "Main Street Decays as Vacancies Rise," *Rochester Business Journal,* December 7, 2001; "Lender's Bid for Midtown Affirmed," *Rochester Business Journal,* June 19, 2001; and "Sibley Centre Sees Challenges Mounting as Plaza Saga Ending," *Rochester Business Journal,* July 13, 2001.

51. "History," *Nineteenth Ward Community Association,* 1999, at www.19thward.org/history.html (accessed May 26, 2002).

52. Michael Pyatok, "Martha Stewart vs. Studs Terkel?: New Urbanism and Inner City Neighborhoods that Work," *Places* 13 (Winter 2000): 40–43.

53. James Wilson McGrew and Arthur Bruce Winter, *A Study of the Fringe Areas of Modesto* (Denver: University of Denver, September 1948).

54. Dave Cummerow, "Growing Pains," in *Modesto on My Mind,* 24, reprint from *Modesto Bee,* April 18, 1987.

55. Quoted in Andrew Ross, *The Celebration Chronicles: Life, Liberty, and the Pursuit of Property Value in Disney's New Town* (New York: Ballantine, 1999), 18.

56. Dave Cummerow, "All in Favor . . . ," in *Modesto on My Mind,* 66, reprint from *Modesto Bee,* October 19, 1985.

A Conversation with Don Chen and Elizabeth Humphrey

Don Chen is the executive director of Smart Growth America (www.smartgrowthamerica.org). Elizabeth Humphrey was the associate director of Smart Growth America at the time of this interview; she is now the executive director of Growth Management Leadership Alliance (www.gmla.org).

What is your personal background with suburban sprawl and smart growth? Why are these issues important to you, and how did you end up in the positions you are in now?

Humphrey: My college degree was in social anthropology, and I entered into the field of planning because I thought that it was important to make communities better for the people who lived in them. I started out doing basic planning and then went to the transit agency and from the transit agency into policy—I went from designing bus stops to federal policy work. Smart growth is a tremendous field with all sorts of policy areas from transportation and transit, where a lot of us came from, to affordable housing policy, social equity, and farmers markets—things that people care about. Smart growth is not just policy work; it means something to people. I could see doing this forever.

Chen: I started my career working as an antipoverty activist working under homeless issues, and from an academic standpoint I also studied environmental studies and was interested in [the] science of environmental quality, ecology, etcetera. I started to merge those two in my career working for environmental justice, particularly with regard to urban pollution and its effect on communities, and then moving into transportation policies and finally realizing that transportation policy can't be improved to better serve people in communities unless you deal with land use, and that brought me to the issue of smart growth.

What is smart growth? Why did you choose to use this term?

Chen: One of the reasons that smart growth has been so successful is because it has been branded well. It is something that sounds good. It is important to be careful with messages and words . . . if you look at any major political initiative, whether it's in Congress or in a state, [whether it's the] Patients' Bill of Rights or the Contract with America, they all have a fancy name that has a good-sounding ring to it. That is part of the reason we chose this term. We chose to name the group Smart Growth America because there were already a lot of people talking about smart growth.

Beyond the surface, I think it is important to emphasize two things: One, efforts to improve communities are not about stopping growth—that's a significant departure from what a lot of activities in the past have pursued. Two, that there is a better way to do things than what we are currently doing. I do believe there is dumb growth out there. There are obsolete practices that were once appropriate to the times of 1950s, but they are being applied today in a completely different context and are resulting in dumb outcomes. That's why I think our message is very important in emphasizing a smarter way to go and emphasizing that growth is also our goal.

Why is smart growth at the top of your agenda, and why should it be at the top of agendas at the federal, state, and local levels?

Chen: For me, smart growth represents a confluence of a lot of different issues that I care about—poverty, environmental quality, making communities better, making them thrive—and it appears to be a task that is at its prime for opportunity to make change. I think smart growth is probably the most viable alternative to come along in half a century to really improve upon the old model of building communities—which have been sprawl. In terms of public officials, lots of public opinions surveys indicate that sprawl and traffic and the combined issues within that ball of wax are at the top of peoples' agendas, and we've seen that from the Pew Centers for Civic Journalism and in our own surveys.

It is becoming such a hot issue among Americans because they are tired of the consequences of sprawl, the traffic, the runaway taxes, the abandoned central cities, the eaten-up open space and farmland, and, as a result, they are counting on their elected officials to do something about it. They are realizing that single entities can't handle it by themselves; there needs to be regional cooperation, and that generally comes from the public sector.

Humphrey: We can talk about smart growth as an issue that should be at the top, but it is much more useful to think of it as a new way to look at public policy altogether. Public policy should be about urban form as much as it is about how we spend federal money because those two things are linked.

The time to put issues in silos—water, air, transportation, and housing policy—has passed. We know that they are all linked, and we have to get much better at understanding the implications of one kind of policy on another policy. You can't do that if you continue to pretend that they don't relate to each other.

Who are your major opponents, and what are their primary criticisms?

Chen: The groups are in four categories. There are people who are against smart growth because it is against their ideology, and those are the people who tend to be opposed to big governments and in favor of markets. The second group represents people who want to improve communities but see a potential downside to smart growth—people who are working on equity issues and see problems with gentrification, with regard to improving communities, problems with housing affordability, and those types of things.

Then I'd say in a very political way there are opponents who tend to lose something if the system changes. And the fourth category are people who are uninformed, who either have a false conception of what smart growth is or what it is trying to achieve or they just don't know enough about it to trust it.

In terms of the first category, the sort of libertarian activist, they are tough to deal with because they are well organized, well financed, and very verbal. They go out and communicate and get printed in the paper. Their work tends not to be based on academic juried research; they tend to come up with their own numbers and say what they want to say. And that is difficult to combat because in the marketplace of ideas, it is the media that governs, not the academy.

The second category represents the equity activists. The whole purpose of smart growth is to bring equity activists together with environmental activists and housing activists in a coalition to accomplish mutual goals. It's not something that is ever done; it's like an alcoholic—you always have to be working on being sober for the rest of your life. With regards to our coalition, even though we have a lot of people together with a nice balance of environmental and equity groups, we have to keep working at it.

The third category, the people who stand to lose, includes home builders and others who fear the effects of smart growth because they see themselves losing revenues, losing jobs, losing this or that. We need to produce evidence that smart growth will produce as robust economic outcomes and environmental outcomes and other outcomes as sprawl does. It's something that we have been successful in communicating, and now we really have to produce the evidence.

Regarding the fourth category of uninformed people, ignorance is often the enemy of the good; all we can do is work to inform people about what the truth is and what real reliable research and data tell us about how to grow.

4

Lawns as Artifacts: The Evolution of Social and Environmental Implications of Suburban Residential Land Use

Robert Messia

"ON YOUR MARK, get set, get ready, mow!" And they're off, middle-aged men darting across the dirt track at the Dacotah Speedway, machines roaring with a deafening sound. Usually in races like these, men would be riding stock cars or all-terrain vehicles, but for this special race held in Mandan, North Dakota, these suburban warriors are putting the pedal to the metal, sometimes exceeding speeds of sixty miles an hour, on souped-up riding lawn mowers. The *New York Times* reported on the events: "Lawn mower racing is becoming a regular sport. Local newspapers report the results. Local businesses sponsor many of the racers . . . and races draw thousands of fans."[1] Is lawn mower racing a cult phenomenon? Perhaps. But it might signify a larger trend in American culture: the importance of the lawn as the quintessential suburban ecology and icon.

Suburbia may be best recognized for its sprawling nature. Though the actual structure of the domicile is a defining characteristic of the suburban, it is important to include the vast spans of land adjacent to homes, wide driveways, private swimming pools, private swing sets, and grills as just as, if not more, indicative of the nature of suburban life. Front and backyards are expressions of larger patterns of suburban life. The well-kept, prim and proper, ornamented front yards and the hedonistic nature of the backyard, where individuals seek refuge from the world in a very protective and intimate playground of leisure and relative luxury, are important indicators of American suburban living patterns. Using a historical framework to look at the social and environmental impact of land use in suburbia will draw important conclusions on the nature of suburban life. To do so entails looking at the origins of the suburbs and the importance of the post–World War II period as establishing an American suburban model and paying particular attention to the sociological trends of the late twentieth century.

The importance of the lawn to American culture has been relatively marginalized. In *Crabgrass Frontier,* Kenneth Jackson defined the yard as a "functionless carpet of green."[2] His work, considered by many to be the definitive volume on the evolution of American suburbs, may very well have defined scholarly study of the American lawn in a restrictive manner. However, an examination of several important pieces of evidence reveals that yards are the most fundamental and function-filled component of the suburban landscape and that social and environmental implications of the lawn are exceptionally important to suburban studies.

Early American Lawns: Patterns and Ideals

In terms of human history, the lawn is not an old tradition per se.[3] By most accounts, the lawn became popular in Europe during the eighteenth century, but "its antecedents are deeply embedded in humankind's struggle to understand and control nature."[4] This struggle for the general American population did not take a substantial form until after the Revolutionary War, as most families did not have individually owned plots of land in front and in back of their homes until long after the war.[5] The grassy areas that did exist were typically held in communal ownership with houses surrounding the patch of land. These open spaces followed two general patterns: open fields, used for animal grazing, and gardens, used to grow fruits, vegetables, or flowers, typically with both an aesthetic and a utilitarian orientation.

Debate rages on the question of the origins of our contemporary idea of the lawn. Some argue that a practical open space used for grazing and cultivation marked the origins of the American lawn, while others argue that the American lawn is an outgrowth of the desire to achieve the European aristocratic ideal of tamed and beautiful open space.[6] Thorstein Veblen argued that this emulation of higher-class lawn care tendencies can be found in the American social structure as well. Veblen explains that the lawn is a true manifestation of "conspicuous consumption," a term popularized by that author arguing that showy displays of money and property were the conventional basis of social status in America, beginning with the nation's founding and being exemplified later during the Gilded Age. Veblen wrote that the lawn "unquestionably has an element of sensuous beauty, simply as an object of appreciation and as such no doubt appeals pretty directly to the eye of nearly all races and classes."[7]

While the lawn of the colonial and Revolutionary period was rarely the "green velvet carpet portrayed in treatise literature,"[8] the key attractiveness of a piece of land to colonists was its grassiness.[9] And though lawns were not a standard feature of every citizen's home, they were found at homes of members of the political and cultural elite and were slowly being found at homes of the upper-middle class.[10] This trendsetting was advanced by two of this nation's most important revolutionaries and land planners, George Washington and Thomas Jefferson. Washington was extremely involved in the maintenance of the grounds of his home at Mount Vernon.[11] He was particularly interested in keeping the grass cut short, but in a time before lawn mowers were invented, Washington tested several methods, eventually finding himself satisfied with the idea of using grazing deer to keep the green expanse short and tamed.[12] Jefferson, who has been praised in his design of the lawn at the University of Virginia and similarly for his residence at Monticello, was perhaps a more direct exemplification of the influence of the lawn on the American landscape. At both sites, Jefferson exemplified the idea that landscape architecture could act as a "civilizing force."[13] Jefferson clearly wanted to change the American landscape, as did Washington, to better meet aesthetic visions that would create a lawn framework for the budding young nation. Washington and Jefferson were two privileged landowners who had immense public and symbolic stature. As O'Malley points out, there is "no doubt the images of the great private house, as epitomized by Mount Vernon and Monticello, and readily available through prints and illustrated books, contributed to the status of the American lawn for the individual homeowner."[14] Further, their dichotomous choice of influences, Washington a British model and Jefferson a French model, demonstrates a distinction that would forever influence American landscape architecture and eventually lead to the synergism of domination and beauty that is the contemporary American lawn.

Roots of the Crabgrass: Nineteenth- and Early Twentieth-Century Lawns

According to Kenneth Jackson, the mowed lawn appeared in the mid-nineteenth century aside the proliferation of the American suburb. Between 1825 and 1875, middle-class America changed the way they looked at residential land use. As Jackson stated, "They no longer needed herbs and vegetables from gardens, and, thanks to the mowing machine, a smooth lawn replaced the rough meadow cut by scythe or sheep."[15] The lawn, "carrying the English connotations of nature with it, became a symbol of prestige in the nineteenth-century suburbs."[16] Following the Civil War, suburbs and consequently lawns flourished as the direct result of the proliferation of the railroad and later the electric trolley transportation revolutions.[17] This suburbanization—and its correlated proliferation of the lawn—was sparked by several well-documented reasons, such as the desire to leave troubled urban areas, the desire for healthier living provided through the open space and cleaner air, and a desire to separate work from home and leisure.

There are several reasons for the "need" of the suburban lawn. One reason is a desire to remove one's family away from the rest of the population. This is exemplified in the fact that the middle class deliberately reshaped the landscape by surrounding single-family homes with yards in their new communities to strengthen the power of the family.[18] Another reason was the desire for upward mobility and its manifestation in the lawn. As Virginia Jenkins, author of *The Lawn,* put it quite bluntly, "Upper middle-class Americans emulated aristocratic society with their own small, semirural estates."[19] In general, the lawn was one of the primary selling points of these new suburban homes, as it shifted social class designations from the equity and ubiquity of urban homes connected to the streets with the upper-middle class designation of a "healthy" green space and the status symbol that is the front lawn.[20]

The first to lay out the genuine American suburban landscape was planner and landscape architect Fredrick Law Olmstead in his 1868 plan for the community of Riverside, Illinois.[21] In Riverside, Olmstead required that developers place each house thirty feet away from the sidewalk, planting trees along the street to create the sense of place most usually identified with a park.[22] With the proliferation of neighborhoods such as Olmstead's Riverside, mowing of lawns became an increasingly important issue. Throughout the nineteenth century, many different innovations were attempted to cut the lawn, and most were unsuccessful.[23] By 1881, only 47,661 lawn mowers had been manufactured in the United States, meaning that fewer than half a percent of the households recorded in the 1880 census would have owned a mower.[24] Adding to the issue was the fact that lawn mowers that were available at the time were "heavy, unwieldy and backbreaking."[25] However, amazing advances were made in the 1880s, leading to the proliferation of rudimentary push lawn mowers.[26] Fascinatingly, Butterworth, writing in the time period, describes the connectedness of a mowed lawn and social status in the late nineteenth century: "A smoothly-shaven lawn is as necessary an adjunct to the houses of the rich and tasteful as the moat and precipitous paths used to be to the castles of the feudal barons."[27] Nearly ninety years later, Kenneth Jackson echoed similar sentiments, stating, "Although visually open to the street, the lawn was a barrier, a kind of verdant moat separating the household from the threats and temptations of the city."[28] Jenkins further describes the lawns of the period attached to middle-class homes as mimicking those of higher social elites, designed to show "the passerby that the homeowner was well-to-do and aesthetically advanced."[29] This demonstrates that lawns are status symbols and a form of fortification. As such, the lawn is an expression of sophistication and wealth that is emulated down the social hierarchy, influencing the values and habits of Americans from the social aristocracy to the nouveau riche and down to the middle and lower classes.

The proliferation of mail-order catalogs, from such companies as Montgomery Ward and Sears, Roebuck, helped fuel the national craze for lush, beautiful, green lawns.[30] Mail-order catalogs had an extremely high circulation in the late nineteenth century, a circulation that would increase even more with the regular mail distribution of the early twentieth century that allowed lawn care companies to disseminate advertising about their products.[31] The lawn, unlike almost all the other products advertised in mail-order catalogs, was not yet mass-produced. That is, the lawn, while a desirable end, was not as easily gratifiable in a tangible sense of sending payment and receiving product. Rather, the mail-order catalogs propagated an idea more than a single product in regards to the lawn. Further, these catalogs had a receptive audience as the nation became increasingly urbanized, industrialized, and communicatively connected.[32] It was the substantive growth of the middle class in the late nineteenth century that led to the initial dramatic proliferation of the lawn and the connectivity of the social ideal of land ownership to the newly industrialized economic climate whereby middle-class workers were better able to achieve the lawn ideal.[33]

The Great Depression and World War II challenged the lawn's proliferation. The Great Depression's 95 percent decline in residential housing construction[34] stopped the lawn in its tracks. World War II did not hinder the growth of suburban housing, nor consequently did the lawn, in the same fashion the Great Depression did, but it did change the ways Americans purchased and maintained their homes. World War II shifted but did not stop the suburbanization of America as big businesses benefited from the war through implementation of mass production techniques.[35] During the war, women were urged by Scott's Lawn Corporation to care for the lawn in the absence of their husbands, fathers, and sons. The company said in a 1943 advertisement that "the maintenance of lawns may fall into new hands this year but there will be ample incentive to carry on valiantly until those on furlough from the job come home."[36] *Better Homes and Gardens* went further than Scott's, charging women with the ideas of the social and aesthetic importance of a well-kept lawn, even during wartime. An article in that publication from 1944 stated, "About your lawn, remember this—we have lawns for their good looks and what they do for the whole place. An unmowed lawn looks as bad as a man without a shave."[37]

Front Lawns: Ambiguity, Duality, and Proliferation

Expanding on nineteenth- and early twentieth-century ideas, the front lawn came into its modern fruition after World War II with proliferation of the suburban lifestyle. As Kenneth Jackson wrote, "The new suburban yard in the United States followed a naturalistic or romantic approach."[38] That is, the yard, particularly the front lawn, was viewed as a manifestation of the quixotic ideals of beauty and order in nature, tamed by man in honor of God and nature itself. This honoring of God and nature is quite paradoxical, as this homage was demonstrated through the razing and later improvement of the natural space created for man; therefore, honoring God and nature came from the human desires to conquer and control, making the expression of the reverence to God and nature supposedly better than the original.

The front lawn presents an interesting mix of public and private space. The lawn in and of itself is a piece of land, privately owned and maintained, yet is in another way considered communal property whose beauty is to be enjoyed by those who live around the domicile and adds to the social and physical environment that is the neighborhood. As lawn historian Georges Teyssot noted, "The ambiguity of the lawn, of the threshold between the public space of the street and the private, familial, domestic space, has remained a constant of the American landscape since the moment of its colonization."[39] The front lawn makes the separation of the public and private realm purposefully blurry. Jackson wrote that "unlike Europeans, jealous of their possessions, and of their privacy, Americans did not build walls around their houses."[40] This distinctly American and markedly ambiguous use of space allowed for the scale and view of land that created a communal parklike area defined by the facades of the suburban homes.

In one sense, the combined totality of a neighborhood or a suburban development's front lawns creates an integrated social and physical community. What is an individual plot of grass, trees, shrubs, flowers, and cement can be viewed as part of a collective whole, a parklike community space, shared aesthetically but based on intensely individual landownership patterns. It is this ambiguous nature of the front lawn that brings about the informal social regulations on the aesthetics of the land. In post–World War II suburbs, it was not uncommon that neighbors would shun their fellow citizens for failing to maintain a well-mowed lawn or for generally not caring for their lawns.[41]

In America's quintessential suburban community, Levittown, lawns, and front lawns in particular were viewed as exceptionally important to the citizens, to the developers, and to a general sense of community. For Abraham Levitt, one of the brothers who created the "town," the "lawn [was] the most important feature" of his housing development.[42] The front lawn's prominence in Levittown was limited by its relative small size, but it was nonetheless an important component to the development, as many home buyers viewed the achievement of their own plot of land as an important milestone in their achievement of the American dream. It was not only Levitt who knew the implications of lawn ownership; those who lived in Levittown also understood the social importance of a well-kept lawn. Levitt's belief in the importance of lawns was put into action. For homes that Levittown Corporation rented, the contract stipulated that "the tenant agrees to cut or cause to be cut the lawn . . . at least once a week between April fifteenth and November fifteenth."[43]

The informal and formal arrangements established to regulate lawn care have long been an assumed characteristic of suburban life. As a 1969 article in *Life* magazine acknowledged, "Let a man drink or default, cheat on his taxes, cheat on his wife, and the community will find forgiveness in its heart. But let him fail to keep his front lawn mowed, and to be seen doing it, and those hearts will turn to stone."[44] A 1999 study conducted by Robert Feagan and Michael Ripmeester found that there is "social machinery" that does regulate the lawn care habits of neighbors within a community.[45] The interviews that Feagan and Ripmeester conducted were revealing. One suburban resident stated that "people who have nice lawns are nice people, hardworking. They care for their property and for themselves."[46] From this statement it can be derived that those who have a nice lawn are reflecting the good character of their individuality, their home, and their community in the keeping of their lawn. Further evidence is found in another resident's statement: "If even one person lets their lawn go, it makes the neighborhood look disgraceful."[47] This statement implies that the manner in which an individual takes care of his or her lawn helps determine the overall quality and character of a neighborhood, underlining the connectivity and communal nature of the individual lawn. Feagan and Ripmeester conclude that the lawn "is almost unquestioned, or ideologically naturalized, as the appropriate landscape form for private green space . . . the lawn maintains its status as a symbol of order and industriousness."[48] Extending Feagan and Ripmeester's conclusions, one can see that lawns today, in particular front lawns, are symbols of "order and industriousness" and further as an expansion of the beauty and goodness of individuals and communities.

Grills, Play Sets, and Pools: Rest and Relaxation?

If the front yard represented the romantic tradition of beauty, order, and putting one's best foot forward, then the backyard represents the medieval notions of utility, chaos, and a lack of concern for the opinion of others. One need only look at the structure of a "typical" backyard to understand the various values that are at the backyard's core. Backyards tend to be more enclosed than front yards. Further, access and the ability of others to see in the yard is regulated by this enclosure. Because of this enclosed structure, the backyard has taken on the role of private retreat. There are two general areas that reveal the nature of human interaction with backyards. The first are sociological elements, which consist largely of lawn accessories, such as grills, play sets, pools, and fences. The second are the ecological elements to this interaction of human and land as embodied in the use of chemicals on lawns.

According to authors Herbert Bormann, Diana Balmori, and Gordon Geballe, "In medieval times, gardens were a form of environmental control: surrounded by walls, they provided a psychological sanctuary for human activity."[49] This desire to have control over one's environment and to feel a sense of independence on one's own land is at the heart of the backyard and is a direct expression of medieval tendencies. The walls, created by fences, define not only space but also the behavior that occurs within that space. With the feeling that one is isolated both physically and psychologically by fences, there is a feeling of increased self-determination and decreased inhibitions. Individuals rationalize the need for fences to surround their yards as a matter of protection of property. Jenkins documented that "fence manufacturers sold fences to protect lawns from neighbors' dogs and children."[50] With this evidence, one could conclude that the lawn is such an intensely private and closely treasured piece of the suburban home that residents do not want it spoiled by the use of others to whom the land does not rightly belong but who may put the grassy area to more practical use, such as children's play or animals' natural fertilizer.

One of the most dangerous activities associated with the backyard is that of barbecue grilling. Grilling, in popular perception, is commonly associated with a white, middle-class, beer-bellied man wearing a "kiss the cook" apron. This common notion of the male dominance over the grill has been a part of American culture throughout the post–World War II period. A period of substantial growth in the use of barbecue grills came about in the late 1980s and early 1990s as the popularity of propane-gas grills rose with that product's declining prices. In 1984, 22 percent of American households used their barbecue grill for at least one meal during a typical two-week period.[51] And eight years later, that share was up 10 percent, marking a significant proliferation of grill usage among American families.[52] But what is thinly veiled behind this popular and easy method of cooking dinner on an open flame is the need to establish dominance over one's environment. That is, in grilling meat, a person is reasserting his position in the environmental hierarchy, marking his position at the top of the food chain. And who best to assert this dominance as the head of the household but a man? Balzer captured this relationship between men and grill quite well: "How many women boast to their relatives, neighbors, friends and just about anybody who will listen that their husbands are the best backyard cooks? Just take a look at where barbecue grills are sold. They are visually displayed alongside lawn equipment, reinforcing the male dominance of this appliance."[53] Grilling can be very dangerous work; according to the *Journal of the American Medical Association,* there were about 2,000 burn injuries at the height of the mid-1990s grill craze.[54]

But in the backyard, we do not only endanger the welfare of our husbands and fathers at the grill, as we allow our children to play on "equipment" that has been documented as having prolific minor and some major injuries associated with its use. On trampolines alone, from 1990 to 1995, the number of children age eighteen and younger treated in emergency rooms for trampoline related injuries rose 98 percent from 29,600 to 58,400, with an average of 41,600 injuries per year.[55] In addition, on backyard play sets of all kinds, 60 percent of injuries are the result of falls,[56] but these private playgrounds are reaching into the sky, sometimes as high as two stories.[57] Here we see playfulness and fun overtaking safety concerns, as is typical of backyard activity. Playgrounds not only are the manifestation of children's desires but are also the engineering result of adult labor and planning; therefore, we can see that parents and designers understand the playground more in terms of hedonism than in terms of safe play. The personal plastic and metal playgrounds that parents have been erecting in their backyards can today cost upwards of $3,000,[58] but there is a "design and size to fit every budget and backyard."[59] These amazingly deluxe and engaging playgrounds represent a fundamental change in American society, as these private retreats for children have been neatly tucked away in the confines of the private backyard, while traditionally playgrounds have been a public good, offered in neighborhood parks for all children that could be enjoyed by all regardless of family income. Today the playground has taken a much more individualistic and seemingly more American twist as children play on their backyard playgrounds by themselves or with family members but almost never with children they do not know. This social isolation of children in the protected backyard further marks a potential connectivity to a decline in social capital and general involvement in community affairs outside one's own personal grassy sphere.

The backyard swimming pool may very well be, as swimming pool historian Thomas van Leeuwen noted, "a hallmark of American life," as there are more swimming pools in the United States than in the rest of the world.[60] It is the prototypical American suburban city of Los Angeles that has the "largest density of private swimming pools in the world."[61] The swimming pool is an interesting element of the backyard, as it involves both the hedonism and the danger components that seem so central to backyard leisure. The physical pool is an interesting artifact, as it is "the architectural outcome of man's desire to become one with the element of water, privately, and free of danger."[62] Further, there are many psychological interpretations of swimming that seem important in this discussion, as "a swim in the pool is a complex and curious activity, one that oscillates between joy and fear, between domination and submission, for the swimmer delivers himself with the controlled abandonment on the forces of gravity, resulting in the sensations of weightlessness and timelessness."[63] Note the male-normative language in reference to pleasure and danger in the backyard—a further exemplification of the man's place in the backyard. In addition, there is a strong historical connection between swimming and military training, particularly in the eighteenth century. It was this military background that gave rise to the rectangular swimming pools as Austria-Hungary and Prussia structured their swimming according to the rules of exercise in the field: marching in straight lines and turning at sharp angles.[64] Leeuwen stated that the pool can be viewed as an "aquatic parade ground."[65] The pool's combination of danger, dominance, submission, militarism, and self-indulgence makes it exemplary of this barbaric, medieval backyard notion that is so prevalent among actions and attitudes in the semi-enclosed private space.

Drug-Addicted Lawns

"The quest for the perfect lawn has gotten out of hand," wrote Dan Johnson in the May 1998 edition of *The Futurist.*[66] Essentially, the social drive to achieve the "perfect lawn" has led to the environmental degradation of the land that composes the lawn. Therefore, the environmental component of the lawn has been viewed primarily as a by-product of this social quest. This chapter is an analysis of the social and environmental implications and manifestations of suburban residential land use. However, notably absent from the discussion thus far has been substantive discussion of the environmental component to the lawn. This has been a conscious choice, as the popular conceptualization of the lawn as an environmental artifact has come about only since the end of World War II and more significantly since Rachel Carson's *Silent Spring* was published in 1962, when public health was connected to the environment.[67]

Since Carson's definitive work, countless other scholars have contributed to the research on environmental degradation and human actions, particularly lawn chemicals. The variety of chemicals used is so great—as is, consequently, their potential health impact—that enormous volumes have been compiled detailing the most up-to-date information available.[68] The widespread nature of the threat posed by lawn chemicals is widely accepted and is compounded by the very fact that sixty-seven million pounds of pesticides are applied yearly to American lawns.[69] Historically, lawn care programs were designed with a "one treatment fits all" approach, based on blanket applications of pesticides over an entire lawn.[70] Therefore, from this fact we can conclude that pesticides have been overused and spread over too large an area, killing not only targeted pests and weeds but also healthy plants and insects that support our environment. However, organic lawn care is not always a feasible alternative, according to some lawn enthusiasts. As one lawn treatment expert stated, "Quit your job. That's how much time you'd need to maintain a healthy lawn without chemicals."[71] While this may sound a bit extreme, the fact that organic lawn care most likely does take up more time and effort than chemically treated lawns has been well documented and is often cited as a determining factor in the choice of lawn treatments.[72]

While some are still reluctant to use organic alternatives, others are returning their lawns to their "natural" state, a practice that has gained substantial press coverage in recent years. A June 2001 article in *Time* magazine documented a couple's lawn in Las Vegas, Nevada, that was transformed from the generic green grass of anywhere USA to more traditional desert plants.[73] While this couple made the decision on the basis of aesthetics and financial considerations, others in the Midwest and on the East Coast, the traditional havens of lawns, have also brought native plants back to the lawn. Lorrie Otto, a longtime Wisconsin environmental activist, decided one day to let her lawn go natural, letting "weeds" overtake her front and backyards. This was not an act of laziness but rather a conscious choice to preserve nature in her own small way.[74] She went so far as to cut down giant old Norwegian spruce trees from her front lawn, as they were not native plants. Because her lawn does not fit in with her neighbors', she has been subject to complaints from neighbors, reflecting the collective or public good aspect to the suburban front lawn. As Otto stated, "Most Americans have become so alienated from the land that they don't know how to treat it."[75] But while Otto claims that Americans are not connected to the idea of nature and the lawn, others have argued that the American lawn has a positive effect on the environment.

A major advocate of the contemporary lawn is the lawn care industry's single largest corporation. The ServiceMaster Corporation, a $6 billion Fortune 500 company and the owner of TruGreen, ChemLawn, and Terminix, was founded in 1947 by an evangelical Baptist and has a unique, if not ironic, company mission: "to honor God in all we do."[76] While honoring God, this gigantic corporation raked in profits over $150 million annually each year since 1996 and has increased its market share considerably in recent years, indicating a growing interest in chemical lawn services for its 3.5 million customers.[77] What is so fascinating about this corporation is its dual commitment to God, the creator, and also its commitment to killing insects and weeds. There is, in my view, some hypocrisy in these two commitments when grouped under one umbrella. But this signifies a greater trend, as many God-loving Americans do not view contradictions between the use of chemical lawn care products and environmental degradation. But by no means do the decent motivations of lawn enthusiasts outweigh the damage they do to the environment. As Bormann, Balmori, and Geballe stated quite eloquently, "In our efforts to make it [the lawn] greener, to make it all grass, to keep it closely mowed, and to make it a constant companion of suburban development, we are unnecessarily contributing to some of the most severe environmental problems facing the world today.[78]

Conclusions

Lawns are profound statements on American culture. The sheer area that the American lawns occupy signifies this cultural significance. If stitched together, America's lawns would occupy some 50,000 square miles, an area equal to the size of the Maine, Massachusetts, Rhode Island, Connecticut, and New Hampshire combined.[79] Specifically, they are real indicators of our social and environmental values. The lawn is an intensely American invention in its modern form; while it draws on European traditions, the post–World War II lawn has taken a ubiquity and social import as never before. Jefferson and Washington's vision of landownership and all that this ownership entails is essentially American; in addition, as our society has evolved throughout the past 200-plus years, we have come to see the lawn in a vein very similar to these Founding Fathers. While Americans may have developed a taste for front lawns out of the aristocratic and estatelike qualities that are presented in this type of landownership, the front lawn ultimately serves a more functional use as well. The front lawn as a physical separator demonstrates the importance of both physical and social distance between neighbors in suburban communities. It is this combination of social and physical distance that has come to define suburbia and that has become an important if unfortunate part of American culture.

Notes

1. Peter Kilborn, "Gentlemen, Start Your Lawn Mower Engines," *New York Times*, June 12, 2000, available through Qpass at www.nytimes.com.

2. Kenneth T. Jackson, *Crabgrass Frontier: The Suburbanization of the United States* (New York: Oxford University Press), 60.

3. Herbert F. Bormann, Diana Balmori, and Gordon Geballe, *Redesigning the American Lawn: A Search for Environmental Harmony* (New Haven, Conn.: Yale University Press, 1993), 13.

4. Botmann et al., *Redesigning the American Lawn,* 13.

5. Therese O'Malley, "The Lawn in Early American Landscape and Garden Design," in *The American Lawn,* ed. Georges Teyssot (Princeton, N.J.: Princeton Architectural Press, 1999), 84.

6. Georges Teyssot, "The American Lawn," in *The American Lawn,* ed. Georges Teyssot (Princeton, N.J.: Princeton Architectural Press, 1999), 20.

7. Thorstein Veblen, *The Theory of the Leisure Class* (New York: Random House, 1934), 133–34.

8. O'Malley, "The Lawn," 84.

9. Joseph S. Wood, *The New England Village* (Baltimore: The Johns Hopkins University Press, 1997), 7.

10. O'Malley, "The Lawn," 84.

11. O'Malley, "The Lawn," 79.

12. Bormann et al., *Redesigning the American Lawn,* 14.

13. James Marston Fitch, "The Lawn, America's Greatest Architectural Achievement," *American Heritage* 35, no. 4 (1984): 55.

14. O'Malley, "The Lawn," 79.

15. Jackson, *Crabgrass Frontier,* 54.

16. Bormann et al., *Redesigning the American Lawn,* 22.

17. Dolores Hayden, "Model Houses for the Millions: The Making of the American Suburban Landscapes, 1820–2000," Working Paper, Lincoln Institute of Land Policy, 2000, 5; Jackson, *Crabgrass Frontier,* 87–102; Sara Lowen, "The Tyranny of the Lawn," *American Heritage* 42, no. 5 (1991): 48; Jane Holtz Kay, *Asphalt Nation: How the Automobile Took Over America and How We Can Take It Back* (Berkeley: University of California Press, 1997), 147; Lewis Mumford, *The City in History* (New York: Harcourt, Brace and World, 1961), 504.

18. Clifford E. Clark, *The American Family Home, 1800–1960* (Chapel Hill: University of North Carolina Press, 1986), 238.

19. Virginia Scott Jenkins, *The Lawn: A History of an American Obsession* (Washington, D.C.: Smithsonian Institution Press, 1994), 21.

20. Jenkins, *The Lawn,* 27.

21. James Howard Kunstler, *The Geography of Nowhere: The Rise and Decline of America's Man-Made Landscape* (New York: Simon & Schuster, 1993), 48–52; George P. Tatum, "Emergence of an American School of Landscape Design," *Historic Preservation,* April–June 1973, 41.

22. Jenkins, *The Lawn,* 25.

23. Jenkins, *The Lawn,* 29.

24. Benjamin Butterworth, *The Growth of Industrial Art* (Washington, D.C.: Government Printing Office, 1892), 13.

25. Jenkins, *The Lawn,* 30.

26. Jenkins, *The Lawn,* 30.

27. Butterworth, *The Growth of Industrial Art,* 13.

28. Jackson, *Crabgrass Frontier,* 58.

29. Jenkins, *The Lawn,* 32.

30. Harvey Wish, *Society and Thought in Modern America: A Social and Intellectual History of the American People from 1865* (New York: David McKay Co., 1962), 105.

31. Frank B. Latham, *1872–1972: A Century of Serving Consumers: The Story of Montgomery Ward* (2nd ed.) (Chicago: Montgomery Ward, 1972).

32. Alan Trachtenberg, *The Incorporation of America: Culture and Society in the Gilded Age* (New York: Hill & Wang, 1982).

33. Bormann et al., *Redesigning the American Lawn,* 30.

34. Jackson, *Crabgrass Frontier,* 187.

35. Jackson, *Crabgrass Frontier,* 233.

36. Scott and Sons Co., *Lawn Care* 16, no. 73 (1943).

37. Harvey Phillips Dean, "Keeping the Home Place Trim," *Better Homes and Gardens,* August 1944, 27.

38. Jackson, *Crabgrass Frontier,* 59.

39. Teyssot, "The American Lawn," 15.

40. Jackson, *Crabgrass Frontier,* 59.

41. Lowen, "The Tyranny of the Lawn," 51.

42. Abraham Levitt, "Chats on Gardening," *The Levittown Eagle,* April 24, 1952, 8.

43. Teyssot, "The American Lawn," 26.

44. W. Zissner, "Electronic Coup de Grass: The Mowing Ethic," *Life,* August 10, 1969, 10.

45. Robert Feagan and Michael Ripmeester, "Contesting Natural(ized) Lawns: A Geography of Private Green Space in the Niagara Region," *Urban Geography* 20, no. 7 (1999): 630.

46. Feagan and Ripmeester, "Contesting Natural(ized) Lawns," 629.

47. Feagan and Ripmeester, "Contesting Natural(ized) Lawns," 629.

48. Feagan and Ripmeester, "Contesting Natural(ized) Lawns," 630.

49. Bormann et al., *Redesigning the American Lawn,* 14.

50. Jenkins, *The Lawn,* 184.

51. Harry Balzer, "The Ultimate Cooking Appliance," *American Demographics,* July 1993, 40.

52. Balzer, "The Ultimate Cooking Appliance," 40.

53. Balzer, "The Ultimate Cooking Appliance," 43.

54. Richard A. Schieber and Donald W. Switzer, "Injuries from Propane Gas Grills," *Journal of the American Medical Association,* March 20, 1996, 886.

55. Julia VanTime, "Danger in Backyard Bouncing: Trampoline Injuries Reach Epidemic Proportions," *Prevention,* July 1998, 36.

56. Fran J. Donegan, "Swing Time," *Today's Homeowner,* June 1998, 32.

57. Rebecca Burton, "Ready, Set Play!," *Parents,* July 2001, 191.

58. Donegan, "Swing Time," 29.

59. Burton, "Ready, Set Play!," 191.

60. Thomas Leeuwen, "Waterworld," *Psychology Today* 32, no. 4 (1999): 62.

61. Thomas Leeuwen, *Springboard in the Pond* (Cambridge, Mass.: MIT Press, 1998), 225.
62. Leeuwen, "Waterworld," 62.
63. Leeuwen, "Waterworld," 62.
64. Leeuwen, *Springboard in the Pond,* 38.
65. Leeuwen, "Waterworld," 63.
66. Dan Johnson, "Chemical-Free Lawns and Gardens," *The Futurist,* May 1998, 12.
67. Bormann et al., *Redesigning the American Lawn,* 47.
68. Michael Kamrin, ed., *Pesticide Profile: Toxicity, Environmental Impact and Fate* (Boca Raton, Fla.: Lewis, 1997); George W. A. Milne, *Ashgate Handbook of Pesticides and Agricultural Chemicals* (Burlington, Vt.: Ashgate, 2000).
69. Cathrine Lemp and Anne Garland, "Garden-Variety Environmentalism," *The Amicus Journal,* Summer 1994, 55.
70. Philip Catron, "Fighting Clean, Green in Modern Turf Wars," *Forum for Applied Research and Public Policy,* Spring 1996, 72.
71. J. Kirk, "Turf Tips from the Professionals," *Home Mechanix,* May 1996, 62.
72. Lemp and Garland, "Garden-Variety Environmentalism," 55.
73. Michele Orecklin, "Say Goodbye to Grass," *Time,* July 2, 2001, 56.
74. Steve Lerner, "Suburban Wilderness," *The Amicus Journal,* Spring 1994, 14.
75. Lerner, "Suburban Wilderness," 16.
76. David Barboza, "In This Company's Struggle, God Has Many Proxies," *New York Times,* November 21, 2001, C1.
77. Barboza, "In This Company's Struggle," C1.
78. Bormann et al., *Redesigning the American Lawn,* 117.
79. Lerner, "Suburban Wilderness," 15.

A Conversation with Parris Glendening

Parris Glendening was the governor of Maryland from 1995 to 2003. In addition, he led the National Governors' Association and was a political science professor at the University of Maryland.

How did you become interested in suburban sprawl and smart growth?

Glendening: My interest is both personal and political. I grew up in Florida, and just in a few years, I saw a road that went through the Everglades become almost a mainstream of suburban development on both sides on what used to be the Everglades. It is now mile after mile of subdivisions and strip malls. I didn't consider myself an environmentalist, but it was so glaring to me that something was terribly wrong.

To be candid, I think I forgot about that for a bit until I got elected to the city council in Heightsville [Maryland]. It had U.S. 1 running through the middle of it, and we were trying desperately to get redevelopment and reinvestment [in the older part of town] because the area had become a superhighway with abandoned stores. We found it was hard to get investments there. Basically the [big-box retail] could go elsewhere in the county and take over a farm or tear down a forest cheaper than they could in-fill in an older community that had its roots all the way back to 1860s.

When I became county councilman and [later] county executive in Prince George's County, we started fighting these battles. It was a huge battle to preserve not only farmland but also the forestland and open space. I realized by the time I became governor that my personal views on the environment were so much more focused. The only way we were going to preserve that space was to make it financially attractive so that it is easier to invest in existing communities than it is to tear up the farm.

How do you see the combination of environmental and economic goals?

Glendening: There used to be this old rule that you are either for the environment or you are for prosperity. That is absolute nonsense, a false dichotomy. You have to be for both. Secondly, we are trying to say what affects these decisions. You could say that it is the zoning boards, but that is not where the decisions are made—maybe in an ideal world where you could draw lines rigidly and say this is forestland forever and this will be for development. And a few states have something like that, but that is just not part of our political culture. If you can't do that, what I call the European model, which you really can't do, then what can you do?

It seems to me more than anything else that growth decisions are bottom-line decisions—people make bottom-line decisions, investors do, builders do, and home buyers do. So let's change the bottom line. The way that you change the bottom line is to say we will give a series of incentives, whether they are tax credits or low-interest loans, to build in designated growth areas, and we will also make it more expensive [to build sprawl development]. So if the state will no longer subsidize school construction or water construction or roads, [developers will] have to pay for it.

Although studies have shown that sprawl has slowed down, it certainly has not stopped. What it means is presumably to build the same project in an already established area, you are not paying for roads, or water lines, or sewer, and getting tax benefits. You can build for probably 60 percent of the costs for building it [on the fringe area].

The media likes to portray me as one of the more progressive governors in the country, but I would like to remind people that the idea of smart growth is actually fiscally conservative. I say it that way because Maryland state and local governments [have historically spent] billions of dollars in the infrastructure just to build out there somewhere, and then we put hundreds of millions of dollars in established areas to deal with social problems because of poverty, crime, and lack of investment and jobs.

If you think about our state and multiply it nationwide, hundreds of billions of dollars are going into infrastructure to subsidize sprawl. The act of sprawl pulls both the human vitality and the economic vitality out of existing communities, and so then we have to put these tens of billions of dollars into programs to deal with the social problems that result from [sprawl]. So my argument is, I may be a progressive governor, but this is a conservative idea because sprawl is fiscally irresponsible.

One might also say smart growth is partly conservative because smart growth seeks to conserve historic buildings and spaces as well as preserve traditional community customs, values, and traditions.

Glendening: We can't have strong farming communities if every third farm gets subdivided and the rural, agricultural way of life is disrupted. Likewise, we have found it difficult to reuse or in-fill [urban centers] because most of the legal codes are stacked against this happening. So we have adopted a reuse preservation code that tries to deal with the issues of the building community. You actually could not build another Annapolis [Maryland] under most codes. There are setback requirements, parking requirements, and mixed use [is not encouraged].

Part of [smart growth] is conserving the American family and the American community. I stress this because we have a hard time evaluating what really causes the violence in schools, but one of the things that takes place is that families are moving farther and farther away from one another [which does not lead to] a sense of community where you know the neighbors.

Now in order to just get a quart of milk, you have to hop in the car and drive down to the convenience store. For the younger teens, instead of walking down the street and picking up their friends as they go along, you go to the shopping mall to meet them. The sense of community is being lost. We put ourselves in gated communities with five-acre lots, and then we say, "I wonder why we've lost the strength." I'm hoping that [with] the revitalization—not just in the big cities, which most people focus on, but all of the smaller and midsize communities across the state—that we'll do the right thing environmentally, we'll make better use of our tax dollars, and we'll get stronger communities to deal with the social pressures.

What types of political opposition have you encountered?

Glendening: When we started, the first opposition was [from] local officials. There is in America a strong tradition of local government and [a belief that] the state shouldn't be involved in land use. But at the same time when you make all these zoning decisions, the first thing you do is turn to the states and say we need more school construction money, we need more roads. But there was a lot of opposition, particularly from the counties who are afraid of being involved in land use. Municipalities, which under our plan would be given automatic smart-growth centers, were very much in favor. This helped to politically offset the counties.

Another source was some of the building communities that said, "We're building [sprawl] because some people want them; you should let people buy where they want to, and you're interfering with a person's rights." I don't argue with that; I say that's fine, but why should the rest of us subsidize your project? If you want to go ahead and pay for the three-million-dollar road to get them out there or for the six-million-dollar elementary school or the ten-million-dollar sewer lines, go ahead and do it [but the state's] not going to do it. Others immediately grasped that it doesn't just benefit the private sector, but it saves taxpayers a lot of money.

We can't say we're going to stop sprawl but we're not going to have higher nodes of density. I committed to the building community that I'll be an advocate for stopping sprawl and I'll also be an advocate for well-planned, well-designed higher density. There was a little bit of opposition [at] the state level of partisan opposition, but I think that was the normal give-and-take of the in party–out party. Across the country, many Republican governors have picked up a great deal of enthusiasm, for example, Governor Levitt in Utah.

[Republican] Governor Huckabee of Arkansas had an interesting conference and asked why Arkansas wasn't developing high-tech jobs. One of the things they found was that high-tech [employers] want a quality of life as well. He called it "fly-fishing to cyberoptic," which was about the connection of the two. Governor Taft of Ohio, recognizing the loss of open space, got the voters to approve a four-million-dollar bond issue, which was very atypical.

Then you have a number of Democrats. Governor [Ray] Barnes of Georgia got through a very strong bill creating an authority that could actually overturn [local] land use decisions. He said the key votes came from Republican legislators from the suburbs who recognize that it wasn't about downtown Atlanta but their constituents who were spending an hour and a half each way in traffic in Atlanta. Even Jesse Ventura [governor of Minnesota from the Independent Party] is enacting several innovative approaches.

II

Contesting Theories of Sprawl: Race, Class, and Culture

THE RELATIONSHIP BETWEEN CONTESTED ECOLOGICAL VALUES and development patterns is at the forefront of contemporary battles over suburban sprawl's effects on metropolitan regions and cities. As growing communities continue to consume in the low-density scattered sprawl model, questions regarding environmental quality as well as quality of life occur with increasing frequency. This part explores these issues within the context of domesticated ecological landscapes such as lawns and streetscapes as well as humanity's transformation of mountain and desert wilderness. Each chapter in this part illustrates how individual and commercial values shape environment quality albeit in very different settings. In addition, each chapter examines the important ways public policies and market choices are influenced by people's values and perceptions of the suburban "good life."

As other commentators in this volume point out, suburban sprawl is a paradoxical play between human desires for the green open space of the suburbs (often manifested as a backyard or soccer fields) and the hyperindividualistic, automobile-centered consumer juggernaut that eats away fifty acres of farmland an hour, according to the American Farmland Trust. In many respects, we are truly "loving the countryside to death"—a contradiction that is rapidly rising to the top of many local and state government policy agendas as sprawl increases traffic congestion and air pollution, destroys wildlife habitat, and sucks the economic and social vitality out of city centers.

In chapter 5, Amanda Rees critiques New Urbanism, an emerging trend in architecture and planning that attempts to reenvision physical, social, and cultural space to create renewed senses of community. New Urbanism and smart growth involve both public and private sector interest and investment. New Urbanism is a philosophy that can be adopted by anyone. However, Rees analyzes New Urbanist developments and evaluates their compatibility to the stated goals of the New Urbanism philosophy. Because the New Urbanist philosophy matches the goals of smart growth and seeks to limit sprawl, it can only be improved with critiques such as that of Rees.

In chapter 6, Milton Curry reminds us that suburbia and the inner city cannot be thought of in isolation; rather, the urban/suburban dynamic is complex and mutually constitutive. Curry specifically offers a critique of the U.S. Department of Housing and Urban Development's (HUD's) recent embrace of New Urbanism through its Hope VI initiative. New Urbanism, as we have encountered in previous chapters in this volume, emerged as an alternative planning doctrine in the 1980s specifically within the suburban context. Its popularity coincided with growing problems with public housing that occurred in the aftermath of post–World War II federally subsidized housing developments. These developments, such as the Robert Taylor Homes and Cabrini Green in Chicago, were large, modernist compounds that often served as incubators for crime and violence. By the 1990s, the efficacy of these housing developments was being questioned from a number of perspectives, and the New Urbanism doctrine of mixed-use development was endorsed by the Clinton administration's first HUD secretary, Henry Cisneros. For Curry, the embrace of New Urbanism by HUD must be understood within the context of race and class relations in the United States and recent trends of gentrification in inner cities. Much of the rhetoric of New Urbanism, Curry argues, either skirts around race and class or problematically assigns racial and class inequity in cities to the inadequacy of the physical environment. New Urbanism is then employed as a panacea for solving the problems of the city without recognizing the structural components of racism and class oppression. Curry examines the more nefarious implications of HUD's Hope VI project, which replaces modernist housing with New Urbanist–inspired alternatives. In practice, Hope VI has been unable to accommodate the numbers of residents displaced when the modernist buildings are demolished. For Curry, the effect of these projects has been to "suburbanize the city" through the forced removal of people of color and lower socioeconomic classes.

In chapter 7, Ron Hayduk shows how race relations in the United States are affected by suburban development and sprawl. The historic nature of racial segregation in the United States in employment, housing, and commerce is evident in the sprawled landscape where minority, low-income communities are separated from places of employment on the suburban fringe, making transportation often challenging and expensive. Hayduk also discusses how suburban sprawl is subsidized at the expense of investment in inner cities, challenging American ideological notions of "equality of opportunity." Hayduk argues that the only effective way to understand and reform the suburbanized sprawling environment is to critically examine and challenge the structural components of racial inequality in the United States.

In chapter 8, Josh Protas discusses this country's ability to love wilderness to death as well as attempt to protect and preserve wilderness. This story elaborates on the notion of a "middle landscape" wherein the Jeffersonian pastoral ideal merges with the urban metropolis in a constantly negotiated suburban landscape. Moreover, this chapter explains an early effort at conserving wilderness and stopping the threat of sprawled development.

This part's interdisciplinary approaches to the same questions indicate a need for further discussion about how we value nature, communities, and the effects of sprawl on the ecological and human landscapes. The interviews are meant to augment and, in some cases, critique the ideas presented in the chapters. It is abundantly clear that various approaches to addressing suburban sprawl evoke a series of important values and questions to explore.

5

New Urbanism: Visionary Landscapes in the Twenty-First Century

Amanda Rees

In the early 1980s, I took classes from an American studies professor who was convinced that America's archetypal landscape was the shopping mall. At the beginning of the twenty-first century, it is difficult to argue with his conclusion, but as over half the U.S. population lives in suburbia, his definition should be expanded beyond shopping malls to include the suburban sprawl that surrounds them. Suburbia, this increasingly ubiquitous physical, social, and cultural space that lies in that middle landscape between urban and rural life, is the dominant American icon of lived space. Some of the most provocative debates in contemporary culture are concerned with the environmental, social, cultural, and economic costs of post–World War II suburban sprawl. One particular planning movement has coalesced in order to reenvision this physical, social, and cultural space: New Urbanism.

Drawing on pre–World War II planning and architectural practices, New Urbanism seeks to change the ways in which the American suburban and urban landscape is developed and redeveloped. New Urban communities are characterized as compact, walkable, mixed-use, human-scale projects that, it is argued, create a sense of community. *New York Times* architecture critic Herbert Muchamp characterizes New Urbanism as "the most important phenomenon to emerge in American architecture in the post–Cold War era."[1] What makes New Urbanism different from a number of other utopian visions is that rather than remaining on the drawing board, it is being built and lived in. Seaside, the first New Urbanist development, was designed as a resort community in the panhandle of Florida in the early 1980s. Featured more recently in the movie *The Truman Show* (1998), Seaside is perhaps eclipsed in fame only by the Disney Company's development of Celebration in Orlando, Florida. By 2001, there were approximately 213 New Urban developments either in the planning stage or completed.[2]

The movement originated with a small number of architects, including Peter Calthorpe, Andres Duany, Elizabeth Moule, Elizabeth Plater-Zyberk, Stephanos Polyzides, and Daniel Solomon. New Urbanism found its political voice in the Congress for the New Urbanism, established in 1993. Broadening to include planners, developers, and educators, in 1996 the Congress drafted the Charter for New Urbanism, outlining the major tenets of the movement, and at the turn of the twenty-first century the movement has over 2,000 members.[3] It has received great attention in such varied national publications as *U.S. News and World Report, Time,* the *New York Times,* and *National Geographic;* in texts created by some of the original leaders and spokespeople of the movement; and in various academic analyses.[4]

New Urban principles have been applied to a variety of communities, including stand-alone townships such as Seaside, Florida, and urban environments such as downtown Providence, Rhode Island, and they have been used to retrofit older, first-ring suburbs built between 1945 and 1965. However, it is the suburban green-field developments such as Kentlands, Maryland (see interview with Kentlands' planner Mike Watson), and Celebration, Florida (see interview with Celebration newspaper publisher), that make up the majority of New Urban communities. New Urbanism has found surprisingly fertile ground within the public and private sectors. City and federal governments are making significant investments of public moneys in New Urban communities and in regional planning that utilizes New Urban thinking. New Urbanism has been an important influence on many regional development plans, including Kansas City, Missouri's, recent FOCUS (Forging Our Comprehensive Urban Strategy) study. At the federal level in 1996, Henry Cisneros, then secretary of the U.S. Department of Housing and Urban Development (HUD), signed the Charter of New Urbanism. HUD's Hope VI initiative, begun in 1993 (mixing public and private development), incorporated many New Urban principles in shaping its projects, and in 2002, HOPE VI was granted almost $500 million.[5] HUD's primary application of New Urban ideas is in Louisville, Kentucky. The Park DuValle neighborhood is the largest public–private, rental–sale development in the United States. Though the movement is having its greatest effect in shaping private, suburban development, it will continue to play an increasingly important part in influencing our built environment.

First, this chapter sketches New Urbanism's underlying tenets to establish the movement's relationship to history, focusing particularly on its rhetorical strategies and historical antecedents. Second, it explores New Urbanism's contemporary context with particular attention paid to its social, communal, fiscal, environmental, preservationist, aesthetic, and democratic aspirations, thought to be achieved through physical design. Finally, it assesses the future for New Urbanism, exploring some of the limitations and possibilities at the beginning of the twenty-first century.

Defining New Urbanism

New Urbanists are often characterized by their two most trenchant dislikes: suburban sprawl and the impact of the car. New Urbanists seek to revolutionize a deeply entrenched system of planning and architectural design that shapes the majority of American lives. Drawing on the work of historians such as Kenneth Jackson, New Urbanists point to two trends that brought this about: late nineteenth-century city zoning and post–World Wart II fiscal and transportation policy. Pointing to Victorian urban plans developed in response to pollution and slums, it was the zoning of the landscape—the separation of factories from residential areas—that is seen as one of the central causes of contemporary suburban sprawl and inner-city blight. In the United States, the City Beautiful movement, which formed the foundation of the new planning profession, promoted segregation of every land use, placing housing separate from industry, low-density housing separate from medium- and high-density housing, medical offices separate from general office space, and restaurants separate from shopping. In addition, postwar Federal Housing Administration and the Veterans Administration loan programs made buying new single-family suburban houses cheaper than renting or renovating existing housing stock or constructing row houses and other mixed-use or multifamily buildings. The provision of cheap loans focused on suburban development, coupled with heavy federal investment in interstate highways, and the neglect of mass transit made car-based commuting affordable and convenient for middle-class Americans. Zoning, combined with postwar housing and generous road subsidies, propelled the movement of primarily affluent white people from a high-density urban core to a lower-density suburban landscape.

Author James Kunstler, one of the more vehement antisuburban voices of New Urbanism, has inspired many New Urbanists with his dramatic criticism of the contemporary suburban landscape:

> We drive up and down the gruesome, tragic suburban boulevards of commerce, and we're overwhelmed at the fantastic, awesome, stupefying ugliness of absolutely everything in sight—the fry pits, the big-box stores, the office units, the lube joints, the carpet warehouses, the parking lagoons, the jive plastic townhouse

> clusters, the uproar of signs, the highway itself clouded with cars—as though the whole thing had been designed by some diabolical force bent on making human beings miserable. And naturally, this experience can make us feel glum about the nature and future of our civilization. . . . When we drive around and look at all this cartoon architecture and other junk that we've smeared all over the landscape, we register it as ugliness. This ugliness is the surface expression of a deeper problem—problems that are related to the issue of our national character. The highway strip is not just a sequence of eyesores. The pattern it represents is also economically catastrophic, an environmental calamity, socially devastating, and spiritually degrading.[6]

Kunstler claims that the misery and social, economic, environmental, and spiritual degradation of the American national character can be placed at the door of suburbia. What about the postwar built environment causes this national cultural degradation? Drawing on the work of urban activists such as Jane Jacobs, New Urbanists point to the following as factors that have discouraged social engagement: the destruction of the city, the reliance on the car to travel between different rigidly articulated zones of retail (malls, strip malls, and big-box retail), single-family dwellings (which are subzoned by house price), retirement accommodations, multifamily apartment accommodations, public housing, industrial zones, office parks, and poorly articulated transportation corridors with no interspersed public, civic, or green spaces.[7]

New Urban leaders Andres Duany, Elizabeth Plater-Zyberk, and Jeff Speck argue that in the rush to apply rational planning techniques to the massive postwar suburban expansion, zoning regulations were developed without attending to a sense of place:

> Rather, it feels like what it is: an uncoordinated agglomeration of standardized single-use zones with little pedestrian life and even less civic identification, connected only by an overtaxed network of roads. Perhaps the most regrettable fact of all is that exactly the same ingredients—the houses, shops, offices, civic buildings, and roads—could instead have been assembled as new neighborhoods and cities. Countless residents of unincorporated counties could instead be citizens of real towns, enjoying the quality of life and civic involvement that such places would provide.[8]

According to Duany, Plater-Zyberk, and Speck, these placeless agglomerations cannot efficiently service society or preserve the environment. To address "placelessness," New Urbanists seek to reconfigure the landscape at three levels—metropolitan region, neighborhood, and street[9]—in order to encourage certain behaviors and attitudes that result in the following:

- *Social benefits:* The promotion of mixed classes, races, and ages
- *Community benefits:* An increased sense of community where residents will know each other and care about collective security
- *Financial benefits:* A reduction of infrastructure investment and its equitable sharing across a region
- *Environmental benefits:* High-density populations that promote the use of public transportation and decrease pollution and high-density development that saves agricultural land and promotes green spaces and green corridors
- *Preservation benefits:* Preserving the historical patterns and boundaries of existing communities
- *Aesthetic benefits:* Linked with utilizing historic architectural design and use of space and a rejection of modernism
- *Democratic benefits:* That by being in close contact with neighbors and having distinct communal spaces and places, democratic initiatives will occur

New Urban practitioners clearly connect the physical design and creation of community with the outcome of myriad benefits that affect the social, communal, financial, environmental, preservationist, and democratic lives of its residents. While rejecting the term "architectural determinism," New Urbanists certainly seem to be applying the rubric of environmental affordance, the belief that environments can both support and constrain activities and meanings. In other words, the physical design can promote and discourage behaviors and attitudes. In order to create this relationship, New Urbanism has developed a set of codes that are designed to promote and discourage behavior and attitudes, including the following:

- Compact walkable neighborhoods/districts, no more than a quarter mile from center to edge
- A center that should include a public space (square, green public building, and important street intersections) and streets organized as an interconnected network (grid or modified grid)
- A diverse mix of activities (homes, shops, schools, workplaces, and parks) that should occur in proximity to one another
- A wide spectrum of housing options for a broad range of incomes, ages, and family types in a single neighborhood

In a growing mass of critical observations on New Urbanism, commentators have brought attention to a number of perils and possibilities for this movement.

Discussions range from New Urbanism's visceral dislike of modernism to an aesthetic critique of New Urban architectural styles, the use of "natural" biological metaphors to articulate social and cultural communities, an analysis of the movement's historical antecedents, the romanticization of "village" life, the belief in the connection between design and behavior, and, finally, the argument that the movement is not radical enough to meet its own stated utopian goals. To explore these issues more directly, it is useful to divide the critical analysis of the movement into two camps: New Urbanism's relationship to history and its contemporary milieu.

New Urbanism and History

Hand in hand with their dislike of sprawl and auto-driven suburban landscapes, New Urbanists have a trenchant dislike of modernism. According to commentator Douglas Kelbaugh, New Urbanists define modernism as less an architectural movement such as Gothic or Baroque and more a specific historical moment, that is, the fifty years stretching from the end of World War I to the Vietnam War. This period is characterized by New Urbanists as "a polemical and radical rupture with hundreds of years of tradition."[10] However, in understanding modernism in its broader cultural context beyond Kelbaugh's definition, it is useful to think of modernism as a set of cultural beliefs that shaped lives. Modernism has been described as a radical utopian impulse, a desire to reject the old in that turbulent period after World War I, when the senselessness and devastation of that conflict became obvious. In architectural terms, this included a rejection of the fin de siècle Beaux-Arts movement and neoclassicism, the rich, overwrought architecture that shaped the landscape of the late nineteenth and early twentieth centuries. These architectural styles were seen to symbolize corruption, inefficiency, and outmoded thinking. In terms of the built environment, modernism was seen as the antidote to a rotten culture, and form followed function as modernists imagined a radical alternative to the twin evils of rich opulence and grinding poverty. Thus, modernism became a utopian desire that helped shape twentieth-century Western culture.

Critics have variously placed New Urbanism as part of a break with modernism, locating it within postmodern thinking, while others have wondered whether it is yet another modernist project. Before New Urbanism even had a name, Edward Relph had placed New Urban architectural traits within postmodernism. Arguing that by the mid-1970s there were few people left with a kind word for modernism, Relph characterizes postmodern urbanization (in which New Urbanism can be included) as a self-conscious and selective revival of elements of older styles, a contrasting frame of mind in comparison with modernism. Arising among the tensions of the social and political climate of the early 1970s, Relph argues that postmodern architecture

> emerged more or less simultaneously with attempts to revitalize the old fabric of inner city areas, with a rise of interest in heritage preservation, and with new approaches to urban design and community planning. Post-modern architecture literally refers to what comes after modernism, but it is largely based on the self-conscious and selective revival of elements of older styles, and this is exactly what has been happening in revitalization, preservation and urban design.[11]

Offering two possibilities for the future of postmodern architecture, possibilities that are certainly applicable to New Urbanism, Relph argues that they might provide a set of sensitive and varied alternatives, or they might merely be decorative or stylistic shifts that merely offer "imagineered disguises for continued corporatisation."[12] How ironic Relph's use of the term "imagineering" is, as Disney's imaginers envisioned Celebration twenty years later.

Like Relph, Kelbaugh places what we now know as New Urbanism firmly in the realm of postmodernism. In particular, he argues that the movement is an example of the postmodern desire for variety versus standardization and for customizing an architecture that provides options for materials, colors, and shapes and the play of various architectural styles. Defining postmodernism as a mix of historicism, contextualism, neoclassicism, and neotraditionalism, all characteristics of New Urbanism, Kelbaugh suggests that the final difference between postmodernism and modernism is the celebration of figurative and representational forms to symbolize and signify ideas. New Urbanism rejects modernism's abstract forms that are based on geometry and logic and not associated with any particular place or instance. Kelbaugh connects New Urbanism with the theoretical perspective of phenomenology, a philosophy that celebrates a sense of place, revealed through active engagement with place rather than its detached observation.

Where Kelbaugh interprets New Urbanism as a postmodern expression, there are others, such as the critic David Harvey, who suggest that the New Urban desire for community is an antidote to the postmodern desire for fragmentation. Taking a slightly different direction, Robert Shibley wonders whether the New Urban desire to reshape society might be yet another type of modernist project that may have a totalizing and potentially oppressive ideology that modernism exhibited. Characterizing modern architecture as the belief in the total control of a project that left no room for challenging the dominant culture and social themes underpinning that project, Shibley wonders whether New Urbanism's codification of community is yet another iteration of modernist tendencies. This concern is made greater because of New Urbanism's anti-intellectual tendencies. It would seem that intellectualism is associated with modernism, and many New Urbanists like to see themselves as eclectic pragmatists working outside an ideological construct. Shibley concludes by arguing that if the movement wants to realize the possibility of creating communities, it needs to be just as much an intellectual project as it is a program of physical design. The location of New Urbanism both inside and outside postmodernism is as much a suggestion of the tensions within the definitions of postmodernism developed among architectural critics and cultural critics as it is a reflection of the movement.

Pointing out the revival of traditional architectural styles creates plenty of reactionary criticism that labels New Urbanism as merely romantic and nostalgic; such critiques also point out that it is a cosmetic activity that lacks depth and responsiveness. Shibley believes that the movement has "created a potentially pluralistic space where real conversation about places and good living can occur."[13] So that the movement's potential can be realized, New Urbanism should problematize New Urbanism each time a project begins; otherwise, the styles, derived from traditional or classical design, will become mere stereotypical reiteration. This will, in turn, feed the already rather aggressive critiques of style over substance that New Urbanism has already generated.

The lack of a historical awareness within the New Urban movement leads to some rather reductive and unnuanced analysis. For example, Kunstler often creates a simplistic dichotomy by comparing the "good" prewar urban versus the "bad" postwar suburban communities. In New Urban writing, prewar communities are articulated as organic and traditional, whereas postwar communities are defined as unnatural in that they break with tradition. Many, though not all, New Urbanists use the rhetorical strategy of bifurcation, splitting communities into two types—the natural, organic, and traditional communities of prewar and the unnatural and inorganic communities of postwar modernism. What effect does the bifurcation of community have on our understanding of New Urbanism? By identifying natural organic communities as "good," they make any communities that do not fit the definition of organic "bad." In many ways, they demonize those communities that do not echo New Urban principles, identifying those communities as the "other" and thus privileging their own vision. As Duany, one of the primary architects of New Urbanism, makes clear, postwar modernist communities are

> an invention, conceived by architects, engineers, and planners, and promoted by developers in the great sweeping aside of the old that occurred after the Second World War. Unlike the traditional neighborhood model, which evolved organically as a response to human needs, suburban sprawl is an idealized artificial sys-

> tem. As the ring of suburbia grows around most of our cities, so grows the void at the center.[14]

Thus, the American landscape is divided up into traditional neighborhoods that are attuned to human needs and an artificial system of suburban sprawl that creates a voided or abject city space. By creating such a black-and-white landscape scenario, there would seem to be no negotiated space in the middle to reenvision and renegotiate the relationship between people and place. Indeed, using the natural-versus-unnatural rhetorical strategy risks alienating the very suburban population whose landscape New Urbanism seeks to change.

Second, using the term "organic" to characterize prewar communities suggests that these human settlements developed naturally without a plan and acknowledges the role of power in the creation of lived landscapes.[15] Indeed, the celebration of organic communities echoes the work of the Chicago School's urban sociology that rose to prominence at the beginning of the twentieth century. The Chicago School's proponents articulated the urban experience as a natural evolution, as an urban ecology rather than as the product of a sequence of political, economic, raced, classed, and gendered decisions. The city was not seen as an outcome of power functioning in a social system; instead, social processes were naturalized, and those making the decisions about the shape and life of the city were ignored. The Chicago School's perspective, underpinned by an unquestioned belief in scientific neutrality, was central to progressive thinking in turn-of-the-century American culture. Indeed, the Chicago School is an excellent example of modernist ideology: the belief in space and form, a faith in technological progress and rationalist methodology, and the standardization of solutions. As the critic Susan Feinstein ably points out, this belief consequently supported a politically conservative outlook that failed to allow for the exploration of systemic constraints shaped by race, class, gender, and ethnicity that produced cities. This vision was certainly problematic because of its lack of critical self-awareness in its celebration of objectivity. Indeed, it was only in the 1960s and 1970s, with the examination of the impact of urban development on class, race, ethnicity, democratic decision making, and environmental sustainability, that modernity and the Chicago School of urban sociology came into question.[16]

One ecological metaphor applied to New Urbanism is the transect. According to Andres Duany and Emily Talen, the transect is

> a system that seeks to organize the elements of urbanism—building, lot, land use, street, and all of the other physical elements of the human habitat—in ways that 1) link urban elements to natural ecologies in one integrated and continuous system; and 2) create immersive environments that preserve the integrity of

> place at each location within the system. The two approaches are interconnected: cities are seen as having a place in nature's order, but it is also recognized that they must find their own internal ordering system that binds them to that order. This is a matter of finding an appropriate spatial allocation of the elements that make up the human habitat. Rural elements must find their place in rural locations, while urban elements must find their place in more urban locations—not unlike natural ecological systems where plant and animal species coexist within habitats that best support them. Urban development must somehow be distributed such that it strengthens rather than stresses the integrity of each immersive environment.[17]

By adapting ecological theory, New Urbanists seek to place urban systems as a seamless aspect of the natural transect continuum, "embedding urban development within the larger ecosystem on which it depends."[18] It is not clear whether Feinstein's concerns over the similarities between the ecological perspective taken by the Chicago School and New Urbanism will be born out. New Urbanists seem open to and aware of the work of contemporary urban ecologists who are developing models of urban expansion that include social, cultural, demographic, and institutional constraints. However, the collapsing of social, cultural, and economic theory with ecological theory is fraught with danger, and this particular feature of New Urbanism bears further scrutiny as the transect concept develops.

Other critics have turned to the historical antecedents and inspirations shaping New Urbanism in order to more fully understand some of the possibilities and perils of the movement. The architect and teacher Vincent Scully makes a brief note that New Urbanism is a revival of the classical and vernacular planning traditions "before the impact of International Style Modernism perverted methods and objectives of such planning."[19] Tom Bressi goes further in articulating the historical influences on this movement by saying that New Urbanism revives the principles on which communities were built, including the City Beautiful and Garden City movements and the work of Camillo Sitte, Werner Hegemann and Elbert Peets, and Clarence Perry.[20] Indeed, this tantalizingly brief sojourn through New Urban antecedents calls for a more detailed analysis of the connections and disconnections between late nineteenth- and late twentieth-century utopian visions of community.

In one of the few studies comparing New Urbanism and other utopian planning movements, the critic Robert Campbell point to turn-of-the-twentieth-century British visionary Ebenezer Howard and the realization of his vision in the Garden City movement as a significant influence on New Urbanism. Indeed, though many utopian communities never make it beyond a paper plan, garden cities, like New Urbanist developments, were realized in numerous locations. However, as Campbell points out, Howard's vision, based on specific utopian vision of politics, self-sufficiency, and social behavior, was never realized in his various garden suburb communities. By drawing on New Urbanism's historical antecedents, Campbell asks whether New Urbanism will suffer the same fate as the Garden City movement by substituting the appearance of radical change for substantive social transformation.

Having been accused of romanticizing the past and constructing a problematic and reductive dichotomy between New Urbanism and traditional suburban sprawl, what is it about prewar landscapes that New Urbanists want to mimic? Scale is perhaps the primary focus. New Urbanists seek to echo the dense scale of the walking city. They call this landscape the traditional neighborhood and its replication traditional neighborhood design:

> The traditional neighborhood was the fundamental form of European settlement on this continent through the Second World War, from St. Augustine to Seattle. It continues to be the dominant pattern of habitation outside the United States. . . . The traditional neighborhood—represented by mixed-use, pedestrian-friendly communities of varied population, either standing free as villages or grouped into towns and cities—has proved to be a sustainable form of growth. It allowed us to settle the continent without bankrupting the country or destroying the countryside in the process.[21]

Critics have questioned the historical model on which New Urbanism bases itself, both specifically and in more general terms. David Schuyler points out that it is the "celebration of the design vocabulary of the early twentieth century, particularly the 1920s, which Duany has termed the apogee of residential planning in the United States."[22] The 1920s, Schuyler tells us, was fraught with its own problems with the dissolution of so-called traditional communities as the car became a viable alternative to mass-transportation-serviced suburbs and zoning was applied with blunt force to shape American cities.

In more general terms, the desire to replicate prewar aesthetics has some commentators calling New Urbanism a middle-class conservative movement. Some have labeled New Urbanism "family values architecture" that fits neatly into the developers' aspirations to meet what they see as the desire for simpler times in their customers' minds. There are still other commentators who question whether suburbia is more complicated and varied than its stereotype, a stereotype that New Urbanism exploits. Indeed, as Robert Wilson argues, the term "suburbia" is manipulated by the opinion makers in the cities at the edge of the American continent and becomes realized in films such as *American Beauty* and *Arlington Road:*

> The s-word has become so ubiquitous and so baggage-laden that it barely means anything anymore. There is a paradox lurking here. The word suburbia has been

> used to describe the increasingly varied places where more and more of us live—the gritty inner suburbs that share many of the problems of their urban neighbors, immigrant neighborhoods at every economic level, and new Greenfield developments sporting one McMansion bigger than the next. Yet our definition of the word remains fixed in a former time, decades ago, when women worked at home and men commuted to work. The biggest problem with suburbia is that we are all so certain that we know what it means . . . suburbia is a dull, sterile, unhappy place.[23]

As we have seen previously, uncritical suburbia bashing is certainly a central thrust of New Urbanism. For the critic Witold Rybczynski, the re-creation of eighteenth- and nineteenth-century urban neighborhood design is merely an appeal to the fantasy of a more ordered harmonious past—the village and the green. Specifically, Rybczynski points to New Urbanism's first development, Seaside, as a hodgepodge of vaguely Victorian and Georgian architecture mixed with picket fences that is not only bland but ultimately the movie set for the remake of *It's a Wonderful Life.*[24] Ironically enough, Seaside did not play host to a wonderful life but instead provided the movie set for *The Truman Show,* a film that used the town to signify controlled perfection as part of a larger, damning critique of the vacuity of contemporary life. Michael Southworth takes Rybczynski's critique further in asking whether the romanticized notion of a village is appropriate for contemporary urban and regional circumstances. Is the village the right way to think about a community that lies close to and has complex interactions with a larger region?[25]

New Urbanism and Its Historical Milieu

New Urbanism's dance with history opens it up to a series of thoughtful analyses and comparisons. However, New Urbanism's vision of contemporary culture also leaves it vulnerable to another set of critical responses. In articulating contemporary culture as harboring the desire to return to a prewar physical space, Campbell wonders whether neighborhood centers can function in a community where efficiency propels the design and functionality of community facilities, such as libraries or supermarkets, to be designed to serve a much larger community than the quarter-mile walking radius articulated in New Urban code. Indeed, New Urbanism raises useful questions about the role of propinquity in creating turn-of-the-twenty-first-century community. New Urbanists assume that propinquity, or the proximity and closeness of things, can result in the creation of community. However, this assumption has been queried for several decades in that society, and critics have argued that communities seem to build social networks in terms of communities of interest rather than communities of physical proximity.[26] The Internet is a useful example of what critics both hail and lament as a medium that propels communities of interest that, at least for some commentators, dissolves the importance of physical neighborhood. Though propinquity may not be the only thing that knits community, it has certainly not been completely negated either. Perhaps a more useful way to understand the individual and community is that community is not one thing; the individual can be an active member of a number of communities that may or may not rely on physical proximity.

There are a number of critics who have rejected New Urbanism because of its codified rules, in particular the writer Maccannell.[27] Focusing primarily on the Disney development of Celebration, Maccannell berates the development's rules as a marker of paternalism. There is no doubt that Celebration houses some unique issues, and it would seem that Maccannell may be conflating this somewhat unique corporate development with the larger movement. Maccannell criticizes New Urban communities as regimented, suggesting that they are places where difference is suppressed. In rather heated terms, Maccannell claims that New Urbanism opposes "naturally" occurring cultural variation. However, the author seems to be unfamiliar with the constraints placed on traditional suburban development at both the city planning and the self-governing levels of home-owners' associations. In battling the transportation and city governance planning regulations, New Urbanists reveal the network of rules that constrain postwar suburban life—wide streets, deep setbacks, elliptical road systems, single-use designations, and so on. In addition, much of suburban private housing is based on common interest developments and is administered by home-owners' associations that are propelled by yet another category of "covenants, conditions, and restrictions formalizing behavior and aesthetic norms."[28] The fiction of unity that Maccannell accuses the movement of creating does not reside solely in the realm of New Urbanism.

Whereas Maccannell rails against the constraints of New Urbanism, the geographer Emily Talen questions the movement's social doctrine, in particular the assumption that the built environment can create a sense of community. Pointing out that there are little data that can back up New Urbanist claims of a link between design and behavior, she argues that

> the social claims of new urbanists are weakened by the fact that sense of community, specifically a shared emotional connection, have been found to exist and even thrive under a variety of conditions, some of which appear to be adverse to new urbanist design ideology (for example within dispersed, auto-oriented suburban environments). One way out of this dilemma would be for new urbanists to tone down their social aspirations and declare that they are simply meeting the human requirements of physical design, rather than actively creating certain

> behaviors. Physical design need not create a sense of community, but rather, it can increase its probability.[29]

Like Shibley, Talen is concerned with the claims New Urbanism makes. Unlike Shibley, Talen calls on its practitioners to constrain their social ideology.

There are several critics who believe that while New Urbanism has articulated a number of well-intentioned social desires in a commercially and environmentally viable manner, its theoretical foundations are too shallow. Indeed, they argue that it will ultimately fail to change the forces it so vehemently criticizes. As the critic Daniel Willis makes clear,

> When avant-garde architects claim to disrupt the societal status quo by instilling "unease" with their disturbing, dislocating shapes, and new urbanists claim to produce social harmony by carefully prescribing sidewalks, picket fences, and house facades, each accepts an insupportable degree of spatial determinism.[30]

For Willis, both modernism and New Urbanism believed in the ability to create community through the codification of architecture. In the case of New Urbanism, Willis suggests that its codes describe only transient aspects, such as colors, styles, materials, minimums, and maximums, and he concludes that New Urbanism cannot articulate or control the intangible aspects of both places and social relationships.

Where Willis is concerned with the role of codification in creating community, David Harvey argues that New Urbanism seems to be one solution to the cultural desire to "recuperate history, traditional, collective memory, and identity."[31] Harvey defines New Urbanism as the desire to improve urban living to make it more authentic and less placeless by returning to the idea of neighborhood and community that "once upon a time gave such vibrancy, coherence, continuity and stability to urban life. Collective memory of a more civic past can be recaptured by a proper appeal to traditional symbols."[32] Harvey commends New Urbanism for thinking about place in a more organic, holistic, and interrelated manner. In addition, he suggests that the focus on the public space (the street or civic architecture) as areas of sociability offer ways of thinking differently about relations between work and living as well as an ecological perspective with which to ask serious questions about the living spaces created in an automobile-based society.

Harvey also raises the question of whether those who can afford the mostly green-field New Urban developments are choosing community or the image and purchase of community. Indeed, Harvey argues that New Urbanism echoes the errors of all utopian visions by placing spatial form over social process, suggesting that urban planners must recognize the limitations of codification and developers what can be prefabricated. Harvey calls for a utopia that coalesces both spatial form and social process because communities are not just physical space; they are also a living and breathing process and cannot be fixed spatially or purchased like a commodity.[33] Harvey's concern about the relationship between commodification and community is most clearly realized in Andrew Ross's analysis of Celebration. Having lived for a year in Celebration, Ross suggests that Celebration was a particularly interesting form of privatized community that eschews public involvement:

> Many spoke to me of their loss of faith in public institutions and public government, and described democratic public process as laborious, wasteful, and inept. . . . The rage for privatization that has swept the country, and much of the developed world, routinely sacrifices justice and accountability at the altar of efficiency. In practice, the efficiency of most forms of private governance is easily subverted, especially when its member-consumers take legal action. . . . More and more of what had been public sector was being turned over to private and corporate interests. Could a large private developer be persuaded to respond to the call to restore civic and community life, especially if it meant going against the grain of industry behavior? The changes seemed unlikely. Only a corporation like Disney—a company whose core business lay in culture and values—would feel it could benefit from taking on the challenge in a high profile way.[34]

Celebration is indeed a fascinating example of an enormous corporation that shapes the values associated with its products. Disney saw in New Urbanism the very values it sought to establish in the creation of community. It is not the only large-scale organization interested in the relationship between built space and values. Indeed, there are a number of religious organizations interested in New Urbanism as is witnessed in the proposed development in Kansas City, Missouri, by the Mormon Church.[35] For Ross, the silver lining in Disney's manufactured community was that instead of being an instant, purchased, and rigid utopia, the various obstacles that residents met living in Celebration "helped them forge community bounds for which there was no planning blueprint." For Ross, there was a space for community beyond the physically produced and consumed product of Celebration.[36]

Above all, it is the uncritical use of the term "community" that Harvey takes most exception to in the work of the New Urbanism, and his criticism offers us a useful set of questions with which to examine the movement. As he thoughtfully points out, "community" means different things to different people, and the untheorized, uncritical use of the term is problematic. When talking about community, he points out that there is an implicit vision of the city as a teeming uncontrolled mass that could be controlled by becoming a series of interlinked urban village communities where everyone can engage each other in a more civil fashion but that throughout the history of industrialization and the concomitant urbanization, "the spirit of community" has always been seen as the antidote to threats of social disorder, class war, and revolutionary violence."[37] In an odd sort of reversal, the nostalgic withdrawal advocated by communitarianism (the philosophical movement most closely allied with New Urbanism) risks replicating some of the least desirable communal aspects of vernacular societies. At the same time, the movement's idealized communities seem most effective as retreats from, not solutions to, late capitalist development. Community thus becomes a site of control and surveillance that Harvey argues borders on social repression. Communities act to create boards, exclude, define themselves in opposition to others, and create various "Keep Out" signs. In this way racism, class difference, and ethnic chauvinism can be propelled in part by the desire for community. Thus, community can become a barrier rather than a promoter of the progressive social change, the very social change that New Urbanism calls for. In contrasting cities to the coded world of New Urban communities, Harvey argues that what makes cities so exciting, liberating, and ultimately more democratic is that they allow the unexpected, the conflict, and the unknown. The city allows space for the mixing of peoples that promotes a sense of tentativeness rather than absolutism. According to Harvey, what New Urbanism does not seem to allow for is the concept of urbanization as a set of fluid dialectical relationships. New Urbanism, he suggests, should be a utopianism of process as well as spatial form.

Finally, there are those critics who find New Urbanism an almost visceral blow to race, class, and gender equality. Neil Smith makes plain that there

> is no mystery about for whom this new urbanism is built. The design styles distill the most traditional social assumptions of gender, class, and race. Dripping like candle wax with sentimentality for "the human scale," a mushy metaphor that hides more than it reveals, Seaside openly and exuberantly celebrates the 19th-century urban ideal of yeoman New England. The past evoked in the promise of a new urban future is the narrowest and most elitist of founding fantasies, and the resulting landscape naturalizes a wide plant of privileged presumptions of the social norm. In its discreetly bounded single-family homes, assumptions about gender roles are neatly kept up as the postage-sized gardens. As you enter Seaside, there is no sign on the road to say "No Irish need apply" or its less verbalized 20th-century equivalents "If you're black stay back," "If you're working class, be out by five," "Women in the kitchen, please." The design style already speaks the exclusionary message with delicate, handkerchiefed smugness.[38]

Smith sees New Urbanism, at least in the form articulated at Seaside, as a scourge for women and racial and ethnic minorities and as promoting the division of economic classes.

Where there may be an increased mixing of income and age levels, race remains stubbornly resistant to mixing in New Urban communities. Racial segregation seems to be prominent in Ross's discussion of Celebration in that he describes the Celebration community as almost completely white. There are a few New Urbanist developments or, more accurately, redevelopments, that have drawn African American interest, such as the Louisville, Kentucky, development of Park DuValle. However, in terms of racial integration, HUD's Park DuValle is almost completely African American in both owned and rented accommodation.

In terms of economic class, Christopher Swope's examination of New Urban developments in Atlanta is a useful if narrow analysis. There are several urban developments that were once public housing projects, such as Atlanta's Little Vietnam. These communities are now mixed-income developments that include poor and middle-income families. But the development now incorporates a fraction of its former "poor" population. In the former Little Vietnam, now known as the Villages of East Lake, only 79 of the 428 families who were screened and agreed to strict rules moved back in once construction was complete.[39] In Atlanta, less than 15 percent of original residents of the community returned to the redeveloped site, and the demand for homeless shelters has increased. Whereas some see this community rehabilitation as an opportunity, others compare this mass removal to the urban policies of the mid-twentieth century, when cities flattened low-income neighborhoods. Swope points out that this low rate of return is reflected in other cities, an issue that recently led HUD's inspector general to comment that although the physical revitalization of Hope VI sites is impressive, improvements to the lives of residents were markedly less obvious.[40] Finally, the critic David Schuyler points out that the large-scale systemic problems of the decline in industrialism, hand in hand with disinvestments in American cities, cannot be addressed merely by better design.[41]

Ironically, one of the limitations of New Urbanism's desire for mixed-income neighborhoods has been its success. Developments such as Seaside have been so popular that there is no chance that a mix of income level in the population can be maintained. Indeed, Seaside's developer, Robert Davis, discusses his technique of completing streets one at a time to accelerate the growth in value of the remaining unsold or undeveloped land.[42] Taking the focus on house purchase and the increase of property values, we can see this dynamic play out in HUD's hope for Park DuValle, where it is hoped that the rental property will ultimately be purchased and that, along with the other already purchased homes, that will act like a catalyst for the revitalization of the neighborhood and increase property values. If this is the only HUD-funded type of development, this begs the question, Where would individuals and families find affordable housing? Perhaps the answer is to rethink the concept of tenancy, providing more options for partial owners, as evidenced in the Joseph Rowntree Foundation's work in communities such as New Earswick, England.[43] It would seem that maintaining a mix of incomes is one of New Urbanism's primary challenges over the long term.

Conclusion

New Urbanism encompasses some very real limitations: its rather blunt, bifurcated rhetorical strategy; its application of environmental metaphors and concepts; the lack of historical grounding; and its more general anti-intellectualism. These limitations mean that both its physical application and its intellectual acceptance will remain problematic. In particular, alienating everyone already living in post–World War II suburbia by simply labeling their physical, social, and cultural environment as "bad" does little to persuade people of its merits. For those in academia, a more rigorous analysis of the ideological underpinnings of the movement is certainly required. The collapsing of social, cultural, and economic theory with ecological theory within New Urbanism's discussion of the transect demands further study.

Does New Urbanism have something meaningful to offer the ways in which Americans live their lives? Absolutely. Most clear, and perhaps most important, is the call for the critical "place-based" application of community. The movement certainly offers some possibilities in its "process" of negotiating community rather than the codification of its physical form. It remains debatable whether New Urbanism falls into the realm of modernism or postmodernism. It exhibits characteristics of both ideological positions, meaning that it can be a utopian ideal, in the best sense of the modernist tradition, while challenging the rigid limitations of that tradition in its practice, one of the gifts of postmodernism. More particularly, the mere application of a reductive codification of form will not allow for the notion of community as a fluid dialectical relationship. Indeed, the tension between control and fluidity seems central to understanding both the possibilities and the limitations of the movement. The raced, classed, and gendered implications for New Urbanism remain both exciting and troubling.

Perhaps what is most exciting about New Urbanism is that as I write, it is a changing movement. Tensions between its generous application to green-field sites allow New Urbanism to remain vulnerable to its derisive nickname, New Suburbanism. Its application in urban areas will perhaps be the best test, though it seems that New Urbanism may be losing support from HUD under the George W. Bush administration. New Urbanism is without doubt one of the most exciting concepts to come out of the architectural and planning arena in thirty years, and it offers us a fascinating lens through which to examine the cultural, political, economic, environmental, and material life of the majority of those who live in the United States.

Notes

1. Herbert Muchamp, *New York Times,* June 2, 1996, Arts and Entertainment section, 27.

2. "New Urbanist Project Construction Starts to Soar," *New Urban News,* October–November 2001, 1–5. To be included in the definition of a New Urban project, the development must be more than fifteen acres and be defined as having a mix of uses and housing types, an interconnected network of streets, a town center, formal civic spaces and squares, residential areas, and pedestrian-oriented design.

3. Ellen Dunham-Jones, "Seventy-Five Percent: The Next Big Architectural Project," *Harvard Design Magazine,* Fall 2000, 8.

4. For the national media, see Richard Polen, "Town-Building Is No Mickey Mouse Operation," *New York Times Magazine,* December 14, 1997; Jay Tolson, "Putting the Brakes on Suburban Sprawl," *U.S. News & World Report,* March 20, 2000; Tim Padgett, "Saving Suburbia," *Time,* August 16, 1999; Herbert Muschamp, "Can New Urbanism Find Room for the Old?" *New York Times,* June 2, 1996; Sarah Boxer, "A Remedy for the Rootlessness of Modern Suburban Life?" *New York Times,* August 1, 1998; and John G. Mitchell, "Urban Sprawl," *National Geographic* 200, no. 1 (2001). For leaders and spokespersons of the New Urbanism movement, see Peter Calthorpe, *The Regional City: Planning for the End of Sprawl* (Washington, D.C.: Island Press, 2001), and *The Next American Metropolis: Ecology, Community, and the American Dream* (New York: Princeton Architectural Press, 1993); Andres Duany, Elizabeth Plater-Zyberk, and Jeff Speck, *Suburban Nation: The Rise of Sprawl and the Decline of the American Dream* (New York: North Point Press, 2000); James Howard Kunstler, *Home from Nowhere: Remaking Our Everyday World for the Twenty-First Century* (New York: Simon & Schuster, 1996); Peter Katz, *The New Urbanism: Toward an Architecture of Community* (New York: McGraw-Hill, 1995); and Douglas Kelbaugh *Common Place: Towards Neighborhood and Regional Design* (Seattle: University of Washington Press, 1997). For examples of various academic analyses, see Charles Bohl, "New Urbanism and the City: Potential Applications and Implications for Distressed Inner-City Neighborhoods," *Housing Policy Debate* 11, issue 4; Mark J. Eppli and Charles C. Tu, *Valuing the New Urbanism: The Impact of the New Urbanism on Prices of Single-Family Homes* (Washington, D.C.: Urban Land Institute, 1999); Susan Feinstein, "New Directions in Planning Theory," *Urban Affairs Review* 35, no. 4 (2000); Tom Peyser, "Looking Back at Looking Backward," *Reason* 32, no. 4 (2000); Andrew Ross, *The Celebration Chronicles: Life, Liberty and the Pursuit of Property Values in Disney's New Town* (New York: Ballantine, 1999); David Schuyler, "The New Urbanism and the Modern Metropolis," *Urban History* 24, no. 3 (1997); Robert Shibley, "The Complete New Urbanism and the

Partial Practices of Placemaking," *Utopian Studies* 9, no. 1 (1998); Neil Smith, "Which New Urbanism? New York City and the Revanchist 1990s," in *The Urban Moment: Cosmopolitan Essays on the Late 20th-Century City,* ed. Robert A. Beauregard and Sophie Body Gendrot (Thousand Oaks, Calif.: Sage, 1999); and Emily Talen, "Sense of Community and Neighbourhood Form: An Assessment of the Social Doctrine of New Urbanism," *Urban Studies* 36, no. 8 (1999).

5. "Hope VI Funds New Urban Neighborhoods," *New Urban News,* January–February 2002.

6. James Howard Kunstler, "Home from Nowhere," *Atlantic Monthly,* Fall 1996, at www.theatlantic.com//issues96sept/hunstler/kunstler.htm (accessed February 20, 2002).

7. Duany et al., *Suburban Nation,* 5–7.

8. Duany et al., *Suburban Nation,* 12.

9. Defining the metropolis as a geographically, economically, environmentally, and culturally bound space, New Urbanism looks to maintain those boundaries rather than blur them with suburban sprawl by calling for in-fill rather than new developments. When new development is required, New Urbanists state that they seek to place them adjacent to existing urban communities and organize them into neighborhoods and districts that should be integrated with existing urban patterns. Noncontiguous developments would be organized as towns and villages with their own boundaries reflecting respect for historical patterns, boundaries, equal distribution of affordable housing, transportation alternatives, and revenue and resource sharing within the region to discourage intraregional competition.

At the district and neighborhood levels, the New Urban tenets require that districts emphasize special single uses, whereas neighborhoods should be compact, pedestrian friendly, and mixed use. To link districts and neighborhoods in a coherent manner, ideal New Urban communities should be connected by corridors such as boulevards, rail lines, rivers, or parkways. New Urbanists envision activities occurring within walking distance, that is, only five minutes from the outside of the neighborhood to its center, and streets should be designed on a grid system to facilitate connectivity rather than using the cul-de-sacs. New Urbanists call for a broad range of housing types and prices, encouraging a population of varying ages, races, and incomes to be in daily interaction, leading to stronger personal and civic bonds essential to an "authentic" community. High-density neighborhoods also encourage public transportation rather than a reliance on automobiles. New Urban practitioners desire that educational, civic, institutional, commercial, and recreational activities be part of neighborhoods and districts, not isolated in remote, single-use complexes. Indeed, through the application of design codes, economic health and harmonious evolution of neighborhoods, districts, and corridors can be improved. New Urbanists have shortened these diverse criteria to a list of five: the center; the five-minute walk; the street network; narrow, versatile streets; and special sites for special buildings.

At the microlevel of the block, street, and building, New Urbanists seek to link a development with its surrounding in order to promote the sense of shared public space. New Urbanists seek to reinforce safe environments but not at the expense of accessibility and openness, and automobile access should respect the pedestrian and public transit. Placing the garage at the back of the house and making residential streets narrow and overhung with trees have been two of the strategies to decrease automobile speed and promote pedestrian engagement. New Urban developments are at a high density, with narrow streets and short setbacks between the street and the dwelling, and they often sport front porches. Garages are placed at the back of the property and sometimes include "granny" or "mother-in-law" flats, and services are delivered in alleys behind houses. New Urbanists imagine public spaces as safe, comfortable, and interesting. In addition, New Urbanists believe that design should grow from the locale. In addition, developing distinct architectural forms for civic places and spaces will act to reinforce community identity and a culture of democracy. A more extended articulation of these tenets can be found at the Congress for the New Urbanism website at www.cnu.org.

10. Kelbaugh, *Common Place,* 60.

11. Edward Relph, *Place and Placelessness* (London: Pion, 1976), 213–15.

12. Relph, 213–15.

13. Shibley, "The Complete New Urbanism and the Partial Practices of Placemaking," 10–11.

14. Duany et al., *Suburban Nation,* 4.

15. The tension between those New Urban practitioners who romanticize the past and demonize the present can clearly be seen in the often-contentious on-line discussion list debates. www.listserv.uga.edu.

16. Susan S. Feinstein, "Can We Make the Cities We Want?," in *The Urban Moment: Cosmopolitan Essays on the Late 20th-Century City,* ed. Robert A. Beauregard and Sophie Body Gendrot (Thousand Oaks, Calif.: Sage, 1999).

17. Andres Duany and Emily Talen, "Transect Planning," *Journal of the American Planning Association* 68, no. 3 (Summer 2002): 245–67.

18. Duany and Talen, "Transect Planning."

19. Vincent Scully, "Afterword," in Peter Katz, *The New Urbanism: Toward an Architecture of Community* (New York: McGraw-Hill, 1995).

20. Todd W. Bressi, "Planning the American Dream," in Peter Katz, *The New Urbanism: Toward an Architecture of Community* (New York: McGraw-Hill, 1995).

21. Duany et al., *Suburban Nation,* 4.

22. David Schuyler, "The New Urbanism and the Modern Metropolis," *Urban History* 24, no. 3 (1997).

23. Robert Wilson, "Enough Snickering: Suburbia Is More Complicated and Varied Than We Think," *Architectural Record* 188, no. 5 (2000): 79.

24. Witold Rybczynski, "This Old House," *The New Republic,* May 8, 1995.

25. Michael Southworth, "Walkable Suburbs," *Journal of the American Planning Association* (Winter 1997).

26. Robert Campbell, "New Urbanism: The Debate Goes On," *Record News,* 187, no. 4: 54.

27. Dean Maccannell, "'New Urbanism' and Its Discontents," in *Giving Ground: The Politics of Propinquity,* ed. Joan Copjec and Michael Sorkin (New York: Verso, 1999).

28. Steve Flusty and Michael Dear, "Invitation to Postmodern Urbanism," in *The Urban Moment: Cosmopolitan Essays on the Late 20th-Century City,* ed. Robert A. Beauregard and Sophie Body Gendrot (Thousand Oaks, Calif.: Sage, 1999).

29. Talen, "Sense of Community and Neighbourhood Form," 1374.

30. Daniel Willis, *The Emerald City and Other Essays on the Architectural Imagination* (New York: Princeton Architectural Press, 1999), 166.

31. David Harvey, "The New Urbanism and the Communitarian Trap," *Harvard Design Magazine,* Winter/Spring 1997, 68.

32. Harvey, "The New Urbanism and the Communitarian Trap."

33. David Harvey, *Spaces of Hope* (Berkeley: University of California Press, 2000), 196.

34. Ross, *The Celebration Chronicles,* 310–12.

35. In 2002, New Urbanism's Seaside Institute ran a conference on the application of New Urban tenets to religious communities.

36. Ross, *The Celebration Chronicles,* 318.

37. Harvey, "The New Urbanism and the Communitarian Trap," 69.

38. Smith, "Which New Urbanism?," 200–201.

39. These rules include the following: "If able-bodied, you needed to be working or receiving job training or enrolled in school. You couldn't have a history of skipping out on your rent payment. You and any family members on your lease could not have a violent criminal history or recent conviction. And finally, you had to agree to regular housekeeping checks." Christopher Swope, "Rehab Refugees: America's Worst Public Housing Projects Are Being Fixed Up, and Many of Them Look Pretty Good. There's Just One Puzzling Question: Where Did the Old Tenants Go?" *Governing's,* May 2001.

40. Swope, "Rehab Refugees."

41. Schuyler, "The New Urbanism and the Modern Metropolis," 357.

42. Robert S. Davis, "Developing New Urbanist Communities: The Role of the Town Founder," Seaside Institute, at www.theseasideinstitute.org/notes.asp, January 2002 (accessed February 25, 2002).

43. "In 1988 the Joseph Rowntree Housing Trust [JRHT] pioneered the first 'mixed tenure' scheme in the UK. . . . Since 1995 all residents have the choice of full rental, or shared ownership, at 25%, 50% or 75%, or can opt for 100% ownership eventually if their circumstances allow. Those who buy may also apply to sell back to the JRHT a part or all of the equity, should their circumstances oblige them to do so. In 1997 a 'voluntary purchase grant' from the Government became available for existing tenants to buy their home (or another property owned by the Trust). And some vacant properties were offered for sale on a 'Homebuy' basis. This scheme provides a 25% loan towards the purchase of a property. Applicants need to contribute 75% of the purchase price through a mortgage and/or personal savings. (There are no monthly payments to be made on the 25% loan but it must repaid when the property is sold. The amount to be repaid will be 25% of the value of the property at the time it is sold.)" Joseph Rowntree Foundation, at www.jrf.org.uk/home.asp (accessed April 3, 2002).

A Conversation with Alex Morton

Alex Morton is one of the original residents of Celebration, Florida, the New Urbanist community developed by the Disney Corporation. In 1999, he began publishing the *Celebration Independent,* a newspaper covering events in the town.

When did you move to Celebration, and what about the concept appealed to you?

Morton: I moved up here a couple of months before they opened, and I took an apartment because my house wasn't going to be ready by May and the kids were going to be ready to start school. So we actually moved into our apartment and were one of the first in an apartment on June 28, 1996. I became interested in the community in August of 1995. I read about Celebration in the paper and flew up, checked it out, went to the preview center.

***It is relatively unique in this economic climate, particularly with the journalism industry being so consolidated over the past ten years, for someone to start an independent newspaper for a small town. What motivated you to start the* Independent?**

Morton: It was in 1999 when we started the paper. I had residents approach me since I am in the publishing business. There was a bunch of them who felt very strongly about the way Disney was responding to various issues. They thought they could start their own paper. I said fine, do you have about $50,000 to invest? Everybody backed out. I said that's what it takes. I said I could do it on the assumption that it could turn a profit. Six months after I started the paper, Disney came out with a competitor. Their paper takes a lot of ads away. They thought they would take us out. They didn't because people want the news. There are always the naysayers. We'll always have those.

Your paper tends to be more critical of Disney and the Celebration Company, obviously, than the company's paper. What have been the challenges you have faced in publishing?

Morton: Actually, we are growing. We have been getting more advertising coming over to us because we publish more frequently than they do. We have even switched to start publishing two editions. One goes to the residents, which has the real news in it. And then the other, the street edition, is what you pick up on the newsstand. The difference is that the street edition has a lot of goody-good stuff like the company's paper, in other words, nothing controversial. The street edition focuses on real estate and general news like the Rotary having their pancake breakfast. In other words, as they say, "feel-good news." In the resident edition, we discuss things that are happening around town that would be more newsworthy, such as residents worried about a thirty-two-story hotel overlooking Celebration, problems with the Celebration Foundation, letters to the editor. People use us a lot for a sounding board.

So why don't you put the newsworthy stuff out with the street edition?

Morton: Because I have advertisers—especially the real estate people—asking, "Why are you putting bad things about us in the street edition? The tourists pick it up, and we can't sell." I am not hurting anybody by doing it this way. I'm not cutting back on the real news to the residents.

What effect do you think having the paper specifically has had in terms of influencing some of the developer's plans?

Morton: It's stopped a lot of things. There were so many things stopped dead in their tracks. First, they wanted to impose a $100 fee for DSL [high-speed Internet connection]. We stopped that dead in its tracks because you have a lot of people who don't want a DSL. We stopped the Celebration Foundation for making mandatory a $100-per-year fee. The Foundation is nothing but a company PR mechanism, really. It was started so they wouldn't have to put in low-cost housing. Any development has to make provisions for low-cost housing. The way Disney got around it was to impose a charitable contribution. It was a rip-off. The Celebration Foundation took in $500,000 and spent $9,000 on charities. The rest was offered to executive pay and public relations. It is PR for the Celebration Company. It is controlled by the Celebration Company.

Celebration has grown quite a bit since you moved here over five years ago. Has this growth actually changed the character of the town?

Morton: The growth of the town has slowed down a little bit because of the economy. Where they used to have 400 or 500 homes finished a year, it's now averaging 250. That wasn't what it was the first three years. Growth is down considerably on homes. The second thing you have to remember is the price range is high—we're still considered by some to be elitist compared to the rest of Osceola County. But we make good voters. Celebration residents turn out for votes, and they've made elections. A couple of elected officials have actually been elected because of the votes in Celebration. For Chuck Dennis, the county commissioner, it was Celebration that carried him. Even his home district didn't carry him. Celebration did.

What are some of the issues facing Celebration residents today?

Morton: We know everything Disney did right, but they did some things wrong. Instead of correcting mistakes, they just went on. Let me give you an example. One of the problems was that the alley was too short and garbage trucks, especially recycling trucks, couldn't get in there. They could get in there, but there wasn't enough room. They made the garage apartments so close in the back that a car couldn't park behind the house. Originally, they didn't want any cars parked on the street. They wanted to keep the streets open, which was a great theory. They left that. Later on, they started adding parking spaces along the golf course to make extra space for the golf course, not for the residents. But the residents were finding a lot of people don't park their cars in the garage—that's number one here in Florida especially. Garages become warehouses or basements. They made them so close to the back of the lot that there wasn't enough room to pull in your car. They need to make the alleyway so cars are not sticking out and the garbage trucks can make turns. But today in Celebration's East Village, they are still building the same way they built five years ago instead of learning from their mistakes.

The other problem we're facing relates to the Community Development District. The developer establishes a Community Development District initially to pay for the infrastructure. I pay $1,600 a year on my home to the CDD. That $1,600 is paying for the infrastructure. There is also an EDD, which is Economic Development District. A CDD is supposed to be for the home owners. An EDD is strictly for commercial businesses. However, there are overlaps—like Celebration Boulevard: Who pays for that? On one side of the street, they are saying we pay for it; the CDD and the other side is supposed to be paid for by the EDD. But the reality is both sides are commercial because there are no single-family homes along there. Residents are getting hit with it, and we are paying for the infrastructure for the apartment houses.

Do residents have representation on the CDD?

Morton: No, the board is just appointed. Someday they will be elected, but the damage is done. For example, they have already obligated us for $50 million for the school even though it was a loan. They had no right to do that. The school is a big issue right now because where they put it—in the middle of a district where they want all these hotels. Development is an issue when it concerns what is going to be the impact on the citizens at a later date. No one has a crystal ball, of course, but you should try to learn from other people's mistakes.

6

Racial Critique of Public Housing Redevelopment Strategies

Milton Curry

> In the narrow passage between rootedness and displacement, when the archaic stability of ontology touches the memory of cultural displacement, cultural difference or ethnic location accedes to a social and psychic anxiety at the heart of identification and its locutions.[1]

THE AMERICAN VERSION OF URBANISM has always been connected with a version of racial profiling and economic classification that measures races and spaces in relation to culturally prevailing concepts of whiteness—concepts that provide the ideological basis of federal housing policy and converge with versions of "New Urbanism" that claim to renew inner cities as enclaves of predominantly white and middle-class interlopers reclaiming the terrain of formerly large-scale modernist public housing tower complexes. The Department of Housing and Urban Development (HUD) and the Congress for the New Urbanism (CNU) entered into an alliance early in the Clinton administration when HUD Secretary Henry Cisneros signed on to the CNU Charter in the first three years of his tenure—a charter that lays out in simplistic yet ideologically loaded terms the framework for both reurbanizing the conventional suburb and, I argue, suburbanizing the conventional inner city. This alliance was the most important strategic move in shifting the public housing debate from one based on improving squalid conditions within existing public housing to a debate of how to entirely replace public housing and shift the responsibility for housing the poor (both the transitionary and the structural poor) from government to private development interests.

The basis of the public housing debate should now be squarely focused on the racial and class implications of New Urbanist methodologies that rely on conceptions of race and class originating from specific concepts of community that disenfranchise inner-city residents and render their race and class as neutral yet integral components of an all-out land grab for the property on which they live. My criticism of New Urbanism, the movement and the architecture, falls into two acute categories for the purpose of discussion in this chapter: 1) the use of race as an ideological variable used by the CNU for the purpose of convincing public and private interests to sign on to its principles for inner-city redevelopment and 2) HUD's HOPE VI Public Housing Replacement Fund for public housing projects, initiated in 1992, which is too reliant on New Urbanist principles—principles that, when implemented, lay the groundwork for long-term detrimental effects for the redevelopment of inner-city communities. These two criticisms problematize New Urbanism while reopening a discussion of not "if" but "how" to effectively redevelop public housing properties and/or existing physical structures.

Race as Ideological Variable

The identification of America with white is marked in this excerpt from the *Plessy v. Ferguson* Supreme Court decision: "A statute which implies merely a legal distinction between the black and white races—a distinction which is founded on the color of the two races, and which must always exist so long as white men are distinguished from the other race by color—has no tendency to destroy the legal equality of the races or reestablish a condition of involuntary servitude."[2] As Walter Benn Michaels has stated, "The transformation here of the difference between master and slave into the difference between white and black records the final separation of racism from slavery, racism's emancipation from the forms of a feudal economy."[3] "As 'white' becomes an adjective describing character instead of skin, the invisibility of race reappears, and the physiological obstacles to determining what race someone actually belongs to are transformed into ideological opportunities for finding 'real white men.'[4]

The *New York Times* reported with fanfare on April 30, 2001, "Whites in Minority in Largest Cities, the Census Shows," reporting that there was a 43 percent gain in the Hispanic population and charging that the fast-changing population complicates the challenges facing urban leaders.[5] As a result of this shift, according to the *New York Times,* "non-Hispanic Whites are now a minority of the total population living in the 100 largest urban centers."[6] However, as Orlando Patterson states in his refutation of that article in his May 8,

2001, *New York Times* editorial, "These articles and too many others have failed to take account of the fact that nearly half of the Hispanic population is White in every social sense of the term: 48% of so-called Hispanics classified themselves as solely White. . . . Racial classification and reclassification is not new, even for the Census Bureau. In the early decades of the twentieth century, the Irish, Italians, and Jews were classified as separate races by the federal immigration office. In 1930, Mexicans were classified as a separate race by the Census Bureau, which reclassified them as White in 1940. Between then and the 1960's, people from Latin America were classified as Whites until the onslaught of poor immigrants from Latin America, after which time the Hispanic category emerged."[7] As he states, "The first stage of racial classification, now nearly successfully completed for Hispanics, is naming and consolidating them all together while disingenuously admitting that they can be 'of any race.' Next, the repeated naming and sociological classification of different groups under a single category inevitably leads to the gradual perception and reconstruction of the group as another race."[8]

The same "perceptual geography" that has produced versions of racial classification, reclassification, and evolving definitions of whiteness is also producing a "New Urban(ism)," a movement that reshuffles thinking about race and the city in very troubling ways. At the "Exploring (New) Urbanism" Conference held in March 1999 at the Harvard Graduate School of Design, CNU leader Elizabeth Plater-Zyberk posited that unwed mothers, teenage pregnancies, child care problems, and other social ills have been exacerbated by the physical conditions of American cities brought about by postwar modernist architectural theories and built works.[9] CNU members Ray Gindroz and Robert Davis spoke at the same conference about "reclaiming" the inner cities and creating a more "civil society."[10] The CNU comrades borrow heavily from those who invoke a pastoral nostalgic where common values were shared by all—a rendition of history that evades an alternate and simultaneous reality whereby the American white immigrant native successfully colonized the Other's psyche through racial violence and the provisional colonization of their bodies and desires through legal and racial regimes regulated and endorsed by the state. If only today's contemporary city was tamed by the New Urbanist vision, they argue, one could again inhabit it as one inhabits the civilized and commodified realms of both the public space of the typical older main street of the small town as well as the domestic refuge of the conventional suburban home.

Seductive and all-encompassing words such as "community," "place," "streets," and so on used by the CNU function as floating signifiers—able to be co-opted into a neutral ideological field where the terms themselves become proxies for universal human subjects whose desires cross class, ethnic, and geographically cultural lines. The only hitch to this way of thinking is that you have to accept the assumptions on which this ideology lies—on the capacity of the civilizing process (one that failed to create a uniform Western subject at any other point in time) to be able to magically do its job today.[11] Socially constructed and educable to the ways of the white rational subject, the inner-city residents/laborers, like the land that they live on, are able to be reshuffled and reclassified just as the savages brought from noncivilized worlds were—that is what this brand of New Urbanism is expected to perform.

Under the operative premise that racial and class segregation in the United States is dependent in large part on the dysfunctional relationship between urban centers and their suburban counterparts, alternative conceptions of urbanism that would seek to mitigate this racial and class divide do so under an equally disturbing premise—that housing, one of the most fundamental of human provisions, should be regulated by market forces and that no one municipality should attempt to constitute a "safe haven" for its low- and moderate-income inhabitants because the dispersion of these persons will ultimately dissolve the racial and class segregation in the first place. This premise, popular among "New Urbanists" and urban planners, government policymakers, and private developers, does not withstand the well-formulated critique that economic displacement is fundamentally disruptive to the establishment of home, community, and other meaningful social formations. By conceding that some will get left behind—that public housing will not be a social safety net anymore—HUD has initiated a paradigm shift in its mission and in the strategy of housing the structural and transitionary poor.

The New Urbanist approaches to aesthetic legislation and implicit social controls of domestic and public spatial practices perpetuate racial and class segregation. These approaches put in motion irreversible urban and architectural paradigms that will make it increasingly difficult for cities to accommodate authentic urban growth at a time when population levels and resource allocations with respect to infrastructure and environmental equity necessitate higher urban densification and flexibility for communities that may experience fluctuations in housing demand. Town-house-style developments by their very nature—wood-frame construction, pitched roofs, and two-story density—do not allow for future densification. Alternately, "top-down" construction, concrete and steel construction, and more flexible floor-area-ratio zoning do allow for this kind of future flexibility for higher density and potential reprogramming or reuse of space for different functions. Housing and patterns of growth that surround and produce housing often dictate infrastructure and transportation, patterns of shopping, cultural and recreational activities, and places of work.

HOPE VI Public Housing Replacement Fund

HOPE VI, the HUD program for putting money in the hands of cities to redevelop public housing, sometimes rehouses only one-sixth of the public housing demand.[12] Larry Keating, professor at Georgia Institute of Technology, notes, "Reflecting disagreement over public housing policy, Congress did not produce precise language in the HOPE VI authoring legislation . . . which increased ways that HUD can fund rehabilitation. Consequently, the legislation gave broad latitude to HUD. To be eligible for a revitalization grant, public housing had to be housing that requires major redesign, reconstruction or redevelopment or partial or total demolition to correct serious deficiencies.'"[13] These policies and the vagueness of their application has led to subsequent emphasis on demolition in lieu of redevelopment, even though in the early years of the Clinton administration, HUD Secretary Cisneros stated publicly that many public housing towers could be revitalized at efficient costs, yet Secretary Cisneros signed on to the CNU Charter and the Awahnee Principles.[14] Cisneros's successor at HUD, Andrew Cuomo, continued to abide by the policy that any HOPE VI moneys were contingent on New Urbanist principles. In short, these principles put forth a vision of development denser than conventional suburbia yet provincial and traditional in their look and feel—abiding by strictly defined and enforced zoning guidelines.

The replacement ratio for HOPE VI projects is 74 percent and will approach something closer to 40 percent, according to projections of net losses of 60,000 units as 100,000 units are demolished.[15] In something akin to the educational desegregation cases of the 1960s and 1970s following the *Brown v. Board of Education* decision (1954), the Supreme Court upheld a decision in 1976 in *Hill v. Gautreaux* involving the voluntary relocation of public housing residents in Chicago with the Chicago Housing Authority (CHA) giving local ward leaders the power to prevent public housing projects (filled mostly with blacks) from being sited in their wards. As a remedy, the Supreme Court "sustained an order of a lower court requiring HUD to provide funds to disperse these concentrations of poor black families."[16] The limited Gautreaux remedy gave legitimacy to currently held public policy practice that HUD no longer should sustain its control of public housing, nor should states or local municipal authorities. The subsequent creation of Section 8 housing vouchers is further evidence of the government's desire to eventually "privatize" the housing of the nation's poor, low-income, public housing residents.

Chicago is not only the site of one of the seminal Supreme Court decisions on housing, it is also the site of historic racial tension and the nation's largest public housing complexes—the Cabrini Green and Robert Taylor projects. The core of what this idea of revitalization misses is caught by Richard Ford,

Stanford professor of law: "Wealthier suburbs have strong incentives to exclude poor urbanites and the means by which to do so, both supplied by the legal regime of American local government. . . . The engine of ghettoization is not entirely internal to the ghetto, nor are its roots exclusively historical."[17]

At the same time that the inner city is being declared a dump, not fit for inhabitation by the urban poor, these same places are the new economic frontier for private development concerns under the guise that mixed-income living is the new utopian ideal. The perceived unspoken aesthetic and social codes of the suburbs—classed and raced—are threatening to the urban poor who are not in sync with the aesthetic or social codes that prevail there. The proposition that a psychic domain that is placeless and culturally neutral can be transported into a geographically and culturally specific urbanity is a strategy that was employed by shopping center developers who perceived in the cultural psyche a universal demand for sameness and instantaneous accessibility to consumer products. If it is community that we are seeking, then a more commodified and sanitized version is arguably reproducible; alternately, if it is urbanism that we are seeking, only a recognition of local conditions and "on the ground" innovation can produce that—a process of catalyzing and evolving that cannot be completed in a single construction cycle. What or whom constitutes a community? Is there a collective and universal ability to cohere the new city all at once, the way one understands Williamsburg, Virginia; Disney's Celebration; or Seaside Florida—not as cities but as pure simulation. What role is played by racial identity and its assumed transportability in any discussion of New Urbanism?

The New Urbanists should not be given license to implicitly or explicitly assert that aesthetics exist in the domain of style and that ideologies are a thing of the past. Here again, I fear that New Urbanists are wagering on global capitalism to carry the day: When consumers reduce their notion of choice to the shape or color of a new product container or the carpet colors in their new tract home and consider that choice as taste, not ideology, they as well as the New Urbanists are mistaken. In some cases, aesthetics create ideologies, and in others it provocates or disrupts existing versions of it. The New Urbanist reenactment of the very things that they claim to be critiquing, like a B movie of the Williamsburg colonial parade, is both paradoxical and surreal. The New Urbanists are becoming experts at convincing poor people and the prurient bourgeois class that the "little house on the prairie" is an American entitlement, just as suburbanism was to a generation after the war. They have succeeded in garnering two radically different classes around the same nostalgic vision and have given them something to oppose together—the "chaotic modern architecture" that separated them by race and class in the first place, just as Target and the new "cross-class retailer" have multiplied their revenue streams by speaking to two or three classes of consumers at the same time. Again we should not mistake this for a new political or social compact that links the interests of rich and poor—only a new ideological aesthetic.

Federal Housing Administration and Veterans Administration policies, along with targeted mortgage programs, fueled white flight from city to suburb.[18] The flight of the upper-middle class from the metropolitan core to suburban residential communities and outer-belt office complexes has left many ethnically concentrated and class-concentrated communities in their wake. The communities that remain in the metropolitan inner cities lack sufficient access to quality and affordable housing, viable retail goods and services outlets, adequate public space, or efficient transportation. The transition from a primarily manufacturing-based urban economy to a more service-based economic community in the past twenty years has also taken its toll on these communities. Despite rhetorical efforts to the contrary, the composition, form, and social intentions of New Urbanism rest on very suspicious base impulses about social distance, race, class, entitlement, the continuing privileges of property ownership, and the disproportionate attention given to comforting an already comfortable upper-middle-class establishment. The weak assertion that New Urbanism will create more community, more cross-class interaction via mixed-income housing developments, and thus more socially responsible city making is problematic. New Urbanism ultimately facilitates the developer class as the controller of public properties—this propels gentrification in ethnically low-income communities and produces an artificial ideological terrain that privileges class and racial assimilation.

Chicago: Cabrini Green and Robert Taylor Homes

The convergence of a renewed public imagination in reimaging the American city (exemplified by the mass desire for New Urbanist imitations of Seaside and Celebration, Florida) has connected with federal resources to actually replace the modernist public housing structures built in the 1950s and 1960s, which in turn has resulted in ambitious projects, such as the Robert Taylor and the Cabrini Green redevelopment projects, both in Chicago.[19] At the intersection of identity politics and the public's desire for an imagined city without public housing (at least not in its current form) is the aesthetic legislation that enables these communities and revitalization efforts to actually get built and that will allow them to maintain their sheen over the next series of decades, so we are told. This is the object of my criticism and analysis.

Chicago; Newark, New Jersey; the borough of The Bronx, New York; and a long list of other cities have enrolled in the federal government's HOPE VI programs and are undertaking multiyear, multi-billion-dollar efforts to replace public housing (predominantly the high-rises built in the 1950s and 1960s) with mixed-income housing. The Chicago example is timely, as the efforts to "reclaim" America's inner cities and the properties that accommodate public and subsidized housing are getting grander and grander. The pressures of gentrification and land speculation have for many years been present, but what makes this moment different is that the scale and pace of these redevelopment efforts—which, ironically, end up displacing more residents that they replace—converge with the largest affordable housing crisis in the country's history as well as a realization on the part of developers that the inner city (where these public lands and projects are predominantly located) are high-growth markets.

History and Context: Robert Taylor Homes, Completed 1962

The Robert Taylor Homes in Chicago, named after Robert Rochon Taylor (CHA commissioner from 1938 to 1950 and CHA board chairman in 1943), is the largest public housing development in Chicago and the largest in the nation, consisting of twenty-eight identical sixteen-story buildings, mostly in U-shaped clusters of three.[20] The project opened in several stages and contained 4,415 apartments.[21] Unlike Le Corbusier's Unite d'Habitation in Marseilles, France, built in the 1950s, the Taylor towers relied on the outer neighborhood for social service provisions, whereas Unite–modernist thinking produced a more atomized, self-supportive infrastructure with schools, day care, and other amenities located within the tower itself. Ironically, had more public housing towers been more similar to Le Corbusier's vision, these towers would have arguably functioned more effectively for the residents that they were housing—residents who need basic services and social services in close proximity to their living environment and protected from the streets to some extent.

A side of the housing and New Urbanist debate that you do not hear much about is that, in this particular case of the Robert Taylor Homes, some of the residents of these urban public housing towers actually do not want to leave. Poverty breeds poverty, right? Well, possibly, but according to residents in the Taylor Homes, it also breeds community and the actual control over one's own domain that may not be had even in the New Urbanist visions that are replacing these urban renewal towers.[22] We know by now that these urban towers were used to segregate the black population, but what makes us think that this new paradigm will not simply resegregate the poor and underclass through the displacement that takes place as a result of these redevelopments?

The complexity of the Robert Taylor situation is highlighted in a December 2000 *Wall Street Journal* front-page story, a fact sheet from the Coalition to Protect Public Housing, and the March 2000 issue of *Illinois Welfare News.* In the *Wall Street Journal* article, "A Housing Project Fails, but the Poor Resist Orders to Move Out," residents are depicted as nostalgically attached to a failing and decrepit set of concrete towers, with an enlightened few who have opted to try their luck in the hostile suburbs—with the focus on the codes of conduct that were particularly difficult for the residents to adapt to as new living conditions. The conditions at Robert Taylor are described as so grave that the government will demolish first and figure out what will replace the housing later. The residents' personal narratives weave and bob through the essay, with scant references to the social expectations and codes in effect, moving from an example where a former Taylor resident finds the suburbs difficult (because the concrete walls that allowed noise do not exist in suburban flats) to a resident who feels comfortable in the towers surrounded by friends, family, and an informal support network. The Coalition newsletter lays out its responses to seven different assumptions about public housing; the assertions centralize around the fact that high-end residential high-rises in Chicago are performing well with good maintenance and care and that many are being upgraded for market demand. The tension articulated is between private economic concerns and demands for a "public good" standard for the reuse of these public lands—a legal threshold in all eminent-domain cases involving municipalities and private landholders. It highlights the fact that residents are being pushed out of poorly maintained housing and forced to find their own housing using Section 8 HUD housing vouchers in a tight housing market with insufficient affordable and subsidized housing supply.

Another essay, "Privatizing Public Housing in Chicago: A Case of Willful Neglect" (*Against the Current,* March 1, 2001) by Jamie Owen Daniel of the University of Illinois at Chicago, further articulates the legislating of domestic spatial practices and behavior implicit in these HUD and CHA policies:

> It [CHA] will act on behalf of private developers and maintenance companies to screen out any potential "undesirable" residents whose presence in the new "mixed income developments" might discourage middle-class people able to pay market rates. . . . Who is meant by this is clear in the Plan's new criteria for qualifying for a CHA unit. The new CHA rental policies will no longer offer housing based on need. Instead, it will "employ admissions preferences aimed at families who are working."
>
> As if these economic criteria, all of which imply that residents who aren't working are not worthy of a roof over their heads, weren't enough, low-income potential residents must submit to "housekeeping inspections" where they currently live. . . . Residents must also be willing to submit to "parenting classes" and "lifestyle choice training."

Conclusion

There is, it seems, an assumed ideal unity of consciousness in these public housing projects that is frontally challenged by what is literally and figuratively going down in Chicago and the contestation that the redevelopment efforts are facing by some of the residents at Robert Taylor. New Urbanism relies on a master narrative—legal, punitive, and administrative—whereby the obsession with community (you can never have enough, but of what kind?) itself produces another kind of fiction, one that acts to name public space explicitly and efficiently and that seeks to capture consumer identities into urban identities as a single unit. This produces an ideological and epistemological crisis for the city and the identity of its inhabitants. Richard Sennett, in *The Fall of Public Man,* states that "the city (public arena) ought to be a forum in which it becomes meaningful to join with other persons without the compulsion to know them as persons."[23] New Urbanism is both a symptom and an oversimplification of this vexed condition for the modern city—it neither challenges nor problematizes this in-between position that urbanity occupies, as it is difficult to suture authentic urbanism into a collective logic for replication or simulation.

New Urbanism anticipates a future logic of collectivity, articulated as a suburban condition of explicit comfort. In New Urbanism, we find an explicit ambition that the poor/urban dweller come to know their own subjugation and come to know again the horror of their legislated circumstances so that they may enact that predicament in complicity with the state—with their housing authorities and municipalities and their federal government. We must question the urban subject's cognitive capacity to absorb and classify spatiocultural practices as "presignifying regimes of thought/consciousness" as they really are constituted as such. The inner-city consumer/subject/citizen is the object of capitalist speculation and geographic manipulation and is more and more under the scopic regimes of privatization (schools, community centers, and so on) and rampant surveillance, not to mention their political dissolution through geographic dispersion. The real subject here is social relations of production. New Urbanism posits an architectural process without a humanist subject. We always need a social analysis of form just as we need for form to provocate analysis of the social.

Notes

1. Homi K. Bhabha, "On the Irremovable Strangeness of Being Different," *Modern Language Association Journal,* May 1998, 35.

2. *Plessy v. Ferguson,* 163 U.S. 540-52 (1896), reprinted in *The South since Reconstruction,* ed. Thomas D. Clark (New York: Bobbs-Merrill, 1973), 159.

3. Walter Benn Michaels, "Souls of White Folks," in *Literature and The Body: Essays on Populations and Persons,* ed. Elaine Scarry (Baltimore: The Johns Hopkins University Press, 1988), 189.

4. Michaels, "Souls of White Folks," 193.

5. *New York Times,* April 30, 2001, 1.

6. *New York Times,* April 30, 2001, 1.

7. *New York Times,* May 8, 2001, Editorial page.

8. *New York Times,* May 8, 2001, Editorial page.

9. Harvard Graduate School of Design, "Exploring (New) Urbanism" Conference, March 1999.

10. Harvard Graduate School of Design, "Exploring (New) Urbanism" Conference, March 1999.

11. Biodun Jeyifo, lecture at W. E. B. DuBois Center, Harvard University, March 10, 1999. Jeyifo cited Norbert Elias's *The Civilizing Process* as a reference point to discuss the failure of the Western colonization process to successfully stamp out cultural resistance on the part of enslaved Africans.

12. Larry Keating, "Redeveloping Public Housing: Relearning Urban Renewal's Immutable Lessons," in *APA Journal,* 66, no. 4 (Autumn 2000): 384: "Congress passed HOPE VI legislation . . . and appropriations to provide grants through HUD to public housing authorities that increased funding for the revitalization of the most distressed public housing. In 1995, Congress repealed the longstanding requirement that local authorities provide one-for-one replacement of public housing units eliminated through demolition or disposition."

13. Keating, "Redeveloping Public Housing," 385.

14. See the CNU website at www.cnu.org, the New Urbanism Charter, and the accompanying Awahnee Principles.

15. P. Belluck, "Razing the Slums to Rescue the Residents," *New York Times,* September 6, 1998, 1, 14, 15.

16. Owen Fiss, "What Should Be Done for Those Who Have Been Left Behind?" *Boston Review* 25, no. 3 (Summer 2000): 8.

17. Richard Ford, "Down by Law," *Boston Review* 25, no. 3 (Summer 2000): 11. "Incentives? In most states, American cities and towns fund public services primarily through property taxes. They also are entitled to limit access to those services to residents of the jurisdiction. This means that cities have an overwhelming incentive to encourage in-movers who will increase the value of property (and therefore tax revenues) and consume little in services, and to discourage in-movers whose presence will decrease property values and who will need a lot of public services. It scarcely needs to be said that the urban poor fit the latter description.

"Means? Although American local governments do not have explicit immigration policies, they do have broad powers to restrict land uses. By excluding all or most high density or multi-family housing, middle class and wealthy suburbs can effectively screen out low income potential residents by prohibiting the housing that they can afford. Local governments also can and do resist regional public transportation, halfway houses, group living arrangements, and rehabilitation centers—all services that many low-income people require in order to make the transition from troubled or dysfunctional lifestyles to success in the job market."

18. Joseph Seliga, "Comment: Gautreaux A Generation Later: Remedying the Second Ghetto or Creating a Third," *Northwestern University Law Review* 94, no. 1049 (Spring 2000): 4.

19. Jeff Glasser, "From Big and Ugly to Small and Promising: A Bet on Chicago's Cabrini-Green," *U.S. News & World Report,* September 11, 2000:

> CHICAGO—The North Town Village condo brochure promises a dream neighborhood "minutes" from the downtown Loop. . . . Missing from this pretty picture, however, is any reference to the area's most obvious feature: Cabrini-Green. That's right, the infamous public-housing project long known for gang murders, drug busts, and despair. The eight hulking high-rises that surround North Town like ominous specters are nowhere in the condo brochure. "I find that stunning," says Bob Tack, a local resident who recently looked at the promotional material. "It's buyer beware."
>
> What's even more remarkable is that wealthy professionals are gobbling up new homes in North Town. All but 10 of the development's 131 market-rate units sold on the first four weekends. (An additional 79 are reserved for public housing and 51 for "affordable housing.") Attracted by its convenient, close-in location, cheaper prices, and the promise that the ugly tenement towers will eventually come down, the homebuyers at North Town and four other new communities are changing the fabric of a century-old slum.
>
> Cabrini-Green is the first major test of Mayor Richard M. Daley's $1.5 billion plan to knock down 51 of the city's public-housing high-rises and replace them with "mixed income" housing. At Cabrini, 2,300 units—including North Town—will rise in the first rebuilding phase, with 700 reserved for public housing. If the redevelopment here succeeds, Cabrini will be touted as a national model for a new kind of community where rich and poor live side by side. "Everybody's nervous about Chicago, concerned about whether the housing authority can pull it off," says Susan Popkin, an Urban Institute senior research associate who coauthored *The Hidden War: Crime and the Tragedy of Public Housing in Chicago.* "It's the largest [urban renewal] project in the country, and this is a housing authority that a few years ago couldn't collect rent."
>
> Location, location. The 5,249 public-housing residents at Cabrini are the most apprehensive. Some tenants complain that "mixed income" is simply a code word for their removal. Cabrini borders three of the city's wealthiest neighborhoods, and suspicious residents fear that developers are mostly interested in a gentrification land grab. Their evidence? The first phase of rebuilding calls for a maximum of 30 percent public housing. Should developers, Cabrini leaders, and the city's housing authority continue to limit the revamped housing to that percentage, many Cabrini tenants will likely have to move to poor outlying areas. "We call it urban cleansing," says Deidre Matthews, a community activist. "They're trying to force us out, but we won't leave." Asked about the land-grab charges, a housing authority official laughs nervously. "That is one way of putting it that's not incorrect," says Olusegun Obasanjo, the authority's Cabrini development manager. "Cabrini-Green is highly desirable. The idea of leveraging that desirability to improve the welfare of residents is not necessarily a bad one. If we are able to minimize the number of residents displaced, then perhaps it's not such a bad thing."

20. Shaw, Metz, and Associates designed the development. Alfred Shaw, the head architect, was a prominent Chicagoan and chief architect of the original McCormick Place. Other well-known projects of Shaw are the Morton Wing at the Chicago Institute and the United Insurance Company skyscraper at State and Wacker. Alfred Shaw was born in Dorchester, Massachusetts, and studied architecture at the Boston Architectural Club from 1911 to 1917.

21. Seliga, "Comment," 4.

22. That is, aesthetic and social controls placed on exterior design, urban design, and the interior domestic realm as in Disney's Celebration and other planned communities under the New Urbanist banner.

23. Richard Sennett, *The Fall of Public Man: On the Social Psychology of Capitalism* (New York: Norton, 1976), 340.

A Conversation with Mel Martinez

Mel Martinez was appointed by President George W. Bush in 2001 to be the secretary of Housing and Urban Development (HUD). Prior to that post, Secretary Martinez was the county chairman of Orange County, Florida.

How did you become interested in smart-growth and housing issues?

Martinez: Being a longtime resident of central Florida, I became increasingly concerned about the quality of life. I grew up in central Florida before Disney, and I knew what life was like then. Then I saw the "progress" as we became a tourist destination and what can happen with growth when it takes place so fast and what it does to the quality of life. As it relates to housing itself, my life was shaped by being a refugee, by being in foster homes. Having seen the opportunities that life has to offer in this country and my parents becoming home owners here, I thought, was a transforming kind of experience.

In many respects, suburban sprawl is considered a municipal, local, or, in some instances, state issue. What role do you see for the federal government, and especially HUD, in addressing sprawl?

Martinez: I think that the federal government's role has to be limited and we should never become a national land planning agency or something like that. That would be ridiculous. But there is a federal role in the interaction. It's not like we have nothing to do with local government. We give them a lot of money. But not only we do at HUD, but also Transportation does. I think there's a direct correlation between the decisions that are made at the Department of Transportation as with award dollars for projects that have to do with highways and byways and the consequences of those decisions on growth. I don't think there's any question that the road leads to paths to the development of regions. So some coordination, some level of coherence from HUD and DOT at the federal level about what makes sense for communities, is a proper role.

In addition to that, the federal government [needs to] make funding decisions that encourage regional growth management decision making. I think that would be very, very positive because when I served in local government, it was made very clear to me that I could only impact up to my borders. But the impact of positions that were being made by transportation officials at the state and national level really transcended those borders.

Following up on that, there are very few areas that you have a metropolitan government per se. There are different regional authorities but few metropolitan governments. Would you consider yourself an advocate for metropolitan government?

Martinez: I think it is effective. I think it is something that should happen. I can say, however, that it's fraught with difficulty politically. I think there has to be a hybrid that would work—a hybrid between a political body and sort of a historically cohesive area. For instance, look at Winter Park, Florida. Winter Park should never be anything other than Winter Park, but there are land use decisions that impact Winter Park. Winter Park has horrendous transportation problems that are not because of the residents of Winter Park but because of the people that live on either side of Winter Park. So you have to look at Winter Park as being impacted regionally. Winter Park needs to maintain its ambiance for being the kind of place it is. It is a very special kind of place. But planning and transportation decisions should be made on a more regional basis.

Many of the problems with sprawl and growth have their origins in a wide variety of policy domains: energy use, transportation, land use, housing, environmental preservation, agriculture, and so on. Have there been attempts at the federal level to take an interagency approach to dealing with issues of metropolitan growth?

Martinez: We're starting to make some stabs at that. I hope that we can begin to have a cooperative arrangement to talk about growth issues with Transportation and maybe Agriculture, as well. I think there is a limit to what we can do at the federal government. One thing we have done here is a multiyear study on land use and planning with the cooperation of the American Planning Association. It's a set of guidelines that might be used by local communities.

Would transit-oriented development be a part of those recommendations?

Martinez: I am sure it would be. Although, you know, it isn't even about mass transit. Mass transit obviously has a place. The fact is the cost of light rail is great. The benefit is really somewhat questionable. By telecommuting, you can only make things different. If you were to get 6 percent, 8 percent of the workforce to stay home for no cost, and you would have the same thing as a light rail system, but it's a cheaper solution.

What's your assessment of the HOPE VI program? What are the beneficial elements of it, and what are the areas where it can be improved?

Martinez: I think HOPE VI is a tremendously positive program, and I'm very, very big on it. What it does is it takes out the stock of old and dilapidated and poor housing of a bygone era, and it makes it something new: transformed, more village style, more green spaces reserved, better places for people to live. There are a couple of problems, however. One is that there is a displacement of people who are living in public housing now but have to live somewhere else. Many can come back but not 100 percent usually. That is a problem but not a huge problem. Sometimes the tenants might get very focused on the fact that they can no longer walk to the grocery store that they've walked to for ten years. That's a problem, but you can't make policy based on whether someone who may already be elderly or frankly may not live long is going to be disruptive. That's not good. It's sad.

We fund the relocation, but we have to make policy on a broader basis than that. The new place is going to be a mixed-income community. It's not going to be all public housing types of people, which is a good thing, but then we have to find a way to do something with other types of people. So those are some of the collateral issues that need to be addressed, and we will when we go forward in tweaking this very good program. I'm big on it, and it's a real solution to a lot of the problems.

How does your experience as a municipal government official who advocated smart growth inform your perspective as a cabinet secretary?

Martinez: It's an invaluable experience because you know different areas. I think a lot of these issues really are local. I think having that perspective is wonderful. Having been on the board of a housing authority, I think it's a very valuable experience. I don't define myself as a smart-growth advocate because I don't know if I want to buy into everything that that would imply. I am, rather, someone who is concerned about growth issues and wants to be proactive in how we view land issue decisions. I think the government has a role, but we have to come to a point where we allow communities to redevelop by providing them attractive places for development to take place. I was in Philadelphia a week ago talking to the mayor about a very large redevelopment there. Philadelphia has lost like a million people over the last fifteen years. It is a disaster area. In order for them to bring people back into the city, they have to make it attractive. How do you do that? First of all, you make public safety a given. You cannot have a successful situation if public safety isn't there. You have to make it attractive. You have to have it clean. You have to do the things you can do to clean up brown fields. You have to lay the table in a way that then makes it possible and attractive and financially prudent for developers to make smart development decisions. If we just rely on the government saying, "You will not develop there because you must develop here," that just isn't going to work. There has to be a series of incentives, and growing communities need to insist that the development pay for the true cost of development. The local government should not subsidize the cost of development sprawling outside area.

Describe your ideal vision for the American metropolis.

Martinez: Oh! The ideal metropolis is a place that, after you raise a child and you send him off to college, the community is one that they want to come back to. They are going to want to come back and want to raise a family, and they are going to have a decent job. It is going to have a kind of quality of life that is going to make it a place where people who have choices about where they live want to live there.

7

Race and Suburban Sprawl: Regionalism and Structural Racism

Ronald Hayduk

WHAT IS THE CONNECTION between suburban sprawl and urban decline? This chapter argues that race is an integral—and neglected—part of the answer. This chapter examines the relationship between these two developments—and the myriad problems associated with each phenomenon—focusing on the role race plays in shaping these outcomes. We begin with an example to help illustrate and explain.

Every week, Kimberly travels from her black inner-city neighborhood to work in a suburban mall. Although Kim's hour-long commute via two buses to a low-paying job does not cover her mounting bills, it is the only work she can find. Like most metropolitan areas in the United States, much of the job growth has shifted to the suburbs but with few transportation links. Just out of high school, Kim hopes to save enough money to go to law school someday. As time passes, however, that hope increasingly seems distant and tenuous, much like her job at the mall.

Thomas commutes weekly from a residential neighborhood in the same white suburb where Kim labors in the mall to work at his law firm in the city's central business district. Sometimes Tom drives, while other days he takes a sleek commuter train, neither of which is an option for Kimberly, who cannot afford a car and lives far from the train. Her meager wages would not cover the train fare anyway. Tom's salary handsomely pays not only for his travel costs but also for a home mortgage, his daughter's college tuition, and nearly all his other needs and wants, including shopping at the store where Kim works.

Ironically, Tom and Kim have much in common, but neither realizes it. Tom grew up in a working-class family in the very same neighborhood where

Kim now lives. But changes in the region, including shifts in the economy, declining real estate values, new public programs, and an influx of new residents, led his parents to leave the city and move to the suburbs. What Tom's family left behind was decaying homes and schools and rising crime rates, all of which Kim's family inherited when they moved into the neighborhood. Kim's family fled the Jim Crow South in the late 1950s in search of better work and life in the North, while Tom's fled the decaying city for the suburbs, a decade later, for roughly the same reasons. Thus, similar motivations shaped their decisions and the conditions of their separate lives. But today, when they pass each other at the mall or interact—which revolves around the cash nexus of payment for goods and services—these past life histories and trajectories are not exchanged or known to them. In fact, each sees the other as the "other."

Why, in the same region, do some people like Tom live in good communities that have all sorts of advantages while others like Kim live in neighborhoods with fewer opportunities and poorer services? If Tom and Kim have anything in common, it is that both are part of a metropolitan region whose historical shifts and political economy reflect the maldistribution of power.

This chapter argues that their stories reveal that one's place in a metropolitan area is not just the result of individual preferences or impersonal market forces—as mainstream accounts of racial disparities argue—but is also a consequence of a host of historically created and contemporarily sustained set of public policies and private practices. The chapter shows how a long chain of incentives and disincentives established by public and private actors cumulatively yields spatial segregation and racial disparities, including problems of suburban sprawl.

Part of the reason that communities of color in particular are faced with such enormous problems—from inadequate housing, jobs, schools, transportation and public services to higher crime—are the structural factors that shape their futures within regions. It is no accident that such neighborhoods are cut off from resources and opportunities that would help remedy these problems. Needed assets exist in abundance in the suburban communities around them—often just a few miles from where they are situated. These suburbs grew rapidly during the postwar period, and although they are rapidly diversifying, suburbs remain largely white. Suburbs also score higher than inner cities in nearly every opportunity category, including income, employment, assets, quality of education, and housing, and have lower crime rates. Suburban prosperity is not coincidental either. It has been subsidized by a host of public policies—from the GI bill to Federal Housing Administration (FHA) home mortgages and transportation policies—while urban dwellers, paying rents and riding mass transit, have been shortchanged. In short, concentrated inner-city poverty and suburban prosperity are two sides of the same coin.

Proximate and older suburbs are finding similar problems creeping in that are often explained in the similar terms. Inner-ring suburbs and "edge cities" that experienced mostly white out-migration found themselves ill equipped to handle such problems because of a lack of revenue to adequately finance areas such as economic development ventures or police protection. Consequently, problems once thought to be confined to central cities became more widespread. In addition, white residents in these suburbs often associate such problems with the movement of working- and middle-class blacks and other minorities into these areas. Moreover, because these suburbs are even less able to cope with such problems than cities—partly because of their having an even smaller tax base, political power, and so on—much of these "urban suburban" populations (mostly white) have moved even farther out into the exurbs.

Indeed, suburban communities such as Tom's are rife with new problems, including "sprawl," overdevelopment, congestion, and environmental degradation, that are indirectly related to the devaluation of central cities. In addition, a host of other problems typically associated with inner cities increasingly can be found in suburbs. Drugs and crime are creeping into his son's school, and pockets of poverty, decaying older homes, and abandoned commercial zones dot the highways that connect his suburb to other suburbs and to the city.

These outcomes result from several factors. A mix of historical developments and contemporarily sustained practices created and maintain disparities between cities and suburbs. Powerful public actors and private institutions make key decisions that shape "who gets what when and how," or what social scientists often refer to as the politics of power and governance.[1]

Yet, paradoxically, the fates of both suburbs and inner cities are inextricably linked. It may not be obvious to residents of either community, but central-city disadvantage imposes costs that go beyond municipal boundaries. Ultimately, these costs affect the viability and thus the sustainability of the region as a whole.

To both understand and fight structural forces that produce disparate racial and regional outcomes, analysts and community builders must develop effective tools that can begin to alter these patterns. And if community builders—leaders of community based organizations, community development corporations, foundations, and other intermediary organizations—are going to be successful at achieving their goals, they must begin to take into account racial and regional dynamics. Equitable and sustainable economic development is possible only when all stakeholders (or their representatives) sit at the tables where key decisions are made, that is, when such decisions are made democratically. Fortunately, some in the community-building field have begun to develop analyses and launch initiatives aimed at shaping more equitable outcomes (discussed later in this chapter).

A structural racial analysis provides important insights into why people like Tom live in good communities that provide numerous advantages while others like Kim live in neighborhoods that impose numerous disadvantages. It helps us see beyond just their individual attributes, resources, and behaviors. We are able to see where and how racial and regional dynamics shape one's ability to get a job and acquire income, attain education, live in a safe neighborhood, or become enmeshed in the criminal justice system. We are able to see how racial and regional dynamics affect attitudes, beliefs, and preferences. Decisions made by people like Tom and Kim are, to a significant extent, "structured." Put another way, their menu of options in life differs, just as the range and quality of selections differ from one restaurant to another. The value of a structural racial regional analysis is that it exposes these interconnections. It also can help community builders form effective strategies for change.

Both suburbanites and inner-city residents have a stake in regional developments. While such communities may differ greatly, people like Tom and Kim have shared interests in solving their own as well as each other's problems. Studies show that regional economies prosper or falter as a whole.[2] The constituent parts of metropolitan regions affect each other. Their destinies are intertwined. The problems associated with suburban sprawl are the flip side of urban blight. Thus, it is argued, regional-level solutions are required to effectively address both sets of problems. So community builders must seek solutions that involve all regional stakeholders rather than inner-city residents alone.

The analysis offered here also exposes the racial dynamics that lie at the heart of spatial segregation and individual-level disparities. Institutions and structures are imbued with the racialized power privilege of dominant groups. Efforts aimed at achieving racial equity, therefore, are key to making regions viable and sustainable. And racial equity must become the basis for the sustainability of regions. This chapter argues that analysts need to know about what happens in their broader metropolitan region in order to effectively solve problems affecting them. Leaders and residents in both urban and suburban communities need to "think and link" regionally in order to combat the insidious form of racial sorting that segregates people residentially and malapportions benefits and burdens.

Regional and Racial Disparities: Regional Polarization and Racial Segregation

There is a familiar pattern of social segregation and racial polarization within a region. The Metropolitan Area Research Corporation (www.metroresearch.

org), for example, depicts this phenomenon in a typical fashion: Regions become polarized as private investment and people are pulled outward into the suburbs. Suburbanization has been fueled by large public and private investments in infrastructure and low taxes with comparatively higher per capita spending on better and more expensive public services. These resources and people are simultaneously pushed outward by the concentration of urban poverty and problems—unemployment, crime, poorly performing schools, poor services, decaying infrastructure due to a dwindling tax base, and comparatively low per capita government spending. The concentration of poverty in central-city neighborhoods—where 20 to 40 percent of a typical region's population lives—destabilizes families, schools, and neighborhoods. It produces dramatic increases in a host of social ills and the loss of economic and social opportunity. As population and business flee, poverty and racial segregation grow. Property values and revenue income erode and deplete needed local social services and government capacity.

Older working-class inner-ring and middle-income adjacent suburbs—where 20 to 30 percent of a typical region's population lives—soon become riddled with similar problems. While poverty rates are twice as high in central cities than in the suburbs, 30.5 percent of the nation's poor live in the suburbs.[3] Ironically, however, these areas are less able to address such growing problems because their local governments have fewer resources. Per capita, they have the lowest sales, property, and income tax bases but higher tax rates and lower spending on services. Suburban sprawl spreads out even farther to growing middle-class communities—where another 20 to 40 percent of a typical region's population resides—that often do not have a sufficient property tax base to support the growing needs for schools and other public services. These fiscally and environmentally stressed communities become tomorrow's declining suburbs.

The stable, secure, and affluent suburbs—where only 15 to 30 percent of a region's population live—capture the lion's share of infrastructural investment and spending, economic growth, and jobs, usually paid for in part by other parts of the region. They enjoy many benefits: funding for roads, wastewater treatment, airports, and shared labor and product markets. Their tax base expands, and per capita spending soars, while their housing markets exclude others. But their prosperity is not due only to their hard work and good fortune. It has been subsidized by federal and state policies.

Yet affluent suburbs avoid most regional responsibilities and burdens. They do not pay for city services and infrastructure that commuters especially use on a regular basis (including sanitation, police, bridges, airports, sports complexes, and so on), let alone caring for the poor and providing affordable housing. At the same time, these affluent suburbs deplete remaining green space and endanger fragile and precious environmental resources.

These regional-area dynamics depict how social need is contained in the cities and declining suburbs—concentrated particularly in poor and minority neighborhoods—and how the growing problems of sprawl are intimately connected. Centrifugal forces that produce patterns of geographic polarization disproportionately produce negative impacts on urban centers and in communities of color. Their concentrated effects are seen in education, jobs, housing, health, neighborhood safety, crime, incarceration rates, and environmental conditions. As jobs leave, people follow, social capital and networks decline, community structures (such as schools and housing) deteriorate, safety suffers, and hazardous waste accumulates. Conversely, suburban jurisdictions disproportionately reap the benefits of racial spatialization even if they are not entirely spared of the problems that regional polarization creates. In short, regional-area dynamics shape the distribution of opportunities and burdens geographically.

Suburbanization: The Great Sucking Sound

Suburbanization—the movement of resources and people out of cities—markedly exacerbated extant racial and metropolitan polarization. As Douglas Massey has written, "Opportunities and resources are unevenly distributed in space; some neighborhoods have safer streets, higher home values, better services, more effective schools, and more supportive peer environments than others. As people and families improve their socioeconomic circumstances, they generally move to gain access to these benefits. In doing so, they seek to convert past socioeconomic achievements into improved residential circumstances, yielding tangible immediate benefits and enhancing future prospects for social mobility by providing greater access to residential determined resources."[4] However, because prejudice and discrimination have especially blocked such avenues for African Americans and other racial and ethnic minorities, residential segregation has increased and persisted. Thus, barriers to spatial mobility have been very real barriers to social mobility.

Moreover, geographic shifts of population and resources have also shifted political power outward to the suburbs. The suburbs now possess the largest portion of voters—who also vote at higher rates than urban dwellers—which has given them greater influence in national and state policy. Their greater political clout erodes any political will to address the problems associated with poverty, race, and urban decline, thus further contributing to urban decay and racial polarization. Following World War II, significant portions of the U.S. population increasingly shifted to the suburbs. In 1960, the proportion was roughly equal: 51 percent lived in cities, and 49 percent lived in the suburbs. By 1980, only 40 percent of metropolitan-area populations lived in central cities, while 60 percent resided in the suburbs. These proportions are more or less the same today, although population shifts vary considerably by region. The Northeast and the Midwest witnessed an overall decline in population in their metropolitan regions relative to the South and the West. Moreover, central cities in the Northeast and the Midwest lost a net total of nearly three million people per year between 1988 and 1996, while their suburbs gained about the same number of people per year.[5]

The racial composition of regions and metropolitan areas also shifted dramatically. While residential segregation among blacks and whites in the early part of the twentieth century was primarily between the South and the North—and within states and counties—black migration northward changed the geographic structure of segregation to the neighborhood level within urban settings.[6] Following World War II, black segregation decreased at the state and county levels but rose dramatically in metropolitan areas and within cities especially. While these trends leveled off somewhat between 1970 and 1990, in most metropolitan areas, racial segregation remained very high or even increased.[7] Out of seventy-four of the largest metropolitan areas of the country, only 40 percent of blacks and Hispanics lived outside these central cities in 1990 compared to 67 percent of whites and Asians. Even more telling, only 16 percent of blacks and Hispanics lived in the suburbs.[8]

The suburban exodus left behind a disproportionate number of poor people of color and new immigrants. Moreover, during the past several decades, we have witnessed growing gaps in income and the availability and quality of jobs, education, housing, transportation, health care, crime, and so on both in urban areas and in declining suburbs.[9]

As jobs and opportunity moved to the suburbs, minorities were concentrated within cities. Joblessness, poverty, crime, hazardous waste, and other social ills increased and disproportionately affected racial minorities. Even though legal discrimination was eliminated in the wake of the civil rights movement, race and place remain strong indicators of opportunities and outcomes. Geography has been so intertwined with race that it almost predicts destiny. The lives of millions of people like Tom and Kim are bound up with race and place. In fact, despite the longest sustained economic boom in our nation's history, such disparities have not changed significantly. Moreover, such problems have spilled out into the suburbs. Sprawl is a direct result of these developments. The fates of these areas with a metropolitan region are inextricably linked.

Explanations for Racial and Regional Disparities

Just how did these patterns of regional and racial disparities emerge? How can the different lives of people like Kim and Tom be understood? Many analysts point to a common set of facts in describing the decline of cities and the problems of suburban sprawl. But they diverge in explaining these phenomena. The literature on regional and racial disparities can be grouped into two primary approaches: 1) conventional or mainstream explanations and 2) critical or structural explanations.

Conventional Explanations for Urban Decline, Suburban Prosperity, and Racial Disparities

Conventional explanations can be further broken down into three broad categories:[10]

1. Individual choices, cultural differences, and racial superiority/inferiority
2. Poorly designed public policies—the failure of urban renewal and social programs
3. Deindustrialization, changing market forces, and globalization

Mainstream narratives and research about urban decline and racial disparities generally go along these lines: Cities and older suburbs declined during the middle to the end of the twentieth century—particularly those in the Northeast and the Midwest—by losing millions of residents, businesses, and tax dollars. Whether these residents and business left because of deindustrialization, changes in demographics and labor markets, changes in property values and tax policy, or recent changes in technology and globalization or because of middle- and upper-class desires to flee the decaying urban centers for the greener pastures of suburbia in pursuit of the American Dream, the result has been that cities became the home to growing numbers of poor and minority groups with a lack of resources to deal with the problems of concentrated poverty: joblessness, failing schools, crime, family fragmentation, decaying infrastructure, poor housing, empty lots, limited transportation facilities, and decrepit commercial districts.

Regional economic and political fragmentation resulted. Suburbanization led to the creation of tens of thousands of new local governments. But such divisions, it is argued, are not all bad. The proliferation of political systems generates intergovernmental competition and produces a smaller and more efficient public sector and a larger and more robust private sector and a greater realm for individual choice and residential preferences.[11] Socially and politically fragmented metropolitan areas are merely the result of heterogeneous preferences by individuals and groups for publicly provided goods and services.[12] These results, they contend, are "natural" or "inevitable" outcomes of market processes and group differences that, on balance, are not seen as problematic. In fact, some contend that these conditions have helped the United States flourish, especially economically.

Others focus on individual-level variables. Some researchers describe urban minorities as lacking the requisite "social capital" or "human capital" (education or job skills) to make it in a changing marketplace.[13] Moreover, minorities and the poor purportedly lack the means or motivation to pull themselves out of the hole they find themselves in, and government welfare programs have fostered dependency, leading to a "culture" or "cycle" of poverty and social dysfunctionality.[14] Changing family structures are also seen as a key contributing factor, particularly the decline of the nuclear family and the rise of single-parent (that is, mother) households.[15]

Essentially, such scholars argue that racial minorities and the poor are culturally different: They have different values, make different choices, and act differently than members of the mainstream. Their differences mire them in social problems and poor conditions. Broken families and single-parent homes are more likely to experience unemployment, poverty, ill health, and so on and exhibit behavioral problems, including criminal activity, substance abuse, a "dependence" on welfare, and a variety of "irrational," "deviant," and "immoral" conduct. An "underclass" is the result.[16]

For others, regional and racial disparities are seen as being due to profound economic shifts that eroded the competitive position of cities in important industries, particularly because of increased global competition.[17] Deindustrialization undermined entry-level jobs that historically provided pathways out of poverty for immigrants and some minorities. The loss of these urban manufacturing sectors further segregated poor and minority populations from the places where jobs moved, creating a "spatial mismatch"—or a disjuncture between jobs that are increasingly located in suburban areas and low-income and minority populations who are located in central-city neighborhoods.[18] Similarly, the "skills mismatch" hypothesis argues that the postindustrial service-oriented and technologically sophisticated economy has fewer low-skilled jobs and now requires higher-level skills for growing sectors of the economy that inner-city minorities lack to effectively compete in the marketplace.[19] Minorities and women have a "human capital" deficit—they possess lower and poorer education and lack necessary job skills and work experience—for the new economy. People like Kim just have less of what is needed in the new world economy and live in the wrong place, while people like Tom have more of what it takes and take advantage of their assets.

Shifting migration patterns have also undercut standards of living for urban dwellers and minorities in particular. New immigrants move into cities in search of a better future, and middle-class residents move out for a better quality of living in the suburbs. The out-migration of middle-class residents reduces social capital, while the in-migration of newcomers brings increased competition in labor markets that drives down wages and employment chances for other residents. The resultant racial and ethnic labor market segmentation and spatialization can especially hurt blacks.[20] Conversely, there is evidence that new immigrants are also helping revive cities and blighted neighborhoods.[21] Finally, the return of urban professionals to low-income housing areas has spurned gentrification and created contested turf and displacement.[22]

Critical Analysis of Mainstream Approaches to Urban Decline and Racial Disparities: Toward a More Comprehensive Explanation

While these analyses contribute valuable data and scrutiny to these developments, mainstream approaches end up describing primarily regional and racial disparities rather than actually explaining what are the key factors that have produced this disjuncture and how these outcomes arose originally.[23] At best, they tend only to identify barriers that inner-city blacks face in obtaining jobs, such as a lack of information to suburban job opportunities, requisite job skills, and transportation (cars). Some also acknowledge discrimination patterns in jobs and housing that disproportionately affect minority groups and women.[24] Yet there is little analysis of the history of how such disjunctures arose, what and who created these disjunctures, and how and why they are perpetuated, nor do they present strategies or viable solutions that would adequately address such problems at a fundamental or structural level. When mentioned at all, policy recommendations tend to focus on increasing investments in education and employment, for example, to inner-city residents. In short, mainstream approaches appear to be satisfied, on balance, with the status quo.

Critics contend that mainstream explanations are flawed or misguided. Some critics argue that conventional explanations are not "wrong"; they just do not go far enough. That is, they fall short of a fuller accounting of how and why disparate regional and racial outcomes occur. More pointedly, critics maintain that mainstream approaches misdiagnose the causes of regional and racial problems, which ultimately points them toward unworkable strategies and untenable solutions. What such debate reveals—because regional and racial disparities implicate American social values and policy—are ideological (as well as empirical) differences that are reflected in these divergent approaches.

For example, one of the mainstream explanations for racial segregation is that blacks prefer to live with other blacks. Yet critics present evidence from surveys that show that blacks actually prefer to live in integrated neighborhoods.[25] Even though whites appear to share blacks' commitment to open housing in principle—that anyone should be able to live wherever he or she wants—whites remain uncomfortable with it in practice.[26]

Similarly, class explanations for racial segregation—that blacks have lower incomes on average than whites and cannot afford to live in white neighborhoods—are not sustained by empirical evidence. While this thesis appears to be correct intuitively and is certainly true to some extent, it fails to comprehensively account for segregation when the data are analyzed. Researchers have found that levels of black–white segregation do not vary by social class when computed with income, occupation, or education.[27] Black families earning at least $50,000 were just as segregated as those earning less than $2,500.[28] And while waves of new immigrants has complicated this picture, "Blacks experience by far the greatest likelihood of hostility from other groups [whites, Asians, and Hispanics], and are universally acknowledged to face the most severe housing discrimination. . . . Segregation does not result from Black ethnocentrism so much as from avoidance behavior by other groups, all of whom seek to circumvent potential coresidence with Blacks."[29]

Instead, critics contend that racial segregation results, in large part, from discriminatory policies and practices that were institutionalized by the real estate industry and other public policies beginning in the 1920s and 1940s.[30] Even after the Fair Housing Act was passed in 1968, however, a more subtle process of exclusion ensued, buttressed by a covert series of barriers. Though individual acts of discrimination may be smaller and subtler, they have a powerful cumulative impact. "Racial steering" by real estate agents, for example, continues to occur and perpetuates segregation patterns.[31]

Thus, the argument goes, as segregation increased, so did concentrated poverty. The effects of concentrated poverty have further compounded the problems of racial minorities. Wilson argued that class isolation among blacks created "underclass" conditions that undermine their life chances.[32] Wilson argued that a variety of societal changes raised the bar to success: The loss of jobs and employment opportunities, reduced incomes, and an increased number of single-parent families perpetuate inequality and produce devastating impacts on poor people and communities of color and negatively impact women and children especially. To be sure, these conditions can affect cognitive and social development, educational and employment opportunities, neighborhood safety and survival strategies (including the probability of being involved in the criminal justice system), higher environmental hazards and poorer health, a decline in social networks and social capital, and a broad range of other social behavior that contributes to negative outcomes for inner-city poor and minority residents and positive outcomes for more affluent suburban residents. Numerous studies have subsequently been conducted that support the basic thrust of Wilson's hypothesis, although the specific mechanisms and dynamics that produce such results are probably more complex than Wilson posited.[33] The interaction of racial segregation with concentrated poverty thereby contributes to regional and racial disparities highlighted previously.

In sum, while conventional analyses may acknowledge that important institutional factors are at work in producing regional and racial polarization, the research focuses mainly on individuals and groups themselves. It is a lack of social or human capital or their appropriate cultural, educational, or employment resources necessary to fit into the new economy that is the problem, even while some analysts note that economic and technological restructuring has made this task harder. Fundamentally, these analysts neglect to adequately and realistically depict the people and places they describe or to properly portray the real nature of such people's lived experience. Moreover, conventional explanations do not fully account for why central cities declined and for regional disparities and why poverty and social problems are concentrated among minority groups. Most of this literature mischaracterizes how such conditions arose, why some individuals were able to make certain "choices," and how other options were closed off to communities of color regionally. They fail to identify the racial dynamics and structural dimensions that are central to a more comprehensive understanding of disparate regional and racial outcomes. In the end, the shortcomings of mainstream approaches undermine community-building efforts to arrest inner-city decline.

Structural Approaches to Regional and Racial Disparities

Why are some individuals' life menus—or life choices and opportunities—so markedly different? How is it that people like Kim have fewer options to choose from than those like Tom? Proponents of structural approaches contend that there is a critical disjuncture between perception and reality in mainstream explanations that they aim to rectify. The previous analysis suggests that a broader, more comprehensive—if more complex and nuanced—approach is needed to adequately explain regional and racial disparities. This chapter argues for a structural racial framework. Structural racial explanations improve on the conventional mainstream analyses by expanding on their strengths and incorporating additional key elements:

- *History and power.* These highlight the legacy of slavery and Jim Crow and the legal and extralegal methods of segregating and isolating African Americans and other people of color along a hierarchy of race. They also examine and help one understand the historical origins that illuminate contemporary patterns.

- *Specifying the mechanisms that racially sort and actively marginalize people of color along this hierarchy of race at the individual, spatial, and institutional levels.* Segregation and marginalization is an active process. Individual-level behavior is seen as one of a matrix of factors; macrolevel forces, such as corporate capitalist restructuring and globalization from above (as opposed to from below), are also shown to be powerful sorting processes.
- *Identifying the institutions and actors that have enacted and implemented racialized policies and produce disparate outcomes.* These include government institutions, programs, and processes and private institutions and practices (such as corporate, real estate, and labor).

The mainstream narrative about white ethnic immigrant working-class assimilation and social mobility corresponds to national values of rugged individualism, the Protestant work ethic, and meritocracy. This narrative also posits a story for people of color—as shiftless, lazy, and inferior—that explains their being anomalous from other groups. A counternarrative put forth by critics that posits structural factors that produce racial disparities shows people of color in their fullness, not as victims but as actors, while at the same time revealing the historical underpinnings and processes that produce past and present barriers and disparities.

History and Power

Critics of mainstream approaches point out that community-level outcomes are, in part, a result of historical power dynamics—including at the regional level—where race and structural factors have played a decisive role.[34] The spatial separation of poor inner-city neighborhoods comprised overwhelmingly of people of color from wealthy, mostly white suburbs directly results from historical laws, policies, and practices. Concentrated urban poverty, racial segregation and social marginalization, poor schools, high unemployment, crime, dilapidated housing, political powerlessness, destructive behaviors, negative attitudes, and hopelessness are all consequences of accumulated white power and privilege. What appears to be the sum of individual-level choices or impersonal market forces that result in critical resources leaving cities (jobs, people, funds, and so on) and moving to burgeoning suburbs (or to the South and West or overseas) instead is seen as structured by a set of factors that provide options and opportunities for some (white movers to the suburbs) and limit chances for others (minorities locked in poor urban neighborhoods). These critics argue that, contrary to the prevailing views, racialized community-level outcomes are not accidental, natural, or inevitable. Rather, they are the result of distinct social, economic, political, and cultural historical developments and racialized political institutions and policies.

Critics do not deny that some portion of the spatial distribution of inequality and opportunity may be the result of individual choices and behaviors or economic changes. Yet they contend that the lion's share of regional and racial disparities is the result of a long litany of public policies and private practices that have been institutionalized over time. Government agencies and private actors actively produced disparate conditions whether by design or by default. Racial subordination is the culmination of laws, government policies, and group practices promulgated and exercised throughout our history through a host of national, state, regional, and local institutions and actors.

These analysts point to important developments at key historical junctures that contributed to regional and racial disparities, including policies and programs such as the GI Bill, FHA mortgages, restrictive housing covenants and zoning laws, urban renewal (and "slum removal") programs, transportation policies, and tax subsidies and abatements for business development in central business districts and in suburban areas. All of these provide incentives and pathways for white ethnic working- and middle-class Americans to move up the social ladder and out to the suburbs while at the same time cutting badly needed funds to cities and posing disincentives and barriers that lock people of color in concentrated poverty-stricken inner cities and, increasingly, in decaying older suburbs.

One's place in a region is not merely the result of individual preferences and incomes—as mainstream accounts of racial disparities and regional differences hold—but instead results from a host of historically created and contemporarily sustained public policies and private practices. What may appear to be neutral decisions about transit locations and routes that result in systems that facilitate the movement of (largely) white commuters and constrain the movement of (largely) black inner-city dwellers are products of particular policies that reflect different power relations and contribute to the profoundly disparate outcomes described previously. Critics contend that distinct public policies and private practices that have sharply different consequences affect people's life prospects in vastly divergent ways. Cumulatively, these add up to produce the spatial segregation of people, opportunity, and resources. "In a very real way, barriers to spatial mobility are barriers to social mobility."[35] The value of such structural approaches is that they unmask the role of race in producing these disparate outcomes.

Marginalizing Political Mechanisms

Contrary to mainstream explanations of regional and racial disparities, suburbanization was not simply the logical result of individual preferences for a slice of nature and a two-car garage. Rather, specific federal policies, which are often mistakenly associated with urban dwellers and minorities in particular, are more properly seen as supporting the lifestyle and conditions of suburbanites and whites.

Following World War II, billions of dollars wielded by national, state, and local governments provided pathways out of cities for millions of white working- and middle-class residents who were able to subsequently amass assets through home ownership, increased incomes through better employment, educational attainment, and safe communities. "Certain federal policies, such as the 1956 Interstate Highway Act and Federal Housing Authority and Veterans Administration home mortgage loan program, were key contributors to metropolitan decentralization, or what by the 1970s was being called urban sprawl."[36] Without federal aid for home buying and highway construction, the white middle-class exodus would not have occurred on such a large scale.[37] Similarly, without publicly built housing projects in inner cities and weak enforcement of federal antidiscrimination policy, minority groups might also have been able to follow jobs out to the suburbs more effectively instead of being relegated to inner-city slums.[38]

Between 1978 and 1997, real expenditures on home-owner subsidies (which includes the mortgage interest deductions, property tax deductions, and deferrals of capital gains that better-off suburban home owners enjoy) rose nearly four times, while at the same time Housing and Urban Development (HUD) subsidies declined by more than 80 percent.[39] Dreier calculated that tax "expenditures" (forgone taxes) from mortgage interest deductions totaled four times more than HUD directly spent on housing subsidies in 1997. "Meanwhile, federal funds targeted to already fiscally starved cities declined by 66% in real terms between 1981 and 1993."[40]

The upshot is not only that inner cities increasingly became places for impoverished people of color but also that the suburbs enjoyed higher tax bases and fewer social program costs. These developments deepened the fiscal divisions between cities and suburbs. Moreover, the impacts of these federal policies were only made worse by many state and local measures that further reflected an antiurban bias, such as state statutes that limit urban taxing powers, infrastructural development, and social support. Localities have passed regressive sales taxes to try to recoup some of the losses.

Blacks were shut out of benefiting from most of these federal spending policies and tax deductions primarily through continued practices of housing market discrimination that effectively ensured their poorer urban status. A host of "urban renewal" and public housing programs and state and local zoning laws—coupled with the broad range of discriminatory private practices (including decades of redlining by the banking and real estate developers, restrictive covenants in housing deeds by real estate agents and home-owners' groups, racial steering, blockbusting, and so on)—insulated the middle and upper classes from urban poor minorities who remain trapped in poor urban conditions. Thus, even at the time when the civil rights movement toppled legal racial barriers and established remedial programs for blacks, middle-class white flight and housing discrimination held them back in declining inner cities. On top of these developments, the distribution of hazardous waste has been disproportionately located in minority communities.[41]

Much of these policies and practices were explicit or implicit reactions to the northward migration of blacks during the first third of the twentieth century, such as Kim's parents, who left the South for a variety of reasons, including being forced off their land by the increasing commercialization of agriculture, increased terror by public and private groups (including the Ku Klux Klan), and so on. Therefore, these critics argue, the reason that urban minorities settled in urban centers and look "lazy," "apathetic," or "dysfunctional" (in social, psychological, and behavioral terms) is because powerful institutions and actors actively worked to marginalize or sort regionally poor and minority populations through taxing and spending policies, land use planning, and outright discriminatory behavior and practices. The poor schools, lack of jobs, and crime in neighborhoods such as where Kim lives are a direct result of racialized programs and policies that actively marginalize racial minorities. Similarly, the benefits that people like Tom reap are also products of these same racialized institutional policies and practices.

Thus, for analysts who employ a structural approach, race and racism are central to properly understanding the current disparate patterns of resources across space by racial group (jobs, housing, transportation, schools, safety and prisons, and so on). Segregation, social marginalization, and the decimation of neighborhoods and families are not "natural" phenomena but rather are socially constructed outcomes of historical public policies and private practices. The color line is contemporarily maintained by a set of similar policies and practices, albeit in some new clothing. The power of a structural racial analysis is that it can tie the litany of devastating conditions that plague communities of color to this history and point to key racialized institutions and actors who have perpetrated and perpetuate inequalities. A structural racial approach argues that metropolitan-area dynamics are imbued with racial considerations that are critical factors in accounting for community-level outcomes in any region.

Federalism: Racialized Policies and Disparate Outcomes

An examination of U.S. federalism—the separation of powers among the national, state, and local governments—reveals the contours of American public policy's bias against cities and people of color by showing how such federalism has played and continues to play a central role in our tax code, economic development programs, transportation and housing policy, social welfare policies, patterns of government purchasing, and other public policies—all of which help account for regional and racial disparities.

Federalism is a structural feature of the American political system that essentially fragments political power by dividing it between different levels of government. In fact, federalism has allowed the proliferation of the number and kinds of governments in the United States. There are over 90,000 governments across the country today, most of which are new suburban political jurisdictions that came into being only in the past fifty years. These separate political jurisdictions have encouraged regional fragmentation and urban sprawl and mitigated against efforts to forge regional planning and equity.

Federalism has shaped community- and regional-level outcomes as well as thinking and planning (or the lack thereof) about how to effectively address community- or regional-level problems. Because political jurisdictions and powers are defined by the America federal system, this constitutional feature has important implications for regional-area dynamics and community revitalization efforts, particularly in the current era of privatization and the devolution of federal authority to state and local levels of governance. Federalism—which defines and delimits the distribution of powers and relations among the national government and state and local governments—can decisively set the direction of policy and has had a heavy hand in determining winners and losers at key junctures of American history. The shifting nature of federalism, or intergovernmental relations, has defined key historical periods in American political development, with the federal government playing a bigger or smaller role in shaping state and local policy and conditions and in shaping outcomes for particular regions, communities, and groups.

Race has played a central role in the social and political conflicts surrounding federalism at each critical moment in American history.[42] One need only contrast the New Deal and Great Society programs with the New Federalism begun by President Nixon and continued by the Reagan and Bush administrations and the Republican-led Congress beginning in 1995 along with the second Bush administration. While structural racism flourished under all forms of federalism—essentially operating "normally" to disadvantage minority groups—regional and racial disparities have increased significantly during the latter administrations.

The New Deal and Postwar Period

Under the New Deal—which had broad public support for using an activist national government to revive the economy, create jobs, provide relief, and buffer widespread poverty—racial considerations nevertheless marred the actual policies created.[43] For example, the structure and eligibility requirements of programs designed to achieve these goals were fatally flawed, limiting the type and number of people who received aid. While northern Democrats, pushed further into the arms of organized labor by social unrest, preferred national programs that operated centrally and safe from state government interference, southern Democrats strongly insisted on significant local control as the price for their cooperation in the New Deal coalition. The Roosevelt administration designed its programs to avoid directly altering the structure of the South's white-ruled legal and political system and the black poverty it produced. Old-age insurance, for example, was significantly restricted and excluded the self-employed agricultural and domestic workers, thereby leaving out nearly 90 percent of the black labor force.[44] Similarly, pensions for mothers initially restricted access to benefits to white widows deemed worthy. Southern congressmen who held key committee leadership positions shaped these and other legislation, including Aid to Dependent Children, which they supported only on the condition that states would have the right to set benefit levels and establish criteria for eligibility because federally set payment levels and policies would have threatened the South's labor supply. The Social Security Act left state and local jurisdictions to set unemployment insurance requirements, leaving out many of the neediest agricultural workers, blacks, women, and migrants. These policies and programs embodied economic and racial considerations that further reinforced regional and racial divisions and were the direct results of compromises between these conflicting forces.

The postwar period witnessed an increasing migration of blacks to northern cities, following the commercialization of southern agriculture, which resulted in tighter labor markets and sent blacks northward in search of jobs and heightened tensions between northern white ethnics who had arrived a generation earlier. This set the stage for further conflict as the civil rights movement gained ground.

The Great Society

The Great Society programs in the 1960s represented a political response to increasing tensions and conflict in the New Deal coalition, which was similarly imbued with racial considerations and biases. While these programs increased federal involvement in state affairs—and in the areas of legal segregation and the denial of civil rights acted broadly in the interests of blacks—they fell short and were compromised by similar (and even some of the same) southern conservatives. Indeed, the "War on Poverty," which provided training, education, and community action programs, did not emphasize income maintenance at adequate levels, nor did it adequately address underemployment and poverty. The War on Poverty was funded at much lower levels than the rhetoric surrounding it, was short lived, and was badly coordinated. Poor results—save a few programs such as Head Start—were also associated with the further racialization of the "deserving" and "undeserving" poor, and rising conflict when the civil rights movement grew more militant and urban riots erupted increased whites' associations of such programs with race-based fears. Law-and-order policies began to replace support for racially identified antipoverty programs. President Nixon capitalized on Barry Goldwater's and George Wallace's presidential races, and his New Federalism would soon reorient federal social policy. The result was further concentration of blacks in cities and in poverty.[45]

New Federalism

Over the past twenty years, the Reagan and Bush administrations' "devolution revolution" slashed taxes—particularly for the wealthy and corporate America—and simultaneously reduced the scope and role of the federal government in providing programs for cities and social services for the poor and minorities.[46] The Republican-led Congress in 1994—coupled with a weak "New Democrat" President Clinton—furthered the thrust of such policies, cutting states off from needed revenue and regulations and giving states a freer hand in setting their own policies. In some instances, states responded by raising their own taxes and beefing up their regulatory activity in areas such as economic development, environmental regulation, and welfare reform. More often states—particularly ones that Republicans controlled (which substantially increased in the 1990s)—continued the direction of these national policies in their own states to the detriment of the poor and communities of color. This is even truer today with Republicans more firmly in control of the federal government.

A guiding assumption behind devolution policy has been that democracy is stronger when government is closer to the people. State and local governments, under this view, are less bureaucratic and more accessible to the public than is a centralized government in Washington, D.C. Currently, however, there are no thoroughgoing assessments of the degree to which state and local governments have the resources, culture, and infrastructure to be open, accountable, and responsive under this new devolution. Indeed, devolution resembles the old "states' rights" impetus. A series of questions are implied about the nature of the "New Federalism" and "devolution" and how these new policies have impacted on communities of color and metropolitan-area issues and dynamics. One strategy for community builders has been to test this assumption in specific regions and in various policy areas, such as welfare reform.

But New Federalism has produced profoundly biased outcomes: Many states and localities undertook policies that disproportionately give advantage to some sectors of the population and disadvantage other sectors. At the state level, dominant groups and businesses are more concentrated and effective than at the national level. All too often, the losers at the state level are those sectors and groups of the population who have fewer resources and less political power but are in more need of state assistance, particularly communities of color.

Because federalism both separates and mixes authority between the national and the state and local spheres, federalism will continue to incite conflict in American politics and has particular relevance for regionalism. Therefore, it will be important to highlight how American federalism is imbued with racial bias and how a structural racial analysis can illuminate this system and trace and explain how it contributed to racial disparities. Such outcomes, however, are not inevitable. Indeed, devolution may yet provide pathways for community-based groups to organize and leverage their own power for change, such as community-based living-wage campaigns, microenterprise public and private partnerships, and innovative housing programs.

Political Fragmentation

Meanwhile, the other side of federalism facilitated rapid suburbanization. Federal programs provided pathways for white ethnic working-class residents to move out of cities to achieve assimilation and social mobility in the suburbs.[47] The GI Bill was one a crowning example, providing whites with access to higher education and to better jobs through massive federal expenditures. As mentioned previously, billions of dollars were also spent on FHA mortgage programs, building interstate highways, and so on, allowing millions of mostly white working- and middle-class residents to attain and retain assets through home ownership and increase their incomes through better employment that preceded and followed them to the suburbs. Restrictive state and local zoning laws and discriminatory private practices (such as redlining by banks, real estate developers, and so on) facilitated movement of resources and white flight to the suburbs and at the same time trapped minorities in poor urban conditions.[48] Thus, the federalist structure of the American political system provides mechanisms for disparate outcomes to arise, particularly through political fragmentation.

The rapid expansion of the number of political jurisdictions to over 90,000 today (mostly new suburban jurisdictions) occurred during this time. The rapid expansion of suburban political incorporation allowed suburbs to insulate themselves from cities, protect their tax base and property values, build better schools, siphon off transportation dollars and business investment, and so on. Many local governments formed as a direct result of powerful individuals and groups seeking to separate themselves from existing governments and communities.[49] Miller argues that "bedroom communities" around Los Angeles, for example, formed as a result of local residents' hostility to the taxing and spending decisions of existing city governments; to avoid being annexed, these residents incorporated their own local governments. Such examples are evident across the country.[50] Moreover, many residents who formed such new local governments did so to segregate themselves from racial minorities as much as for economic reasons. Finally, just as African Americans were beginning to win elected offices in urban centers, federal aid was cut back and the political power of urban governments scaled back or made moot.[51]

At nearly every turn, one can see that American public policy—at the federal, state, and local levels—is biased against urban renters in favor of suburban home owners, urban mass-transit users in favor of suburban car owners, and urban infrastructure of most kinds in favor of exurban and rural development projects. Since most suburban regions are not required to pay the costs of maintaining the poor and urban infrastructure, they artificially lower the costs of living and working outside or on the outer fringes of our metropolitan regions. Moreover, they artificially increase the costs of living and working in cities.

Taxing and spending patterns reveal the tremendous magnitude of the subsidy to suburban areas, adding up to tens to possibly hundreds of billions of dollars a year. Federal and state governments have spent trillions of dollars building roads out to the suburbs and between states but only a fraction of that on city roads or mass transit. Annual federal funding for mass transit has been less than a fifth of highway funding. States have done even worse. Similarly, the vast share of federal and state economic development funds goes to nonmetropolitan areas—for more highways, tax credits and subsidies, and low-interest loans for new development.[52] These trends accelerated and deepened during the Reagan and Bush administrations and since the Republicans gained control of Congress in 1995.

The results of such antiurban policies have produced declining central cities and have subjugated and subjected large portions of urban populations—particularly people of color—to harsh conditions that are unsafe, where infant mortality is high and health care is meager, where schools are failing and facilities crumble, where crime is high and neighborhood safety is low, and so on. Such conditions take devastating physical and psychological tolls on their residents and breed despair and hopelessness. Government has become more a means of policing these communities than a vehicle for self-governing, and residents have been further isolated from economic resources and political institutions.

Federalism's Legacy: Racialized Institutions and Disparate Public Policy

These public and private institutions and actors have actively marginalized cities—the poor in general and blacks in particular—and have actively aided white ethnics in suburbia. Moreover, such policies and practices are not just the products of southern racist segregationists, though their imprints are apparent. The racialized institutions that were established to carry out such policies developed bureaucratic cultures that embody the historical developments and still act to reproduce racial biases. That is, policies and institutions may reflect historical racism, but they are also manifested in the behavior of individuals who continue to administer and deliver public services. Thus, part of what a structural racial analysis can provide to community builders is identifying and documenting the makers of public policies, the institutions and programs, the bureaucratic cultures, and the biased behaviors of individuals on the front lines as all tied to a racialized system that produces concentrated poverty and isolated and distressed communities of color.

American public policy is also economically costly and wasteful for suburbs. Sprawl wastes land, water, and energy; it squanders existing assets, with new houses, factories, and schools being built in the suburbs and outer rings of cities while good urban buildings are allowed to decay and get boarded up. This, as we shall see later, is one of the arguments regionalists make for a more rational and productive public policy that sees the fates of cities and suburbs as intertwined. Because economies are regional, their parts can affect each other. They thus have a shared destiny. Regional planning, they contend, can provide a useful means to assist communities of color attain redress.

But some argue that many suburbanites are prepared to pay the costs and forgo the benefits of more integrated regional planning arrangements, especially if racial concerns and equity outcomes are promoted prominently. They contend that suburbanites believe that their walled communities are worth it. But, many regionalists counter, their isolation may be more of an illusion than a reality. The economic fortunes of suburban dwellers are in large part dependent on the health of the region they are within, whether they are aware of it or not. Regions are the economic engines in the global world, and the fates of cities and suburbs are increasingly intertwined. Ultimately, they rise and fall together.[53]

Regionalism

A growing body of research by analysts of metropolitan areas—or regions—argues that the problems we see manifest in urban centers and suburbs are interrelated.[54] The story goes along these lines: Urban decline increases development pressure on the suburban fringe, and government policies that facilitate fringe development and keep poor people and communities of color concentrated in urban neighborhoods make it more difficult for them to maintain social and economic health. Older suburbs are increasingly facing similar problems and, in turn, send more people and problems to the newer suburbs. Whole regions are affected, and their constitutive parts mutually affect each other. Regionalists see "functional" linkages between blighted inner-city neighborhoods and a city's economic and social well-being and between the health of a city and its suburbs or whole regions.

While cities and suburbs are formally separate and independent political and administrative jurisdictions, in reality their economic and social lives overlap in myriad and complex ways. They are increasingly interdependent and have common interests and linkages, even if informally. Metropolitan-area dynamics—the connections and disconnections between inner-city neighborhoods and distressed communities and the adjacent urban and suburban rings—is an increasingly popular and useful way of understanding the common plight of cities and suburbs. Regionalists of various stripes argue that metropolitan-area governance is the key to remedying these problems and to promote "smart growth" or remedy racial inequalities. But governance by whom and growth for what? Where and for whose benefit?

Because powerful overarching regional forces have significant impacts on inner cities and communities of color—both historically and contemporarily—many analysts now argue that theoretical and practical work is needed in this area. The community-building field could proceed with a greater appreciation of regional-level dynamics, which might help forge more effective strategies that address the problems of distressed communities of color.

Regional literature posits that the problems and fates of cities and suburbs are linked. Regionalists argue that most social, economic, and political problems cannot be solved by independent actors and fragmented government jurisdictions acting alone. In other words, regionalists conclude that cross-jurisdictional problems demand cross-jurisdictional solutions at the metropolitan or regional level.[55] Their main point is that there is a commonality of economic and political interests among cities and many suburbs. However, there is significant disagreement about the nature of regional dynamics and problems and what strategies and solutions are best to pursue.

The literature on regionalism—as well as government programs and community-based initiatives—varies widely. Different regionalists focus on different social problems and aspects of metropolitan-area dynamics. Moreover, they hold different views about how regional and racial disparities arose, and they promote different policies or strategies to remedy them.

Some, for instance, are more attuned to racial disparities and dynamics than others. These "democratic" regionalists maintain that community building will be effective only if done from a regional perspective that presses for equity in regional-area dynamics and decisions.[56] Community-building efforts must include some regional-level organizing or at least aim to affect regional-area dynamics because the health of a neighborhood is linked to the health of the region to which it belongs. These metropolitanists argue that regionalism is a critical missing link in effective community building. They contend that structural racism as it operates in regional-area dynamics has cumulative effects that produce and are reflected in the conditions of distressed neighborhoods and at the individual level. These regionalists identify racialized institutions and processes—in both the public and the private sector—that operate to marginalize urban communities of color and privilege white suburbanites. A structural perspective is vital, they maintain, to see how regional-area dynamics function to undermine community builders and their efforts, especially in communities of color. They contend that the power of such an analysis is that it highlights these institutions and processes that can make them clearer targets for community-building efforts. Therefore, such regionalists call on the community-building field to examine how structural racism works at the regional level. They call on community builders to employ a regional analysis in order to forge effective strategies for real and lasting social change.

Approaches to Regionalism

As alluded to earlier, there are two broad approaches to regionalism and regional problems: market-driven regionalism and democratic regionalism. The first sees materially self-interested individuals acting to advance personal benefits and limit their costs. This approach, which draws heavily on economic theory and public choice models, sees regional problems as particularistic and favors market-oriented solutions. Where government intervention is called for, it is in the role of exploiting "natural" comparative advantages in both urban and suburban communities.

The second general approach, democratic regionalism, sees regional problems as the outcomes of long historical processes and favors intervention aimed at structural change. It also sees racial dynamics as intimately bound up with regional disparities and thus posits regional and racial equity as necessary to solve problems and lay the basis for sustainable development.

Both groups see central-city disinvestments as problematic. Both accurately view the federal government's process for allocating funds to states for basic purposes, such as economic development or transportation, as reflecting pragmatic and bureaucratic concerns with the inevitable pork barreling among the political actors and jurisdictions, with dominant groups coming out on top more often than not. But important differences in their diagnoses of regional- and community-level problems lead them to very different strategies for reform and remedy.

Market-Driven Regionalism

The first group argues that some minimal regional planning can promote greater efficiency and better services.[57] Although some in this first group see fragmented metropolitan-area governance as not all bad—that fragmentation can foster greater government competition—many argue that greater cooperation among different governments or special districts can better meet needs by governments with few resources and produce greater efficiency, such as for fire, sewers, police, and so on. Many of these researchers, however, focus primarily on the problems of suburban sprawl and how to limit it and only secondarily on the revival of inner-city communities, if at all. Some regional advocates and policymakers argue that regional or cooperative governance is key to managing mutual economic self-interest, which is the driving force, and to use government regulatory powers and policies to steer market-driven incentives toward efficient and desired ends.[58] Some promote fiscal cooperation through revenue sharing to improve services in cities and suburbs, and this requires legislative alliances. One of the best examples of such regional legislative alliances and governance is exemplified in the Twin Cities Metro Council.[59] Orfield argues that educating suburbanites to see their self-interest as linked to the vitality of cities is a key strategy to achieve popularity for successful regional and legislative alliances. Others argue for using planning methods for "smart growth" (that is, limited growth and suburban sprawl) through establishing boundaries and using zoning and land use policy for resource conservation and environmental protection.[60] Yet there is little focus on the role of community-based organizations in such public policymaking, nor is equity high on these agendas.

Democratic Regionalism

The second general group that advocates for greater regional cooperation focuses more on reviving urban centers and community building.[61] This group tries to bend government policies—particularly the federal government, which can be more redistributive where possible, but also state and local governments—toward making cities more livable through preserving and improving housing, including public housing (such as HUD's HOPE VI program); using transportation funds to make infrastructural improvements that connect communities to jobs; and increasing citizen participation in civic institutions and political action, which can make politicians more accountable and promote racial dialogue about policy issues aimed at improving racial equity and community and regional ties. It is this latter group that sees the separation and segregation of people as deliberate, as generated by particular public policies and private practices over time that reflect powerful economic and political interests. In addition, some in this group see racial considerations as a central dynamic that has driven past and contemporary policy and practice. They hold a broader conception of community and place greater value on equity and democracy. Ultimately, they favor explicitly confronting powerful dominant interests and racialized policies and institutions to change these conditions.

Contemporary Regionalism

The 1990s saw a resurgence of regionalism across political jurisdictions. Growing networks across public (federal, state, and local governments), private, and nonprofit sectors have emerged, largely in response to the increasing challenges involved in revitalizing urban centers that have affected regional growth. In addition, a new force is at work in contemporary regionalism: fighting the spread of sprawl in the suburbs. Environmentalists, real estate interests, urban planners, government officials, academics, and community-based organizations are coming together on issues of "sprawl," "smart growth," and "environmentalism." While neighborhood revitalization or preservation is not new, doing so from a regional perspective and level is.

This revived interest in regionalist solutions during the contemporary period has also come as a result of "globalization," whose impacts are greater in the context of further devolution of federal power. The decreased likelihood of direct federal intervention with an urban agenda to aid older and central cities has fostered greater regionalist efforts by divergent but powerful stakeholders.[62] Globalization simultaneously acts to pull regions together and pit them against each other in the global marketplace (and their component parts of cities, suburbs, and states). Some regions have gained ground, whereas others are losing ground as they jockey for comparative advantage or are blackmailed outright into giving high tax breaks and subsidies to induce investment. Regionalism has gained favor with sectors of the business community and many politicians who felt the negative effects of urban decline and suburban sprawl. Efforts to spur economic development have led to cross-sectional alliances of private–public partnerships. Big-city mayors and other elected officials who faced the enormous challenges of creating jobs, providing a range of services (such as education and policing), and responding to an increasing homeless population, an AIDS epidemic, housing crises, and a loss of revenue became more receptive to joint public–private ventures and regional cooperation with neighboring jurisdictions.

Yet, on balance, privatization further eroded community control of public institutions and policies that affect regions, particularly urban centers and communities of color. Similarly, suburbs experienced an increasing range of problems that they found themselves ill equipped to handle, from having enough revenue to adequately finance economic development ventures to funding police protections. Consequently, problems once thought to be confined to central cities—such as crime, infrastructural decay, and unemployment—became more widespread. Increasing environmental consciousness and concerns have also helped popularize and propel regional planning to a higher place on the political agenda.

As Tietz and Chapple have argued, if urban minority poverty is in part the result of the lack of demand for labor, then one might also argue "that [the] lack is due to a deficit in the creation of new firms."[63] Similarly, if urban minority residents lack adequate educational and labor skills to fit into the market, it is due to the poor educational institutions and job opportunities and employment experiences that racial and regional dynamics generate. Historically, thinking and action aimed at developing local and regional economies have usually meant inducing outside capital investment. All too often, however, such policies are created without the input of communities of color. Instead, corporate investors sit at the tables where such decisions are made. Thus, entrepreneurship is the local indigenous version of similar market-driven strategies. Empowerment might have been the rallying cry, but the results of local development have been disappointing. Capitalists and markets rarely supply the demand for affordable housing, accessible and quality education, health care, employment, and neighborhood safety for poor people and communities of color.

The Promise and Challenge of Democratic Regionalism

Regional problems—particularly sprawl—have increasingly made their way into national political campaigns and state policymaking debates. In 1998, there were 240 ballot measures across the country proposed to limit sprawl or alleviate its impacts on cities and regions. Congress formed bipartisan task forces to investigate sprawl, the Government Accounting Office produced reports examining the causes of sprawl, and the Clinton White House introduced a new "Livability Agenda." These developments sometimes led to informal regional-area networks and formal regional governments.

Vice President Al Gore placed sprawl prominently on his campaign agenda during his 2000 presidential election bid. And on election day in November 2000, there were more than 550 growth-related measures on the ballot in thirty-eight states; 72 percent of these measures passed. A study by the Brookings Institution presents analysis of these growth-related ballot measures. The wide range of ballot measures—covering open space, transportation and infrastructure, economic development, growth management, and governance arrangements—shows that many forces shape development and that citizens and governments are willing to experiment with strategies for growing differently.[64]

These developments have pushed contemporary regionalists to be more comprehensive in the scope of their regional thinking and planning. Increasingly, they describe both domestic and international dynamics and note how centrifugal forces have intensified and threaten the viability of metropolitan areas. Importantly, many point out that central-city decline portends for suburban decline as well. Contemporary regionalists often argue that these new dynamics demand that critical attention be given to the futures of metropolitan areas as a whole. Some regionalists contend that the problems of concentrated urban poverty must be seen as an important aspect of a larger metropolitan crisis, affecting both core cities and the suburban communities to which they are connected. In short, new regionalists see this crisis as the increasing inability of current governance arrangements to control the many centrifugal forces propelling metropolitan problems. Sprawl, for example, needs to be controlled because it is inefficient, wasteful of scarce resources, destructive to the environment, and a drain on core cities. Again, for some democratic regionalists, it is also seen as intimately bound up with the concentration of poverty, minorities, and racial dynamics.

Nevertheless, different metropolitanists propose different solutions. Some want to enhance the functional, fiscal, environmental, and other forms of interdependence that already exist among some metropolitan jurisdictions. They argue that these linkages are the potential basis for a more extensive and enlightened regional cooperation. These new regionalists want to infuse a sense of a shared metropolitan fate across community boundaries, believing that an awareness of mutual self-interest could engender interjurisdictional cooperation around regional policy issues.

However, many of those who are focused more on the problems of distressed urban communities are somewhat skeptical of the mainstream turn toward metropolitanism. One source of their concern lies in the mainstream's tendency to gloss over the significance of structural racism to central-city decline. As mentioned earlier, decades of racist federal and state policy—also manifest in social relations and private practices—have played a fundamental part in the flight of the urban white middle class to the suburbs and consequently in the steady hemorrhage of businesses, jobs, federal subsidies, and political influence in the same direction. New advances in transport and telecommunications technology merely facilitated these trends. Yet such critiques are largely absent from mainstream theorizing and policy discussions of metropolitan-area dynamics and planning.

Moreover, critics contend that the new regionalists too often focus more on the plight of suburbs and only secondarily on the plight of inner-city decline and on race. Many contemporary regionalists have developed theoretical analyses of regional problems with some appreciation of racial inequities, and some have even launched efforts to generate community mobilization on a regional basis aimed at affecting policy and social outcomes. For example, Myron Orfield, a state legislator in Minnesota and author of *Metropolitics*, makes linkages between cities and suburbs—both theoretically and programmatically—but he falls short of the promise of realizing democracy by strategically skirting racial issues and concerns, afraid of running into the problem of how to sell democratic regionalism to privileged white suburbanites. Orfield's dilemma, however, is not to be dismissed lightly. It remains a significant, real challenge that the community-building field must take up thoughtfully and carefully.

Fortunately, some regionalists have posited a regionalism that holds the potential for rebuilding American democracy and that at the same time addresses structural racism. These democratic regionalists explicitly argue that federalism has allowed structural racism to flourish: that the American federal system has failed to resolve racial inequalities in part because its fragmented political decision-making structure allows public policy outcomes to disproportionately benefit the majority and powerful dominant interests. Racial inequalities in employment opportunities, education, crime and punishment, housing, taxation, subsidies, and patterns of spending and service delivery can be attributed directly to the undemocratic distribution of influence within public policy structures. These political structures and processes operate to "normalize" such outcomes to the disadvantage of racial minorities. Thus, to forge a progressive and democratic regionalism, they argue, it is imperative to make this critique explicit through a structural and racial viewpoint and to frame regionalism explicitly as a democratic project aimed at achieving equity. A few such regionalists have explicitly made racial concerns central to their approach to analyzing regional-area dynamics and have developed strategies and tools that can help alleviate racial disparities as well as the problems of sprawl.[65] Indeed, their theoretical and practical work provides valuable models for the future efforts of analysts and the community-building field.

Conclusion

If cross-jurisdictional solutions are required to address the problems identified in this chapter and in this volume, they will need strong cross-jurisdictional coalitions. A region is no one community's neighborhood or locale. Thus, generating action on a regional scale requires collaboration. This may necessitate alignments among groups and interests who may not believe that they share common issues or, even if they know it, who feel little reason to act on it. The challenge that regionalism poses for analysts and community builders is how to forge effective coalitions among community leaders, corporations, and governments to believe in and make racial equity a central part of their everyday operation. It remains to be seen whether this challenge will be taken up and effectively grappled with.

Notes

Research for this chapter was originally commissioned by the Aspen Institute Roundtable on Comprehensive Community Initiatives for its Race and Community Building Project (www.aspenroundtable.org).

1. The phrase comes from the title of Harold Lasswell's book, *Politics: Who Gets What, When, How* (New York: P. Smith, 1936).

2. Manuel Pastor, Peter Dreier, J. Eugene Grigsby III, and Marta Lopez-Garza, *Regions That Work: How Cities and Suburbs Can Grow Together* (Minneapolis: University of Minnesota Press, 2000), chap. 5.

3. Pastor et al., *Regions That Work,* 3.

4. Douglas Massey, "Residential Segregation and Neighborhood Conditions," in *America Becoming: Racial Trends and Their Consequences,* vol. 1, ed. Neil Smelser, William Julius Wilson, and Faith Mitchell, National Research Council (Washington, D.C.: National Academy Press, 2001), 391.

5. Alan Altshuler, William Morrill, Harold Wolman, and Faith Mitchell, eds., *Governance and Opportunity in Metropolitan America,* National Research Council, Committee on Improving the Future of U.S. Cities through Improved Metropolitan Area Governance (Washington, D.C.: National Academy Press, 1999); F. Kaid Benfield, Matthew D. Raimi, and Donald D. T. Chen, *Once There Were Greenfields: How Urban Sprawl Is Undermining America's Environment, Economy and Social Fabric* (Washington, D.C.: National Resources Defense Council, 1999).

6. Massey, "Residential Segregation and Neighborhood Conditions," 395.

7. There are a few exceptions to this trend, most notably in Boston and Los Angeles, where black–white segregation showed a decline. Still, these changes probably reflected the displacement of blacks by the arrival of Latinos and Asians, particularly in Los Angeles (Massey, "Residential Segregation and Neighborhood Conditions," 401).

8. Pastor et al., *Regions That Work,* 437.

9. U.S. Census data and reports (2002); Pastor et al., *Regions That Work;* Altshuler et al., *Governance and Opportunity in Metropolitan America;* Benfield et al., *Once There Were Greenfields;* John Brennan and Edward W. Hill, "Where Are the Jobs?: Cities, Suburbs and the Competition for Employment," Center on Urban and Metropolitan Policy (Washington D.C.: Brookings Institution, 1999).

10. The research associated with each of these explanations generally comes packaged in three theoretical frameworks: public choice theory, pluralism, and regime analysis.

11. V. Ostrom, C. Tiebout, and R. Warren, "The Organization and Governance in Metropolitan Areas," *American Political Science Review* 55 (1961); R. B. Parks and R. J. Oakerson, "Metropolitan Organization and Governance: A Local Political Economy Approach," *Urban Affairs Quarterly* 25 (1989); Paul Peterson, *City Limits* (Chicago: University of Chicago Press, 1981).

12. M. A. Nelson, "Decentralization of the Subnational Public Sector: An Empirical Analysis of the Determinants of Government Structure in Metropolitan Areas in the U.S., *Southern Economic Journal* 57 (1990); J. Martinez-Vazquez, R. Rider, and M. B. Walker, "Race and Structure of School Districts in the United States," *Journal of Urban Economics* 41 (1997); R. C. Fisher and W. Wassmer, "Economic Influences on the Structure of Local Government in U.S. Metropolitan Areas," *Journal of Urban Economics* 43 (1998); R. Stein and Stephanie Post, "The Local Goods Market" (paper presented at the 1998 meeting of the American Political Science Association, Boston).

13. John Kassarda, "Inner-City Concentrated Poverty and Neighborhood Distress: 1970–1990," *Housing Policy Debate* 4 (1993).

14. Oscar Lewis, "The Culture of Poverty," in *On Understanding Poverty: Perspectives from the Social Sciences,* ed. Daniel Patrick Moynihan (New York: Basic, 1968); Charles Murray, *Losing Ground: American Social Policy 1950–1980* (New York: Basic, 1984); Lawrence Mead, *Beyond Entitlement: The Social Obligations of Citizenship* (New York: Free Press, 1986).

15. Nathan Glazer and Daniel Patrick Moynihan, *Beyond the Melting Pot: The Negros, Puerto Ricans, Italians, Jews and Irish of New York City* (Cambridge, Mass.: MIT Press, 1970); Stephanie Coontz, ed., *American Families: A Multicultural Reader* (New York: Routledge, 1998).

16. William Julius Wilson, *The Truly Disadvantaged: The Inner City, the Underclass, and Public Policy* (Chicago: University of Chicago Press, 1987).

17. Barry Bluestone and Bennett Harrison, *The Deindustrialization of America: Plant Closings, Community Abandonment, and the Dismantling of Basic Industries* (New York: Basic, 1982).

18. Wilson, *The Truly Disadvantaged;* Kasarda, "Inner-City Concentrated Poverty and Neighborhood Distress."

19. Kasarda, "Inner-City Concentrated Poverty and Neighborhood Distress."

20. Roger Waldinger, *Still the Promised City? African-Americans and New Immigrants in Postindustrial New York* (Cambridge: Harvard University Press, 1996); and Philip Kasinitz, *Caribbean New York: Black Immigrants and the Politics of Race* (Ithaca, New York: Cornell University Press, 1992).

21. Charles Hirschman, Philip Kasinitz, and Josh DeWind, eds., *The Handbook of International Migration: The American Experience* (New York: Russell Sage Foundation, 1999).

22. Janet L. Abu-Lughod, *From Urban Village to East Village: The Battle for New York's Lower East Side* (Oxford: Blackwell, 1994).

23. John F. Kain, "The Spatial Mismatch Hypothesis: Three Decades Later," *Housing Policy Debate* 3 (1992).

24. Waldinger, *Still the Promised City?,* and Wilson, *The Truly Disadvantaged.*

25. Howard Schuman, Charlotte Steeh, and Lawrence Bobo, *Racial Attitudes in America: Trends and Interpretations* (Cambridge, Mass.: Harvard University Press, 1985); Massey, "Residential Segregation and Neighborhood Conditions."

26. Schuman et al., *Racial Attitudes in America.*

27. Massey, "Residential Segregation and Neighborhood Conditions," 411.

28. Douglass Massey and Nancy Denton, *American Apartheid: Segregation and the Making of the Underclass* (Cambridge, Mass.: Harvard University Press, 1993).

29. Massey, "Residential Segregation and Neighborhood Conditions," 414.

30. Massey and Denton, *American Apartheid.*

31. George Galster, Ronald Mincy, and Mitchell Tobin, "The Disparate Racial Neighborhood Impacts of Metropolitan Economic Restructuring," *Urban Affairs Review* 32, no. 6 (1997).

32. Wilson, *The Truly Disadvantaged.*

33. Massey, "Residential Segregation and Neighborhood Conditions."

34. Massey and Denton, *American Apartheid;* Jon Powell, "Race and Space: What Really Drives Metropolitan Growth," *Brookings Review* (Fall 1998), and "Addressing Regional Dilemmas for Minority Communities," in *Reflections on Regionalism,* ed. Bruce Katz (Washington, D.C.: Brookings Institution, 2000); Pastor et al., *Regions That Work;* Altschuler et al., *Governance and Opportunity in Metropolitan America;* Bennett Harrison and Marcus Weiss, *Workforce Development Networks: Community Based Organizations and Regional Alliances* (Thousand Oaks, Calif.: Sage, 1998); Paul Jargowsky, *Poverty and Place: Ghettos, Barrios, and the American City* (New York: Russell Sage Foundation, 1997); Galster et al., "The Disparate Racial Neighborhood Impacts of Metropolitan Economic Restructuring"; Myron Orfield, *Metropolitics: A Regional Agenda for Community and Stability* (Washington, D.C.: Brookings Institution Press, 1997); Kenneth Jackson, *Crabgrass Frontier: The Suburbanization of the United States* (New York: New York University Press, 1985); David Rusk, *Inside Game/Outside Game: Winning Strategies for Saving Urban America* (Washington, D.C.: Brookings Institution Press, 1999); Margaret Weir, "Coalition Building for Regionalism," in *Reflections on Regionalism,* ed. Bruce Katz (Washington, D.C.: Brookings Institution, 2000).

35. Massey, "Residential Segregation and Neighborhood Conditions," 392.

36. Pastor et al., *Regions That Work,* 445.

37. Jackson, *Crabgrass Frontier.*

38. Massey and Denton, *American Apartheid.*

39. Dreier, as quoted in Pastor et al., *Regions That Work,* 445.

40. Pastor et al., *Regions That Work,* 445–46.

41. Pastor et al., *Regions That Work,* 446.

42. Pamela Winston, "Race in American Federalism: From the Constitutional Convention to the Devolution Revolution" (paper presented at the American Political Science Association annual meeting, Washington, D.C., 1997).

43. Winston, "Race in American Federalism"; Jill Quadagno, "From Old-Age Assistance to Supplemental Security Income: The Political Economy of Relief in the South, 1935–1972," in *The Politics of Social Policy in the United States,* ed. Margaret Weir, Ann Shola Orloff, and Theda Skocpol (Princeton, N.J.: Princeton University Press, 1988); Denis Judd and Todd Swanstrom, *City Politics: Private Power and Public Policy* (New York: Longman, 2002); Frances Fox Piven and Richard Cloward, *Regulating the Poor: The Functions of Public Welfare* (New York: Random House, 1993).

44. Quadagno, "From Old-Age Assistance to Supplemental Security Income."

45. Quadagno, "From Old-Age Assistance to Supplemental Security Income."

46. In the 1960s, corporations paid approximately 23 percent of all federal taxes collected; today, their proportion has dropped to less than 10 percent (Henwood, 2000; 2001, at www.panix.com/~dhenwood/LBO_home.html; Citizens for Tax Justice, at www.ctj.org; and Center for Budget and Policy Priorities, at www.cbpp.org).

47. Judd and Swanstrom, *City Politics.*

48. Massey and Denton, *American Apartheid;* June Manning Thomas, *Redevelopment and Race: Planning a Finer City in Postwar Detroit* (Baltimore: The Johns Hopkins University Press, 1997); June Manning Thomas and Marsha Ritzdorf, eds., *Urban Planning and the African American Community: In the Shadows* (Thousand Oaks, Calif.: Sage, 1997).

49. G. Miller, *Cities by Contract* (Cambridge, Mass.: MIT Press, 1981); Stephanie Shirley Post, "Metropolitan Area Governance Structure and Intergovernmental Cooperation: Can Local Governments in Fragmented Metropolitan Areas Cooperate?" (paper presented at the American Political Science Association annual meeting, Washington, D.C., 2000).

50. Judd and Swanstrom, *City Politics.*

51. Steven P. Erie, *Rainbow's End: Irish Americans and the Dilemmas of Urban Machine Politics, 1840–1985* (Berkeley: University of California Press, 1988).

52. The repeal of the commuter tax to New York City by the state legislature and governor—worth between $400 and $900 million in revenue—is one recent example (*New York Times,* September 9, 2000).

53. Powell, "Race and Space"; Pastor et al., *Regions That Work;* Dreier, as quoted in Pastor et al., *Regions That Work* (Minneapolis: University of Minnesota Press, 2000).

54. While definitions of regions vary, a flexible and organic definition can allow analysis of metropolitan-area issues and questions of governance.

55. Orfield, *Metropolitics;* William R. Dodge, *Regional Excellence: Governing Together to Compete Globally and Flourish Locally* (Washington, D.C.: National League of Cities, 1996); Peter Salins, "Metropolitan Areas: Cities, Suburbs and the Ties That

Bind," in *Interwoven Destinies: Cities and the Nation,* ed. Henry Cisneros (New York: Norton, 1993).

56. Powell, "Race and Space"; Pastor et al., *Regions That Work;* Weir, "Coalition Building for Regionalism."

57. Ostrom et al., "The Organization and Governance in Metropolitan Areas"; Peterson, *City Limits;* Nelson, "Decentralization of the Subnational Public Sector"; Martinez-Vazquez et al., "Race and Structure of School Districts in the United States"; Fisher and Wassmer, "Economic Influences on the Structure of Local Government in U.S. Metropolitan Areas"; Stein and Post, "The Local Goods Market."

58. Anthony Downs, *The Challenge of Our Declining Big Cities* (Washington, D.C.: Brookings Institution, 1996).

59. Orfield, *Metropolitics.*

60. Rusk, *Inside Game/Outside Game;* Orfield, *Metropolitics;* Dodge, *Regional Excellence;* Altshuler et al., *Governance and Opportunity in Metropolitan America.*

61. Judd and Swanstrom, *City Politics;* Powell, "Race and Space"; Pastor et al., *Regions That Work;* Katz, ed., *Reflections on Regionalism;* Harrison and Weiss, *Workforce Development Networks;* Weir, "Coalition Building for Regionalism."

62. The only prominent federal policy aimed at cities in the recent period was Empowerment Zones, which are few in number, limited, market driven, and economically and politically flawed (Judd and Swanstrom, *City Politics*).

63. Michael Teitz and Karen Chappel, "The Causes of Inner-City Poverty: Eight Hypotheses in Search of Reality," *Cityscape: A Journal of Policy and Development Research* 3, no. 3 (1998): 54.

64. Phyllis Myers and Robert Puentes, "Growth at the Ballot Box: Electing the Shape of Communities in November 2000," (Washington, D.C.: Brookings Institution, 2001).

65. Nancy Green-Leigh and Catherine Ross, "Planning, Urban Revitalization and the Inner City: An Exploration of Structural Racism" (paper prepared for the Association of Collegiate Schools of Planning, Chicago, 1999); Powell, "Race and Space"; Pastor et al., *Regions That Work;* Weir, "Coalition Building for Regionalism"; Dreier, as quoted in Pastor et al., *Regions That Work.*

Appendix 7.1

Regional Definitions and Governance Issues

THE CENSUS BUREAU uses metropolitan statistical areas (MSAs) to define a particular area by a set number of census tracks that count a finite geographic area and number of people within it, often a city and several additional counties that contain a number of municipalities and suburbs. Many researchers cite such data and often limit the area of study, as does the Census Bureau. The National Research Council[1] defines regions in a way that allows for making distinctions between "lifestyle" issues and "system maintenance" issues. Lifestyle issues involve access by individuals and groups to jobs, schools, shopping, and so on in a region, whereas system maintenance issues involve the development of infrastructure, such as transportation, water and sewer systems, and environmental protection policies and institutions.

Regions are also discussed in terms of "common-purpose" objectives and interests, some of which are more controversial than others, especially when the redistributive nature of such areawide policies and practices are evident. The distribution of the tax base, income, employment, housing values, social makeup, and status of particular sections within a region are more intrinsically divisive since they often appear to be zero sum in nature and create distinct winners and losers. Thus, regionalists who view benefits accruing to a whole metropolitan area view common-purpose problems and solutions in terms of efficiency rather than redistribution. For example, systemwide maintenance needs and issues that cut across jurisdictional lines have led to the creation of metropolitan or regionwide institutions in the areas of transportation, water and sewer systems, parks, economic development, airports, air quality, and so on. Metropolitan areas with one or more counties—which comprised 60 percent of all MSAs or regions broadly defined—contained thousands to tens of thousands of multicounty government districts, performing functions such as fire protection, water supply, sewage treatment, drainage, libraries, and so on.

Others define regions and regional governance more broadly than merely metropolitan governments. "Regions are organic systems organized in ways surprisingly similar to flowers, fish, mammals and humans. They have evolved out of less complex, but not necessarily lower life forms, especially in urban areas that started with small settlements that grew into cities that, in turn, expanded into regions containing suburbs and exurbs. As a result, regions have one or more vital organs—central business and cultural districts, suburban employment centers and shopping malls, and even regional parks—tied together with the sinews of transportation, the arteries of commerce, and the protoplasm of community."[2] Dodge goes on to explicate how regions have become more important, as has the need for regional governance and decision making, developing visions and strategies for pursuing regional excellence, and analysis of different types of regional governance initiatives in particular places in the United States and around the world. Many regionalists prefer a more flexible and "organic" definition of region, and much more information is needed to accurately assess the nature of a region. No one really has the total picture of any region. No federal governmental entity or institutes have compiled a comprehensive picture or data set on regional-level institutions, functions, and practices. This is even further underscored with respect to evaluating the effects of current policies and practices in assessing causal processes involved in producing disparate effects and examining past and proposed solutions.

Notes

1. Alan Altshuler, William Morrill, Harold Wolman, and Faith Mitchell, eds., *Governance and Opportunity in Metropolitan America,* National Research Council, Committee on Improving the Future of U.S. Cities through Improved Metropolitan Area Governance (Washington, D.C.: National Academy Press, 1999).

2. William R. Dodge, *Regional Excellence: Governing Together to Compete Globally and Flourish Locally* (Washington, D.C.: National League of Cities, 1996).

A Conversation with Geoffrey Anderson

Geoffrey Anderson is director of the Development, Community, and Environment Division in U.S. Environmental Protection Agency.

What is your education background, and how did you become interested in smart-growth issues?

Anderson: My undergraduate education is from Connecticut College. I got a bachelor's in human ecology, which is essentially environmental science with some government and economics thrown in. Then I did my master's work at Duke University [studying] resource economics and policy. The undergraduate work was looking at the natural science side, and the graduate work was the people side.

I started at [the Environmental Protection Agency, or EPA] in 1994, just as the Office of Policy was thinking about what direction it should be headed. At the time we were working with the President's Council for Sustainable Development. It was through working with the hundreds of people involved in that effort that we thought developmental patterns are a big deal. They are a big deal from an environmental perspective in terms of their impact on air, water, land, etcetera. But they are a big deal from a bunch of other perspectives in terms of people's daily lives and travel and taxes, schools, crime, and so forth.

From an environmental perspective, the EPA was very poorly positioned at that time to work on this. We'd basically wait around until things got bad and then say, "Now you've done it," you've violated our standards, so here's your fine. That didn't seem to be the most proactive approach we could take, so we thought we should try to get in on the front end of this thing and really do pollution prevention on a metropolitan scale.

When you look at it for any length of time, you realize a few things: Development decisions and development outcomes are really the result of myriad people making a lot of decisions for a lot of reasons. Even if you had a developer who wanted to do all the right stuff, it can be tough because of what the fire chief wants or what the road guys want or because the local government won't zone for it or financers won't let you build it.

There are a lot of different actors. You also realize that EPA is not particularly influential in the decision making. We come in the end and sort of get the output of that process from the environmental perspective, but we don't really have a role except tangentially maybe in our water decisions or air decisions here or there. We thought, let's go to work with the people who do have a big influence on the outcomes. Let's work with the developers, the local governments, the environmental groups, and the community development organizations and see if we can't find some areas where we all think improvement is possible and a good thing.

What was the impetus for change in EPA's orientation?

Anderson: Basically in the Office of Policy, the previous focus in 1994 had been reviewing regulations that came out of the different program offices. People wanted to be a little more proactive, focusing on the next big environmental issue rather than such an internally focused viewpoint. So we had a lot of latitude to say, alright, this is what we think the next big environmental issue is. So it was really Harriet [Tregoning], myself, and other folks on the staff that said that development is a big issue, and we kind of made that case to our management and said we ought to work on this. We realized that as a federal agency known mostly for regulating, it was going to dicey, that we're not always going to be welcome. So it became important to define our role really well. That came down to doing education and outreach, providing tools and technical assistance, doing research and policy work, looking at our own programs, and at a minimum making sure we are not doing things that lead to perverse outcomes with respect to other local agencies trying to do smart growth.

You mentioned that state and local government officials haven't been excited about the EPA's involvement in the past. Can you speak about some of the responses to your new smart-growth approach?

Anderson: Shock! They are so used to us in a different role that we get a lot of really good responses. After there's a small confirming period of "Are you serious? This is what you're doing?" then [they say] "this is great, the federal government as a partner in helping us figure out how to deal with the issues that affect our day-to-day environment, quality of life, etcetera." I think it helps a lot that we work with the organizations that they trust and communicate with every day [such as] the ICMA [International City/County Management Association], National Association of Counties, and the Conference of Mayors.

One of the impetuses for the work in the Air Office was the Conference of Mayors saying that it seems like there is a potential for conflict between [EPA's toxic waste and brown-field] goals and [EPA's] air quality goals. You want us to redevelop brown fields, but it's hard in nonattainment areas. So the work we did basically said, look, when you redevelop brown fields that could actually have air quality benefits. So we were able to help them negotiate the agency regulatory framework and get an outcome that met environmental needs and met their needs.

From your personal perspective, whom do you hold up as an outstanding leader regarding smart growth?

Anderson: I have several. I tend to admire the people who've made a difference. I think that Christine Todd Whitman (secretary of EPA, former governor of New Jersey) is one of the people. She took very substantive steps to promote smart growth—particularly on the open-space issues but also on brown fields. She has a good understanding of the interconnectedness of the factors that go into growth decision making and took action on a number of them.

I'm also a big fan of Governor Glendening [Parris Glendening, governor of Maryland]. [He has] a very thoughtful approach to using the state's resources.

I also think that Andres Duany has clearly, pound for pound, enlightened and made more people think about it than almost anyone you can name in the country. I don't agree with every piece of his perspective, but in terms of bringing this issue to the public, politicians, and professionals, he's done as well as anyone.

The only other person I would say is Harriet Tregoning [special secretary of the Maryland Office of Smart Growth]. She really was an innovator from within the federal government and just pulled a lot of folks together and took a chance in an environment in which chance taking is not necessarily really rewarded.

8

The Straw That Broke the Camel's Back: Preservation of an Urban Mountain Landscape

Josh Protas

> Brooding, through the hazy distance,
> Listless, indolent, reclined,
> Head extended, drowsing, dreaming,
> 'Gainst a turquoise sky outlined,
> Lies the Camelback, a mountain,
> Age-carved from the upthrust stone,
> In the semblance of a camel,
> Resting, sleeping, lying prone.[1]

Rising above the modern urban metropolis of Phoenix in central Arizona's Salt River Valley, Camelback Mountain is the subject of W. I. Lively's 1928 mythic legend of the "Old Man of the Mountain." According to this tale, which appropriates and generalizes American Indian imagery, the dromedary-shaped mountain served as a sacred site and place of worship for an ancient civilization "long since perished from the land." When the cruel and arrogant chief of the tribe set out to defy the gods by scaling the mountain and bringing it under his rule, he was struck by a bolt of lightning, "chang[ing him] into the stony substance of the mountain he profaned." The camel has remained "lying prone" ever since. A warning to those who would attempt to master Camelback's sacred heights, the moral of this legend has gone largely unnoticed in recent times.

With the modern settlement of the Phoenix metropolitan area, Camelback Mountain has become one of the region's most distinguished landmarks. It functions as a popular outdoor recreational spot and a landscape of natural beauty for both area residents and visitors. Likewise, Camelback serves as an identifying symbol for the city that has grown up around it. Though this urban expansion has brought new threats to the mountain's sanctity, such encroachment has been highly contested over the years. In contrast to the intervention of the gods in the legend, Camelback Mountain was saved most recently by the impassioned efforts of concerned citizens from the Phoenix community. The story of the preservation of Camelback Mountain reveals much about the city's complex and fragile relationship to its surrounding open spaces. Insights into the community's perceptions, attitudes, values, and politics regarding its physical environment can be gleaned from this fascinating chapter in the history of Camelback Mountain.

The story of the mountain's preservation also reflects patterns and processes of urban growth occurring on a broader, regional level. Questions of land use and perception, central to the history of the American West, were played out in the lengthy debates over the mountain's future. The preservation of Camelback Mountain is significant in that it illustrates the contested nature of both the mental and the physical landscapes in Phoenix and in the West. The community's struggle over issues of the meaning, use, and ownership of the mountain has pointed to its conflicting responses to the surrounding landscape. The mountain represents to some a wilderness environment worthy of preservation, whereas for others it is a resource to be developed and transformed. This situation reflects the tensions that followed the rapid urbanization of the American West in the twentieth century. Cities attempted to reconcile people's desires for a regional ideal involving Old West traditions and an unspoiled natural environment with the realities of an urban context. The open spaces and "western" lifestyle that attracted people to the region became increasingly threatened by new urban growth and expansion.[2] As historian Richard White has noted, "There are many possible relationships between us and the land, and such meanings are contested. Despite multiple use, land cannot be simultaneously range, parking lots, and wilderness; discovering which perceptions and which uses of land prevail, and why, has become much of the subject of environmental history and the New Western History." A study of such relationships focuses on the diverse, conflicting interests at play in the debates over the meaning and use of the land. It explores the contesting groups, their perceptions of the land and plans for its use, and the power relationships that shape the contest.[3]

This story holds particular resonance, however, because the community's efforts to resolve its paradoxical relationship with the surrounding landscape did not end with Camelback's preservation. Issues such as the development of the McDowell Mountains, the possible closure of Camelback hiking trails, and the recent arsons of luxury homes built in proximity to the Phoenix Mountain Preserves continue to make the local headlines. The tensions between a regional ideal and the urban reality have remained unreconciled. Although the settling of individual disputes has had some effect in shaping the landscape, the failure to address the underlying ideological issues suggests that continued contestation and conflict await the community's future.

This investigation begins with an exploration of people's perceptions of and attitudes toward the landscape in the hope of portraying the dominant images and identity of the area. How the land is viewed, by whom, and from what perspective are important considerations in understanding the mental geography that frames the contests over the meaning of the landscape. The story continues with a narrative account of the many people, organizations, and agencies involved in the effort to save Camelback Mountain. This instance of the local community rallying together serves as an example for other groups trying to preserve open spaces and natural landscapes; it also offers suggestions about the most effective means to accomplish these goals. Camelback's story offers us guidance to better deal with other contested landscapes within or near our city spaces:

> Came again the feast of springtime;
> And the people of the land
> Came to worship at the mountain,
> Each one bearing in his hand
> Wands of willow, carved and painted,
> Token of a silent prayer
> That the gods would bless their harvest—
> Keep their cornfields green and fair.[4]

Historically, Americans have responded ambiguously to mountain and wilderness landscapes. On one hand, they have been perceived as theological places of evil and temptation. The wilderness was seen as an obstacle and threat to human progress and development—a remote, austere, and ominous place viewed in opposition to the comforts of civilization. On the other hand, inspired by Romantic poets of the nineteenth century, people began to look on mountains and the wilderness in a different way. They saw these environments as sources of sublime beauty, simplicity, and poetic inspiration. Around this time, the wilderness also became associated with the American frontier and was thought to promote toughness, virility, and independence among pioneers who accepted its challenges.[5]

One reason for the shift in attitude toward untamed natural landscapes was a response to the failings of city life. Colonial American cities liberated their citizens from the constant toil of working the land and were regarded as bastions of culture, civilization, comfort, and abundance. However, increasing growth, urbanization, and commercialization transformed the city's environment. Crime, poverty, decay, and overcrowding became common themes in critical images of mid- and late nineteenth-century cities.[6] Like the contrary images of the wilderness, both positive and negative views of the city have coexisted.

The fluctuating images of the wilderness and city continue to influence popular thought and ideas about environment. One reason for this fluctuation is the existence of two antithetical landscapes, the natural and the urban, that exemplify the contrasting environmental ideals in America. The constantly changing attitudes toward these environments occur as people vacillate in their preference of one ideal or the other. The tension between the two images also accounts for the resonance of the idea of a "middle" landscape.[7] Geographer Yi-Fu Tuan described such landscapes: "The American dream is compounded of profoundly ambivalent and even contradictory elements. Nowhere is the dream's dichotomy more evident than in the desire to combine, in the nineteenth century, the antithetical images of an urban empire and an agrarian nation."[8] The desire to combine these ideal landscapes was not limited, however, to the nineteenth century. Americans have attempted throughout this nation's history to reconcile the best of the urban and natural worlds, merging the idea of culture and society with the concept of untouched nature and spaciousness. It is in this ideal middle landscape that we find the most lucid expression of attitudes regarding the relationship between city spaces and natural landscapes.[9]

The concept of the middle landscape in America has its roots in the Jeffersonian pastoral ideal. This type of landscape embodies the desire to bring the natural and human worlds together into a structured, compatible system. Here, the organization and order of the city are imposed on a wilderness setting. However, the mastery over nature is not followed to the extreme of the city environment, and the natural landscape is not entirely left in an unspoiled wilderness state. Instead, a delicate balance is struck, combining the conventions of city life with the vast open expanses found in nature. The modern equivalent of this pastoral ideal is the satellite or suburban community located between the urban metropolis and wilderness areas. In the American West, however, the rapid expansion of urban centers has abruptly brought them in close proximity to surrounding middle landscapes and wilderness areas. As the forces of urbanization extend outward, issues of the ownership, use, and meaning of the land become more hotly contested. Geographer Kevin Blake has commented on this state of affairs: "Increasingly, the urbanite's vision of what a landscape should look like controls the human impacts on mountains."[10] More often than not, the voices representing the urban interests of development and commodification have risen above the pleas to protect and preserve mountain and wilderness landscapes. The sprawling city raises the question of what to do with the open spaces now nearby or within its boundaries. To preserve these spaces as open and natural would disrupt the created order of the city landscape and impede the development of the area. Yet to transform such open spaces to harmonize with the surrounding urban fabric would be to deny the community a valuable natural resource providing solace and relief from the frenetic urban world. Thus, the expansion of urban centers into middle landscapes and wilderness areas transforms them into contested landscapes, centered around the conflict over the use and meaning of their encroached-on open spaces.

In the case of Camelback Mountain, this point of contact between the growing metropolis and the pristine mountain foothills brought to the surface the highly contested nature of the landscape. Prior to the 1950s, the mountain was not immediately threatened by the distant city, and there was little public concern over the mountain's fate. At the founding of the Arizona Territory, Camelback was the property of the federal government. Over time, most of the land later became privately owned and settled under the Homestead Act. However, a quarter section of this area (160 acres) was still owned by the federal government and was given to Arizona on its statehood in 1912. The state later saw fit to dispose of this property and sold the majority of the 160 acres to individuals during the 1920s.[11] The state sold the last publicly owned portion of Camelback Mountain in the mid-1940s.[12]

At this time, Phoenix's residential and commercial areas were far removed from the land surrounding the mountain. By 1948, the city's boundaries only slightly extended north of Indian School Road and east of Twenty-Fourth Street, still several miles away from the piedmont of Camelback. Over the course of the next two decades, however, the Phoenix metropolitan area experienced an explosive growth in population. To keep pace with the rapidly increasing demands for homes and commercial property, the City of Phoenix underwent an aggressive policy of annexation, substantially extending its borders in all directions (see figure 8.1). This period of dramatic urban expansion brought the city in close proximity to the outlying communities and to undeveloped open spaces such as Camelback Mountain. The sudden advancement of city development raised questions about the meaning and use of Camelback's slopes and in the 1950s sparked the first of many attempts to preserve the mountain.

In studying the many efforts to save Camelback, it is helpful to examine the community's perceptions and values of the mountain in order to better understand what was at issue in the origins of the conflict over the landscape. Kevin Blake, in his work on mountain imagery in the American West, has identified three primary archetypes that "form the bedrock of mountain symbolism in metropolitan Phoenix. These representations are mountains as

FIGURE 8.1 Camelback Mountain viewed from downtown Phoenix, 1928. Photograph by E. D. Newcomer. Courtesy of the Arizona Historical Society, Southern Arizona Division, Tucson (AHS# PC 196/f.387/06).

wilderness, playground, and home."[13] These mountain symbols, portraying distinctive features of the urban landscape, have contributed significantly to the identity of the city; they are highly valued because of the images they project and the meanings they connote. Camelback Mountain has, at different times and by different people, been seen in terms of all three mountain archetypes. Each of these representations has informed the controversy surrounding the mountain's meaning, use, and ownership.

The image of Camelback Mountain most often appealed to during the efforts to preserve its upper reaches was that of a wilderness area. The open spaces of such a wilderness preserve were presented in sharp contrast to the rapidly expanding urban environment. The mountain was viewed as a sacred place because of its natural beauty and the refuge it provided from the city lapping at its base. Again and again in writings about cities of the American West, reference has been made to the need for such open spaces. Wallace Stegner noted their value in providing the silence, remoteness, illusion, and solitude absent from city life. Bruce Berger, author of works on southwestern ecology and culture, labeled the mountain and desert spaces around Phoenix as "the wastes we turn to for relief." The functions of mountainous open spaces are clearly articulated in the 1970 Open Space Plan for the Phoenix Mountains: "The grand scale and rugged character of these mountains have set our lifestyle, broadened our perspective, given us space to breathe, and freshened our outlook."[14] Preserved wilderness areas and open spaces also correspond with popular conceptions of the regional ideal—the wide expanses of untouched nature that make possible the carefree "western" lifestyle. Thus, the psychological, spatial, and spiritual qualities of a preserved wilderness have contributed to the debates over Phoenix's mountain landscapes.

Various proposals for Camelback Mountain made in the 1950s included setting the land aside as a bird sanctuary and creating a wildlife preserve on the mountain's peaks. The eventual resolution of the conflict in 1968 led to the preservation of the mountaintop as a scenic outdoor area with no development other than minimal trails for hiking and horseback riding. This plan aimed to protect Camelback as "a natural landmark in perpetuity" and preserve "for all times [its] natural beauty."[15] Yet the very act of preserving the wilderness is steeped in contradiction. As Yi-Fu Tuan has remarked, "Wilderness cannot be defined objectively: it is as much a state of the mind as a description of nature. By the time we can speak of preserving and protecting wilderness, it has already lost much of its meaning."[16] The very acts of defining and designating wilderness impose a human order and value over the natural environment and take some of the "wild" out of the wilderness. For the open spaces and mountains surrounded by or in close proximity to urban areas, however, their preservation is the surest way to keep them in a state as near to wilderness as possible. Camelback Mountain is now an example of this type of protected landscape—kept in a natural state yet bounded and defined by human activity.

The image of the mountain as a playground and recreational area also affected the proposals for the uses of Camelback's slopes. Though community groups fought to protect the upper portions of the mountain from commercial and residential development, they did not want to restrict all access to the peaks. Phoenix City Council Resolution 13059 made clear the intent of the city to "maintain all of the land acquired on the upper-portion of Camelback Mountain . . . as a scenic outdoor area." Included in this plan was a provision for the development of trails, making the scenic landmark more readily accessible to the community.[17]

Although Camelback was located far from the city center during the early years of Phoenix's settlement, it was often frequented by picnickers and was the site of many excursions by adventurous hikers. The mountain spaces were also used as the location for public concerts during the winter of 1926–1927. Ralph J. Murphy, son of prominent Phoenix developer W. J. Murphy, served as the vice president of the Echo Canyon Bowl Association and promoted the canyon as an ideal concert setting. I. E. Behymer, the man given credit for the idea of the Hollywood Bowl, was brought to Phoenix to help pitch the idea of the natural amphitheater. During the one winter of the bowl's existence, a wide variety of entertainers performed on the wooden platform stage before crowds of tourists and locals. The acts that winter included the 158th Infantry Band, a forty-piece orchestra, a seventy-person Mormon choir, a group of Hopi dancers, and the Phoenix Indian School Band. Lack of funds prevented the further use and development of the bowl, but the mountain continued to host other recreational activities through the years.[18]

Many Phoenix natives, newcomers, and winter visitors alike enjoyed outings around Camelback's humps. Of the letters accompanying contributions to the Preservation of Camelback Mountain Foundation's 1965 fund-raising drive, many revealed stories of personal experiences on the mountain. For these people, Camelback was both a playground and a cherished spot. Aurelia Hull of Phoenix wrote, "Being a native of Arizona and the Valley of the Sun, and remembering the many happy outings I have had around and over old Camelback, especially in Echo Canyon, I would like to contribute my little bit toward its preservation." Mr. and Mrs. Herbert Huebach, transplants to Sun City, noted how their son's adventures on the mountain were an early memory of living in Phoenix: "As new residents from Wisconsin in 1950, our young son climbed Camelback Mountain. We'd like to help keep it so other young people might have the same adventure." Visitors also took advantage of the mountainous recreation opportunities. Ms. Murray Johnson of Phoenix wrote, "Winters spent in Arizona exploring the desert, and climbing old Camelback were the highlights of my childhood."[19]

The efforts to save Camelback were motivated by more than the desire to preserve the area as a secluded natural landmark. The mountain had served as the playground for generations of Valley residents and visitors, and many wanted to preserve this aspect of the mountain as well. An important benefit of the mountain was its use as a place for recreational activity. Camelback was a popular destination for hikers, climbers, picnickers, and concertgoers over the years and stood as a landmark for many people not only for its distinctive silhouette but also because of the memories of personal experiences there. One vivid memory for many who have made the arduous hike to the summit is the breathtaking view of the Valley. Camelback is noted both for its famous profile and for the scenic vista to be had from its top. This is one of the few places where one can see a complete picture of the sprawling urban expanse. Bruce Berger commented on this unique perspective from the mountain's heights: "You are at the hub of a great wheel, and flashing about you are the accelerating spokes of the New West."[20] From the mountain's peak, one can feel the energy of the city stirring below yet remain isolated and apart. Perhaps this is why Camelback Mountain has been such a popular playground for the Valley. Although the City of Phoenix did not officially open hiking trails and make the mountain accessible to the public until the early 1970s, the memory and meaning of Camelback Mountain as a recreation area were motivating factors in the efforts to preserve this special place.

The personal nature of people's mountain experiences has also influenced the commodification of mountain imagery and association. Kevin Blake has observed the proliferation of Phoenix subdivisions bearing names with mountain themes over the past twenty years and noted that mountain symbols have come to represent an ideal home site in the popular imagination.[21] The image of the mountain conveys a sense of a majestic beauty and spaciousness associated with the stereotypical "western" lifestyle. Mountainside property has been marketed as a way to buy into this lifestyle and to possess a part of nature's beauty. The personal connection to the peaks is a strong draw in upper-class subdivisions that offer residents the opportunity to own their very own section of the mountain. Proximity to the heights adds to the character, value, and security of such elite homes and sets them apart, both physically and symbolically, from the rest of the city.

Camelback's natural charm and beauty have appealed to the Valley's fashionable resorts and country clubs as well as private home owners. The nearness to the distinctive peaks of the mountain has lent an air of exclusivity to these establishments. The property around the mountain's base became an ideal setting for leisurely walks, poolside conversations, or rounds of golf. Visitors have enjoyed spectacular views without leaving the resort's grounds, and a hike around the mountain's slopes was just a short distance away for the more adventurous. Several resorts and country clubs took advantage of Camelback's images, views, and recreational opportunities as they purchased property in prime locations nestled around the mountain. Phoenix's mountain peaks have thus become valuable symbolic and spatial commodities in the promotion of homes and resorts.

Although much of Camelback's mountainside property was purchased by wealthy home owners and elite resorts during the 1950s and 1960s, the peak continued to be seen as a symbol of community identity. Geographer Yi-Fu Tuan has commented on the different levels of a city's imageability: "A large city is often known at two levels: one of high abstraction and another of specific experience. At one extreme the city is a symbol or an image (captured in a postcard or a slogan) to which one can orient oneself; at the other it is the intimately experienced neighborhood."[22] While the area around Camelback Mountain was increasingly becoming the neighborhood of the city's upper class, the symbol of its peaks remained a regional icon for all residents of the city. The frequent use of Camelback's name and image in local business signs and advertisements points to the widespread community identification with this landmark.

In Phoenix, peaks with a distinctive appearance and those on the fringes of urban development are the most likely to become contested and symbolic landscapes.[23] The multiple meanings and uses of Camelback, including its representations as wilderness, playground, and home and its prominence as a community icon, all contributed to the fiercely contested nature of this landscape. Phoenix's urban expansion and the new developments encroaching on the mountain's base in the 1950s and 1960s aroused the concern of several members of the community and sparked the first efforts to save the mountain:

> Then the brooding cloud drew upward,
> And the Chief stood there alone,
> With his feet forever rooted
> In the firm, unyielding stone;
> Toiling upward, ever upward,
> With no distance ever gained;
> Changed into the stony substance
> Of the Mountain he profaned.[24]

In Lively's *The Legend of Camelback Mountain,* the mighty chief disregarded the warnings of the priests and sought to conquer the mountain so that the gods would bow down to his decree. The people watched helpless from below as the chief strode toward the summit, "where the mighty gods abide." They witnessed on the peak a display of natural power directed against the stubborn leader. The mountain trembled, lightning illuminated the sky, and boulders were sent tumbling down the slopes. In an instantaneous burst of fury, the gods administered justice and transformed the chief "into the stony substance of the mountain he profaned."

Unlike Lively's myth, the threats to Camelback's upper reaches were not caused by the actions of a single individual; rather, it was the widespread pattern of rapid growth and development and the expansion of the burgeoning metropolis that endangered the natural, open spaces surrounding the mountain. The protection of this landmark was not the consequence of a natural disaster or the act of a higher power but resulted from the community's lengthy struggle over its relationship with the surrounding landscape. This struggle was led by a core group of dedicated citizens who took up the cause of the mountain's preservation. The story of their efforts tells of the community rallying together around a common cause and illuminates a shift in its collective values. The traditional defense of individual property rights was weighed more carefully against the public good associated with the mountain's open spaces. Citizens of the sprawling metropolis began to rethink the consequences of its growth and development as expansion endangered areas of natural beauty and recreation. The conflict over the upper reaches of

Camelback Mountain brought to the public's attention new questions regarding the meaning and use of the landscape. The community's struggle with these issues highlighted some of the Valley's devoted organizations and vibrant personalities who led the charge to save the mountain. The stories of their efforts are full of humor and disappointment, joy and frustration.

The first organized efforts to preserve Camelback Mountain began in the mid-1950s. While there was interest in the landmark previous to this time, the cause of saving the mountain was not seen as a pressing issue, and nothing much came about from these early unorganized efforts. In the 1950s, however, the rapid urbanization and expansion of the Phoenix area heightened concern over the mountain's future. As residential and commercial development continued pushing outward and began encroaching on Camelback's foothills, members of the community were driven to take action. The grading of a road on the southeast face of the mountain and the construction of homes on its slopes sparked the initial mobilization of concerned citizens to deal with this problem. In December 1954, the Camelback Improvement Association was incorporated, having as its primary purpose the preservation of Camelback Mountain in its natural state. There were twenty or more prominent citizens in attendance at the group's organizational meeting. The association circulated petitions protesting new development on the mountain and filed these with the Maricopa County Planning and Zoning Commission. The petitions voiced strong public opposition to the continued defacement of Camelback Mountain and urged the commission to take action to prevent this.[25]

In response to these protests, the commission in 1956 set the maximum building elevation on Camelback Mountain for 1,600 feet. It later became clear, however, that there was no legal basis for its zoning regulation. The commission had no power to enforce this informal ruling and attempted to persuade home builders to cooperate with the height restriction. The director of the commission said of this restriction, "There is a somewhat general misconception that construction is legally prohibited above the 1,600-foot level. Such is not the case.... Construction above this level has been limited primarily because of the cost that would be involved in site improvements."[26] Despite the tremendous costs of building on the mountain, several property owners began constructing homes farther up its slopes. Between 1957 and 1961, builders began seeking permits for homes higher than 1,600 feet, and a few started construction.[27] The failure of the commission to contain development below 1,600 feet and the ascending home sites provoked new efforts to protect the mountain.

Reacting to the growing demands for construction, Louise Woolsey, R. C. Saddler, and Bonnie Upchurch took up the campaign to save Camelback. The three women were spurred to action by requests for subdivision zoning and the bulldozing of an area in Red Rock Canyon, located above the 1,600-foot level. "I've never been madder in my life," recalled Woolsey, who lived just a short distance from the base of the mountain. "I watched them dig into the mountain and throw the waste over the side, and then stick a house up there that looks like a boxcar. I told myself, if this is all men can do, maybe its time the women rebelled."[28] Women activists were in fact among the first to take the preservation of Camelback Mountain seriously. From their initial agitation sprang an organized movement that included many of the most prominent figures in the state. In 1958, Mrs. Woolsey and the others met with representatives from thirty different Valley garden clubs to raise support for the cause. The dedicated efforts of these women brought the matter to the attention of Milton Gan, then chairman of the Phoenix Community Council. The garden clubs and the community council enlisted the help of conservationists and other Valley groups, and together they explored different ways and means of preserving Camelback. They also continued to voice their concerns to H. S. "Casey" Abbott, chairman of the Maricopa County Planning and Zoning Commission, who was sympathetic to their cause. Between 1958 and 1960, the groups met many times and considered several proposals for the mountain, including setting the land aside as a bird sanctuary, developing a state or county park, and creating an outdoor symphony bowl.[29]

The major difficulty these groups encountered was the divided ownership of the mountain land. The profiles of the property owners ranged widely and included speculators, future home builders, luxury resorts, and a church group. Because of their notably different plans for and valuations of the land, owners did not agree in their ideas about the mountain's future, and attempts to persuade the property owners to deed their land over to Maricopa County were unsuccessful. Thus, the conflicting land ethics and values of the owners precluded their joining together in the effort to preserve Camelback. The multiple owners and their multiple visions of the mountain exacerbated its highly contested nature. Frustrated after unsuccessfully seeking the cooperation of the property owners, the preservation groups eventually recommended trading publicly held land in exchange for Camelback's peaks or forming a nonprofit corporation to make an outright purchase of the land as the best possibilities for saving the mountain. Growing concern over Camelback Mountain and other conservation issues brought together in 1960 the community councils of Phoenix and Tucson along with a number of other interested groups to discuss the formation of a statewide conservation organization.

In November 1960, the Arizona Conservation Council was founded for the purpose of promoting and encouraging the conservation of natural resources, historic sites, and the scenic beauty of Arizona. Many people and groups with diverse interests joined the council, united by the goal of conservation. Among the first to join were the Arizona Game Protective Association, the Arizona Federation of Women's Clubs, the State Parks Association, and groups representing the interests of bow hunters, bird watchers, yachtsmen, campers, photographers, and marksmen.[30] Protecting Camelback was the conservation council's first order of business, and it spearheaded the campaign to restore public ownership of the upper reaches of the mountain. The conservation council, with its large and diverse membership, intensified the momentum of the cause and pursued a new course of action.

In September 1961, meetings were held with representatives from the governor's office, the attorney general's office, the county attorney's office, county parks and recreation officials, and various property owners in the Camelback area. After meeting with the conservation council to discuss the issues, a majority of the Camelback Mountain property owners expressed that they would be willing to trade their land for government-owned land elsewhere in the state. John McChesney, one of the sixteen owners of the 550 acres of undeveloped land on the mountain's top, spoke on behalf of the owners of roughly two-thirds of the acreage involved when he said that they would be willing to make the trade if it could be arranged legally. However, he also noted their concern over the protection of their private property rights in the process. In the past, McChesney commented, the property rights of the individual were ignored. He stated that "developers were referred to as fast buck operators, which wasn't true. They described residents on the mountain as plutocrats in palatial homes looking out over the peasants in the Valley."[31] This controversy points to the conflicting values at play in the perception and values of the landscape, where the public good is seen in opposition to the rights of the individual. A planning report for the Phoenix Mountains expresses the difficulty this situation presents for the preservation of open spaces:

> The benefits we seek from our natural environment are, in many cases, competing, or even mutually exclusive. Choices and compromises are unavoidable. The interests of the public often collide with those of the individual citizen. Traditional convictions as to the inviolability of private property rights often stand in the way of insuring the inherent right of the public to protect and enjoy its natural environment.[32]

However, with the expressed cooperation of most of Camelback's property owners, the challenge became one of working out the details of a land exchange.

These details proved to be more difficult than originally anticipated when Arizona's attorney general pointed out that the federal enabling act allows the disposal of state lands only by public auction or by trade with the federal government. The conservation council met with members of Arizona's congressional delegation to discuss the possibility of trading federally owned land for the property on Camelback. The investigation of this option was given a boost when, in September 1961, the John H. Page Land Company volunteered to handle the complicated and time-consuming land search involved in the proposed exchange. In addition, the Phoenix Title and Trust Company and the engineering firm of Collar, Williams, and White volunteered their services to help the campaign.[33]

In response to the widespread community interest in preserving Camelback Mountain, Congressman John Rhodes introduced House Resolution 10922 in the U.S. House of Representatives on March 26, 1962. This bill would have authorized the exchange of federal lands for the property on top of Camelback. It was referred to the House Committee on Interior and Insular Affairs, out of which it never passed. Secretary of Interior Stewart Udall commented on the legislation introduced by Rhodes and stated the Department of the Interior's view of the bill: "Because of the location of this property we believe the local community should be encouraged to preserve the mountain top in some manner for public use." Udall expressed concern that the landmark remain in local control; the best way to ensure this was its preservation at the local level. In his letter, Udall suggested local zoning regulations (which had already proved unsuccessful) or the outright purchase of the land by the state or county. He noted that under Title VII of the Housing Act of 1961, there was a possibility that the federal government could share as much as 30 percent of the cost of acquiring the mountaintop.[34] Because of the secretary's comments, the bill failed to make it out of committee. Rhodes responded by saying that he was in general agreement with Udall's opinion on the matter and that he introduced the bill as a means of "bringing the situation to a head." Ironically, Secretary Udall would be the one to seal the fate of Camelback Mountain when he presented a federal grant to the City of Phoenix for the acquisition of the mountain property, nearly six years after his comments on Rhodes's proposed bill. In the end, however, local control and public use of the mountain were secured as Udall had stressed in his earlier observations.

Before the eventual acquisition of the mountain, many different efforts were made to preserve its heights. In 1963, Senator Barry Goldwater introduced in the U.S. Senate a bill similar to the one introduced by Representative Rhodes. Congress again took no action on the measure. In light of the failure of the federal government to assist in the mountain's preservation, the Arizona Conservation Council shifted the focus of its efforts and pushed for legislation at the state level. On February 1, 1963, three members of the Arizona House of Representative, Isabel Burgess, John Pritzlaff, and Don Reese, introduced a bill that proposed to authorize the exchange of certain state lands for properties on Camelback Mountain. According to this proposal, the acquired lands would be managed by the state parks board and preserved as a state landmark. The preservation campaign received the endorsement of numerous groups throughout the community at this time. The backers of the measure to save the mountain included the conservation council, Governor Fannin, Arizona's congressional delegation, the chamber of commerce, and many community organizations, school groups, local businesses, and private citizens.[35] Despite this widespread support, the bill was never reported out of the House Judiciary and Livestock and Public Lands Committees and was never passed.

The community became increasingly frustrated by the unsuccessful attempts to save the mountain and the growing threats of development on its peaks. In 1963, there were between fifty and one hundred owners of the land above the 1,600-foot mark. The multiplying number of property owners and the skyrocketing value of the land made acquisition of the mountaintop begin to appear unlikely. Getting all the parties involved to agree to sell or exchange their lands would be difficult enough; coming up with the price of purchase or a suitable trade was another matter altogether. Don Dedera's columns, which appeared in the *Arizona Republic* during the spring of 1963, described in detail Camelback's unfortunate situation. In his column on May 2 of that year, he listed the possibilities for saving the mountain. Aside from improbable ideas, such as having the city using its powers of eminent domain to condemn the land, soliciting the voluntary contribution of land parcels, and launching a campaign to raise funds to buy the top of the mountain, he maintained that the best hope for Camelback was in the state's acquisition of the Phoenix landmark. Yet in the wake of the failed effort in the last legislative session, even Dedera, the voice of the preservation campaign, saw little hope in the outlook for the mountain. With tongue in cheek yet fearing the accuracy of his predictions, he noted the likelihood that private development would shape the course of Camelback's future. The defacement that Dedera reluctantly envisioned included a nightclub at the summit of the tallest peak, a hotel, a funicular railway, homes, and roads covering the surface of the mountain.

Despite this pessimistic outlook, not everyone gave up hope of saving the mountain. Inspired by Dedera's articles and the uncertain fate of the landmark, Shari Hume, a seventeen-year-old student of Arcadia High School, led a new crusade to save Camelback. In October 1963, Shari drew up a petition and began circulating it around the Arcadia campus. The petition resolved that "the young people of Arizona (less than 21 years old) do respectfully petition the Second Session of the 26th Legislature of the State of Arizona to take appropriate action to permanently preserve Camelback Mountain in its present state for the viewing pleasure of future generations." The high school students focused their efforts on a goal that many before them could not accomplish.

Hume remarked, "The response was terrific. I think the kids are glad to have a chance to succeed where their parents have failed."[36] To help in the campaign, Hume challenged other high schools in the Valley and from around the state to match the number of petitioners. There was a tremendous response to this call to action; more than twenty high schools throughout the state collected signatures in support of this effort. Through November and December 1963, the *Arizona Republic* printed a tally of the signatures collected at participating high schools. The "Teenage Crusade to Save Camelback" continued until February 1964 and reinvigorated community support for saving the mountain. Shari Hume was invited by Representative Isabel Burgess to present the petition to the Arizona House of Representatives on February 21, 1964. The petition was 322½ feet in length and contained the names of 12,679 Arizona high school students. Also on this day, Representatives Burgess, Pritzlaff, and Reese introduced House Bill 312. This bill, like the one introduced the year before, proposed to authorize the state lands commissioner to negotiate the exchange of state lands with the Camelback property owners and to designate the mountain a state landmark. Senators Hilliard Brooke and Paul Singer introduced a similar bill in the Arizona Senate on the previous day.

In addition to the high school students' actions, the blasting of a boulder near the head of the camel provoked stepped-up efforts to preserve the mountain. On February 14, 1964, Mr. and Mrs. Carruth attempted to topple an 18,000-pound boulder that posed a threat to the home the couple was building. The Carruths took out a twenty-four-hour policy with Lloyd's of London to cover any potential damages and then packed seventy sticks of dynamite into thirty-one holes drilled into the base of the sixty-foot rock formation, which was described in the media as both "the ear of the camel" and "the carrot" in front of the camel's nose. Ear or carrot, the boulder moved just four inches and remained standing after the blast. However, the community was outraged by this attack on the mountain and was reminded again of the need to protect the vulnerable landmark. One angry neighbor remarked, "First the ear, then the humps, and then the tail, and finally the camel will be no more."[37] The blasting of the boulder near the camel's head and the tremendous success of the students' petition drive inspired a great showing of public support that boded well for the bills before the state legislature. Don Dedera commented on this state of affairs: "With roads scarring the rump of the old mountain camel, and with dynamite blasts reverberating in its ear, one fact seems clear: the bill that Shari Hume wants passed is the last, best chance to save scenic Camelback."[38]

Yet in a situation all too familiar to the supporters of Camelback's preservation, disappointment was again to be experienced. Various amendments were made to House Bill 312 to quiet the fears of educators that state school land would be diminished by a land exchange. However, the Arizona Education Association (AEA) remained vehemently opposed to the bill and applied pressure on various officials, including Representative Waldo DeWitt, chairman of the Livestock and Public Lands Committee.[39] DeWitt apparently concurred with the AEA's opposition to the land swap and prevented the bill from passing out of his committee. In an ironic twist, the AEA effectively killed the legislation for which Arizona students had worked so hard to introduce. This most recent failure by public officials to approve the measure ensuring the preservation of Camelback Mountain highlighted a lack of strong leadership in the legislature and the degree of influence of Arizona's education lobbying organization. Despite wide public support of the issue, legislators came up short and could not get the bill passed. By contrast, the 1964 Arizona Boys State legislators had no difficulty in deciding this issue. They voted unanimously (36 to 0 in the House of Representatives and 10 to 0 in the Senate) to stop all construction and create a state park on the mountain.[40]

After the defeat of the proposal in the state legislature, the cause of saving Camelback Mountain was next taken up by the high-powered Valley Beautiful Citizens Council (VBCC). As Walter Meek observed in an article on the goals of the Citizens Council, "It may be a sad commentary, but perhaps two dozen bankers, businessmen and publishers can do what couldn't be done by 14,000 dedicated school kids."[41] Former Phoenix City Councilwoman Margaret Kober, who lived on the south side of the mountain, recalled how the VBCC initially got involved in the project:

> I was very loath to be the instigator or the promoter of this [save Camelback campaign] because I was so afraid that it would be misinterpreted; that I was trying to save my own backyard. But I said that I thought we should do something to begin to try to preserve it. . . . Nobody got too excited, and finally Henry Luce [VBCC director and the publishing genius behind the Time Inc. empire] spoke up and he said, "If this organization shouldn't be concerned with saving the likes of Camelback Mountain, then I don't know why we exist." And he's the one who got me off the ground. So we went to work immediately.[42]

The VBCC set the preservation of Camelback Mountain as one of its top three projects and officially announced the formation of the Preservation of Camelback Mountain Foundation (PCMF) as a nonprofit corporation on May 10, 1965.

The PCMF committed itself to the acquisition of the property on Camelback Mountain above 1,800 feet by any and all means possible, including, if necessary, raising funds for its purchase. After the dismal showing of the past legislative efforts, it appeared that the best hope for saving Camelback was to acquire the mountaintop property. PCMF members decided on the 1,800-foot level as their goal because above this height the silhouette of the mountain could be preserved intact, while below this height the land was already subdivided and would be too expensive for acquisition. The foundation next chose its board of directors to lead the campaign. The list of board members read like a Who's Who list of Phoenix's elite citizens: Lewis Ruskin, Henry Luce, Ralph Burbacher Sr., Isabel Burgess, John Pritzlaff, and J. C. Wetzler. The officers selected were Barry Goldwater, chairman; Margaret Kober, vice chair; Harry Montgomery, treasurer; and Harry Coblentz, executive secretary. Under the direction of this prestigious board, the PCMF first attempted to persuade the owners of the roughly 300 acres of property above the 1,800-foot mark to contribute their land for public use. Goldwater, who was staying in Phoenix that winter after having been defeated in his 1964 presidential bid and before returning to the U.S. Senate, became actively involved in the effort and personally contacted many of the property owners to discuss the possible donation of their lots.[43]

When it became clear that funds would be required to purchase the majority of the mountaintop property, the PCMF initiated a drive for cash donations to help meet these costs. Announced on October 9, 1965, this "most promising campaign in 20 years to conserve Camelback Mountain"[44] quickly set out to garner community support. The campaign was officially launched at a public meeting held on October 26 in the Camelback High School gymnasium. Approximately 450 people showed up to hear Goldwater tell the story of the mountain, show photographs, and announce campaign plans. Don Dedera, the outspoken supporter of Camelback's preservation over the years, was the master of ceremonies for the evening. At the rally, it was announced that an estimated $300,000 would be needed to purchase the property on Camelback's summit above 1,800 feet. Kober expressed that the PCMF's goal was to raise this amount by December 25 so that the foundation could give Camelback Mountain to the city and its young people as a Christmas gift. The kickoff rally proved to be a tremendous success. That night there was a great response to the PCMF's campaign to save the mountain, including many donations and pledges of support.[45]

The show of community support after this initial campaign rally was even more impressive. Margaret Kober, chosen as the campaign chairman, led the way by organizing hundreds of volunteers, soliciting donations and in-kind contributions, and arranging media coverage of the group's efforts. Organizations and individuals across the greater Phoenix area got involved in the campaign. Barry Goldwater wrote letters to the residents of the areas near the mountain calling on them to help out a cause very close to home; over 4,000 letters signed by Goldwater were mailed to home owners in Paradise Valley and the Arcadia district bordering the mountain. In addition, he sent letters to all the prominent Valley business firms asking for their support.[46] Various service clubs, fraternal organizations, women's clubs, and garden groups were also called on to help by announcements and leaflets that were distributed at their meetings. The appeal to the business and civic community paid off. In-kind support helped keep the campaign's expenses to a minimum and allowed the PCMF to concentrate on raising funds for the mountain's purchase. Among the contribution of goods and services were printed matter donated by Maricopa Printers, Don McGraw Printers, Arizona Messenger, Andy Chuka, and S. W. Envelope Co.; postage for mailings supplied by Western Savings, Valley National Bank, and Phoenix Newspapers; and engineering services provided free of charge by Collar, Williams, White and Holmquist Engineering Co.[47]

Media coverage also gave a significant boost to the campaign efforts. Kober sent out notices to the newspapers and television and radio stations regarding the activities of the PCMF and other community groups involved in the campaign. The media responded with overwhelming support for the PCMF project. Television and radio news coverage raised community awareness about the fund-raising campaign and called attention to the various projects going on in support of this goal. But the support of the *Phoenix Gazette* and the *Arizona Republic* was truly phenomenal. Between the launching of the campaign in October and its self-set December deadline, the newspapers ran an article, editorial, or cartoon almost daily. During this period, at least sixty-three different articles were published on the topic of Camelback Mountain.[48] *Republic* columnist Don Dedera, who had been so vocal over the years about preserving the mountain, continued to devote his column to this cause. A cartoon by the *Republic*'s Reg Manning, showing a cowering Camelback Mountain about to be struck by an angry-looking steam shovel, became a popular image in the campaign and was reproduced on printed leaflets asking for donations. To individuals or groups making a donation of $10 or more, a certificate designed by Kearney Egerton of the *Republic* was mailed. This media coverage and support significantly helped broaden the appeal of the campaign.

What began as a project of an elite civic organization, many of whose members lived in close proximity to the mountain itself, expanded into a communitywide effort to save Camelback Mountain. This shift recalls Yi-Fu Tuan's distinction between the different levels by which a city is known: "At one extreme the city is a symbol or an image (captured in a postcard or a slogan) to which one can orient oneself; at the other is the intimately experienced neighborhood."[49] While earlier concern over the mountain's fate originated largely from those who intimately experienced the peak from their picture windows or backyard vistas, the later, more widespread activism seemed to focus on protecting Camelback as an icon of the Valley whose silhouette defined the city skyline. The symbolism of a preserved mountain also represented the community's reappraisal of the value and meaning of its surrounding landscape.

In response to the popular appeal of saving the mountain, a broad spectrum of community groups got involved with the PCMF campaign. Some businesses and organizations actively encouraged their employees and members to support the campaign. An article in the *Voice of Motorola* newsletter urged employees and their families to donate to this worthy cause.[50] Phoenix Union High School Superintendent Howard Seymour devoted his space in a district newsletter to heaping praise onto the Valley landmark and noting the reasons why it should be saved. A newspaper article noted the backing of the campaign by the Mobile Home Owners Association.[51] These examples are representative of the broad community support enjoyed by the PCMF.

Yet perhaps no other group was more fervent in their support of the cause of preserving Camelback Mountain than the children of Arizona. Valley high school students, who before were instrumental in introducing legislation to save Camelback, once again came to the mountain's assistance. From articles in school papers to fund-raising drives, high school students demonstrated their serious devotion to this cause. Students from around the Valley pledged their support for the campaign and created "Save Camelback Mountain" chapters at twenty-six local schools.[52] A "Cans for Camelback" contest between Valley high schools was sponsored by KRIZ radio, and other teens participated in a car wash to raise funds for the mountain's preservation. The efforts of Valley teenagers culminated in the Save Camelback Mountain Dance, organized in part by Joanne Holloway, chairman of the Teen Committee to Save Camelback Mountain and sponsored by KRIZ radio. The dance, which took place on December 18 in the State Fairground Exhibition Hall, featured performances by The Wanderers, The Pendleton Sound, Inc., and The Doorknobs. Barry Goldwater showed his support for the teens' enthusiasm by making an appearance at the concert. For his performance, Goldwater wore a Beatles wig and played "Silent Night" on the trombone.[53] In addition to the high school students' efforts, many other school and community groups participated in the PCMF's fund-raising campaign. Bake sales, Pennies for Pebbles drives, and various contests were held to raise money for the mountain. Campfire Girls, Girls Scouts, Boy Scouts, and hundreds of schoolchildren across the Valley made contributions to assist in the preservation of Camelback Mountain.

The PCMF received numerous contributions during this time, many of which were extremely large. At the end of the fund-raising campaign, over 2,700 certificates had been mailed to those contributing over $10, not including groups of schoolchildren. Donations had been received from forty-seven

Arizona towns and cities, twenty-seven states, two foreign countries, and twenty-nine different schools. Contributions ranged from 25 cents to significantly larger amounts. Some of the letters that were mailed along with campaign contributions revealed endearing testimonies of people's love for and support of the mountain. The note by the Smith Park Garden Club of Phoenix is an example of such a personal statement: "The Washington garden Club Jrs. of Smith Park donated all their money [43 cents] to help save Camel[back] Mountain. We can't see it from here but we love it anyway. We would like to save it for the other kids."[54] The most generous gifts to the PCMF included $25,000 by Henry Luce, $25,000 by Barry Goldwater, $25,000 by Mrs. Goldwater (Barry's mother), $25,000 by Henry Galbraith, $10,000 by John Pritzlaff, $10,000 by the *Republic* and the *Gazette,* and $5,000 by the Junior League.[55]

Despite the enormous community support and the generous contributions, the PCMF failed to meet its goal of raising $300,000 by December 25. By Christmas, the foundation had, to the disappointment of its members, reached only two-thirds of its goal. Margaret Kober took the news especially hard: "This has been a blow—those of us who have worked on this since last April are *deflated.* We do not *understand*!"[56] However, the PCMF remained committed to saving the mountain and regrouped its forces to examine new ways to finance the project. In early 1966, the foundation began looking into money available through the Land and Water Conservation Fund Act. Funds from this act were allocated to municipalities and counties through the Arizona Outdoor Recreation Coordinating Commission. The PCMF negotiated with officials from Maricopa County and together applied for $200,000 in federal funds from the Land and Water Conservation Fund Act. The request was turned down in April 1966 because the act was established to promote active participant-type recreation, and the few primitive hiking trails on Camelback failed to meet this requirement. In addition, Public Law 88-578, which established the Land and Water Conservation Fund Act, required that the applicant have in place a recreation and open-spaces use plan, which Maricopa County lacked.[57] Thus, the failure to meet the prerequisites of the act precluded Maricopa County and Camelback Mountain from receiving funds.

After the county request was denied, the PCMF discussed applying for federal funds with the City of Phoenix. The foundation suggested that the city seek a grant to preserve Camelback Mountain through the Open Spaces Program of the Federal Housing and Urban Development Act. It recommended that an application be made for $200,000 to help establish a scenic preserve, the creation of which was the objective of the Open Spaces Program. The PCMF was prepared to match the federal money with the roughly $250,000 it had acquired through contributions and planned to use these funds to complete the purchase of the mountaintop properties. The Phoenix City Council approved a resolution on December 13, 1966, that enabled the city to seek the previously mentioned federal grant.[58] By this time, however, the estimated costs for the purchase of the 352 acres had risen to over $500,000. In its application to the Land and Water Conservation Fund, which was decided on as being the best possible source of funding, the City of Phoenix requested a total of $269,625 in order to cover the higher estimates for the land purchase; according to this plan, the balance of the total amount was to be made up for by the PCMF's funds.[59]

This grant proposal for the purchase of the upper portion of Camelback Mountain for the creation of a scenic preserve was among forty-three other projects requesting funding, four of which were also submitted by the City of Phoenix. In order to better the chances of the project's approval by the Arizona Outdoor Recreation Coordinating Commission (AORCC), the group responsible for reviewing proposals and making recommendations at the state level, the Phoenix City Council decided to give its top priority to obtaining money to preserve Camelback Mountain.[60] The council's move meant the possible delay of Phoenix's four other proposals; however, the urgency of the Camelback project was seen as proper justification for the decision. This strategy paid off. On August 22, 1967, the AORCC voted unanimously to recommend granting $215,700 in matching federal funds to be used to protect Camelback's undeveloped summit, or 80 percent of its initial request of $269,625. In addition, the commission voted to support any appeal the city might make to Secretary of the Interior Stewart Udall for the remaining amount, which could come from the secretary's contingency fund.[61]

Eventually, the Bureau of Outdoor Recreation, the federal bureau overseeing the grant program, approved the proposal for Camelback Mountain and awarded the City of Phoenix the amount of $211,250. The grant was officially presented to the city during a ceremony held nearby the contested mountain at the Racquet Club on May 28, 1968. First Lady Johnson, who visited Arizona to attend the dedications of several new public facilities, announced that the federal funds had been given to match the $250,000 raised by the PCMF for the purchase of the mountaintop above 1,800 feet. Secretary of the Interior Udall was also in attendance at the ceremonies for Camelback Mountain. When presenting the grant to the City of Phoenix, Udall remarked, "I'm sure, Mrs. Johnson, you would realize even, coming into this state, that if you find me and Barry Goldwater in intimate collaboration on some cause, it has to be a good one."[62] To his embarrassment, however, Udall forgot the check that he had promised to hand over to the city.

Check or no check, the preservation of Camelback Mountain was indeed an excellent cause that had engaged so many in the community over such a long period of time. It was fitting that First Lady Johnson, who was so concerned with the beautification of the physical environment, and Secretary Udall, who had commented almost six years earlier that the mountain should remain in local control, be present for the ceremonies that brought the matter to a close. The final hurdle was cleared in the saga of the preservation of Camelback Mountain when the Phoenix City Council adopted Resolution Number 13059 on October 29, 1968. In the resolution, the council agreed to accept the parcels of land already acquired by the PCMF and to purchase the remaining portion of land above 1,800 feet with the money obtained from the federal grant and contributions to the PCMF's campaign. The council also accepted "the ownership and control of Camelback Mountain above eighteen hundred feet subject to the trust and obligation of preserving it for all time in its natural beauty and prohibiting any development other than trails on that upper portion of Camelback Mountain."[63] Finally, the upper reaches of the mountain were safe from the various forces that endangered it; yet the story of urban sprawl threatening natural landscape is one with which Phoenicians and most westerners have become all too familiar. The history of the preservation of Camelback Mountain provides one example of our rethinking the growth and development that have transformed the region and the efforts to save this valued landscape:

If you doubt the ancient legend,
You may see the Chieftain's form,
Ever straining up the mountain
In the sunshine and the storm.[64]

The "Old Man of the Mountain" of Lively's legend stands as a warning to those who would try to defy the mountain as did the mighty chief. The story of the preservation of Camelback Mountain illustrates the lessons of this legend while also highlighting the issues underlying the city's dynamic relationship with its surrounding environment. The efforts to save the mountain were informed largely by the public's perceptions of and attitudes toward the landscape. The environmental values of the Phoenix community reflected the changing physical context of the city and its increasingly urban character. The responses to the mountain's development and the efforts taken to prevent this were revealing of a changing relationship between the city and its open spaces. The contestation over the meaning, use, and ownership of the landscape, as was played out in the struggle over Camelback's future, continues to challenge the community.

The accounts of the numerous efforts over the years to preserve the mountain's peaks also illuminate situations common in Arizona's history. In this story, both federal and state governments failed to act on the matter despite widespread support. Such inability of leaders to accomplish a goal so clearly in the public interest has been, unfortunately, altogether too familiar. In the wake of the disappointing showing by public agencies and officials, private citizens took the matter into their own hands. Although the drive to save the mountain originated among a small group of people with close personal ties to the contested landscape, a communitywide campaign developed as threats to the landmark increased; however, these efforts also turned up short. In a final attempt to protect Camelback Mountain, a partnership of federal, municipal, and private entities joined together to acquire the threatened summit. The combined forces were at last able to accomplish what had frustrated so many individual efforts before. Despite the persistence and dedication exhibited by many who championed Camelback's preservation, it was not until public and private organizations linked together that the community attained its goal of saving the mountain. In a situation typical of Arizona politics, the combination of public and private groups proved best able to get the job done.

Barry Goldwater, a central figure in this story of Camelback Mountain, once noted the importance of history: "I don't think anybody can make progress unless they're constantly aware of what man has been doing, 'cause if I try to do something tomorrow that failed yesterday, I'm a goddamn fool."[65] The history of the preservation of Camelback Mountain offers many insights about the community in the Valley, its dynamic relationship with the surrounding landscape, and the process of change that has shaped this relationship. The lessons from this story offer the guidance to better deal with similar situations in the future. We would do well to take notice of this history lest other threatened landscapes go unprotected.

Notes

The editors gratefully acknowledge permission from the University of Arizona Press and the Southwest Center to reprint portions of this chapter. Another version appeared in their publication *Journal of the Southwest* 43, no. 3 (Autumn 2001).

1. W. I. Lively, *The Legend of Camelback Mountain* (N.p.: A. Truman Helm, 1928), 1.

2. Michael F. Logan, *Fighting Sprawl and City Hall: Resistance to Urban Growth in the Southwest* (Tucson: University of Arizona Press, 1995), 76.

3. Richard White, "Trashing the Trails," in *Trails: Toward a New Western History*, ed. Patricia Nelson Limerick, Clyde A. Milner II, and Charles Rankin (Lawrence: University Press of Kansas, 1991), 37.

4. Lively, *The Legend of Camelback Mountain*, 9.

5. Yi-Fu Tuan, *Topophilia: A Study of Environmental Perception, Attitudes, and Values* (Englewood Cliffs, N.J.: Prentice Hall, 1974; reprint, New York: Columbia University Press, 1990), 102–12 (page references are to reprint edition).

6. Tuan, *Topophilia*, 192–96,

7. The concept of a "middle" landscape is elaborated on in Roderick Nash, *Wilderness and the American Mind* (New Haven, Conn.: Yale University Press, 1967), and in Tuan, *Topophilia*. As they describe it, the middle landscape embodies the conflicting desires for wilderness and civilization. It functions as a compromise between the beauty and simplicity of the natural environment with the order and organization of city spaces.

8. Tuan, *Topophilia*, 196.

9. It must be noted that the "environment" is a cultural construct that is shaped by shared life experiences and differs with ethnicity and class. The ideal landscapes discussed in this chapter reflect the predominantly Anglo, upper-class visions of environment that were projected onto the terrain of Camelback Mountain. These visions were the most influential in directing the discourse over the mountain because they were held by those with the economic and political power to determine the use of this land. Evidence regarding other groups' perceptions of and attitudes toward Camelback Mountain is sparse; these "other" voices were not heard equally in the community's discourse. For a superb discussion of the cultural construction of environmental ideals and of Latino/a environmental discourses and how these differ from mainstream environmentalism, see Barbara Deutsch Lynch, "The Garden and the Sea: U.S. Latino Environmental Discourses and Mainstream Environmentalism," *Social Problems* 40, no. 1 (February 1993).

10. Kevin S. Blake, "Where Eternal Mountains Kneel at Sunset's Gate," *Pacifica*, Fall 1994, 1–10.

11. "Camelback Mountain and Echo Canyon" Box 2-74.10, Folder 5, Save Camelback collection, Arizona Historical Society, Central Arizona Division, Tempe.

12. "Background History and Description of Efforts to Save Camelback Mountain," date unknown, Box 2-74.10, Folder 5, Save Camelback collection, Arizona Historical Society, Central Arizona Division, Tempe.

13. Blake, "Where Eternal Mountains Kneel at Sunset's Gate," 6.

14. Wallace Stegner, *The American West as Living Space* (Ann Arbor: University of Michigan Press, 1987), 52, 81; Bruce Berger, *The Telling Distance: Conversations with the American Desert* (Portland, OR: Breitenbush Books, 1990), 2; City of Phoenix, *An Open Space Plan for the Phoenix Mountains*, prepared by Van Cleve Associates, Inc., 1970, 69.

15. Phoenix City Council, Resolution No. 13059, October 29, 1968.

16. Tuan, *Topophilia*, 112.

17. Phoenix City Council, Resolution Number 13059, October 29, 1968.

18. James E. Cook, "Echo Canyon's Bowl Pioneered Rock Concerts," *Arizona Republic*, May 11, 1989.

19. Box 2-74.10, Folder 1, Save Camelback collection, Arizona Historical Society, Central Arizona Division, Tempe.

20. Berger, *The Telling Distance*, 99.

21. Blake, "Where Eternal Mountains Kneel at Sunset's Gate," 9.

22. Tuan, *Topophilia*, 224.

23. Blake, "Where Eternal Mountains Kneel at Sunset's Gate," 10.

24. Lively, *The Legend of Camelback Mountain,* 12.

25. "Background History and Description of Efforts to Save Camelback Mountain."

26. Don Dedera, "Camelback Controversy at Crucial Stage," *Arizona Republic,* April 28, 1963.

27. Henry Fuller, "The Cry Went Up Years Ago," *Arizona Republic,* April 10, 1966.

28. Don Dedera, "Women Rebel Trying to Save Camelback," *Arizona Republic,* April 29, 1963.

29. "Background History and Description of Efforts to Save Camelback Mountain."

30. Dedera, "Women Rebel Trying to Save Camelback."

31. "Land Trade Believed Way to Save Camelback Scene," *Arizona Republic,* September 13, 1961.

32. City of Phoenix, *An Open Space Plan for the Phoenix Mountains,* 6–7.

33. "Background History and Description of Efforts to Save Camelback Mountain."

34. Ben Cole, "Udall Says Camelback Up to City," *Arizona Republic,* September 28, 1962.

35. Don Dedera, "Phoenix Upmanship: Camelback's Tops," *Arizona Republic,* May 1, 1963.

36. Don Dedera, "Children Crusade to Save Camelback," *Arizona Republic,* October 20, 1963.

37. *Arizona Republic,* February 15, 1964.

38. Don Dedera, *Arizona Republic,* February 21, 1964.

39. For a more detailed discussion of the AEA's position on the proposed Camelback land swap, see Don Dedera, "AEA Camelback Opposition Aired," *Arizona Republic,* March 5, 1964. Dedera questioned Dix W. Price, executive director of the AEA, and Olas Lunt, member of the AEA public lands committee, about their reasons for fighting House Bill 312.

40. *Arizona Republic,* June 12, 1964.

41. Walter W. Meek, "Save Camelback Mountain," *Arizona Republic,* December 8, 1964.

42. Margaret Kober, interview by Sylvia Laughlin, June 18, 1976, Phoenix History Project, Arizona Historical Society, Central Arizona Division, Tempe.

43. Margaret Kober collection (unprocessed), Arizona Historical Foundation, Tempe.

44. "New, Promising Campaign to Preserve Camelback Mountain Begins," *Arizona Republic,* October 10, 1965.

45. "Save Camelback Meeting Tonight," *Arizona Republic,* October 26, 1965.

46. Margaret Kober collection.

47. Margaret Kober collection.

48. Margaret Kober collection.

49. Tuan, *Topophilia,* 224.

50. *Voice of Motorola,* December 15, 1965.

51. *Phoenix Gazette,* January 3, 1966.

52. *Arizona Republic,* October 30, 1965.

53. "Barry Blares Out for Camelback," *Arizona Republic,* December 18, 1965.

54. Box 2-74.10, Folder 1, Save Camelback collection, Arizona Historical Society, Central Arizona Division, Tempe.

55. Margaret Kober collection.

56. Margaret Kober collection.

57. *Phoenix Gazette,* April 22, 1966.

58. "Council Seeks Grant to Buy Camelback Top," *Arizona Republic,* December 14, 1966.

59. Harold R. Cousland, "Camelback Gets Fund Priority," *Arizona Republic,* August 2, 1967.

60. Cousland, "Camelback Gets Fund Priority."

61. Clarence W. Bailey, "Camelback's Hump Spared by Funds," *Arizona Republic,* August 23, 1967.

62. *Arizona Republic,* May 29, 1968.

63. Phoenix City Council, Resolution Number 13059.

64. Lively, *The Legend of Camelback Mountain,* 13.

65. Barry Goldwater, interview by G. Wesley Johnson, November 16, 1978, Phoenix History Project, Arizona Historical Society, Central Arizona Division, Tempe.

A Conversation with Richard Moe

Richard Moe is president of National Trust for Historic Preservation (www.nthp.org).

Explain your personal interest in preservation. What motivated you to get involved with the National Trust for Historic Preservation?

Moe: It was entirely unplanned and unanticipated. I was practicing law here in Washington after I left the White House, and in the late 1980s early 1990s, I decided that I wanted to pursue an interest I had in American history, so I wrote a book about the Minnesota Regiment that served in the Civil War. They had a very tragic experience at Gettysburg, and I read the letters and diaries, and in the course of researching this book, I discovered how so many Civil War battlefields were endangered, mostly by sprawl, and I got on the board of the Civil War Trust, which was in the business of protecting Civil War battlefields.

It was just a short jump from there to the National Trust because the chairman of that group was on the search committee of the National Trust looking for a new president, and he encouraged me to think about this, and I did. I hadn't really thought of preservation earlier, but once I learned more about the Trust, it became an immediate attraction to me as another form of public service. So I've been here almost nine years now and feel very strongly about the mission of this organization.

What criteria are used to determine the worthiness, so to speak, of preserving buildings, monuments, and open space? The notion of being historically significant is somewhat subjective.

Moe: It is subjective. Now, in order to be listed with the National Registrar, a structure must be fifty years old and have either architectural or historical significance, so there are pretty clear definitions of what that means. But, much more importantly in terms of what each community or each individual wants to preserve, that's in the eye of the beholder, and it is subjective as you say. What we try to do is to encourage every community to preserve what it views as important to its heritage and to determine significance on its own.

In the past fifty years, many of the newer developments have included such things as malls, fast-food places, mom-and-pop gas stations, drive-in movie theaters, this sort of thing. Do you think these kinds of developments would be worthy of preserving or protecting in the next fifty years?

Moe: That's for another generation to decide. We did help to preserve the first McDonald's down in California, but that was because it was emblematic of that particular phenomenon (we're not trying to save all McDonald's). So I don't think the strip malls that we see occupying so many highway interchanges today will be preserved or should be preserved.

They're not meant to last or built to last like so much of what we see going up today. We're building these things to last only for a certain amount of time. And they're unattractive, and they're built to get people's attention as you're driving by. It's all fashioned around the automobile culture.

You said that preservation isn't about saving buildings or necessarily protecting buildings; it's about lives and livelihoods. Can you expand on that a bit?

Moe: What it really means is that saving historic buildings or historic neighborhoods is important in and of itself, but it's more important in terms of contributing to the livability of communities. We think that communities are a lot better off by having within their midst older structures, older neighborhoods that can not only allow people to commune with their past but which can continue to contribute to the vitality and the culture of the community by bringing great architecture and interesting structures. It's a mix.

I know you've also quoted the economist Robert Solow's comment that livability is not some middle-class luxury but an economic imperative.

Moe: That's right. That's increasingly true because people now have a lot of choices as to where they can live. Companies have a lot of choices as to where they can locate. Livability is more important to more people now than ever before. We know people want to live in attractive, livable communities. So if the community wants to thrive or even survive, it has to pay attention to what people want in those communities, and increasingly people want pedestrian-friendly, attractive communities where they don't have to drive everywhere.

Who are your heroes? Beside yourself, whom would you consider the national or local leaders who are really leading the way and coming up with innovative policies and really trying to invigorate downtown?

Moe: That's a really good question. I don't get asked that often enough. The list of my heroes has to include those preservationists who really discovered how to use preservation as a tool to revitalize older communities, and that includes people like Arthur Ziegler and Stanley Lowe from Pittsburgh, Lee Adler from Savannah, and many others of that generation. There are a number of those individuals, many of who are still around but, back in the 1950s, 1960s, and 1970s, were pioneers.

Today there are a lot of people who are advocating this. Fortunately, we have a much larger and more effective movement and organization all over the country. But there are a number of public leaders giving a real voice to this, and Governor Glendening of Maryland is an outstanding example of someone who gets it. I mean he really invented smart growth as far as I'm concerned. He's shown the way. It's not a perfect solution that he's initiated, but it's better than anything else that has [been] tried in the last twenty-five years. I mean he realizes that smart growth does not just involve saving open space but involves revitalizing older communities.

[In order to] stop the demand for sprawl, he came up with this brilliant strategy of saying, We're not going to subsidize sprawl. You can build wherever you want, but don't look for state support for roads, schools, [and] structures, unless you do it in existing communities and those places designated for growth.

III

Development, Equity, and Policy Options: Theory and Cases

ONE QUESTION FACING CRITICS, scholars, and practitioners interested in reforming dominant strategies of suburban development is, What is to be done? While critics of sprawl have existed since the inception of modern suburbanization, it is only in the past decade that the issue has attained a sustained level of prominence in national and local policy debates. Contemporary sprawl did not appear overnight. The character of our suburban landscapes has developed over a long period of time, and its dimensions and appearance have been influenced by conscious political decisions backed by substantial appropriations. Additionally, sprawl cannot be looked at in isolation from our corporate capitalist economy. Dominant patterns of sprawl create numerous opportunities for a variety of very powerful forces that may not be interested in upsetting the status quo. Automobile manufacturers, the energy industry, housing developers, manufacturers, and retailers are just a few of the special interests that profit from dominant patterns of sprawl.

In the final part of this volume, we seek to assess the prospects for managing sprawl from a variety of perspectives. Mindful of the historical conditions that inform contemporary predicaments, we combine case studies with general critiques of the policies that facilitate sprawl. This approach encourages the development of a structural understanding of the phenomenon of sprawl, but it also illuminates the specific and varied ways different communities have met the challenges posed by sprawling suburbanization. As with the previous parts, the interviews with diverse practitioners provide insight into the latest thinking and actions of individuals directly engaged with managing the contemporary sprawled frontier.

In chapter 9, Patricia E. Salkin looks at the legal aspects of the legislating of metropolitan growth. The movement for smart growth has taken on numerous proponents in recent years, and Salkin offers an assessment of how the U.S. legal context relating to private property rights makes growth legislation difficult to legally enact and defend. The historic relegation of land use control to local municipalities, furthermore, makes effective smart growth initiatives difficult to implement since such fragmented regulation and decision-making processes cannot adequately address the regional nature of sprawl. Salkin provides a comprehensive overview of ways that municipalities and states are trying to avoid the obstacles of municipal fragmentation in order to develop regional approaches toward managing metropolitan growth. These include voluntary programs such as "compact" planning and intermunicipal cooperation agreements that often include state incentives for regional management as well as the creation of special governing structures dedicated to managing a particular domain (such as transportation or a watershed) that encompasses multiple municipalities. Salkin also discusses the various initiatives from the federal government and state governments that encourage regional planning for growth.

In chapter 10, H. William Batt explains sprawl from an economic standpoint, arguing that it is an unnatural form of metropolitan development based on flawed understandings of land valuation. Policies of suburbanization have been driven by an overemphasis on the logic of mobility at the expense of accessibility. Batt cites literature in geography to argue that both mobility and accessibility are necessary for urban life but that the latter has been ignored. Resources are funneled toward encouraging mobility through the construction of highways and encouraging traffic, but the lack of concern for accessibility results in people having to travel farther away to access homes, workplaces, and centers of consumption. Batt suggests that the way to remedy the social costs of sprawl is to have pricing mechanisms that reflect the true costs of expansive land use. Because our contemporary sprawled environment privileges mobility to the detriment of accessibility, Batt argues that the true costs of mobility should be borne by transportation users. This arrangement would result in a much different form of suburban landscape.

In chapter 11, Mark Edward Braun provides a historical treatment of the metropolitan development of southeastern Wisconsin as a prototypical case study of the effects of particular policies that facilitated sprawl. Braun argues that "white flight" from Milwaukee, disinvestments in the urban core, and job movement created economic disadvantages for inner-city residents—whose changing demographics indicate a growing percentage of minorities—while simultaneously transforming the character of southeastern Wisconsin's once-flourishing agricultural communities. One of the policies highlighted by

Braun that contributed to this transformation was a disproportionate allocation of state highway funds to new highway construction. This occurred at the expense of the repair and maintenance of existing roadways—which were often situated closer to the region's urban core—and was undertaken without adequate development of public transportation alternatives. Simultaneously, an affordable housing crunch has ensued, as large minimum lot sizes mandated in some of Milwaukee's suburbs makes owning a home difficult for families with average household incomes. Braun critically assesses the role that locally mandated impact fees on new housing have in perpetuating affordable housing scarcity.

In chapter 12 on Atlanta, Ulf Zimmermann, Göktuğ Morçöl, and Bethany Stich provide a historical look at how this apotheosis of the sprawl city developed and analyze the current ways in which the issue of sprawl is being discussed and managed in the region. The authors argue that the recent creation of the Georgia Regional Transportation Authority (GRTA) follows Molotch's "growth machine" theory. This theory talks of how business leaders, who often are the cause of sprawl, will jump on the "smart-growth" bandwagon once the threat of zero growth presents itself. The chapter outlines the historical role business played in the politics of transportation and land use planning in Atlanta and documents the role of the business elite in the creation of the GRTA. In addition, it discusses the peculiar role race has played in the Atlanta metropolitan region's development and how the interests of business engaged in a complex balance of accommodation of African American interests while being cognizant of white suburban resentment of perceptions of African American political power. Ironically for the authors, the GRTA—while dominated by business interests—is a progressive force, particularly when seen within the context of local governmental officials' questioning of the GRTA's legitimacy. The implications of this chapter are important, for it challenges notions about the efficacy of grassroots initiatives at changing sprawling development without having the support of local elites.

The interviews chosen for this part emphasize the divergent opinions of practitioners and policymakers dealing with sprawl and urban development on a daily basis. Their varied perspectives speak to the complexity of sprawl and the various challenges faced in reforming dominant patterns of metropolitan development.

9

Smart Growth and the Law

Patricia E. Salkin

To best understand the legal underpinnings of smart growth, or the laws that regulate land use and development that can support sustainable development, it is important to examine the history of both the development of land use law in the United States and the historical development of the philosophy of landownership. Although both of these concepts are clearly separate and distinct, they seemingly merge when discussing the policies needed to support sustainable metropolitan growth and development.

The Concept of Landownership

The system of landownership in the United States has resulted in a widespread belief by individual property owners that title to the land (or a deed) is tantamount to a right to do whatever the owner desires with the property. Historically, government regulation over the use of property did little more than separate incompatible uses (such as separating residential areas from commercial areas). Even this limited measure of government regulation has met with resistance over the years from the growing property rights movement. Land use regulation and control in the United States fails to promote the notion that landowners are simply the stewards of the land for future generations, and the notion of a common public resource in privately owned land simply does not exist. Basic common law principles of waste (not destroying the rich resources of the land) are often irrelevant to landowners.

Little success has been achieved by public leadership addressing the environmental degradation of land. Following the Earth Summit, U.S. Senator Paul Simon (D-Ill.) remarked that "the responsibility to preserve our natural resources for future generations must become one of our highest priorities."[1] Unlike other countries where land use policies emanate from the national government, in the United States land use controls have been viewed by most states and by the federal government as a matter of local concern. This proved problematic immediately in the area of environmental protection and preservation as local governments almost uniformly failed to take into account regional needs and concerns regarding impacts on issues such as drinking water and air quality since it was not mandated.

The notion that land use controls and decision making are best left to local governments presents a challenge when admittedly the air and water pass through the arbitrary boundary lines drawn on a map. Restrictive covenants that prohibit the use of land in certain stated ways and siting decisions for what may be viewed as locally unwanted land uses resulted in settlement patterns whereby minority communities and communities of predominantly low-income individuals were located in industrial areas and other blighted areas that in hindsight have proven to pose varying degrees of health, safety, and welfare concerns (today, the environmental justice movement is attempting to address these issues). Furthermore, certain public infrastructure, such as highways and roads that have been built, are interjurisdictional, meaning that they cross over the political boundary lines of more than one unit of government. Whereas people once lived in the small communities where they worked, today people live and work in separate jurisdictions. The economic health of one community is dependent, for better and for worse, on its neighboring municipalities. Thus, to achieve economic, environmental, and social sustainability, the United States is forced to revisit the land use control system that has been at work for nearly a century.

The Early Foundation of Land Use Law and Zoning

The authority to control the use of land in the United States is typically passed by state governments to local governments through what are referred to as "enabling acts." Much of the current state planning and zoning enabling acts are based on 1920s-model statutes promulgated by the U.S. Department of Commerce under Secretary Herbert Hoover. Consider that more than eighty years later, cities, counties, towns, and villages are limited by the statutes that were enacted prior to television, computers, and massive expansion in our built-up infrastructure. The first zoning ordinances were enacted just at the start of the industrial revolution. Overcrowding in the cities was a paramount concern because it impacted numerous public health, safety, and welfare issues (such as the spread of disease and fire). There was relatively sparse development at the urban fringes, and in hindsight the challenges of the day were simple. The last decade has witnessed an unprecedented level of state legislative activity and interest in modernizing outdated planning and zoning enabling acts.[2]

A discussion of the political evolution of local environmental land use controls can begin only by starting with *Euclid v. Ambler,* the seminal U.S. Supreme Court decision that upheld the constitutionality of local zoning as a valid exercise of the police power (the power of government to enact laws to protect the public health, safety, and welfare). In the early part of the twentieth century, zoning was viewed as a means to an end—the end was to separate incompatible land uses because there was an inherent conflict between uses that were not identical (such as residential, agricultural, business, and commercial). This is referred to as "Euclidean zoning," which describes the historical use of zoning as merely a tool to separate what had been viewed as incompatible land uses.

Fast-forward approximately eighty years. The cities are on a continuing population decline. Infrastructure investments have shifted from the urban core to the suburban and rural communities. Where families were once lucky if they owned a car, today consumers demand two- and three-car attached garages. Manufacturing plants and other industrial facilities once located in the cities next to railroads and/or ports have found it more desirable and economical to relocate to suburban communities, and as a nation we consume acreage at a rapid rate far exceeding our population growth. Home owners and businesses in our suburban and rural communities desire fiber-optics cabling and other costly amenities to support the technology boom.

These changes are among those that have exposed the shortcomings of the early-model planning and zoning enabling acts. These acts reflect society in a very different generation. What may have seemed a rational approach to addressing issues such as overcrowding is simply incapable of addressing the loss of balance in the pursuit of sustainable land development. While it is true that across the country land use controls are viewed as a matter of local concern, municipalities possess only those powers given to them by the states. No matter how creative a city, town, or village desires to be, the statewide planning and zoning enabling act often presents a challenge for advocates who support change.

An effort to modernize these acts in the 1970s by the American Law Institute produced a publication, "A Model Land Development Code," but there was little practical impact realized from this work beyond the academic exercise of debating drafts and promulgating a model code. In reality, the model code became little more than a shelf document. Just as environmental statutes and regulations began to flourish at the federal and state levels, our country's planning and zoning enabling acts lay dormant. No significant connections were made early on between land use laws and environmental laws. Perhaps because these two types of regulation were initially conceived to address different problems at different times, they became for many years mutually independent.

At the dawn of the twenty-first century, the federal, state, and local governments, as well as the private and the nonprofit sectors, have begun to realize that achieving sustainable development means changing our land use policies. Sprawl has become the identified problem responsible for driving up the cost of infrastructure, raising both housing prices and local property taxes; eating up prime agricultural land and once-treasured green space; threatening the integrity of significant natural and cultural resources; and emasculating what is left of the urban core. Proof positive that the public has rallied around the antisprawl movement is evident from a recently released national poll by the Pew Center for Civic Journalism, which found that local concerns about sprawl and growth are now exceeding more traditional issues such as crime.[3] The smart-growth movement is proving to be, at least in rhetoric, not only the solution to correct the disorganized and inefficient system of land use controls of the past but also a framework to set a new paradigm for the future, one that merges land use law and environmental law.

Regional Planning in the United States

Brief Overview

A common thread in both the proposed and the recently enacted land use reform initiatives is the realization that the impacts of local land use decisions know no political boundaries. Addressing the political ramifications of upsetting a tradition of purely locally based land use decision making emanating from the model state and city planning and zoning enabling acts continues to be a challenge. Just how to balance the political need for interjurisdictional cooperation while respecting the valued tradition of local control with its attendant built-in intergovernmental tensions and rivalries is a monumental task, one that often presents a barrier to meaningful land use reform.[4]

States have taken varied approaches to dealing with the concept of regionalism in land use control. For example, some states have opted to mandate that local governments work together to achieve horizontal consistency while at the same time mandating that all levels of government (local, regional, and state) work together to achieve vertical consistency. Other states choose not to mandate regional cooperation but rather authorize various forms of regional or intermunicipal arrangements that may be created at local option. There is no one best way to address the issue of regionalism other than to find the best methods that will be acceptable within the political landscape of each state and region. Presented next is a brief discussion of some of the history of regional land use planning in the United States, followed by some examples of how intermunicipal cooperation may be achieved across the country.

The Quiet Revolution

As a result of the growing interest in addressing environmental concerns, some states began to adopt major land use reform in the 1970s.[5] The result was a "quiet revolution"[6] in land use law wherein states, including Vermont (1970 and 1988), Florida (1972 and 1985), Oregon (1973), and Hawaii (1978), made significant modifications to their systems of land use control, giving more power to the regional and state governments to deal with environmental protection through land use controls. Four more states made reforms in the 1980s (New Jersey, 1985; Maine, 1988; Rhode Island, 1988; and Georgia, 1988). The interest in and lessons learned from these early experiments led to the creation of the modern smart-growth movement promoting the reform of state and local land use laws to address more directly the continued need to balance land development with notions of sustainable economic development and environmental protection. One notable difference is that the reforms of the 1970s and 1980s yielded state legislative efforts that gave the states a greater role in what had traditionally been purely locally based land use decision making.[7] Today, the smart-growth movement focuses more on bottom-up than on top-down processes. Under these approaches, the states provide authorization, guidance, and incentives to local governments to promote better local land use planning and decision making to, among other things, protect environmental interests.

Different Types of Legal Arrangements

This section offers a review of some of the different methods that could promote intermunicipal cooperation in land use planning. The one common theme in each of the items discussed is that participation by municipalities is voluntary. While this approach is politically more appealing—as it may, among other things, serve to protect home-rule interests and facilitate local decision making—it does not guarantee that regional planning will occur. A majority of the states have said that if local governments desire to work together, then they can, and that if local governments do not wish to work together, then so be it.

This approach, of course, may not be as successful in achieving sustainable development as a more hands-on approach to requiring regional cooperation and partnerships.

Compact Planning

Compact planning, a voluntary agreement whereby local governments agree to plan consistently with one another and with regionwide vision, offers a viable option in the search to redefine the local role in planning in the context of regional and statewide concerns. Most recently, New York State has been experimenting with a regional planning and land use management approach called the "compact" for the Hudson River Valley Greenway[8] and the Long Island Pine Barrens.[9] Somewhat similar to these applications of the compact approach has been the planning process and implementation of the New York City Watershed Agreement, which created watershed protection programs addressing land use and economic issues for a 2,000-square-mile, mostly rural watershed area serving the New York City water supply system.[10] This regional plan and program is a compact negotiated between the governor, New York City, upstate watershed communities, certain environmental organizations, and the U.S. Environmental Protection Agency.

Compact areas may be defined to be geographic regions or areas based on environmental, economic, and social factors. Typically, units of local government within the compact area voluntarily agree to form a compact where they express the good-faith intentions to work together to make planning and zoning decisions in accordance with an agreed-on "compact plan." In the case of New York, the only state to specifically authorize some compact planning, the state provides certain incentives to the municipalities for their voluntary participation. Incentives may be grants, technical assistance, indemnification from lawsuits, and other desirable rewards.

Intermunicipal Cooperative Arrangements

Every state, either through its constitution or via statute, authorizes local governments to enter into voluntary intermunicipal agreements. These agreements, which essentially are negotiated contracts among and between two or more units of local government, may address issues such as the development of a joint comprehensive land use plan, the establishment of a joint planning or zoning board, or the sharing of a professional planner. Unlike the compact approach that offers state incentives for participation, intermunicipal cooperative agreements tend to materialize because enlightened local officials realize cost savings, economies of scale, and a better use of resources with a regional picture in mind. Other examples of state laws that promote regionalism are the authority to voluntarily establish planning federations (these may be groups of counties that get together for education, training, and technical assistance), the authority to contract out for services from another municipality (for example, a small village might contract with the county planning department for technical expertise), and the establishment of regional planning agencies (appointed agencies with representatives from two or more counties that typically function as information gatherers and disseminators and that may be asked to develop regional plans). Again, all these approaches offer voluntary ways for municipalities to work together.

Special-Purpose Regional Planning

When states create special "regional" government entities to protect and preserve significant natural and environmental resources, this is a form of special-purpose regional planning. From the Tahoe Regional Planning Agency in California and Nevada to the New Jersey Pinelands Commission and the Adirondack Park Agency in New York, there are hundreds of examples across the country of special state laws creating new government entities vested with sometimes broad land use control powers to protect a certain stretch of land or habitat. Greenway trails and heritage corridors are additional examples of where government might create specialized commissions to protect and preserve significant scenic vistas or environmentally sensitive areas and/or to create ways in which the public might access these natural resources. The powers and duties of these special-purpose agencies are as diverse and varied as the states and regions.

Smart Growth for the Twenty-First Century

The Role of the Federal Government

While this chapter begins with the understanding that the legal environment of land use controls is something that is delegated from the states to the local governments, there is an important role for the federal government in the smart-growth arena. Specifically, the federal government has long had involvement "influencing" the activities of state and local governments in areas critical to sustainable development, such as the environment, housing, and transportation. The federal involvement may be through laws and regulations that require compliance with certain activities. Perhaps more subtle and powerful are federal government subsidies and funding opportunities that require state and local governments to behave in certain ways in order to reap the economic reward. Following are some historical examples of these different approaches.

National Environmental Policy Act

In 1969, Congress enacted the National Environmental Policy Act (NEPA), which sets forth a framework for considering the environmental impacts of certain government decision making. In general, while the strength of the law is in the process it provides for environmental review, its enforcement by the courts has been somewhat weak.[11] The Council on Environmental Quality, the entity responsible for implementing the NEPA, has examined sprawl and smart-growth issues in the past. For example, in 1974, the council released a report titled "The Costs of Sprawl," which studied the impacts of sprawl.[12] In 1981, the council, in its "National Agricultural Lands Study," examined the loss of agricultural lands due to sprawl.[13] Currently, a legislative proposal has been introduced that will require the council to update these studies and analyze how well recent environmental impact assessments and environmental assessments have examined the impacts of proposed federal actions on growth and suburban sprawl.[14]

Recognizing that the NEPA was limited in scope to environmental impacts and that, while this was important and necessary, it was only part of the solution, Senator Henry Jackson introduced legislation titled the National Land Use Policy Act (NLUPA).[15] The proposal, meant to be a bookend with the NEPA, was buried after it twice passed the U.S. Senate but failed to win support in the House of Representatives.[16] The NLUPA would have provided states with incentives in the form of funding for the purpose of preparing state land use plans. It would also have established a national data system that would have given state and local governments access to data for the purposes of sound land use planning. The NLUPA also would have established a single federal agency to ensure that all other federal agencies were complying with state plans.

The HUD 701 Program

Under the 1954 Housing Act, the Section 701 planning grant program of the U.S. Department of Housing and Urban Development (HUD) promoted urban planning by providing money to the states for the development of regional and local comprehensive land use plans.[17] The 1965 Housing and Urban Development Act, which created HUD to coordinate urban planning at the federal level,[18] extended and expanded the Section 701 grants. Although funding through this program has long dried up, congressional efforts in 2000 and 2001 to pass the Community Character Act (discussed later in this chapter) would in many ways reintroduce this initiative.

Department of Transportation

With the enactment of the Federal Highway Act in 1921,[19] the stage was set for the building of more than 200,000 miles of road, which represented just the beginning of the interstate highway system that critics have argued has had a long-term negative effect on our cities and that has contributed significantly to sprawl. Under the Eisenhower administration, the Interstate Highway Act was enacted in 1958 creating, among other things, a 41,000-mile highway system with 90 percent of the costs for construction and maintenance borne by the federal government.[20] In terms of investment dollars, the federal government has historically spent more money on the construction of new roads than on public transit, with recent spending on roads outstripping transit by almost 5 to 1.[21] Today, the national highway system consists of 120,229 miles of rural highways and 45,826 miles of interstate highways.[22]

Transportation policies have contributed to sprawl by a providing a steady stream of funding to support the construction of highways and roads. Although this activity provided jobs, "government's obsession with road building has degraded cities and accelerated suburban sprawl . . . by physical destruction of city neighborhoods and by making suburban life more convenient."[23]

Department of the Interior

Within the Department of the Interior, a number of federal bureaus are housed that have all contributed to the growth of the country and that impact our land development patterns. For example, in 1946, the department's General Land Office and the Grazing Service (resulting from the 1934 Taylor Grazing Act) were merged into the Bureau of Land Management, an office that now administers 264 million acres of public lands in twelve western states. The Fish and Wildlife Service was created in 1940, and today this bureau manages approximately ninety-three million acres of land, including coastal lands.[24] Classifying itself as the "Nation's Principal Conservation Agency," the Department of the Interior today manages approximately 20 percent of the land in the United States in the form of public lands, parks, and refuges. The magnitude of the land management by the department through its various bureaus sets the stage for important smart-growth, conservation, and sprawl-related policies through a regulatory agenda and funding for various programs and initiatives.

Department of Defense

Often an overlooked player in the land development and conservation communities, the Department of Defense is one of the largest landholders in the United States with approximately thirty million acres under its management.[25] The impact of these holdings on community development, smart growth, and environmental conservation has been great over the years. With 250 military bases scheduled for closure since 1988, the federal government has turned over extensive land areas to communities who have been challenged to craft reuse and development strategies, particularly in light of potential serious environmental problems on some of the lands.

Other

Scholars have documented myriad federal laws and programs that affect state and local land use, including federal spending on highways, tax benefits and mortgage insurance, inner-city housing, urban renewal, block grants, and enterprise and empowerment zones.[26] In addition to spending programs that clearly influence land use, various agencies have promoted preservation efforts that, while laudable in public purpose, fail to produce anything other than a disconnected and haphazard puzzle of preserved parcels sprinkled across the landscape.

For example, commentators have criticized as pro-suburban the government's policies in the areas of housing, transportation, and education.[27] In fairness, however, these may have been well-intentioned programs that simply produced the unintended results of urban decay. For example, Federal Housing Administration (FHA) mortgage insurance programs during the New Deal era guaranteed home loans only in areas that were "low risk" and, by definition, not inner-city properties.[28] Furthermore, the FHA policies favored new construction as opposed to renovations, and programs that followed under the guise of urban renewal resulted in "white flight" from the cities by infusing capital to the poor and by building public housing in the once-vibrant cities.[29]

There are a host of other examples of how policies and programs from federal agencies over the years have demonstrated profound impacts on sustainable development.

Policies Designed to Specifically Preempt State and Local Land Use Decision Making

A number of federal laws and agency regulations limit and/or preempt local government land use decision making. This is exemplified most recently by the Religious Land Use and Institutionalized Persons Act of 2000, a law prohibiting any government from imposing or implementing a land use regulation in a manner that imposes a substantial burden on the religious exercise of a person, including a religious assembly or institution, unless the government demonstrates that imposition of the burden on that person, assembly, or institution 1) is in furtherance of a compelling governmental interest and 2) is the least restrictive means of furthering that compelling governmental interest.[30] Traditionally, state common law has guided municipal decision making on land use issues that involve the siting, alteration, and expansion of religious uses.

The Telecommunications Act of 1996 offers a mechanism to fast-track the siting of thousands of wireless towers across the national landscape.[31] The Fair Housing Act Amendments of 1988 place a number of restrictions on local governments' ability to decide on the siting of group homes and other traditionally locally unwanted land uses.[32] Other federal laws that impact state and local land use regulations include the Americans with Disabilities Act, the Clean Air Act, the Clean Water Act, ISTEA, and TEA-21. While these are not discussed in this chapter, they are noted to make the point that a litany of federal laws and implementing regulations affect and restrict state and local land use decision making.

The Appropriate Federal Role in Land Use Reform

The most appropriate role for the federal government in land use issues is embodied not in a national zoning scheme but rather in facilitating community planning through technical assistance, guidelines, and funding. There is no doubt that a need exists for more comprehensive federal legislation on land use.[33] Can Congress provide funding and necessary assistance without its guidelines crossing the line from guidance to directives?

The Proposed Community Character Act

In April and May 2001, Representative Earl Blumenauer (D-Ore.) and Senator Lincoln Chafee (R-R.I.) introduced the Community Character Act of 2001 (HR 1433/S 975) "to assist States with land use planning in order to promote improved quality of life, regionalism, sustainable economic development, and environmental stewardship." Reiterating the federal government's belief that land use planning should be conducted at the state and local level, the act asserts that there is an important role for the federal government in supporting state and local comprehensive planning and community development.[34]

The two bills have a common goal of revamping outmoded land use policy; however, the programs would be administered differently. The Senate bill charges the secretary of commerce with the responsibility of establishing a program to award grants to the states. In the House bill, the HUD secretary is responsible for enacting the program. Both bills cap an award to $1 million. However, under the Senate bill, the secretary may award an additional $100,000 to fund pilot programs. The cap was raised over the 2000 proposal, which would have authorized grants only up to $500,000 to states for the purpose of assisting in the development or revision of land use planning legislation in the states where the enabling acts are inadequate or outmoded; and, as a second priority, for states that do have updated land use planning legislation, the grants could support the creation or revision of state comprehensive land use plans or plan elements.[35] Either way, the Community Character Act represents a potential annual appropriation of $50 million.

To be eligible for funding, the act requires that states demonstrate consistency with the following: citizen participation in the development, adoption, and updating of land use plans; a routine schedule of plan updates; multijurisdictional cooperation in the development of the plans to provide for resource sustainability; an implementation element in the state plan that provides timetables for action, definition of roles, consistency with state capital budget objectives, and future infrastructure needs; land use plans that are consistent with established professional planning standards; and comprehensive planning that would 1) promote sustainable economic development and social equity; 2) enhance community character; 3) coordinate transportation, housing, education, and social equity; 4) conserve historic resources, scenic resources, and the environment; and 5) sustainably manage natural resources.

A congressional hearing on the Community Character Act was held on March 6, 2002, before the Senate Committee on Environment and Public Works.[36] Senator Lincoln Chafee, a cosponsor of the bill, reiterated the belief that land use control is best left to the state and local levels.[37] He pointed out that "through enactment of numerous and often-times incompatible laws regarding transportation, housing, environment, energy, and economic development, the federal government has created a demand for state and local planning."[38] Not everyone is enthusiastic, however, about the proposed act. David A. Sampson, assistant secretary for economic development at the U.S. Department of Commerce, testified that "the Administration cannot support S. 975 because it calls for resources that are not included in the President's budget to support activities that can be accomplished through existing authorities and appropriations, and a centralized approach to land use planning is not the most effective solution to address issues of sprawl and unfocused economic development."[39] The assistant secretary may have misunderstood the proposed legislation in that it does support and enable a decentralized local land use planning and control function by providing the necessary funding to facilitate better planned and more strategic land development.

Elizabeth Humstone, executive director of the Vermont Forum on Sprawl, testifying on behalf of the American Planning Association, pointed out that "unlike the Hoover model, the Community Character Act does not suggest imposing a single model on all of the states but rather supports reform and implementation that is developed based on the unique needs and context of individual states and communities."[40] She makes the environmental connection in explaining the reason for the act's strong support, offering, "It responds to widespread citizen interest in smart growth by providing critical resources to help state and local leaders, business and environmental interests, and concerned citizens bring about positive change in their communities through better planning."[41] Humstone pointed out the need to promote multi-state cooperation on these issues "because natural resources, watershed, city borders, and development impacts do not stop at artificial political boundaries."[42] She reminded the committee that Environmental Protection Agency Administrator Christie Todd Whitman expressed administration support when she remarked, "Addressing new environmental challenges requires us to manage all of our resources better—economic, social and environmental—and manage them for the long term. That is why Smart Growth is so important—it is critical to economic growth, the development of healthy communities, and the protection of our environment all at the same time. The Bush Administration—and the EPA especially—understands the importance of Smart Growth."[43]

On April 25, 2002, the Senate committee approved the act by a vote of 12 to 7.[44] Voting in favor of the measure were Republican Senators Lincoln Chafee (R.I.) and Arlen Specter (Pa.) and Democratic Senators Max Baucus (Mont.), Harry Reid (Nev.), Bob Graham (Fla.), Joseph Lieberman (Conn.), Barbara Boxer (Calif.), Ron Wyden (Ore.), Thomas Carper (Del.), Hillary Rodham Clinton (N.Y.), Jon Corzine (N.J.), and James Jeffords (Vt.).[45] It is worth noting that there have been significant smart-growth reforms introduced and/or enacted in each of the states that these members represent. Senators who voted against the act at the committee meeting included the remaining Republican members of the committee: Michael Crapo (Id.), Ben Nighthorse Campbell (Colo.), Christopher Bond (Mo.), George Voinovich (Ohio), Robert Smith (N.H.), James Inhofe (Okla.),[46] and John Warner (Va.).[47] None of these votes were surprising based on the national "state of the states" research recently completed by the American Planning Association,[48] except for the senator from Colorado, who seemed to go against the smart-growth movement in his state.

The Role of State Governments

Leadership for Reform Starts with Governors and State Legislators

In just the past two years, there have been thirteen gubernatorial executive orders promulgated to address the issues of growth and development within the states. Noteworthy is the fact that this interest is bipartisan in nature. Six of the executive orders were issued by Democratic governors and seven by Republican governors. The executive orders exemplify different approaches to managing smart-growth reform. In some states, the executive order was used to create a task force or study commission,[49] in other states it was used to require state agencies to submit smart-growth implementation plans to the governor,[50] and in other states it was used to follow up on and monitor recently enacted smart-growth legislation.[51]

The statistics regarding the level of reform activity across the country are astounding. The following is from a summary report of the American Planning Association:

- Approximately one-quarter of the states are implementing moderate to substantial statewide comprehensive planning reforms (these states include Delaware, Florida, Georgia, Maryland, New Jersey, Oregon, Pennsylvania, Rhode Island, Tennessee, Vermont, Washington, and Wisconsin).
- One-fifth of the states are pursuing additional statewide amendments strengthening local planning requirements or are working to improve regional or local planning reforms already adopted (these states include Arizona, California, Hawaii, Maine, Nevada, New Hampshire, New York, Texas, Utah, and Virginia).
- Nearly one-third of the states are actively pursuing their first major statewide planning reforms for effective smart growth (these states include Arkansas, Colorado, Connecticut, Idaho, Illinois, Iowa, Kentucky, Massachusetts, Michigan, Minnesota, Mississippi, Missouri, New Mexico, North Carolina, and South Carolina).
- Approximately one-quarter of the states have not made and are not currently pursuing significant statewide planning reforms (these states include Alabama, Alaska, Indiana, Kansas, Louisiana, Montana, Nebraska, North Dakota, Ohio, Oklahoma, South Dakota, West Virginia, and Wyoming).[52]

Growing Smart: The Legislative Guidebook

In January 2002, the American Planning Association released its long-awaited *Growing Smart Legislative Guidebook: Model Statutes for Planning and the Management of Change* (available on-line at www.planning.org). This two-volume reference book is the culmination of a seven-year effort to study and build consensus on new models for state planning and zoning enabling legislation. Funded through a combination of public, private, and nonprofit support, this document promises to be the seminal resource on land use regulation during this century. The model statutory language offered throughout the document is "intended to provide governors, state legislators, state legislative research bureaus, local elected and appointed officials, planners, citizens, and advocates for statutory change with ideas, principles, methods, procedures, phraseology, and alternative legislative approaches drawn from various states, regions and local governments across the country."

The introduction offers an eleven-point philosophy that guided the drafting of the document:

1. There is no single "one size fits all" model for planning statutes.
2. Model statutes should provide for planning that goes beyond the shaping and guidance of physical development.
3. Model statutes should build on the strengths of existing organizations that undertake and implement planning.
4. Planning statute reform should look not just at regulation but also at provision of infrastructure and property taxation.
5. Model statutes should account for the intergovernmental dimension of planning and development control.
6. Model statutes should prescribe the substantive content of plans.
7. Model statutes should anticipate the potential for abuse of planning tools and correct for it.
8. Model statutes should use familiar terminology.
9. Model statutes should expressly provide for citizen involvement.
10. Model statutes should allow flexibility in planning administration.
11. Model statutes should be based on an appraisal of what has worked.[53]

The *Guidebook* also provides a checklist of what can be accomplished through statutory reform. The following seven goals for statutory planning and zoning enabling law reform are identified:

1. Certainty and efficiency in the development review and approval process can be improved.
2. Statutes will contain a mix of carrots and sticks to promote planning.
3. People affected by the planning process can be involved early in the process.
4. Plans can address the interrelationships of employment, housing, fiscal impacts, transportation, environment, and social equity.

5. Governments are empowered with a range of planning tools to manage growth and change locally to create quality communities.
6. The timing, location, and intensity of development can be linked to existing or planned infrastructure.
7. Mechanisms to monitor the ongoing performance of planning systems can be created.[54]

Organized into fifteen chapters, the *Guidebook* maintains that it is important to reform planning enabling legislation because of today's more significant intergovernmental dimension for planning, a marked shift in society's view of land, a more active citizenry, and a more challenging legal environment.[55] Major topics covered in the *Guidebook* address the planning process and implementing plans (at the state, regional, and local levels), development controls (including zoning, subdivision, site plan, uniform development standards, vested rights, nonconforming uses, and development agreements), siting of state facilities, infrastructure and capital improvement plans, special and environmental land development regulations and incentives (such as historic preservation, transfer of development rights, conservation easements, purchase of development rights), mitigation, administration and judicial review of land use decisions enforcement, taxation, financing planning, geographic information systems, and public records.

Will Growing Smart Make a Difference? The short answer is yes. The *Growing Smart Legislative Guidebook* will and has already had an impact on state land use reform. Although the final version of the *Guidebook* was released in January 2002, the American Planning Association released a first interim edition in 1996 and a second interim edition in 1998. In just over the five years that have passed since the early publication of a working draft, it has been easy to track the profound impact of the documents as assessed through adopted statutory language in many state statutes.

Planning for Smart Growth: 2002 State of the States (available at www.planning.org) reports on the recent trends and extent of legislative efforts to reform outdated planning and zoning enabling legislation. The report identifies eight trends that consistently emerged in state activities related to planning and smart-growth reform. For example, implementing recently enacted reforms has proven to be an ongoing challenge as many states continue to work toward full implementation that balances competing needs and interests. Identifying and sustaining political leadership has proven critical to realizing meaningful reform. State governors and key legislators must commit to staying with the process for the long haul and not lose interest after the first couple of years. Linking smart-growth planning reforms with issues such as traffic congestion, housing, affordability, environmental protection, and other quality-of-life issues has helped secure a spot for the issues on the various government reform platforms. To better ensure success, coalitions have been built and time has been expended to develop consensus among the various stakeholders. Many states have opted to create task forces and commissions to further study the issues and offer recommendations for further action. There has been an increased level of citizen activity at the ballot box on smart-growth-related initiatives, indicating that if government is not yet prepared to move forward, their constituents are happy to push the agenda in another arena. Although many would advocate for a comprehensive overhaul to planning and zoning enabling acts in one fell swoop, the fact remains that most of the states have made progress through a piecemeal approach to statutory reform. Finally, there has been the need to offer some responses to backlash from groups that are of the opinion that land use reforms may impinge on property rights.

The Role of Local Governments

Local governments—our counties, cities, towns, and villages—in most instances control the ability to make real grassroots change happen. While it is true that state governments have a role to play in providing appropriate legislative authority to the local governments and it is true that the federal government could assist by providing coordinated incentives to promote appropriate modifications and reforms, the bottom line is that in most states the land use planning and land use decision-making controls are legally viewed as matters of "local concern." The notion of "home rule" is important in the control of land use because in home-rule states, local governments are empowered to tend to their "local property, affairs, and government." The concept of home rule is sometimes used by local governments as an impediment to smart growth, as it can be used to prevent neighboring local governments from having input into land use decision making. It is also used effectively in some states to prevent state legislators from enacting laws that would require or seriously promote intergovernmental cooperation.

A second impediment to the ability of local governments to implement meaningful land use reforms is the "not in my backyard" (NIMBY) syndrome. While it is true that local government is governance closest to the people, a corollary follows that local government officials will most often do what their constituents who sent them into public service demand of them to do. While political scientists discuss and debate the delegate and trustee methods of how elected officials represent those who elected them, the fact remains that, as former Speaker of the House Tip O'Neill so aptly put it, "all politics is local." Just as landowners in a town are more likely to know personally the supervisor or a member of a town body (as opposed to their state and federal legislators), people can put more political pressure on their local officials to carry out the wishes of the "vocal majority." These are too often self-promoting goals that fail to take into account regional and statewide needs, as local landowners tend to focus on "what's in it for me?" and "how will this action affect my property value?"

On the positive side, however, local governments present thousands of laboratories for experimentation with smart-growth policies. The fact remains that local governments are empowered to make a difference. They have tremendous authority and flexibility to be innovative with design standards, coordinated reviews, and decision making that is coordinated in the best interests of the neighborhood and region. In fact, local governments are limited only by their own creativity. Many grassroots groups that support and promote smart-growth activities are just now starting to document and offer case studies on successful local smart-growth initiatives.

Conclusion

The United States is experiencing a major overhaul in its land use system in large part because of the activities of the smart-growth movement. Because the system of land use control in the United States is fragmented at the local government level, benchmarking actual meaningful progress will require more time. While clearly the federal government has promoted sustainable land use policies through some funding and technical assistance, the major responsibility rests with state governments to provide workable statutory frameworks that both enable and encourage local implementation of sustainable land development laws and policies. Through the smart-growth movement, states are just starting to do their part to at least "talk the talk" of sustainable land use. It remains to be seen whether enough states and the political jurisdictions therein will "walk the talk" to truly create sustainable communities where economic, environmental, and social policies are fairly integrated into the decision-making landscape. Smart growth is about the law—seeking legislative and sometimes regulatory reforms so that together we can grow with the land and leave a legacy of green space and lands that allow for sustainability for the future generations.

Notes

This chapter is a compilation of various sections from Patricia Salkin's recent writings on smart-growth issues. The works used in assembling this chapter are from the following sources:

Salkin, Patricia. "From Euclid to Growing Smart: The Transformation of the American Local Land Use Ethic into Local Land Use and Environmental Controls." *Pace Environmental Law Review* (Spring 2002).

———. "Land Use." In *Stumbling Toward Sustainability*, ed. John C. Dernbach (Washington, D.C.: ELI, 2002).

———. "The Next Generation of Planning & Zoning Enabling Acts Is on the Horizon: 2002 Growing Smart Legislative Guidebook Is a Must-Read for Land Use Practitioners." *Real Estate Law Journal* 30, no. 353 (Spring 2002).

———. "The Smart Growth Agenda: A Snapshot of State Activity at the Turn of the Century." *St. Louis Public Law Review* 21, no. 2 (Spring 2002).

———. "Smart Growth and Sustainable Development: Threads of a National Land Use Policy." *Valparaiso Law Review* 36, no. 1 (Spring 2002).

Salkin, Patricia and Paul Bray. "Compact Planning Offers a Fresh Approach for Regional Planning and Smart Growth: A New York Model." *Real Estate Law Journal* 30, no. 121 (Fall 2001).

1. Senator Paul Simon, "Introduction," in *Agenda 21: The Earth Summit Strategy to Save Our Planet*, ed. Daniel Sitarz (Boulder, Colo.: EarthPress 1994), x.

2. See generally American Planning Association, "Planning for Smart Growth: 2002 State of the States—A Survey of State Planning Reforms and Smart Growth Measures in Order to Manage Growth and Development" (February 2002) (Denny Johnson, Patricia Salkin, Jason Jordan, and Karen Finucan, coauthors).

3. "Managing Growth Is a Major Interest of Governors in Their State-of-the-State Addresses," National Governor's Association Online, at www.nga.org/Releases/SOS2000224 (accessed March 1, 2000). See generally www.nga.org/center/topics/1,188,c_CENTER_ISSUE^D_404,00.html (accessed July 23, 2002).

4. Douglas Porter, "Reinventing Growth Management for the 21st Century," *William & Mary Environmental Law and Policy Review* 23, no. 705 (Fall 1999).

5. See John M. DeGrove, "The Emergence of State Planning and Growth Management Systems: An Overview," in *State and Regional Comprehensive Planning: Implementing New Methods for Growth Management*, ed. Peter A. Buchsbaum and Larry J. Smith (Chicago: ABA Press, 1993); see also George W. Liebman, "The Modernization of Zoning: Enabling Act Revision as a Means to Reform," *The Urban Lawyer* 23, no. 1 (1991).

6. See Fred Bosselman and David Callies, *The Quiet Revolution in Land Use Control* (Washington, D.C.: Council on Environmental Quality, 1971).

7. For an excellent review and comparison of growth management programs in seven states (Florida, Georgia, Maryland, New Jersey, Oregon, Tennessee, and Washington), see Department of Community Affairs (Fla.), *Growth Management Programs: A Comparison of Selected States* (July 31, 2000), www.floridagrowth.org (accessed July 23, 2002).

8. Act of December 31, 1991, chap. 748, sec. 10, 1991 N.Y. Laws 1451 (codified at New York Environmental Conservation Law, secs. 44-0101 et seq.).

9. Act of July 25, 1990, chap. 814, sec. 1, 1990 N.Y. Laws 1645, 1646 (codified at New York Environmental Conservation Law, sec. 57-0103).

10. See David Markell, "Lessons from the New York City Watershed Agreement," *Environmental Outlook* 2, no. 2 (Winter 1996).

11. Matthew Lindstrom, *The National Environmental Policy Act: Judicial Misconstruction, Legislative Indifference, and Executive Neglect* (College Station: Texas A&M University Press, 2001).

12. Real Estate Research Corporation, *The Costs of Sprawl: Environmental and Economic Costs of Alternative Residential Development Patterns at the Urban Fringe: Detailed Cost Analysis* (Washington, D.C.: Real Estate Research Corporation, 1974).

13. United States Department of Agriculture and Council on Environmental Quality, *National Agricultural Lands Study, Final Report* (Washington, D.C.: U.S. Government Printing Office, 1981).

14. 147 *Congressional Record* E 729 (May 3, 2001).

15. See John R. Nolon, "The National Land Use Policy Act," *Pace Environmental Law Review* 13, no. 519 (1996), citing the National Land Use Policy Act, S. 3354, 91st Cong., 2d sess. (1970).

16. Nolon, "The National Land Use Policy Act," 520.

17. 40 U.S.C. sec. 461 (1954) (repealed 1981). See also John C. Whitaker, *Striking a Balance: Environmental and Natural Resources Policy in the Nixon-Ford Years* (1976), and Charles E. Connerly and Marc Smith, "Developing a Fair Share Housing Policy for Florida," *Journal of Land Use and Environmental Law* 12, no. 63 (Fall 1996).

18. See Mark Solof, *History of Metropolitan Planning Organizations—Part II* (1998).

19. Federal Highway Act, P.L. 67-87, 42 Sta. 212 (1921).

20. Federal Highway Act, citing the Interstate Highway Act, P.L. 85-767, 72 Stat. 885 (1958).

21. Federal Highway Act, citing Liam A. McCann, "Tea-21: Paving Over Efforts to Stem Urban Sprawl and Reduce America's Dependence on the Automobile," *William & Mary Environmental Law and Policy Review* 23, no. 857 (1999). According to the *Washington Post,* spending on new roads has recently decreased, while improvement spending has increased. See Edward Walsh, "Is the Road to State Sprawl Paved with U.S. Highway Funds?" *Washington Post,* May 26, 1998.

22. See Patricia Salkin, "Smart Growth and Sustainable Development: Threads of a National Land Use Policy," *Valparaiso Law Review* 36, no. 1 (Spring 2002), citing www.fhwa.dot.gov/tea21/sumauth.htm (accessed September 2001).

23. Salkin, "Smart Growth and Sustainable Development."

24. www.fws.gov (accessed July 23, 2002).

25. www.whitehouse.gov/omb/budget/fy2003/pdf/bud12.pdf (accessed July 23, 2002).

26. Shelby Green, "The Search for a National Land Use Policy: For the Cities' Sake," *Fordham Urban Law Journal* 26, no. 69 (1998).

27. Michael Lewyn, "Suburban Sprawl: Not Just an Environmental Issue," *Marquette Law Review* 84, no. 301 (2000).

28. Lewyn, "Suburban Sprawl."

29. Lewyn, "Suburban Sprawl."

30. P.L. 106-274 (September 22, 2001).

31. Telecommunications Act of 1996, sec. 704; 47 U.S.C.A. sec. 332, et seq. (1996).
32. 42 U.S.C. secs. 3601–3619 (1988).
33. Green, "The Search for a National Land Use Policy."
34. The act makes the following findings in section 2:

(1) inadequate land use planning at the State and tribal levels contributes to
  (a) increased public and private capital costs for public works infrastructure development;
  (b) environmental degradation;
  (c) weakened regional economic development; and
  (d) loss of community character
(2) land use planning is rightfully within the jurisdiction of State, tribal and local governments;
(3) comprehensive land use planning and community development should be supported by the Federal, State and tribal governments;
(4) State and tribal governments should provide a proper climate and context through legislation in order for appropriate comprehensive land use planning, community development, and environmental protection to occur;
(5) (A) many States and tribal governments have outmoded land use planning legislation, and (B) many States and tribal governments are undertaking efforts to update and reform land use planning legislation;
(6) the federal government and States should support the efforts of tribal governments to develop and implement land use plans to improve environmental protection, housing opportunities and socioeconomic conditions for Indian tribes; and
(7) the coordination of use of State and tribal resources with local land use plans require additional planning at the State and tribal levels.

35. S. 2995, sec. 4 (July 27, 2000).
36. See www.senate.gov/epw/stm1_107.htm (accessed April 4, 2002).
37. In his statement to the Senate committee, Senator Chafee explained, "The bill recognizes that land use planning is appropriately vested at the state and local levels. . . . The bill does not prescribe any particular approach to land use planning, because each community must decide for itself what is appropriate." See www.senate.gov/epw/cha_030602.htm (accessed April 4, 2002).
38. The senator also offered that "the Community Character Act should be viewed as providing the federal payment for an unfunded mandate whose account in overdue."
39. Testimony of David A. Sampson, March 6, 2002; see www.senate.gov/epw/Sampson_030602.htm (accessed April 4, 2002). Given the statements made by Administrator Whitman and others, one can surmise that perhaps the Department of Commerce is facing a political issue; to wit, the original Hoover model acts came from the Department of Commerce in the 1920s, and today the reform efforts to modernize those acts are being led not by the Department of Commerce but rather by the Environmental Protection Agency and HUD.
40. Testimony of Elizabeth Humstone, March 6, 2002; see www.senate.gov/epw/Humstone_030602.htm (accessed April 4, 2002).
41. Testimony of Elizabeth Humstone.
42. Testimony of Elizabeth Humstone.

43. Testimony of Elizabeth Humstone.

44. See Audrey Hudson, "Bill to Give Feds Control of Zoning Kept Private," *Washington Times*, April 26, 2002.

45. Hudson, "Bill to Give Feds Control of Zoning Kept Private."

46. Senator Inhofe issued a press release announcing that he is leading the fight against the Community Character Act over his concerns that the legislation transfers too much power to the federal government at the expense of states and local communities. He argues that although proponents insist that the federal grant program would be voluntary, "this ignores the fact that such a program creates a strong incentive for conducting planning activities solely in accord with federally-imposed guidelines." See www.senate.gov/inhofe/pr042502b.html (accessed May 28, 2002).

47. See www.senate.gov/inhofe/pr042502b.html.

48. Denny Johnson et al., *Planning for Smart Growth: 2002 State of the States* (Washington, D.C.: American Planning Association, 2002).

49. For example, see New York Executive Order 102 (2000) creating the Quality Communities Task Force.

50. For example, see Delaware Executive Order 2001-14 directing state agencies to submit implementation plans for the governor's Livable Delaware agenda.

51. For example, see Arizona Executive Order 2001-02 creating the Growing Smarter Oversight Council.

52. See Johnson et al., *Planning for Smart Growth.*

53. *Growing Smart Legislative Guidebook: Model Statutes for Planning and the Management of Change* (Washington, D.C.: American Planning Association, 2002), xlii–xlviii. Each of these principles is discussed in detail in the introduction to the *Guidebook.*

54. *Growing Smart Legislative Guidebook,* xlv.

55. *Growing Smart Legislative Guidebook,* xxix.

A Conversation with Earl Blumenauer

Earl Blumenauer is a member of the U.S. House of Representatives and chair of the U.S. House of Representatives Smart Growth Task Force.

What prompted your interest in livable communities and questions and issues around that nature?

Blumenauer: Largely my early experience in Oregon. My hometown, Portland, Oregon, had hit rock bottom. The big transportation solution was to plan an eight-lane freeway through the heart of southeast Portland. Our bus system was failing. I had come to the conclusion after having worked on some national issues that the federal level was not where it was at but rather the state and local level. I got involved in the freeway issue, ran for the state legislature. I offered legislation that created a comprehensive statewide transportation plan and planning legislation at the state level. So it just sort of led naturally.

You've stated that the most important domestic issue of the new millennium is making our communities more livable. Why is this on the top of your political agenda?

Blumenauer: Actually, it's also, I think, the most important international issue. People today are organized around metropolitan areas. We're told there are 564 cities around the world with a million or more. We have a couple dozen megacities. And actually much of the population growth that we anticipate for the world for the next fifty years is going to occur in metropolitan areas. In the United States, it combines protection of air and water quality; it is making our urban areas function at definable boundaries in a good relationship to the surrounding farmland [which] is key to protecting our farm base. It's an economic and energy issue. And at home and abroad, it's key to giving people open connections rather than a sense of alienation, frustration, poverty, and disease.

Livable communities and issues around smart growth are not new for you by any means, but nationally speaking, it is sort of an emerging issue. How have you been able to convince your constituencies of the importance of this issue and what sort of policy learning has occurred among your fellow decision makers at the national level?

Blumenauer: I think this is cyclical. I really do believe that these issues actually have persisted over time. We haven't called it the same; our prescriptions have shifted. But people have been struggling with ways to make communities work better for decades. I think what has occurred most recently is the cumulative effect of our frustrations, our goals, and our failures coupled with some bright spots. I would think that what's happened in Oregon is one of the bright spots in terms of protecting farmland, focusing investments. We're also finding people are appreciating the types of communities that work. Because almost every place has a little gem, a little neighborhood, a small town, something that really shows on a human scale connectivity and how the pieces can be fit together. Jane Jacobs was talking about this forty years ago.

Most recently I have used the term "livable communities." So many of the other terms carry baggage. Even things like "smart growth." "Growth" for some people is a loaded term. So by focusing on livable communities and the ways that government partnerships on all levels can empower individual citizens, business, and just the very process of development and redevelopment, I think it's helped people appreciate what the possibilities are. I find that there are so many competing interests that are better financed and have seemingly more imperative nomenclature. But it's a matter of getting people's attention. Once you get people's attention, talk about the goals in a sense that a community can define and design its own vision of the future. I kind of use a common language that cuts across philosophical, geographic, levels of government, but it's a matter of getting people's attention and using examples that people can relate to. One of the reasons that I think this is gaining momentum is that we now have so many good examples.

The Livable Communities Task Force seems to be made up entirely of Democrats (or if not entirely then almost exclusively). Is this a partisan issue?

Blumenauer: What we have done is developed a variety of different mechanisms. Yes, we have a task force that is made up of the Democratic caucus. There was a Democratic administration that was interested in this issue, so it made sense to have a vehicle around which the party that is most involved could organize. But we've also developed a bipartisan caucus for sustainable development. We worked with the Senate's smart growth caucus that was bipartisan, so we do things that are bicameral and bipartisan. All the legislation that I worked on is all bipartisan. This does not have to be a partisan issue. I hope that there will be a Republican livable communities task force.

What obstacles and possibilities does working on the federal level give to advocates of livable communities?

Blumenauer: Well, we try and make clear that the federal government has been involved with land use and infrastructure from the very beginning since we first started taking land away from Native Americans and giving it to European farmers. This is part and parcel of what our legacy is in the federal government. Today it is as strong as ever. The federal government is the largest landlord, landowner, and employer. One of the most important things we argue is the federal government ought to model the behavior that we expect from the rest of America. It spends hundreds of billions of dollars on ground transportation, air transportation, and construction.

We establish the fiscal policy. We make it easier to borrow money for development and home ownership. It's been federal policy regarding finance and lending, for example, that promoted suburbanization and segregation. So it has not been popular of late to talk about the critical federal role, but upon reflection almost everybody acknowledges that it remains and that it doesn't require a lot of new rules and regulations, taxes, and fees to be transformational.

10

Stemming Sprawl: The Fiscal Approach

H. William Batt

SPRAWL DEVELOPMENT CONFIGURATIONS are not natural. Were it not for incentives to the contrary, people would choose to live and work in close proximity. This has been well documented in studies of every era and place.[1] Only when incentives are put in place that induce people to live in other circumstances do they choose settlement patterns that are remote, less accessible, and alienating. Only in the industrial era and after have outlying areas become more attractive. Tracing the history of such developments makes it clear that they are a response to less livable conditions of urban life as they have evolved—the pollution of air and water, loss of nature, loss of privacy, housing deficiencies, and so on. In more recent years, differentials in taxation and the quality of services (such as schools) have also played a role in making the suburbs more attractive.

Those differentials are explained by public policies that were never understood or envisioned by their designers. Lacking an appreciation of land economics or the relationship between land value and transportation service, governments have put into place a system of taxes and subsidies that amplify and exacerbate whatever impulses already exist to escape the pathologies of urban environments. The polluting industries of the nineteenth and early twentieth centuries are largely gone, but the impulses to leave cities behind continue, driven now by policies for which governments themselves are responsible.

It is important to understand how closely linked transportation costs and land costs are. There are fixed costs involved in locating a home or a business in either place: the costs of building a home, office, or factory and the costs of purchasing

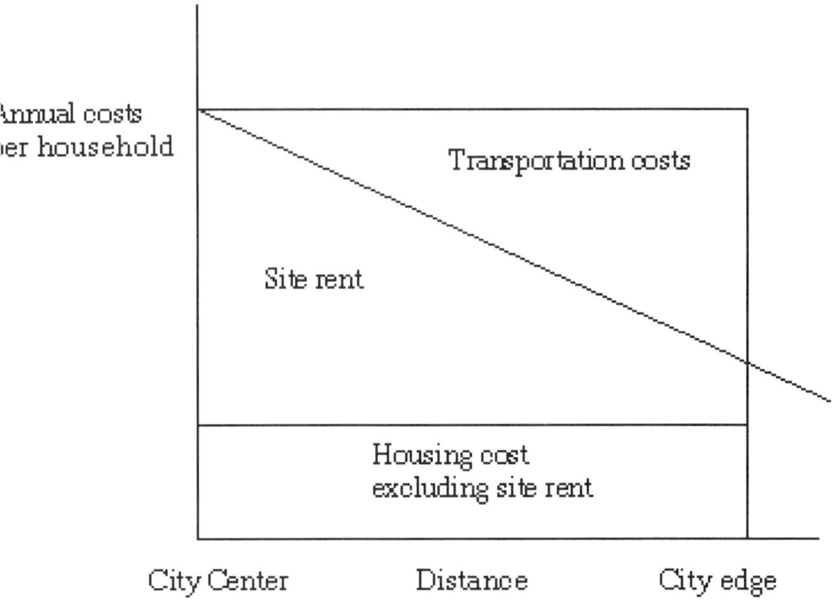

FIGURE 10.1.

a car or a truck. Leaving those costs aside for the moment, consider the relationship between the variable operating costs due to locating in an urban center versus those in locating at the periphery, expressed conceptually in figure 10.1.

Figure 10.1 shows that a household or business is likely to incur costs by locating at either site, whether at a city's center or at the city's edge. At a center site, the costs will take the form of higher land rent; at the city's edge, the costs will be transportation related. If this is not readily apparent, it is because society provides subsidies to titleholders and travelers beyond what are directly experienced or understood.

Transportation Costs

Consider first the costs of transportation in remote areas; such costs are necessarily higher. The way in which geographers and some land economists understand transportation is by using the terms "accessibility" and "mobility." As explained in one basic textbook,

> *Accessibility* refers to the number of opportunities, also called activity sites, available within a certain distance or travel time. *Mobility* refers to the ability to move between different activity sites (e.g., from home to a grocery store).[2]

American transportation planners have focused excessively on mobility with almost total disregard for accessibility. The result is that we are frequently hard put to accomplish our transactions for lack of easy access, even though it is easy to travel great distances with facility. One old joke will serve as a metaphor to better illustrate the dilemma:

> A man ordered a cup of coffee at a lunch counter and shortly then ordered a second cup. After quickly drinking that cup, he ordered a third cup, and then a fourth, and then a fifth. The waitress, astonished at this man's requests, finally said to him, "My Sir! You certainly do like coffee." "I certainly do," he replied. "Otherwise I wouldn't be drinking all this water just to get a little."

The analogy is apparent: Water is to mobility as coffee is to accessibility. We do an awful lot of driving just to do what we need to do. This is because transportation engineers and land use planners have confused two fundamental concepts: access and mobility.

By confusing these two principles, we spend an inordinate amount of money on transportation services, most of it on roads and highways. One 1993 study calculated that the total costs of motor vehicle transportation to our society equal approximately a fourth of our gross domestic product (GDP).[3] The study concluded that "when the full range of costs of transportation are tallied, passenger ground transportation costs the American public a total of $1.2 to $1.6 trillion each year. Just the costs of automobile crashes represents a figure equal to 8 percent of the American GDP.[4] Japan, by way of comparison, spends an estimated 10.4 percent to satisfy all its transportation requirements, although the figure might be a bit low because not all externalities are included in the calculation.[5] Road user fees in 1991 totaled only about $33 billion, whereas the true costs to society were ten times that;[6] put another way, drivers pay only 10 percent of the true costs of their motor vehicle use.[7] The balance is paid by society, effectively subsidizing highway use by paying for all but the marginal out-of-pocket operating costs.

The relationship between transportation costs and land values can be made even clearer by empirical study of how land values increase as one moves toward the center of the city. In an investigation for the Urban Land Institute, the author concluded that, for Portland, Oregon,

> each additional mile [traveled] translated into slightly more than $5,000 in housing costs; closer-in locations command a premium, those farther out save money. A ten-mile difference, all other things being equal, would amount to about $56,000 in new home value.
>
> For a household in which one worker drives downtown (or at least to a more central location) to work, that ten-mile difference may amount to 4,600 miles annually, assuming 230 days of commuting and a round-trip of 20 miles each

> day. Moreover, if non-work trips to the central area and elsewhere doubled that amount, the tradeoff would be about 9,000 miles annually, which could mean a higher/lower driving cost of $3,000 annually, not counting the time saved/spent.[8]

Such are the savings for living closer to the urban center by ten miles. If the urban resident has to rely on a car nonetheless, subtracting some $3,000 annual travel expenses will still leave him paying again that much (and likely more) to own a car. Author James Kunstler put the true costs along with other experts at about $6,100 annually seven years ago.[9] The American Automobile Association calculated that a car driven 15,000 miles in 2001 cost 51 cents per mile, or $7,650.[10] This figure reflects only direct costs to the driver, not the additional costs passed on to society.

The latter figures include externalities such as pollution and the costs of highway crashes. Hortatory public pleas for people to tune up their engines so that they pollute less, to inflate tires properly, and to drive more safely are not likely to change the reality that people are forgetful and fallible. Pollution-free cars are not available; people must drive to participate in this society. The consequences of sulfur dioxide, carbon dioxide, and ozone are no longer a matter of debate; they are scientific fact. Despite frequent headlines about replacing the internal combustion engine, all the realistic substitutes also ultimately rely on fossil fuel power; solar-powered cars are far in the future, if at all, and also fail to deal with any transition. And every person driving his or her own car multiplies the probabilities of accidents. When people step into a car, they are seldom mindful of such odds. Yet if the direct pecuniary costs of driving increase in any substantial way, there will surely be significant changes in the trade-offs involved in housing/transportation choices. As will be made clear later, making costs visible and linking them to private personal behavior is one way to ensure that transportation pays its own way.

Sooner than Americans are likely to bear the real burden of global warming's environmental consequences, they are likely to experience the onset of price rises for petroleum. Experts are divided, but among those best insulated from the pressures of bias, there is increasing consensus that the peak of oil extraction worldwide will come sometime around 2010 if not sooner.[11] Rising prices will not induce greater supply; it will not change the fact that the world will have passed the point of most easily extracted oil and will enter a long and increasingly steep period of declining availability. It is rather a matter of physics: When it costs more in energy to bring oil from deep in the earth than what can be extracted, it is not worth the investment. Even the greater wealth of American society will not insulate it from world competition over what is a limited and fungible commodity. How this alters the calculations Americans make about where to live and work will increasingly depend on the price they are willing to pay for transportation service.

Looking at figure 10.1 once more, it is likely that the slope of the line reflecting land rent and transportation costs will become steeper in time, making each factor greater relative to the other. The century during which motor vehicle transportation was dominant tended to flatten that line, but the greater and growing transportation costs will tend to make land values at urban centers higher relative to remote locales, much as occurred in preindustrial times or during the railroad and canal eras. George Kennan notes in one of his books that

> The railway . . . was capable of accepting and disgorging its loads, whether of passengers or freight, only at fixed points. This being the case, it tended to gather together, and to concentrate around its urban terminus and railhead, all activity that was in any way related to movements of freight or passengers into or out of the city. It was in this quality that it had made major and in some ways decisive contributions to the development not only of the great railway metropolises of the Victorian age—particularly of such inland cities as Moscow, Berlin, Paris, and Chicago—but even certain of the great maritime turnover ports, such as London and New York.
>
> The automobile, on the other hand, had precisely the opposite qualities. Incapable, in view of its own cumbersomeness and requirements for space, of accepting or releasing large loads at any concentrated points anywhere, but peculiarly capable of accepting and releasing them at multitudes of unconcentrated points anywhere else, the automobile tended to disintegrate and to explode all that the railway had brought together. It was, in fact, the enemy of the concentrated city. Thus it was destined to destroy the great densely populated urban centers of the nineteenth century, with all the glories of economic and cultural life that had flowed from their very unity and compactness.[12]

Land Rent

From the standpoint of an economic geographer and for some land economists, land rent is simply capitalized transportation cost. Land rent is the surplus generated by social activity on or in the vicinity of locational sites that accrues to titleholders of those parcels. Whether or not it is recaptured by public policy, rent is a natural factor deriving from the intensive use of natural capital. One must return to nineteenth-century classical economics to appreciate the importance of economic rent or land rent; neoclassical economic frameworks have largely discarded it.[13] More intensive use of high-value land sites leads to site configurations that are less dependent on transportation services. Land rent is highest where the greatest traffic and market exchanges occur, that being at the center of large conurbations. Comparing land values of urban property parcels, the highest land rent in the urban cores and traffic junctures are analogous to the contours of land elevations. Mountain peaks gradually slope down to valleys and flatland regions and continue outward until at distant points—perhaps at the poles of the earth—land sites have no market value at all.

The differentials in land values are profound, even more than most people realize. In 1995, in the small city of Ithaca, New York, the highest quintile of land had a value of over $56,000 per acre in the downtown center, whereas the lowest quintile only a mile away falls to less than $3,000.[14] Large city centers have far higher site prices. Even in Polk County, Iowa (which includes Des Moines), in the middle of cornfields where I did a study two years ago, the highest urban value land site was $31.3 million per acre, which quickly declined to about $20,000 per acre only about a mile away. In the spring of 1998, one land parcel (the building was to be razed) of less than an acre in New York City's Times Square and split in two pieces by Broadway was sold by Prudential Life to Disney for roughly $240 million.[15] To take another instance, a nine-acre tract on the East River in New York City occupied by an obsolete power plant was purchased by Mort Zuckerman to build high-rise condominiums two years ago. The sale price was in the neighborhood of $680 million and would have been higher were it not for some enormous costs associated with the demolition of the old structures.[16] It should be noted that the overwhelming proportion of land value is in cities; relatively speaking, the site values of peripheral lands, typically used for agriculture and timber growth, are negligible.

Land values are high in urban areas because, over time, rent accrues to a site. Each improvement in proximity to a property parcel enhances the value of all other parcels. This makes even unimproved sites attractive objects for speculation, particularly when land sites surrounding it are to be improved by adding either transportation service or new structures. One nine-mile stretch of interstate highway in Albany, New York, costing $125 million to construct, has yielded $3.8 billion in increased land values (constant dollars) within just two miles of its corridor in the forty years of its existence.[17] This is a thirty-fold return in a time span typically used for bond repayment! The Washington *Metro* created increments in land value along much of the 101-mile system completed by 1980 that easily exceeded $3.5 billion, compared with the $2.7 billion of federal funds invested in *Metro* up until that time.[18] Any major building construction project, private or public, will have a similar effect on adjacent land sites. Differentials in land value can have a profound effect on decisions made by titleholders, either positively by inducing appropriate development in urban cores or negatively by giving monopoly titleholders power to hold sites out of use for long-term speculative gain. Such decisions of course determine the character of urban configurations and society as well.

Stemming Sprawl: Command-and-Control Measures

Policymakers have two modes of leverage by which to implement public will: 1) so-called command-and-control approaches that are typically enforced by what state and federal constitutions group under "police powers" and 2) fiscal approaches that typically involve a variety of taxes, fees, fines, and other charges that derive constitutionally from either police powers or "tax powers." When governments administer either of these powers, they are legitimate and authoritative. Fiscal measures available to governments can come from either ground. The charges that the private sector usually impose differ in that they usually are responsive to market forces. Prices that are established by government, however, are not necessarily responsive to market forces, nor are they intended to be. Rather, they are set in order to accomplish specific public policy goals.[19] They can be no less efficient, however, when responsibly instituted.

Governments face the challenge of knowing which of the tools at their disposal—command-and-control approaches or "pricing" approaches—will best serve effective and efficient achievement of public policies. Only in recent years, however, has there been a renewed interest in fiscal levers to achieve goals that policymakers seek to achieve. There is particular interest among students of welfare economics in incorporating costs earlier regarded as externalities, especially in designing environmental policies. Moreover, the use of pricing approaches to recover costs of government services that have a high level of private good about them can bring about more attractive and achievable goals than reliance on conventional police power approaches. User fees, environmental fees, and other such fiscal tools have become more fascinating—at least to students of public policy—than conventional taxes.

The renewed interest in fiscal approaches comes in recognition of the fact that traditional command-and-control approaches have not been successful. Government authority is far more effective at prohibiting and controlling than it is inducing and channeling.[20] Three illustrations of failed command-and-control approaches will demonstrate this: zoning, urban growth boundaries, and altering (usually expanding) political jurisdictions.

Zoning

The largest single and impartial study of zoning, a 1969 report to the National Commission on Urban Problems (the Douglas Commission), conceded that zoning is of questionable value. A part titled "Fragmentation in Land-Use Planning and Control" quoted with approval a (then) recent study that had held the following:

> 1) While a great deal has been said about what zoning ought to do, very little has been said about what zoning actually does to the city and its inhabitants.

2) Although zoning is the most widespread tool of land-use control and urban planning in the United States, there is almost no evidence, logical or empirical, to indicate whether or not zoning accomplishes the goals and purposes attributed to it by planners and other proponents.
3) There is almost no evidence to indicate that the unzoned city is substantially different from, or substantially similar to, the zoned city.[21]

Planners, of course, respond by saying that they have been given too little power and that their designs needed to be incorporated more widely, comprehensively, and stringently over broader regions. To their way of thinking, it is the balkanization of municipal plans, as well as their tepid injunctions, that account for failure. Zoning, they argue, needs the even more fundamental support of "master plans," that is, more command-and-control instruments.

Zoning becomes captive of parochial interests—home owners, speculators, the highway industry, and building contractors—who naturally either resist or exploit the inexorable and evolutionary patterns of change. The political Right criticizes zoning for interfering with individual choice and rational land use,[22] and the Progressive Center criticizes it for being outdated and rigid at best, unresponsive and destructive at worst. Alan Ehrenhalt, columnist for *Governing Magazine,* said,

> The postwar zoning codes discouraged the old pedestrian-scale Main Street corridors that had flourished before World War II, and encouraged their replacement with strip-mall-like businesses that provided large amounts of parking. They took the idea of segregated uses and pressed it much further than the original versions had dared go. The more distance they could create between residential, commercial and industrial uses, planners reasoned, the easier it would be to dissuade residents from escaping to greener pastures.[23]

Implicit in all this is an authoritarian approach to land use decisions. It arises out of the notion that professionals—in this case planners—know best and that fragmented land use is an outgrowth of "excessive localism" and fragmented decision making and an inability to see the "big picture." The report recognized the continuing influence of the classic approach of planners first put forth in the (congressional) Standard City Planning Act of 1928 and defined in detail in Edward Bassett's classic book *The Master Plan.* In that text, to influence planners for decades to come, three criteria determined the scope of a good plan: "Each of the elements of the plan relates to land areas; has been stamped on land areas by the community for the community use; [and] can be shown on a map."[24] Particularly revealing, and no doubt deliberate, is the use of the word "stamp." The approach is autocratic, static rather than organic, and governmentally expensive.

Urban Growth Boundaries

Urban growth boundaries (UGBs) are another panacea receiving great attention: the attempt to curtail outward growth by imposing a constraining girdle on development. Portland, Oregon, and Boulder, Colorado, are the exemplars, both having instituted their policies decades ago. In Boulder, however, the results are more in consequence of factors relating to topography and infrastructure service than to prohibition of outward extension.[25] And Portland has been pressured to alter its boundary repeatedly as differential land values within and beyond the boundary induce growth patterns both unnatural and inefficient.[26] Landholders within the city endorsed it because it doubled their site values in a decade, which has meant that, relative to local income, housing is now more expensive than in any city except San Francisco.[27] Inevitably, the economic pressures grew to the point of political crisis, at which time the policies were relaxed. This is because UGBs deal with symptoms rather than the root economic causes of the problem. In 1996, six Bay Area communities "locked in" long-term protection for the greenbelt by adopting a UGB covering a total of 3.75 million acres.[28] For perspective, this translates to 5,860 square miles, an expanse equal to that of Connecticut and Rhode Island together. But only 731,000 acres, 1,142 square miles, are urbanized[29] at the present time, and it could be a century before "build-out" and any significant impact from such measures occur. It was politically impossible to impose any smaller design, which illustrates the difficulty, and indeed the fallacy, of using a command-and-control device to constrain an inexorable economic force.

Elastic City Boundaries

The former mayor of Albuquerque, New Mexico, David Rusk, has made a name for himself promoting what he calls "elastic cities."[30] His answer is for municipalities to expand or combine their political boundaries in order to "capture" suburban growth in their tax base. In some cases, state laws must be passed to authorize this, overcoming the reluctance of suburbs to relinquish their privileged status. In those states where such annexation is permissible and has occurred, it might momentarily help address a shrinking tax base, but the urban configuration is unaltered and perhaps bloated. Consider, for example, the case of Columbus, Ohio, which in 1950 had an incorporated area of only 39.9 square miles.[31] The total number of square miles by 1967 had grown to 114 and in 1996 had almost doubled again to 206.[32] One unwelcome consequence, however, is the reduction of farmland, which the city is now realizing.

Stemming Sprawl: Pricing Measures for Transportation

From the foregoing, it is clear that insofar as the causes of sprawl development are economic, the solution needs to be economic as well. The equilibrium of forces can be restored in two ways: 1) by charging the true marginal costs of motor vehicle transportation to users and 2) by recovering the economic rent from urban site owners that is really the socially created value.

It is easy to distinguish five elements of transportation service cost: capital investment, maintenance costs, regulation costs, environmental externalities, and congestion costs. Each of these calls for a different treatment with respect to revenue design. Capital costs are best recovered by recapturing the land rent proximate to the highway corridors. This is socially created value, which is better used to honor debt service of infrastructure investment than allowing it to be retained as windfall gains by titleholders to property close by. User fees, most aptly linked to the purchase of motor fuel and tire wear, serve as a proxy for the use of the roads and can be designed to be commensurate with use. As the wear and tear of roads as well as police patrol, snow and ice control, and signaling all involve operating and maintenance costs, such charges are easily linked with benefits received. In the future, still more accurate systems of service charges are likely to appear: Singapore, Hong Kong, and New Zealand are already reliant on electronic devices that record road use by time, place, and vehicle weight.

Ensuring the safety of drivers and vehicles through licenses, registrations, and inspections is most appropriately financed by fees commensurate with the costs of their administration. This way, if a vehicle is used but seldom, it is charged on the basis of its identification rather than assuming any projected level of use. Environmental externalities such as pollution costs can be linked to the polluting source, such as diesel fuel and gasoline consumption, to the full extent necessary to equilibrate air quality and other environmental ambiences. Congestion costs, the last of the major components of a pricing design for highway use, are partially paid for by the time loss of those caught in traffic. The costs of time lost due to highway congestion are enormous: In 2000, the average driver spent 62 hours sitting in traffic at a nationwide cost of $68 billion in gas and time lost. In Los Angeles, the average driver spent 136 hours stalled in traffic at an average cost of $2,510.[33] Commuting times were also 20 percent longer than they were a decade ago, about 22 minutes one way nationally on average but as high as 32 minutes on average in New York.[34] But not all people's time is valued equally, and people themselves value their time differently at different times, and it is unfair to require people to impose their congestion on others. Therefore, congestion pricing, being explored in several urban regions, provides a rationing of limited highway space. In a sense, that payment for space usage, in time or money, is a form of land rent.

Stemming Sprawl: Pricing Measures for Land Use

Just as recovering the costs of transportation service equilibrates costs and benefits on one side of the equation, recovering the economic rent accruing to land value facilitates efficient space configurations on the other side. Figure 10.2, again conceptually, portrays how the collection of various transportation user fees as well as the recovery of land rent corrects the economic distortions that today result in sprawl development. The shaded area indicates the pricing correctives necessary to ensure that neither urban nor rural land sites are disadvantaged in travel or location choices that individuals make for either residential or commercial purposes.

As it happens, collecting land rent is a relatively simple operation: It involves a small computer adjustment in the assessment base of what is now the local real property tax. The real property tax to an economist is really two separate taxes: that put on land value and that put on improvement values. A gradual phaseout of the tax on the improvement component, shifting totally to a tax on the land, recovers economic rent in a way that satisfies all the principles of sound tax theory.[35] It is efficient, neutral, equitable, administrable, stable, and simple. It is also absolutely foolproof: One cannot hide land or take

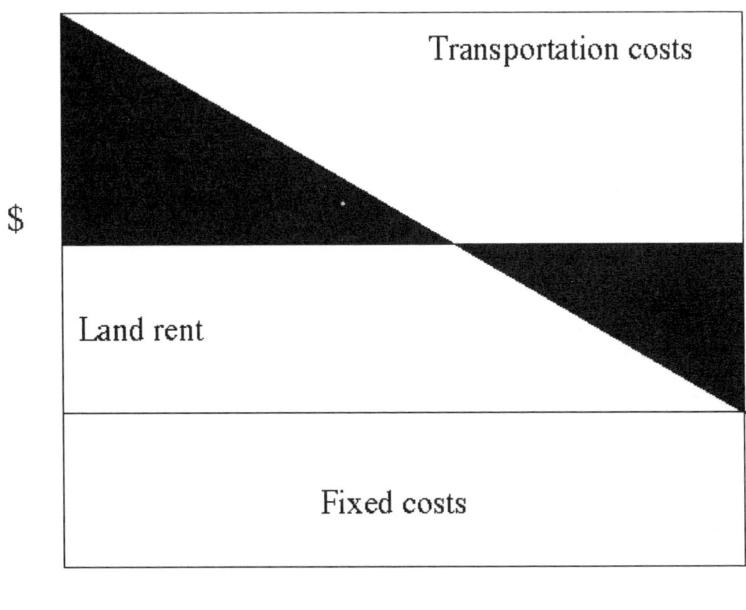

FIGURE 10.2.

it to a remote tax haven. It relieves poor households (who typically own no land) of any tax burden and rewards those titleholders who use their sites efficiently. High-value sites are induced to construct high-value improvements, and low-value sites are left alone. In this way, central locations, where commercial enterprises typically locate, pay according to their intensity; home owners, who typically locate at the periphery of a neighborhood community, pay moderately; and agricultural land and forestlands pay little if anything. By an automatic and natural process, the centrifugal forces of sprawl development are reversed, and investment is encouraged in core locales. The higher density resulting affords the necessary ten to twelve households per acre (or the commercial equivalent) that makes public transportation service economically viable, lessening the prospect of automobile dependency.[36]

In addition, a tax on site value (that is, the collection of economic rent) restores moral principle to tax theory. By collecting rent on that value that is generated by the collective activity of the community, it offers the opportunity to relieve tax burdens on value that is generated by individual effort. Put another way, any value that individuals create by their own bodies and minds is left for them to keep; that which is socially created value is recovered by the community to pay for its collective purposes. "Tax what you take, not what you make," is one way to say it. "Tax bads, not goods," or "Tax waste, not work," is another way. At the heart of this approach is a very profound message: The earth is the common heritage of humanity; it belongs to everyone. That which grows out of our own personal efforts and ingenuity is ours to keep, and no part of it should be subject to taxation.[37] Taxes on income, sales, savings, structures, and things that come from the sweat of our brow can be replaced by taxes on land rent—which, when all forms of it are included, is revenue source that can fully pay for the full services of government and is nonetheless essentially burdenless to taxpayers.[38] What economists call the "excess burden" or "deadweight loss" of the current tax structure—by many calculations at least 25 percent[39]—is reduced to zero, thereby increasing our collective productivity by that amount. That effectively makes us all 20 percent wealthier.

John Houseman, an actor perhaps most widely known as Professor Kingsfield in the film and long-running television series, *The Paper Chase,* later became the pitchman for Oppenheimer Mutual Funds. In that advertisement, his tag line was "We get our money the old-fashioned way—we *earn* it." That we should earn our money rather than live off the efforts of others seems a simple enough moral tenet. But it seems to have lost its cogency in contemporary economic thought. More than a century ago, John Stuart Mill noted that

> landlords grow richer in their sleep without working, risking or economizing. The increase in the value of land, arising as it does from the efforts of an entire

community, should belong to the community and not to the individual who might hold title.[40]

Notes

1. Brian K. Roberts, *Landscapes of Settlement: Prehistory to the Present* (London: Routledge, 1996); Spiro Kostof, *The City Shaped: Urban Patterns and Meanings through History* (Boston: Little, Brown, 1991).

2. Susan Hanson, ed., *The Geography of Urban Transportation* (2nd ed.) (New York: Guilford, 1995), 5. See also Elliott Sclar, *Access for All: Transportation and Urban Growth* (New York: Columbia University Press, 1980).

3. Peter Miller and John Moffet, *The Price of Mobility: Uncovering the Hidden Costs of Transportation* (Washington, D.C.: Natural Resources Defense Council, 1993). This is somewhat more than the U.S. Department of Transportation's own calculation. The latter uses only direct measurable pecuniary costs and estimates that the figure was in the neighborhood of $1 trillion for 1992, about 17 percent of gross national product (converting to GDP would make it somewhat higher). Since it fails to include externalities such as pollution, accidents, and other associated costs, it seems a reasonable estimate (U.S. Department of Transportation, *Transportation Statistics Annual Report, 1994* [Washington, D.C.: U.S. Department of Transportation, Bureau of Transportation Statistics, 1994], 4–5).

4. In 1988, a study by the Urban Institute calculated that $71 billion were borne in out-of-pocket costs, another $46 billion in lost wages and household production, and $217 billion in pain, suffering, and lost quality of life. Translated into vernacular, this is a total of $334 billion in lost property, work time, and injuries and deaths (T. Miller et al., *The Costs of Highway Crashes* [Washington, D.C.: Urban Institute, October 1991]).

5. Walter Hook, "Counting on Cars, Counting Out People," Institute for Transportation Development Policy Paper, Winter 1994, 28. Another author puts the figure at 9.2 percent of personal expenditure in Japan versus 22 percent in the United States (Michael Replogle, "Improving Access for the Poor in Urban Areas," *Appropriate Technology* 20, no. 1 [1993]: 21–23).

6. James J. MacKenzie et al., *The Going Rate: What It Really Costs to Drive* (Washington, D.C.: World Resources Institute, 1992).

7. *Road Kill: How Solo Driving Runs Down the Economy* (Boston: Conservation Law Foundation, May 1994), 7. This study is a summary of a larger study done by Apogee Research, Inc., funded by the Joyce Foundation.

8. Robert T. Dunphy, "The Cost of Being Close: Land Values and Housing Prices in Portland's High Tech Corridor," ULI Working Paper No. 660, October 1998, at www.uli.org/Pub/Pages/a_issues/660/a_trl44_cost.html (accessed December 2000).

9. James Howard Kunstler, *Home from Nowhere: Remaking Our Everyday World for the 21st Century* (New York: Simon & Schuster, 1996), chap. 3, at www.isd.net/msp00050/driving.html (accessed January 2001).

10. See www.ouraaa.com/news/library/drivingcost (accessed January 2001). Driving 10,000 miles per year will typically cost 64.5 cents per mile, or $6,450, and driving 20,000 miles per year will cost 45.8 cents per mile, or $9,160.

11. See, for example, www.oilcrisis.org, listing inter alia Kenneth S. Deffeyes, *Hubbert's Peak: The Impending World Oil Shortage* (Princeton, N.J.: Princeton University Press, 2001); Walter Youngquist, *Geodestinies* (Portland, Ore.: National Book Company, 1997); and www.dieoff.org, maintained by Dr. Jay Hanson (Cornell University, retired).

12. George Kennan, *Around the Cragged Hill: A Personal and Political Philosophy* (New York: Norton, 1993), 160–61.

13. Explanation of the failure to recognize the law of rent, as understood by classical economists, is explained in Mason Gaffney and Fred Harrison, *The Corruption of Economics* (London: Shepheard-Walwyn, 1994). See also H. William Batt, "How the Railroads Got Us on the Wrong Economic Track," *Torch Magazine,* Spring 1998, at www.geocities.com/Athens/Acropolis/5148/batt_railroad_1.html (accessed February 2001).

14. These data come from other work I have done.

15. *New York Times,* March 7, 1998.

16. Charles V. Bagli, "In Manhattan, a Battle over Nine Acres with River View," *New York Times,* December 29, 1999; Charles V. Bagli, "Winning Bid to Develop Nine Acres Near U.N.," *New York Times,* January 2, 2000.

17. H. William Batt, "Value Capture as a Policy Tool in Transportation Economics: An Exploration in Public Finance in the Tradition of Henry George," *American Journal of Economics and Sociology* 60, no. 1 (January 2001): 195–228 (reprinted in Laurence S. Moss, ed., *City and Country* [Malden, Mass.: Blackwell, 2001]).

18. Walter Rybeck, "Transit-Induced Land Values: Development and Revenue Implications," *Economic Development Commentary* 5, no. 1 (October 1981): 23–27.

19. One recent exploration of this is a chapter titled "Catalytic Government: Steering Rather Than Rowing," in *Reinventing Government: How the Entrepreneurial Spirit Is Transforming the Public Sector,* ed. David Osborne and Ted Gaebler (New York: Penguin, 1993).

20. This was explored in powerful detail in a book that is now regarded as a classic study: Robert A. Dahl and Charles E. Lindblom, *Politics, Economics and Welfare: Planning and Politico-Economic Systems Resolved into Basic Social Processes* (New York: Harper & Row, 1953, updated in 1992).

21. James G. Coke and John J. Gargan, "Fragmentation in Land-Use Planning and Control," Research Report No. 18 (prepared for the consideration of the National Commission on Urban Problems, Washington, D.C., 1969), 11.

22. Linda Fantin, "Libertarian Candidate Says Government Is Root of Most Planning Ills," *Tribune* (Salt Lake City), March 28, 1998.

23. Alan Ehrenhalt, "The Trouble with Zoning," *Governing Magazine,* February 1998, 28–34.

24. Coke and Gargan, "Fragmentation in Land-Use Planning and Control," 61.

25. Peter Pollock, "Controlling Sprawl in Boulder: Benefits and Pitfalls," *Landlines,* January 1998, 1 ff., at www.lincolninst.edu/main.html (accessed February 2000).

26. The studies of Portland's UGB are myriad, so many that one is better served by surfing the Internet anew rather than enumerate citations here. The Portland *Oregonian,* however, has had extensive and balanced coverage of the issues and offers the best single source of material.

27. Alan Ehrenhalt points out that "Portland land prices, 19 percent below the U.S. average in 1985, were 6 percent above it by 1994, and that while Portland was the nation's 55th most affordable city just six years ago, it now ranks 165th out of 179." He points out that the increased land values have encouraged both in-filling and higher densities inside the growth boundary, while the individual lot sizes have gone from an average of 13,200 square feet when the growth boundary was first established to an average 8,700 square feet in the mid-1990s. This increased density has been an attraction to many residents, and it is now possible for 40 percent of the workers commuting to work in Portland to rely on public transportation (Alan Ehrenhalt, "The Great Wall of Portland," *Governing Magazine,* May 1997, 20–24).

28. Urban Growth Boundaries—New Report and Factsheet, at www.rahul.net/gba/ugb (accessed January 2001), and www.metroactive.com/papers/sonoma/07.11.96/urban-9268.html (accessed January 2001); Zack Stentz, "Inward Bound," *Sonoma County Independent,* July 11, 1996.

29. One square mile converts to roughly 640 acres. San Francisco covers 30,000 acres (46.8 square miles), Santa Rosa 22,000 (34.4 square miles), and San Jose more than 100,000 (156 square miles). More than 864,000 acres (1,350 square miles), an area larger than Yosemite National Park, are publicly owned, mostly in parks and watersheds; see www.rahul.net/gba/aboutgb.html (accessed February 2001).

30. David Rusk, *Cities without Suburbs* (Baltimore: Woodrow Wilson Center, The Johns Hopkins University Press, 1993). See also Myron Orfield, *Metropolitics: A Regional Agenda for Community and Stability* (rev. ed.) (Washington, D.C.: Brookings Institution Press; Cambridge, Mass.: Lincoln Institute of Land Policy, 1997).

31. City of Columbus, *Growth Statement, 1993,* 37.

32. Communication with Dr. Barbara Brugman, Development Department, City of Columbus, Spring 1998.

35. Texas Transportation Institute study, reported in the *Christian Science Monitor,* June 24, 2002, 14.

36. Laurent Belsie, "Commutes Get Longer, More Rural," *Christian Science Monitor,* May 31, 2002, 1 ff.

37. See H. William Batt, "Principles of Sound Tax Theory as Have Evolved over 200 and More Years," *Groundswell,* at www.progress.org/cg/battprincip02.htm (accessed February 2001).

38. Parsons Brinkerhoff, "Transit and Urban Form," TCRP Report No. 16, Transportation Research Board, Washington, D.C., 1996.

39. See www.earthrights.net for greater elaboration of the theory underlying this approach.

40. Classical economic theory employed the word "land" as a factor of production, the others being labor and capital. Land was taken to mean any valued good in nature and today includes highly valued items, such as hydrocarbons and hard-rock minerals, fisheries, water for irrigation and power, the electromagnetic spectrum, geosynchronous

satellite orbits, and airport landing and takeoff time slots. All these yield economic rent that today is being captured by private corporate interests but that should be the entitlement of all humankind according to the theories of what is coming to be known variously as geonomy, geoclassical liberalism, Georgism (after the writings of nineteenth-century self-taught economist Henry George), and natural taxation. For further references to this school of political economy, see, for example, www.henrygeorge.org, www.schalkenbach.org, www.urbantools.org, www.cooperativeindividualism.org, www.progress.org, and the search engine for all these and more: www.askhenry.org.

41. Fred Harrison, ed., *The Losses of Nations: Deadweight Politics versus Public Rent Dividends* (London: Othila Press, 1998). See also National Center for Policy Analysis, "The Deadweight Loss of Income Taxes," where it is argued that "the efficiency loss from current income taxes is more than 30 percent. If Social Security taxes are included, there is a 50 percent efficiency loss" (at www.ncpa.org/pi/taxes/pd053000g.html; accessed February 2001).

42. John Stuart Mill, *Principles of Political Economy,* bk. 5, chap. 2, sec. 5.

A Conversation with Greg LeRoy

Greg LeRoy is executive director of Good Jobs First.

What was the genesis of Good Jobs First?

LeRoy: Good Jobs started up in July of 1998, so it's a little over three years old. I founded it after winning the Public Interest Pioneer Award of the Stern Family Fund, a small foundation over in Arlington [Virginia]. We now have ten staff people and offices in Washington, D.C., and in New York and Chicago.

The genesis of the issue comes out of the plant-closing movement. For a dozen years from the early 1980s to the mid-1990s, I consulted nationally against plant closings. I worked for a nonprofit research group that was the technical assistance hub of the network of plant-closing groups. We found over and over again that the factories that were shutting down had been subsidized. So we made as much hay as we could about that fact. We used a couple of exotic legal cases that actually stopped a shutdown in Duluth, Minnesota, and won severance in another case and figured in other ways and other strategies to try to arrest or ameliorate shutdowns. I sort of became known in labor community organizing circles as the guy who knew how to do this—investigate subsidies. I actually started my first research paper on subsidies in the late 1970s, when I worked for a community organizing network in Chicago. So I collected horror stories and remedies in this book I wrote in 1994 called *No More Candy Store.* The theory of that book is that economic incentives have been multiplying like rabbits for twenty years. They are ubiquitous, but they are very loose. Most of them are not monitored effectively, there is no money-back guarantee language built into them, they don't have wage standards attached to them, they're not really transparent, and they didn't result from healthy civic engagement.

Where and how did Good Jobs First start discussing and writing about smart-growth issues?

LeRoy: Most explicitly, in May of 1999, I talked my way into the founding meeting of what is now Smart Growth America, what was then called the National Smart Growth Coalition. It was a very impressive meeting. There were sixty organizations sitting around the room, and everyone did a one-minute speech on who they were and what kind of issues they were working on. I said that we're Good Jobs First and we're very concerned that economic development subsidies are an overlooked aspect of what causes sprawl.

We also got hired by a business civic association in Chicago called Chicago Metropolis 20/20 to create a curriculum for labor union leaders on sprawl for the leaders of the Chicago Federation of Labor (CFL). The CFL is an old client of mine, and the president, Don Turner, is very passionate about this issue; he really thinks it's the issue for the next twenty years. So we actually ended up in April 2000 staging a daylong conference for more than a hundred local union leaders in Chicago, the first such event that anyone has ever staged. The Metropolis 20/20 people have been very pleased by the outcome because now they have labor support for a bunch of very cool stuff they're doing in the state legislature and in the Cook County metro region. So we're interested in promoting effective, accountable development. To me, you can't talk about sprawl without looking at subsidies that foster job migration to the fringe.

Unions are often thought of as being pro–economic growth, pro-development. Have you met resistance in the union communities?

LeRoy: Sure. I try to be very candid. The delicate political position for us is the building trades. There are occasions where, most recently in Arizona, the State Federation of Labor with the building trades went on record opposing a smart-growth voter initiative. But when you break down the story, it's not a simple story. The self-interests of the different building trade unions vary a great deal. For instance, the operating engineers get a lot of work from highway construction. They run the graters and the cranes and the pavers. The carpenters don't get a lot of work from highway construction, the electricians don't get a lot of work from the highway construction, and the pipefitters don't get much either. [Unions] get much more work from mixed-use, high-density, ground-field reclamation, condo, in-town, transit-oriented development projects, renovations.

Likewise, except for very few markets like Chicago and St. Louis, the track-style development, track-style housing construction, is uniformly nonunion in this country. The only segment of the activity generated at the fringe that the building trade might get is some of the resulting commercial and retailing construction. [**Au: The following sentence is still confusing. ce**]If [housing construction] was an equivalent number of units in a high-rise condo building or in mixed-use townhouses high-density development [the building trade unions] are much more likely to get that work, and a lot of them know that.

Carpenters, pipefitters, masons, and painters understand that there is a geographic correlation with the likelihood that they're going to get the work. There are other factors that effect unionization and construction—the size of the project, whether or not there is going to be public money involved, and especially who the contractors are because there is a union world of contractors and a nonunion world, and they compete all the time.

11

Suburban Sprawl in Southeastern Wisconsin: Planning, Politics, and the Lack of Affordable Housing

Mark Edward Braun

THE NEW FRONTIERS of suburban development in southeastern Wisconsin are a far cry from the American frontiers of yesteryear. Thousands of years ago, American Indians were attracted to the natural resources and abundant clean water found in the nearby marshes, rivers, and lakes. Three hundreds of years ago, the first white men who reached the area were Jesuit missionaries, but settlers did not reach the area until the 1830s, when Yankees traveled west along the Great Lakes to Milwaukee. Along the banks of the Milwaukee, Fox, Root, and Rock Rivers, they found thinly scattered Native Americans, such as the Winnebago, Potowatomie, and Menomonee. From 1850 to 1950, housing development was a fairly traditional pattern that was contiguous to urban areas and was accommodated by extending existing infrastructure. By 1963, however, development occurred at lower densities in more isolated areas where the provision of services cost more. As discussed in this chapter, housing sprawl in southeastern Wisconsin had an enormous impact on land use during the last part of the twentieth century and continues to impact housing, farming, and other social and economic factors.

The economic hub of this 2,700-square-mile region is Milwaukee with 154 smaller municipalities situated on its edges. In 1990, southeastern Wisconsin had a population of 1.8 million. Over time, the rural population decreased as the nonrural population increased, and the area has lost 367 square miles of open spaces since 1950.[1] Southeastern Wisconsin contains seven counties—Kenosha, Milwaukee, Ozaukee, Racine, Walworth, Washington, and Waukesha—that encompass eleven major watersheds. It is bounded to the east by Lake Michigan, to the south by Chicago, to the west by agricultural lands, and to the north by forests. Politics of suburban sprawl in southeastern Wisconsin has had cultural, economic, and social impacts that directly resulted in the creation of very little housing that people on low incomes could afford. In short, the sprawling pattern of postwar growth has resulted in social, environmental, and economic problems that transcend the geographic limits of local units of government.

As developers, planners, and politicians helped create the expansion of freeways after World War II, large numbers of subdivisions rapidly appeared in southeastern Wisconsin. These suburbs became bedroom communities for people who could more easily commute to work in Milwaukee since the interstate system allowed commuters easy passage from Milwaukee to the outlying suburbs. Since many of these suburbs lacked public transportation, they remain extremely automobile-oriented places.

After the freeways were constructed, predominantly white, middle-class citizens moved out to the suburbs. As a result of this demographic shift, it diminished Milwaukee's tax base and deteriorated the quality of education provided at public schools, and many leading manufacturing firms moved their operations out of the central city to where employees lived. Indeed, following World War II, there were twenty-three factories employing at least 1,000 people located in Milwaukee County. As the "crabgrass frontier" became suburbanized, those who remained in the central city inherited enormous social problems, including hypersegregation and increasing concentrations of poverty.[2]

The construction of freeways hurt Milwaukee and, in particular, the citizens of the inner city. As people moved to the suburbs, poor residents of color became highly concentrated in Milwaukee's inner city, creating an underclass. There was also a political power shift as the population outside Milwaukee County increased three times faster than that of the city. Generally, suburban dwellers had high incomes and were likely to vote for the Republican Party. In contrast, the predominantly Democratic working-class poor were constrained by economic forces, preventing their flight to the suburbs. Suburbanization created an "iron ring" of eighteen suburbs around Milwaukee, separating two polar opposite political parties.

With the completion of Interstate Highway 43, the construction of cookie-cutter "McMansions" quickly spread to the north and south of Milwaukee County. Some of the reasons people moved to suburbs included the demand for modern houses with large lawns and less crime. But others were concerned about declining property values and the diminished quality of education and were unwilling to live near a rising population of African Americans in particular. Since many of the suburbs offered little in the way of affordable housing and public transportation, low- and moderate-income racial minorities were extremely unlikely to live there.[3] As people demand bigger lots and a

TABLE 11.1
Change in Residential Land Use by County, 1963–1985

County	*No. of Acres Devoted to Residential, 1963–1970*	*No. of Acres Devoted to Residential, 1970–1985*	*Ranking by County as Percentage of Total Acres, 1963–1985*
Kenosha	1,554	3,054	7
Milwaukee	2,398	4,031	3
Ozaukee	2,419	3,711	4
Racine	2,781	3,516	5
Walworth	1,199	3,491	6
Washington	2,617	6,117	2
Waukesha	7,184	17,992	1

Source: Southeastern Wisconsin Regional Planning Commission, *A Regional Land Use Plan for Southeastern Wisconsin—2010* (Waukesha, Wis.: SEWRPC, 1992), 185.

"better view," subdivision developers supplied this lifestyle and built subdivisions next to subdivisions. Consequently, the open view was obstructed, the farmland disappeared, and the drive to work in the city was gridlocked. This process was exemplified by Waukesha County. As shown in table 11.1, it had the most land devoted to residential use from 1963 to 1985.

Besides interstate development and increased suburbanization, another force that transformed urban life was the relocation of jobs out of the city. As employers and employees moved to the suburbs, employment opportunities fell in the inner city, which coincided with more people of color moving into the inner city. Deindustrialization also reduced the number of manufacturing firms in Milwaukee to thirteen.[4] Between 1960 and 1970, there were 10 percent fewer jobs available for people looking for work in the central city, while the number of jobs outside the inner city increased by 75 percent.[5] Because of the lack of affordable housing, one-third of those who worked in the suburbs had to live elsewhere because of a lack of affordable housing, which contributed to traffic congestion, air pollution, and energy waste.[6] People of color, if they had jobs, were more vulnerable to economic changes than whites because they were often the first to be fired. Moreover, they were adversely affected by layoffs, plant closings, and the relocation of business firms to the Republican-controlled suburbs known for lower tax rates.

The data assembled for this research on sprawl included personal interviews, university studies, newspaper articles, planning documents, government reports, and other primary and secondary documentation. Materials were gathered from employers, historical societies, and the University of Wisconsin–Milwaukee. The author also talked to experts and residents and witnessed firsthand many issues discussed in this chapter.

TABLE 11.2
Loss of Open Space in Acres by County, 1963–1985

County	*Loss of Open Space in Acres, 1963–1970*	*Loss of Open Space in Acres, 1970–1985*	*Total Acres Lost, 1963–1985*
Kenosha	2,675	5,432	8,107
Milwaukee	5,649	6,276	11,925
Ozaukee	4,495	6,304	10,799
Racine	5,412	5,391	10,803
Walworth	3,680	6,815	10,495
Washington	4,224	9,059	13,283
Waukesha	13,766	24,902	38,668
Totals	39,901	64,179	104,080

Source: Southeastern Wisconsin Regional Planning Commission, *A Regional Land Use Plan for Southeastern Wisconsin—2010* (Waukesha, Wis.: SEWRPC, 1992), 181.

The findings demonstrated that in addition to socioeconomic consequences, another long-term impact of sprawl was its encroachment on farmland. According to a recent study by the U.S. Department of Agriculture, between 1982 and 1997, more than 2.3 million acres of Wisconsin farmlands were lost because of development. The majority of the loss occurred in southeastern Wisconsin. Every year, sprawl devoured ten square miles of farmland in southeastern Wisconsin.[7] Tables 11.2 and 11.3 depict, respectively, the number of acres of open space lost to development from 1963 to 1985 as well as projections for the next twenty years. In the past four decades, southeastern Wisconsin has lost over 100,000 acres of open spaces and is projected to lose another 14,000 by 2010.

TABLE 11.3
Projected Number of Open Spaces in Acres Lost by 2010 or 2020

Municipality	*Projected No. of Open Acres Lost by 2010 or 2020*	*Total No. of Acres in Municipality*	*Percentage of Open Acres Lost*
Sussex	1,739	5,445	31.9
West Bend	3,392	13,074	25.9
Troy	570	22,749	2.5
Rochester	943	11,343	8.3
Saukville	1,227	2,830	43.3
Waukesha	6,575	27,250	24.1

Sources: Southeastern Wisconsin Regional Planning Commission, *A Land Use Plan for the Town of Rochester—2020* (Waukesha, Wis.: SEWRPC, 1999); *A Land Use Plan for the Town of Saukville—2010* (1998); *A Regional Land Use Plan for Southeastern Wisconsin—2010* (1992); *A Land Use Plan for the Town of Troy—2020* (1999); *A Land Use Plan for the City of Waukesha—2010* (1993); and *A Land Use Plan for the City of West Bend—2010* (1992).

Three generations ago, Waukesha County had more purebred dairy cattle per square mile than anyplace in the country. Today, "Cow Country USA" has lost its cows and country. According to the Southeastern Wisconsin Regional Planning Commission, 90 of the 580 square miles of land in Waukesha County became sprawling suburban developments.[8] Between 1963 and 1990, sprawling development removed sixty farms just from Waukesha County.[9] In addition to the sixty family farms lost, scholars have argued that the destruction of farmland increases tensions between remaining farmers and suburban neighbors, leads to higher tax burdens, and puts pressure on environmental areas around the world.[10]

Although politicians wrote legislation in 1968 requiring environmental corridors to protect woodlands, wetlands, and floodplains from being destroyed, developers found loopholes, and in 1999 this legislation was strengthened to mandate that zoning reform of such lands first be approved by the Department of Natural Resources.[11]

Rather than being driven by the free market, developers of sprawl were given incentives by legislation that provided public subsidies for the automobile and highways. During the past twenty-five years, the sprawl model has become institutionalized and self-replicating throughout America. Along with new subdivisions and roads came business parks, sewers, and big-box strip malls. They were a natural consequence of the sprawl model. Faced with the high costs of providing infrastructure and services to new residential subdivisions, many suburban planners allowed the development of strip malls.[12]

Over time, sprawling development in southeastern Wisconsin reduced the amount of nature and solitude that drew wealthy home owners in the first place. It is ironic that the people who were attracted to the suburbs because of its pristine natural resources would have to move increasingly farther out to find their peace and quiet.[13] Large lot requirements precluded low-income families to obtain building permits for new construction. Many regional planners were critical of suburban officials who consciously sought out economic development through corporate parks without providing affordable housing for employees who might work there.[14] As table 11.4 demonstrates, over 75 percent of all permits issued in Waukesha and Ozaukee Counties in 1997 were for single-family detached housing units.

Wisconsin's governor at the time was Tommy Thompson, whose conservative political ideology permitted the use of septic tanks in environmentally sensitive areas that were previously illegal. According to an interview with Department of Natural Resources agent Dan Hellenberg, matters were made worse by the fact that few, if any, additional resources were available for county inspectors to monitor the 500,000 septic tanks in the state.[15]

TABLE 11.4
Metro Milwaukee Housing Trends, 1977, 1987, and 1997, by County

	Single-Family Permits as a Percentage of Total Permits						*Total Permits*		
County	*1977*	*%*	*1987*	*%*	*1997*	*%*	*1977*	*1987*	*1997*
Milwaukee	1,044	28	563	28	556	37	3,713	2,047	1,523
Waukesha	2,693	63	1,644	60	1,506	61	4,152	2,760	2,471
Washington	938	42	503	53	647	76	2,212	946	856
Ozaukee	489	58	351	73	238	78	840	482	306

Sources: M. Derus, "Wide-Open Spaces Are Closing in on Homeowners and More Find Themselves Hemmed in by Sprawl," *Milwaukee Journal Sentinel,* February 1, 1998, B1, and Waukesha County Economic Development Corporation, "Demographic Profiles," at www.wcedonline.org/demo.html (accessed April 12, 2001).

Years ago, to protect water quality, all private sewer systems were forbidden on steep slopes and in areas with unsuitable soils. However, that reality has recently changed as pro-growth politicians and planning officials embrace new wastewater technologies. Legislation known as COMM 83 created the "mound" sewer system, which used aboveground earthen mounds instead of drain fields. The introduction of this technology meant that subdivisions could be accommodated almost anywhere.[16] Prior to this invention, suburbs had to be linked into the Milwaukee Metropolitan Sewerage District system. During the 1980s, several wealthy suburban communities tried to shift their sewage costs to the poor. One political observer characterized the subsidy attempt as "an effort to shift a heavy burden from the bedroom suburbs to the central city."[17] Local experts claimed that when miniature sewage treatment plants were hooked up to larger municipal systems, it resulted in less affordable housing and more sprawling subdivisions.[18]

Affordable housing is defined as a residence that a family with a median income can afford. In 2000, median family income meant that the average family could afford a home valued at $140,000. In the high-income suburb of Mequon located in Ozaukee County, average house prices are so large that the probability of finding an affordable house is extremely low. According to data from the Chamber of Commerce, the average price in 2000 was $319,000.[19] In contrast, within the five-county region, Milwaukee had the lowest per capita tax base, approximately one-quarter the amount of the elite suburbs and one-half as large as the remaining sixty-seven municipalities.[20]

The political economics behind the deficiency of affordable housing in the suburbs were straightforward. The average cost of small lots cost $80,000, and a half-acre lot often can cost $200,000. This aspect of the affordable housing debate was clearly described by one expert: "Even if many of the suburbs were to allow quarter-acre lots in a specified area, the price of a lot would be around

$40,000. The average price per-square-foot for single-family residential construction is $44. To come in at a price of $80,000 for a lot and house, the residence would be 900 square feet, or 300 square-feet smaller than many suburban minimum house requirements."[21]

Housing advocates claimed that planners and politicians were to blame for the meager existence of affordable housing. The director of the Wisconsin Fair Lending Coalition acknowledged that few suburban politicians or planning officials discussed developments for affordable housing since the majority of suburbs had floor-area and lot-size requirements that reduced the supply of affordable housing.[22] Furthermore, city officials in the town of Lisbon in Waukesha County were set on one-acre lots. Despite open communication, regional planners could not persuade Lisbon political officials to conserve farmland. Local officials argued that farmers had a right to develop their land as they deemed fit and that attempts to save farms were unrealistic.[23]

Just south of Milwaukee in Racine County, open spaces were subdivided so hastily that local political officials declared the situation a disaster. In the city of Caledonia, over 1,000 homes were built between 1993 and 1998, with 1,500 additional children attending public schools. Planners claimed that it was difficult to provide services for police, fire, garbage pickup, mail delivery, and education. In nearby Waterford, the village administrator exclaimed, "From 1990 to 1997, the town changed dramatically. It's like a completely different community. Over the years we haven't been trying to stop growth since that would be just about impossible."[24]

As more subdivisions are developed, prices for farmland have soared to record highs, which is a boon for farmers who want to sell and retire but bad news for anyone who wants to get into farming. The causes behind the steady growth in land prices include a booming economy and a strong demand for farmland to be used for nonfarming purposes, exemplified by the city of Mequon in Ozaukee County.[25]

The development of expensive McMansions that must occupy large lots because of restrictive zoning requirements also created subdivisions farther away from the existing infrastructure. As a result, the costs associated for additional civil servants, police officers, firefighters, and road maintenance to serve people in the hinterlands skyrocketed. Some communities found that sprawling residential developments did not even generate enough taxes to educate the children who lived there. One study concluded that for every $1 increase gained in tax base, each new house cost $1.33 to provide services to.[26]

Subsequently, Wisconsin politicians introduced a new tax law in 1995. Although the tax break aimed to help farmers, it had the unintended consequences of reaping profits for land speculators. According to dairy farmer Robert Loduha, a common result is that the farmer reluctantly sells his or her land in order to pay taxes.[27] Consequently, the numbers of McMansions continue to proliferate in former farm fields. As a result, in 1995 state politicians enacted a use-value assessment law requiring agricultural property to be taxed according to its value as cropland, not land destined to be made into subdivisions. Use-value assessment was promoted largely by representatives of farmers on the edges of growing urban areas in Wisconsin. They argued that property tax rates based on the potential for development drove farmers near cities out of farming and hastened suburban sprawl.[28]

Over time, the tax legislation created a loophole for land speculators. David Dueholm, a land assessor in southeastern Wisconsin, pointed out, "Many of these so-called farmers do not even know the working end of a cow. It's a bad law. Farmers have received about $37 million in tax relief during the first two years of the freeze."[29] The state assessor's association charged that it accelerated sprawl by granting property owners a tax break until the land is sold for development. Dueholm provided several examples: In Roxbury, lots would normally sell for $26,000, but a North Carolina real estate speculator leased the land to a farmer despite the fact that it was already subdivided into lots. Dueholm added, "Unfortunately when I got there, it had corn growing on it, so I have to place a value of $4,800 per acre on it."[30] Just north of Milwaukee County, a 140-acre abandoned farm was taxed at $1,200 per acre even though it was divided into one-third-acre lots that were valued at $8,600 each. In Port Washington, a 116-acre estate owned by one of the wealthiest families in the state also enjoyed the agricultural tax break because some chickens and goats were raised on the property. Its tax assessment was 2,000 percent lower when compared to its neighbor's thirteen-acre parcel. The president of the Wisconsin Association of Assessing Officers agreed: "The law is for those who profit most from land speculation. We're not opposed to giving true farmers a tax break but we do not want that tax break to go to developers at the expense of other taxpayers."[31] In the end, those who challenged the law lost.

The state should encourage farmland preservation, but political lobbying efforts by developers over impact fees made this objective more difficult. The Metropolitan Builders Association of Greater Milwaukee argued that because each subdivision had different impact fees, it forced "leapfrog" development as developers had an incentive to build in areas with the lowest fees. Impact fees made builders responsible for the public costs of roads, sewers, and libraries created by each new development. Some suburbs raised the impact fee for single-family homes from $1,500 to $10,000, increasing the disparity in home prices between city and suburbs. Impact fees up to $10,000 add to the walls of segregation around Milwaukee. Housing expert Gregory Squires claimed in an interview that any expense that increased the cost of housing had a disproportionately negative effect on people of color since they have lower incomes.[32]

Impact fees represented a substantial shift in the traditional thinking about community growth. The traditional thinking was that growth created jobs and tax revenue, thereby improving the local quality of life. Experts believed that growth did not necessarily mean jobs, but it did mean having to provide services for people. Growth also meant added pollution, more demand on public facilities, and, as a result, higher taxes and a less desirable quality of life. Other scholars argued that impact fees raised assessments, increased rents, and reduced housing quality as developers looked for ways to cut corners.[33] Three external forces have been significant in the use of impact fees. First, members of the environmental movement have argued that growth may not be good. Second, most citizens do not want to pay more taxes. Finally, construction costs for infrastructure have increased while federal funds for such improvements have decreased.[34]

Impact fees were a major stumbling block for affordable housing in suburban communities. Both the developer and the buyer might share in the payment of the impact fee. However, in communities with high buyer demand, home buyers pay all the fees that developers would normally have to pay. Impact fees do not treat all households equally because it is a regressive fee; that is, there is a higher burden for those with lower incomes. Moreover, existing home owners who purchased property before the inauguration of impact fees added financial gains at the expense of new home owners.[35] Impact fees kept out low-income citizens because some developers profited when they tripled the cost of the impact fee and added it to the price of a new house. Housing specialist Sammis White argued that the buyer, not the developer, often paid the impact fees at inflated rates and that impact fees were a form of taxation without representation that increased rents for low-income people while they provided no benefits to the renters.[36]

It is undeniable that impact fees of thousands of dollars added another impediment to the creation of affordable housing. In many suburbs, city employees, such as teachers, firefighters, and sanitation workers, could not afford to live where they worked. And some children of parents who grew up in a community had to move out when they became young adults. Research has also shown that the lack of affordable housing often forced elderly residents to relocate. Low-income service workers needed to endure long commutes to get to their jobs. The commuters, in turn, added to freeway congestion and air pollution.[37]

In 1990, Ozaukee County political officials rejected the Milwaukee City Housing Authority's plan for affordable housing in the suburbs. Milwaukee politicians offered to buy one home in each suburb to use as low-income housing. One Ozaukee County Board supervisor remarked, "There's no way in hell would we want to participate with Milwaukee County communities. I said our foxholes will be dug right at the county line. . . . While many of the suburbs' residents can empathize with Milwaukee's problems, they don't want to pay for them."[38] The nonexistence of political cooperation between Ozaukee and Milwaukee regarding affordable housing later included the rejection of a proposed regional transportation authority as well as opposition to a regional cultural tax for the Milwaukee Zoo and the Performing Arts Center. This political attitude represented a recent exclusionary phenomenon in which citizens desired the cultural aspects associated with a big city but in their own backyards want it rural.

Some of the suburban difficulties associated with affordable housing could be attributed to its planning. Were the political officials who required large lot requirements trying "to price out low- and middle-income homebuyers? According to William Tisdale, director of Metropolitan Milwaukee's Fair Housing Council, the answer is yes."[39] Nonetheless, developer J. Michael Mooney claimed, "What it comes down to is economic and racial bigotry."[40] The extent of racism should not be surprising since across America it has been argued that restrictive zoning laws were examples of a phenomenon in which an elite used its political power to exclude outsiders. The real reason for growth management was to increase the property values of existing owners.[41]

The lack of affordable housing has prohibited numerous people of color from living in the suburbs. According to U.S. Census data, blacks accounted for 0.7 percent of the population in suburban Ozaukee County. The president of the Ozaukee chapter of the National Association for the Advancement of Colored People explained, "In one case, there was a subdivision where the owners had design restrictions. A black couple submitted blueprints for their home. Design changes were suggested and revisions were made but the homeowner's association design committee cited additional problems. The couple tried to fix the design but in each case, they were turned down and were struck by the similarity between existing houses and their blueprints that were repeatedly rejected. Then the police stopped them for driving in another neighborhood without substantial cause. These kinds of messages send signals to people that they're not welcome."[42]

Many city dwellers fled to the suburbs to jettison urban social problems and later resisted bringing in low-income and minority families. During the 1950–1980 period, those persons who could afford to "moved out of Milwaukee's central city in part due to crime and racism."[43] Resistance to people of color moving to the suburbs occasionally took the form of racism. For example, large-lot zoning restrictions prevented the construction of affordable houses. In addition, racist lending practices and steering techniques used by real estate agents discriminated against people of color and low-income people of all races. Real estate lawyer Robert Koenig attested, "Segregation, de facto, is pervasive in Milwaukee's suburbs. They have a multitude of laws that have the effect of keeping low- and moderate-income people out of the suburbs. The statistical reality is that barriers to affordability have a disproportionate effect on minorities. Racism exists in the suburbs."[44] It was not surprising that only 2 percent of African Americans in the Milwaukee metropolitan area lived in the suburbs. As a consequence, at 1990s lending rates, it would take 141 years to racially integrate Milwaukee's suburbs.[45]

By building on smaller lots, affordable housing becomes available to people who normally could not afford a bigger lot. Just like investors in the stock market, the suburbs need to diversify their portfolios of residential types to include affordable housing in case of future downward cycles in the economy. A somewhat contradictory trend uncovered in this study was the fact that many officials were quick to raise the fact that affordable housing should be market driven and that government should not interfere. Yet many of the suburbs' zoning of large minimum lot sizes amounts to heavy government interference in the housing market. Would not the housing market be completely free without restrictive zoning? In a more sustainable era, why are we unable to use our finite resources more efficiently? Research has shown that subdivisions using smaller lot sizes, reduced street widths, and decreased front-yard setbacks can provide savings over 50 percent when compared to more restrictive zoning subdivisions, as shown in table 11.5.

TABLE 11.5
Cost Savings in Dollars with Reduced Minimum Zoning Laws

Municipality	*Cost without Reduced Minimums*	*Cost with Reduced Minimums*	*Percentage Savings with Reduced Minimums*
Brookfield	6,173	3,086	50
Lisbon	4,497	2,172	52
Mukwonago	9,341	4,517	52
Pewaukee	9,090	4,517	50
Waukesha	1,613	739	54
Eagle	9,188	3,086	66
Merton	6,173	3,086	50
Ottawa	3,591	1,796	50

Source: Mary Kay Schuetz and Sammis White, *Identifying and Mitigating Regulatory Barriers to Affordable Housing in Waukesha County Wisconsin* (Milwaukee: University of Wisconsin–Milwaukee Urban Research Center, 1992), table 2.

Solutions for the Future

Several recommendations can be made to reduce sprawl and increase affordable housing units. First, we must encourage more compact development because it allows for the preservation of open spaces. Second, we must find solutions to improve inner-city neighborhoods and give incentives to keep people living in the metropolitan area when their incomes rise. Next, suburbs must be willing to allot a certain percentage of new housing permits, perhaps 10 percent, to affordable housing units. In addition, we need to enact laws that provide funds to purchase the development rights of rural lands. Finally, we must strive for greater regional cooperation in order to reduce leapfrog developments.

Planners and political officials need to also consider the health and welfare of children. Those who examine the needs of children often look at threats posed by air bags, food poisoning, and accidental shootings. However, transportation and medical researchers have recently declared that "more children were hit by a car and killed than died as a result of those other tragedies combined . . . [and] the US Centers for Disease Control warned, we discourage routine physical activity, such as walking. The consequences of this lifestyle are alarming; an increased risk of obesity, heart disease, diabetes, high blood pressure, and other chronic diseases. Only 10 percent of children now walk to school. . . . It's a wake-up call to local governments to require new developments to be more pedestrian friendly."[46]

Besides children's safety, the growing need for regional planning and cooperation is a worthwhile solution. As long as Wisconsin makes do with more than hundreds of separate land use policies and little or no coordination among them, our attempt at a comprehensive land ethic will be tenuous. Several scholars have exclaimed that cookie-cutter development rarely works. The suburbs are not isolated communities in which planners can throw up barriers to the things they fear. If you fail to think in regional terms, you end up destroying the region since citizens generally have self-interest in mind.[47]

Finding answers to today's regional land use questions requires a wide focus, and one worthwhile solution being used around the country is the purchase of development rights. This allows a property owner to voluntarily sell the right to develop his or her land to a municipality or to a land trust. The landowner receives a payment equal to the difference between the land's market value and its agricultural value. In return, the land remains private property, and the buyer receives a conservation easement that permanently restricts use of the parcel to farming, open space, or wildlife habitat.[48] Near Madison, the town of Dunn was the first community in Wisconsin to use conservation easements. Consequently, Dunn officials were able to keep taxes significantly lower than surrounding municipalities. In southeastern Wisconsin, there are dozens of groups saving open spaces through acquisition or conservation easements. For example, the Waukesha Land Conservancy has protected more than 200 acres throughout the county, including woodlands, prairies, and wetlands. The Ozaukee Land Trust has saved some forests and stream corridors. In Port Washington, the trust was one of several groups that worked to establish a twenty-seven-acre nature preserve along the banks of the stream that bisects the city.[49]

In order for affordable houses to be built, restrictive zoning laws must allow for higher densities. One study found that single-family residences could be built at as many as twelve units per acre and townhouses at fifty-seven units per acre.[50] Indeed, many renowned architects have built as many as forty to fifty housing units per acre in U.S. cities.[51]

Conclusion

Unless Americans push for affordable housing, experience suggests that only legal action at the state or federal level will cause local politicians to seriously consider this issue. Elected officials must block attempts by pro-growth politicians to speed suburban sprawl, diminish wetlands, and gobble up farmland in the name of free enterprise. Instead citizens, political officials, and planners must try to create a balance of activities that do not favor cars. Currently, most of the suburban housing, shops, and restaurants associated with sprawl are inaccessible to half the population who are unable to drive. The elderly, children, and low-income citizens in particular depend on others for mobility. And in the face of ever increasing expansion of highways, open places are rapidly dwindling. Modification of the rural landscape has outreached our ability to come to terms with capital market structures. As we become more affluent and populated, development pressures will continue; therefore, smart growth complements the community, conserves natural areas, preserves agricultural lands and small farms, and creates financial incentives that encourage developers to build more affordable housing.

Looking into the future, the political, economic, and social implications of sprawl and affordable housing are extremely important. Southeastern Wisconsin, like many locations west of the Mississippi, has a beautiful yet fragile landscape. However, the question for many public officials in the outlying regions is not when will people arrive but how much space will they consume? We must recognize the idea that there is something intangible in certain open places—a kind of quality that makes these places worth defending. Open places must be preserved in every community in order to give people a sense of orientation and inspiration for future generations. It is not too late to protect open places and encourage affordable housing.

Notes

1. Southeastern Wisconsin Regional Planning Commission, *A Regional Land Use Plan for Southeastern Wisconsin—2010* (Waukesha, Wis.: SEWRPC, 1992), 82.
2. Douglas Massey and Nancy Denton, *American Apartheid* (Cambridge, Mass.: Harvard University Press, 1993), 221.
3. Mark Edward Braun, *Social Change and the Empowerment of the Poor* (Lanham, Md.: Lexington Books, 2001).
4. Metropolitan Milwaukee Association of Commerce, *Economic Fact Sheet,* June, 2000.
5. Henry Reuss, *To Save Our Cities: What Needs to Be Done* [**Au: Pls. supply city.** ce](N.J.: Public Affairs Press, 1977), 2.
6. Gregory Squires, *Capital and Communities in Black and White: The Intersections of Race, Class, and Uneven Development* (Albany: State University of New York Press, 1994).
7. Wisconsin Farm Bureau Federation, "Wisconsin Farm Facts," at www.wfbf.com/FarmFacts.htm (accessed April 12, 2001).
8. Southeastern Wisconsin Regional Planning Commission, *A Land Use Plan for the City of Waukesha—2010* (Waukesha, WI: SEWRPC, 1993).
9. Elaine Middleton, *Agricultural Impact Statement for Waukesha County* (Madison, Wis.: State of Wisconsin Department of Agriculture, Trade and Consumer Protection, 1993).
10. Thomas Daniels, "The Purchase of Development Rights—Preserving Agricultural Land and Open Space," *Journal of the American Planning Association* 57 (1991): 421–31. See also Adam Rome, *The Bulldozer in the Countryside: Suburban Sprawl and the Rise of American Environmentalism* (New York: Cambridge University Press, 2001).
11. Wisconsin Department of Natural Resources, "Protecting Precious Natural Resources, Discouraging Urban Sprawl, and Encouraging Compact Development" (1999).
12. Al Norman, *Slam Dunking Wal-Mart: How You Can Stop Superstore Sprawl* (Greenfield, Mass.: Raphael Marketing, 1999).
13. Thomas Kindschi and Charles Causier, "Preserving Endangered Rural Character" (presentation at the National Planning Conference, Seattle, 1999).
14. Constance Beaumont, *How Superstore Sprawl Can Harm Communities* (Washington, D.C.: National Trust for Historic Preservation, 1994).
15. Personal interview with Dan Hellenberg, August 15, 2001.
16. Wisconsin Department of Industry, Labor and Human Resources.
17. Richard Cutler, *Greater Milwaukee's Growing Pains, 1950–2000: An Insider's View* (Milwaukee, Wis.: Milwaukee County Historical Society, 2001), 184.
18. Robert Burchell and Naveed Shad, *The Benefits and Costs of Growth* (Milwaukee, Wis.: Milwaukee Metropolitan Sewerage District Symposium, n.d.).

19. Mequon-Thiensville Chamber of Commerce, "Area Demographics," at www.mtchamber.org/profile/demographics.asp (accessed November 21, 2000).

20. Public Policy Forum, "2000 Spending and Taxing Report," *Research Brief* 88 (2000): 3.

21. Sammis White, *An Assessment of Impact Fees* (Milwaukee, Wis.: Urban Research Center, University of Wisconsin–Milwaukee, 1993), 31.

22. M. Derus, "In Search of Cheaper Lots There's Rush to Find Land Under $40,000," *Milwaukee Journal Sentinel*, May 25, 1997, B1.

23. Don Walker, "Waukesha Searches for Ways to Put the Brakes on Sprawl," *Milwaukee Journal Sentinel*, May 9, 1995, B1.

24. S. Tunkiwicz, "Officials Make Tough Decisions on Growth," *Milwaukee Journal Sentinel*, September 13, 1998, B1.

25. Mark Edward Braun, "A Social History of a Suburban Community: Mequon, Wisconsin 1957–2000," in *The Small City and Regional Community*, vol. 14, ed. Ronald Shaffer and William Ryan (Madison, Wis.: Center for Community Economic Development, 2001), 333–46.

26. American Farmland Trust, "Farming on the Edge," at www.farmland.org/edge.html (accessed November 21, 2000).

27. Personal interview with Robert Loduha, June 15, 2001.

28. League of Wisconsin Municipalities, "Conferences and Meetings: 1998 Approved League Resolutions," at www.lwm-info.org/calendar/annual98/resolutions.html (accessed April 12, 2001).

29. Vanden Brook, "Farmers Not Alone in Getting Tax Break," *Milwaukee Journal Sentinel*, August 10, 1997, B1.

30. Brook, "Farmers Not Alone in Getting Tax Break."

31. Kenneth Cook and Andrew Art, *City Slickers: Farm Subsidy Recipients in America's Big Cities* (Washington, D.C.: Environmental Working Group, 1995).

32. Personal interview with Greg Squires, March 22, 2001.

33. T. I. Miller, "Must Growth Restrictions Eliminate Moderate-Priced Housing?" *Journal of the American Planning Association* 52 (1986): 319–25. See also J. M. Armentano, "As Local Governments Struggle to Finance Cost of New Construction, More and More Turn to the Option of Requiring Developers to Pay Impact Fees," in: *2000 Zoning and Planning Law Handbook*, ed. D. Mans (New York: West Group, 2000), 569–81.

34. G. Bauman and W. Ethier, "Development Exactions and Impact Fees: A Study of American Practices," *Law and Contemporary Problems* 50 (1987): 51–68.

35. Forrest E. Huffman et al., "Who Bears the Burden of Development Impact Fees?" *Journal of the American Planning Association* 54 (1988): 49–55.

36. Telephone interview with Sammis White, January 28, 2001.

37. Marc Levine, *Suburban Sprawl and the Secession of the Affluent. Metropolitan Polarization in Milwaukee: 1987–1997* (Milwaukee: University of Wisconsin–Milwaukee Center for Economic Development, 1999).

38. M. Devine, "Milwaukee's on Its Own, Ozaukee County Says," *Milwaukee Journal*, September 5, 1993, B1.

39. William Tisdale, "Fair Housing Strategies for the Future," *Cityscape* 4 (1999): 153.

40. Telephone interview with J. Michael Mooney, February 21, 2001.

41. Rolf Pendall, "Local Land Use Regulation and the Chain of Exclusion," *Journal of the American Planning Association* 66 (2000): 125–42.

42. P. Nero, "Ozaukee, Washington Still Draw Few Blacks," *Milwaukee Journal*, March 4, 1991, B1.

43. Richard Cutler, *Greater Milwaukee's Growing Pains* (Milwaukee, Wis.: Milwaukee County Historical Society, 2001), 184.

44. Derus, "In Search of Cheaper Lots There's Rush to Find Land Under $40,000."

45. Stanley Battle, ed., *The State of Black Milwaukee* (Milwaukee, Wis.: Milwaukee Urban League, 2000). See also Gary Delgado, "The Real Test Is Race," *Colorlines* 2 (1999): 22–24, and Bruce Katz, "Race, Poverty and Sprawl," *Poverty and Race* 7 (1998): 1–5.

46. Surface Transportation Policy Project, "Cars, Kids, and Sprawl: A Deadly Combination," *STPP Transfer Newsletter* 4 (1998): 3.

47. Myron Orfield, *Metropolitics: A Regional Agenda for Community and Stability* (Washington, D.C.: Brookings Institution Press, 1996); Thomas Daniels, *When City and Country Collide* (Washington, D.C.: Island Press, 1999).

48. Don Behm, "Sprawl-Fighters Seek Truce in City-town Border Wars," *Milwaukee Journal Sentinel*, January 31, 2000, A11.

49. Whitney Gould, "Growing Smarter," *Milwaukee Journal Sentinel*, January 30, 2000, A1.

50. E. Alexander, K. Reed, and P. Murphy, *Density Measures and Their Relation to Urban Form* (Madison, Wis.: Center for Architecture and Urban Planning Research, 1988).

51. Peter Calthorpe, *The Next American Metropolis* (Princeton, N.J.: Princeton University Press, 1993); Peter Hall, "Urban Renaissance/New Urbanism," *Journal of the American Planning Association* 66 (2000): 359–60; Peter Katz, *New Urbanism: Toward an Architecture of Community* (New York: McGraw-Hill, 1994).

A Conversation with Ted Mondale

Ted Mondale is chair of the Metropolitan Council, Minneapolis–St. Paul.

What led you to become interested in smart growth?

Mondale: When I ran for the legislature in 1990, my district was a first- and second-string suburban district, and we also had more Superfund sites than any legislative district in the state. It became very clear to me that there was a set of forces in play driven by government regulation and spending policy that created a market upon which older communities would fail. Or to put it another way, to be successful as a community, we needed to have resources that in the normal course of business we could renew ourselves. When the commercial becomes outdated, how do you upgrade it? How do you make sure the parks are nice places to be? How do you make those connections?

We had a debate around here in the early 1990s driven by the census. If I may characterize it, you had the far-right wing saying, "Look, this is about prosperity; the death of the center city and older suburbs is inevitable. This is a natural part of America. You have a $100 billion housing market; let government get [out] of the way."

And on the far-left wing, [Representative Myron] Orfield was the lightning rod for the debate and argued for a punitive damage approach to these issues. So if a city didn't build affordable housing, you would take their local government aids away. The growing cities said, "You know I'm losing 40 percent of my commercial industrial tax base, so where do you want it to be?"

We came to a consensus that we would create market choices for businesses and individuals with limited government dollars. We passed the Livable Communities Act with $12 to $14 million a year in redevelopment funds. On top of that, we opened up tax increment financing laws to polluted lands. We moved ahead with our first light-rail line.

Five years later after that market experiment, it's incredible what's happened here. When we had our first set of grants that were for mixed-use transit-oriented development, there was no market. Cities came back with, "Well we'd like to do a clock tower, or we want to do light posts with flowers hanging." Now we are overexpired. We could now do $50 to $60 million in [smart-growth development]. The market has changed. There is clearly a premium for living near services. The market is making its choice, frankly ahead of the politicians. Almost every suburban community in the Twin Cities metropolitan area is planning a downtown. They get it now. They hear from their residents that people would like to walk around their community. They get it that folks want better access to local parks. They get it that they want new retail;

they don't want the gang task force in their community. They want unique, cool restaurants.

We now have a smart-growth screen on our bonding that [encourages the use of] existing infrastructure. There is a countervailing force now.

The Twin Cities are often cited as one of the nation's leading sprawl areas. Why have the Twin Cities sprawled so much?

Mondale: Number one, we're on the tundra up here. There are no natural barriers to growth other than water and natural resources on the ground. Second, we are a younger city. A lot of growth is within [the sprawl] model, and we have a high number of baby boomers in peak earning years with children. Third, most analyses of these things are wrong. If you factor in all the land and water we've preserved along with our park systems and bike trails, I think you'd see a different number. Give me an ocean, and I'll show you land management.

What kind of tools does the Metropolitan Council have that allows it to control sprawl?

Mondale: Unlike anywhere but Portland, we have a system whereby there is a systemic way we interact with local government. We have a massive wastewater system, transit, GIS [geographic information survey]; we have the redevelopment arm; and we are the MPO (Metropolitan Planning Organization) for the area.

We implement the Livable Communities Act, which is voluntary. You need to have resources to say to local governments, "We're going to put a new wastewater project in your town, and you can get it in the next few years or the next twenty years, but we need to know where is the housing going to be? Where's your commercial going to be? Here's a $75,000 planning grant for your new infrastructure project, and here are the three things we want back—we want to see a mix of house, local street projects, and where your transit is going to be. If you say, "Here's what I want you to do," in most of these communities you'll get met by pitchforks and shotguns. But if you say, "Hey, I've got a $20 million asset we're going to give you plus a planning grant to do these few things," they say, "Hey, this is great."

The day of government making unilateral decisions on things and expecting everyone to follow is gone. There are very few voices saying we need to reinstitute large, unresponsive bureaucracies.

12

From Sprawl to Smart Growth: The Case of Atlanta

Ulf Zimmermann, Göktuğ Morçöl, and Bethany Stich

BETWEEN 1980 AND 2000, the Atlanta metropolitan area's population doubled, its built environment doubled, and it is considered the most rapidly expanding and largest human settlement ever constructed, consuming 500 acres of undeveloped land a week.[1] In those last two decades, metropolitan Atlanta's reach has spread to 110 miles from one end to the other, and average commuting times have risen to national highs of thirty-one minutes, ahead of Chicago, Los Angeles, and Houston,[2] with this traffic producing 250 tons of nitrogen oxide a day,[3] making Atlanta the media's "poster child of sprawl."

To get a grip on this growth, the Georgia Regional Transportation Authority (GRTA)[4] was created in 1999. The creation of GRTA is significant not only because it is one of the boldest attempts in the nation to solve regional problems directly through state intervention but also because the metro Atlanta business community played a leading role in the process. The metro business community reacted, collectively and decisively, to the escalating threats to the region's economic vitality in the late 1990s and took the lead in efforts to curb sprawl and to promote "smart growth."

This concerted behavior of the business community is in fact a continuation of its traditional role in Atlanta politics. As in most American cities, the dominant cultural norm in Atlanta is that what is good for business is good for the city.[5] The Atlanta business community has a strong sense of collective self-interest, and as the area's best organized social group, it is seen as natural that it exercises leadership in public policymaking.

For more than a century, city boosters promoted unfettered growth. Their role in the creation of GRTA signifies an important turnabout. They have not abandoned growth but have begun promoting restrained and planned growth (smart growth). In this chapter, we delineate these developments in metropolitan Atlanta and discuss the implications for regional politics.

These developments will be better understood in the context of national politics and culture, the legal status of local governments in Georgia, and the region's social and economic dynamics. Federal transportation policies and America's car-dependent transportation culture, which mutually produced and perpetuated one another for decades, have been hugely influential in the economic and geographic development patterns in Atlanta as in many other metropolitan areas. As a home-rule state, Georgia constitutionally vests land use authority in counties and municipalities, and the resulting competition among the metro area's jurisdictions for economic growth has thus propelled sprawl. Race relations always played a large role in the area's social and economic dynamics and influenced transportation policies. Although Atlanta has traditionally projected a more progressive image in race relations compared to its peers in the South, "white flight" to the northern suburbs nonetheless intensified both racial segregation and urban sprawl in the metro area.

Business Interests and Urban Politics

The rigorous planning requirements and restrictions that are the norm in European countries are all but nonexistent in American cities because of a political culture that is antigovernment and "privatist" and that enshrines private persons' rights to develop and dispose of their property as they see fit.[6] This American privatism enables organized business interests to play powerful roles in policymaking in urban areas.

The role of business interests in city politics has long been debated by the "elitist"[7] and "pluralist" theorists.[8] Later Clarence Stone's and Harvey Molotch's theories emphasized that urban politics is complex and involves multiple actors, but the economic resources held by certain groups place them in more powerful positions. In his study of Atlanta, Stone argues that businesses did not necessarily control the decisions of elected officials directly, but their economic resources made them the more powerful partners in the informal biracial coalition, the "urban regime," which they formed with the middle-class blacks who commanded the African American majority's electoral power.[9]

Molotch's "growth machine" theory also emphasizes that municipal governments serve the needs of capital, particularly the needs of the "land-based elite" whose property interests are closely tied to the economic growth of the city.[10] Unlike corporations whose interests in any particular urban area are not strong because of the mobility of their investment capital, real estate developers, property-financing institutions, media, and utilities have strong interests in the economic growth of their cities and therefore pursue leading roles in their governance.[11]

In our discussion of the transportation policies in metropolitan Atlanta, we use Molotch's and Stone's theoretical frameworks. Molotch's growth machine metaphor aptly describes the role of the business community in Atlanta. We propose two "upgrades," however: First, the growth machine has been transformed into a "smart-growth machine." Second, it is not the city (and hence an urban regime) but rather the metropolitan region that should be the unit of analysis since the focus of the business elite has become regional and a new "regional regime" may thus emerge. And as the sphere of politics has become regional, the role of the African American community, so central to Atlanta's urban regime in the past, has thus also undergone a transformation.

The Business Elite, Race Relations, and the Evolution of Transportation Policies

While Atlanta owed its origins and early growth to the railroad, it might have stayed little more than a mere "Terminus," as it was first called, had this early growth not sufficiently whetted its business community's appetite for more growth to trump its racial distastes. For when the then capital's innkeepers in Milledgeville refused, after the Civil War, to house the newly elected African American legislators, Atlanta was quick to assume the role of capital.[12] This marked the beginning of Atlanta's efforts to put economic growth before racial considerations, and while racial problems in Atlanta may not have been less than in other southern cities, Atlanta continued to do everything to promote its business interests first and to cultivate an image of racial accommodation, enabling it to attract a vast influx of northern capital.

That Atlanta's business community did not practice the most benign race relations and that it would seek to influence policy accordingly was demonstrated in an early transportation issue. The electric streetcars operated by the Georgia Power Company in Atlanta beginning in the late nineteenth century got their first competition in 1915 from jitneys. Small vanlike motor vehicles, jitneys offered passengers faster and more flexible transportation at modest fares and seriously threatened the streetcar business.[13] When in 1922 an African American–owned and –operated jitney business also started up,[14] the Georgia Power Company used its influence to convince the city's aldermen to pass an ordinance effectively eliminating the jitney in 1925.[15]

As the battle between jitneys and streetcars was going on, automobiles were making profound inroads onto the Atlanta transportation scene. The state of Georgia attempted to deal with the influx of automobiles with the creation of a state highway commission in 1916. However, the seemingly endless reorganizations of the commission until it reached its current form as the Georgia Department of Transportation (GDOT) in 1972 created a policy vacuum that in effect left transportation planning in the city to its economic and political leaders who in the process pushed for more use of automobiles.

In the 1940s, the Atlanta business community, as represented by the Chamber of Commerce, underwent a transformation in which the leaders of the big businesses downtown (such as Coca-Cola) established a separate organization to promote their more systematic and comprehensive vision of the future of downtown Atlanta. This was the Central Atlanta Improvement Association (CAIA), later renamed Central Atlanta Progress (CAP).[16]

In this era, race relations entered a new phase as well. Thanks to the 1946 federal court mandate to end Georgia's all-white primaries, African Americans mobilized a voter drive that made them more than a quarter of the Atlanta electorate.[17] The white business elite, particularly the CAIA's prominent property holders, recognized that future economic growth would require abandoning segregation and courting the emerging political power of African Americans.[18] This view, combined with the racially pragmatic and pro-business political leadership of Mayor William B. Hartsfield (1937–1941, 1943–1961), laid the foundation for the biracial urban regime of Atlanta.

This did not, however, mean that this elite would promote integration. Its policies promoted spatial segregation via transportation policies. Thus, for example, they pushed for the construction of a north–south expressway that would curve around downtown in such a way as to form a "buffer between the business district and the black neighborhoods."[19]

Impacts of Federal Legislation

The most important federal legislation affecting transportation developments and hence the direction of growth were the acts that launched the construction of the National System of Interstate and Defense Highways and the creation of the Highway Trust Fund (that is, the Federal-Aid Highway and Highway Revenue Acts of 1956).[20]

While these acts made massive amounts of federal money available to states and cities, the placement of these federal highways was, as noted, dictated by local racial politics. As Stone points out, "The original north-south and east-west expressways [I-75/I-85] mostly disrupted black neighborhoods, especially those close to the CBD,"[21] and, as Bayor notes, Interstate 20 was built immediately south of the CBD to limit African American access to it.[22] The African American community initially protested these highway plans but was placated by the city's offer to hire minority contractors in the construction.

The early frenzy of highway building was tempered in the 1960s, particularly by the federal legislation that came in response to the "Freeway Revolt" that had arisen in threatened neighborhoods and included environmentalists and African Americans. Subsequent acts required relocation assistance that would begin to diminish the destruction of poor neighborhoods, which had been the cheapest way for Georgia highway builders to go, and preservation of parks and historic sites, which had also been cheap for the state to build across, but the main racial transportation patterns had already been put into place.

African American Power in Atlanta and Mass Transit Redivivus

During the 1960s, when the last white mayors of Atlanta—Ivan Allen Jr., a member of a liberal business elite family, and Sam Massell, the first Jewish mayor—governed the city, Atlanta's official support for civil rights and the African American universities, which gave it its "Black Mecca" reputation, spurred a tremendous influx of African Americans to Atlanta. The growth of this population and the continuing white flight to suburbs in the 1960s created the conditions for the election of Maynard Jackson as Atlanta's first African American mayor in 1973. Whereas before African Americans could only bargain with city hall, they now controlled it, but Atlanta's white business elite was still able to exert their influence because of their control over resources. African Americans needed the white elite for economic opportunities, and this elite continued to work with African Americans for the sake of a progressive image and thus growth.[23] The relations between the partners of the regime were not always smooth, however.

African American electoral power had been demonstrated in the 1968 and 1971 referenda on the Metropolitan Atlanta Rapid Transit Authority (MARTA). The first MARTA campaign was energetically backed by downtown business leaders and the Allen administration, but forgetting that this was not the 1920s, they ignored the African American community's insistence that MARTA had to be more than "a rapid rail system for white suburbanites working downtown."[24] The referendum lost in all four jurisdictions—Fulton, DeKalb, Gwinnett, and Cobb Counties—and its leaders learned a lesson: They added an African American who had been a vocal critic of the 1968 proposal to the MARTA board and incorporated the African American community's concerns into the text of the second referendum. This passed in 1971, though only in Fulton and DeKalb Counties, where African Americans constituted substantial percentages of the populations, and not in predominantly white Gwinnett and Cobb Counties.

The MARTA referenda illustrate the geographic limits of the power of the downtown business elite. Its policy of racial accommodation was not widely endorsed by white suburbanites. This racial divide between the city and the core metropolitan counties of Fulton and DeKalb on the one hand and suburban counties on the other has influenced metro Atlanta politics for decades and has hampered regionwide approaches to social and economic problems in the multiple jurisdictions of metro Atlanta.

Metropolitan Planning and the Atlanta Regional Commission

Atlanta has a long tradition of metropolitan planning. The Atlanta Regional Commission (ARC) is a federally recognized metropolitan planning organization whose predecessor, the Metropolitan Planning Commission, was created by the legislature in 1947 as the nation's first multicounty planning agency (and it received part of its funding from private businesses).[25] Why then, one might ask, the Georgia Regional Transportation Authority, with its largely overlapping jurisdiction? The answer lies in the legal limitations on the ARC's power and political composition of its board.

The ARC does not have the legal authority to enforce its plans. The ARC's power is limited to leveraging the planning decisions of its member governments by allocating federal and state funds among them. Its power is further limited by the composition of its board: Of its thirty-eight voting members and one nonvoting member, twenty-three are elected public officials (county commission chairs, mayors, and an Atlanta City Council member) from the ARC's member governments, and the remaining fifteen are private citizens chosen by them from multijurisdictional districts in the metro area. As board member Claire Mueller put it, "Developing a consensus . . . [is] virtually impossible with a board that is dominated by county commission chairs who are elected to represent their counties and not the region as a whole."[26]

The Georgia Regional Transportation Authority

A Changing Environment in the 1990s

Between the ARC's incapacity to solve the region's problems and the steady worsening of these, something had to change. Atlanta had failed to meet clean air standards ever since the Environmental Protection Agency (EPA) began monitoring ozone in 1980, but no one in the region or in the state had taken any serious action.[27] Under the Clean Air Act Amendments of 1990, the area was classified as a "serious" violator of the National Ambient Air Quality Standards,[28] and in 1996 the EPA threatened to withhold federal funds for highway construction. Funds were finally withheld in 1998, except for "grandfathered" projects.[29]

The classification of Atlanta as a "serious" violator of these standards was a problem not only because of the threat of losing federal money for highway projects. More important was the prospect of projecting an image of pollution and sprawl that could discourage outside investment in the region's further growth. Leading business groups, such as the Regional Business Coalition of Metro Atlanta and, particularly, the Metro Atlanta Chamber of Commerce, had thus been watching these developments for some time, and the newspaper attention these regional problems were getting had been steadily increasing with major *Atlanta Journal-Constitution* editorials in the fall of 1997.[30] In its January 1998 issue, *Atlanta* magazine answered its bold-print rhetorical question, "Is Traffic Killing Atlanta?" with a resounding "yes."[31] A survey of national real estate investors had rated Atlanta fifteenth among eighteen cities in investment potential for 1998. Two years before, it had been ranked first. By May 1998, the *Journal-Constitution* was shouting "SMOGLANTA" in a huge headline.

As it turned out, the day after the very June 18 that the whole country saw the *Wall Street Journal* ask on its front page, "Is Traffic-Clogged Atlanta The New Los Angeles?" A. D. "Pete" Correll, chairman of the Metro Atlanta Chamber of Commerce, announced the chamber's plan to address the issue.[32]

The Metropolitan Atlanta Transportation Initiative

With the stage set for major policy change and no one else taking the lead, the Metro Atlanta Chamber of Commerce, a public policy–oriented organization of business leaders with a regional vision, stepped in and formed an ad hoc committee—the Metro Atlanta Transportation Initiative (MATI)—to study the region's air quality, sprawl, and economic development problems and to recommend solutions. The membership of the MATI board was quite diverse—including university presidents, local government leaders, and representatives of state agencies—but the preponderant leadership role of the businesses was unmistakable. The executive summary of MATI's full report stated,

> In times of crisis, the metro Atlanta business community has often led and championed change. Recognizing its unique ability to galvanize the community,

> the Metro Atlanta Chamber of Commerce gathered a diverse set of leaders from the region's businesses, universities, and government agencies to address the growing traffic congestion problem.[33]

MATI observed that the rapid population growth, suburban expansion, exclusionary zoning policies, and the limited availability of transit alternatives had increased the dependency on cars and the total vehicle miles traveled in the region. Although metro Atlanta had added more road capacity than any other metro region in the country, all these factors had overwhelmed that capacity, and traffic congestion had gotten worse. The report also pointed out that while all related agencies in Atlanta worked to relieve congestion, there was no agreed-on regional target for congestion relief that drove the planning process. Therefore, it called for empowering

> one regionally focused agency with integrated responsibility for planning, resource allocation/authority, and monitoring of implementation for all forms of transportation in the Atlanta region to achieve a stronger alignment of authority and accountability for meeting regional transportation system aspirations.[34]

Governor Roy Barnes, elected in November 1998, quickly adopted MATI's recommendations and proposed the creation of GRTA. The resulting bill was steered through the Georgia General Assembly in the 1999 legislative session so forcefully and swiftly that no serious opposition formed, although many of the state representatives and senators were from districts in which county commissioners and mayors would be strongly opposed to any interference in their home-rule prerogatives.[35]

The Structure and Powers of GRTA

The GRTA legislation stipulated a fifteen-member board, all appointed by the governor. From the beginning, it was quite clear that an overwhelming majority of the board members would be representatives of the metro Atlanta business community, and indeed, only three were not (one community activist, one professor, and one environmentalist).

Granted large direct and indirect powers, GRTA was given authority over all transportation projects in the thirteen counties (the ARC's ten plus three adjacent ones) that had been declared in nonattainment by the EPA, and it has the authority to plan, coordinate, or directly operate transit systems in its jurisdiction. It does not have direct land use planning authority—that would require a risky attempt to amend the state constitution—but it can influence planning and zoning through its authority to withhold state and federal funds from counties and municipalities that do not comply with its standards. The broad authority of this "superagency" has caused some apprehension, especially among leaders of the wealthy northern metropolitan counties who are particularly sensitive to any signs of interference with their planning authority and its implications for economic growth.

To diminish this apprehension, GRTA has taken a cautious approach. In December 1999, Executive Director Catherine Ross stressed that GRTA would not "dictate to local governments or other agencies about how they should grow and how people get around." It would "avoid pitting cities against suburbs and car commuters against transit riders," and it "won't evolve into the big, bad actor that many are worried about. Instead GRTA wants to step in to fill gaps left by other agencies . . . [such as the ARC and GDOT]."[36] GRTA policies have, however, gotten somewhat more decisive, as in the example of its board's decision to link the amount of state funding a local government receives for transportation to its acceptance of GRTA's mass-transit and dense land use policies, and these "impositions" are resented by some local governments.[37]

While the GRTA board has broad powers and autonomy legally, its policy decisions are largely beholden to the political will of the governor, as is perhaps most signally illustrated by the "Northern Arc." The GRTA board approved a long-term Regional Transportation Plan (RTP) in 2000 and a three-year Transportation Improvement Program (TIP) in 2002. Both the RTP and the TIP heavily favor building and improving alternative transportation systems for mass transit, bikes, and pedestrians along the lines of ISTEA and TEA-21, but among the proposed investments there is also the highly controversial Northern Arc project—a highway that would connect metro Atlanta's northeastern and northwestern exurbs. The Northern Arc was placed in the RTP, and the funding process was hastened by GRTA[38] despite the fact that it was heavily criticized for enabling further sprawl in the region in editorials of the *Atlanta Journal-Constitution* time and again (for example, "Northern Arc would do one thing: Enable sprawl"[39]), and that a coalition of environmentalists and suburban neighborhood associations was strongly opposed it.[40] The governor and GRTA present the Northern Arc as a solution to sprawl (and, of course, it may be a sop to his supporters among developers).

Conclusions

GRTA's success in curbing sprawl in metro Atlanta is yet to be determined. Its current structure and functions may also evolve into different ones. One possible future direction of GRTA's development is that it turns into a more comprehensive regional government, such as Portland's Metro. In its 2001 session, the Georgia General Assembly, once again heeding the advice of the Metro Atlanta Chamber of Commerce,[41] created another regional board—the Metropolitan North Georgia Water Planning District (MNGWPD)—to address water problems within sixteen metro area counties. In the long term, a regional government structure may emerge from a merger of these two and, say, the ARC in the manner that Portland's Metro emerged from the merger of a voluntary association of local governments and a metropolitan service district.[42] To judge by a lead editorial in the *Atlanta Journal-Constitution* advocating a "metro council" modeled after Portland's Metro, this idea had gained some currency even before the creation of the MNGWPD.[43]

On the other hand, of course, strong opposition from local jurisdictions may render GRTA and the MNGWPD nonfunctional or dysfunctional. County leaders' grumbling about GRTA's "power grab" has already been in the news, as mentioned previously. This opposition may effectively stymie regional solutions to the metro area's problems.

In the face of the opposition from local governments, the regional smart-growth orientation of the business leaders is, perhaps ironically, a progressive one. They have recognized and articulated that improved quality of life is the chief criterion for economic growth in this era, and only they seem to be capable of providing concerted leadership in the area. Environmental groups have not been very effective in grassroots organizing and mobilizing, although they have shown some signs of strength in the recent Northern Arc controversy. In a loose coalition with some neighborhood groups and local politicians, they forced the governor to suspend the building of the road, at least temporarily.[44]

The general public is at best ambivalent about regional solutions, particularly regional mass transit. On the one hand, there is increasing public support for mass-transit alternatives. A poll conducted by the U.S. Conference of Mayors and the Mortgage Bankers Association in seven booming metropolitan areas—Atlanta, Boston, New Orleans, Phoenix, St. Louis, San Jose, and Washington, D.C.—shows that substantial majorities of people support using public dollars for improving public transportation and that they would be willing to take smaller homes for a reduced commute time.[45] On the other hand, people in metro Atlanta still love their cars, and the "not-in-my-backyard" (NIMBY) phenomenon is strong indeed. When MARTA announced its plans to extend its rail lines in 1999, neighborhood groups in northern DeKalb County—one of the two metro counties with MARTA rail lines and otherwise the most liberal and transit-friendly county in the region—organized strong opposition against the plans.[46]

Since it is not likely for there to be a progressive grassroots coalition representing the whole region, the business elite is bound to play a progressive role in cultivating regional solutions. But that does not guarantee success; its skills in building regional coalitions will determine the outcomes. Stone points out that the business elite of the city of Atlanta were forced to acknowledge that they needed the support of African American groups in the 1960s and forged a coalition with them.[47] The political economy and demographics of metro Atlanta have changed substantially since the 1960s. Suburbs have attracted new businesses, and their populations increased at much faster rates than the city's (in fact, the population of the city declined after 1970 until the late 1990s). New centers of business power emerged in the suburbs, and the traditional business elite of the city, although still powerful, had to take this new regional reality into account.[48] Today's business elite, now regional in nature, acknowledges the need to collaborate not only with its own members but also with local jurisdictions throughout the metro area. Hence, the question is whether a larger, more diverse group, such as the Metro Chamber, can play as forceful a role in the region as the closely knit elite of CAP were able to play in the city.

The regional scope of the economy in metro Atlanta has also affected race relations. While African Americans constitute the majority of the electorate in the city (about 68 percent as of 2000), they represent less than 27 percent of the metro area. During the 1990s, the long-standing rift between the black city and white suburbs was accentuated by the behavior of Atlanta Mayor Bill Campbell, who was criticized for ethical impropriety by the African American editors of the *Atlanta Journal-Constitution* and who refused to attend ARC board meetings beginning in May 1999. The newly elected mayor, Shirley Franklin, a businesswoman and former member of the GRTA board, not only took actions to ensure ethical functioning in city government but also began attending the ARC meetings, which is welcomed by the ARC executive director as a sign of the city's recognition of its place in the region.[49] This may be a sign of a new relationship between the city and suburbs.

As a final and further encouraging point, we must note that the role the Atlanta area business leaders have played in creation of GRTA and are likely to play in the future is not unique. It is illustrative of larger trends in metropolitan areas. Rusk observes that while religious leaders, universities, grassroots activists, and business communities have all been involved in attempts to solve metropolitan problems, his examples from different metropolitan areas in the United States show that among these four groups, the business community is by far the most effective in influencing legislation for regional solutions.[50]

Rusk points out, "Business leaders are practically the only natural constituency for regionalism. Business groups tend to think in terms of economic regions and labor market areas."[51] He also observes that the nature of the leadership among local businesses has changed. Like Molotch, he points out that leaders come from businesses that are more dependent on the local market—the gas, electric, and telephone companies; locally owned banks; local newspapers; and local hospitals—the land-based concerns.

These business leaders today do not have that much power individually or as a small clique, as was much the case in the city of Atlanta's urban regime, and they therefore have to build and work in larger-scale coalitions. Accordingly, the future of regionalism in Georgia seems to depend on the coalitions the metro Atlanta business leaders will be able to build. And it remains to be seen whether they succeed in maintaining an operative smart-growth machine and, even further down the horizon, creating a regional regime.

Notes

1. Richard Lacayo, "The Brawl over Sprawl," *Time,* March 22, 1999, 42–48.
2. *Atlanta Journal-Constitution* (hereafter *AJC*), June 3, 2002.
3. Alan Ehrenhalt, "The Czar of Gridlock: Can Roy Barnes Save Atlanta?" *Governing,* May 1999, 20–27.
4. GRTA is pronounced "Greta."
5. Dennis R. Judd and Todd Swanstrom, *City Politics: Private Power and Public Policy* (3rd ed.) (New York: Longman, 2002), 1–12.
6. Bernard H. Ross and Myron A. Levine, *Urban Politics: Power in Metropolitan America* (6th ed.) (Itasca, Ill.: F. E. Peacock, 2001), 10.
7. Robert S. Lynd and Helen M. Lynd, *Middletown* (New York: Harcourt, Brace, 1929), and Floyd Hunter, *Community Power Structure* (Garden City, N.Y.: Anchor Books, 1963 [originally published in 1953]).
8. Robert A. Dahl, *Who Governs? Democracy and Power in an American City* (New Haven, Conn.: Yale University Press, 1961); Nelson W. Polsby, *Community Power and Political Theory* (New Haven, Conn.: Yale University Press, 1963).
9. Clarence N. Stone, *Regime Politics: Governing Atlanta, 1946–1988* (Lawrence: University Press of Kansas, 1989).
10. Harvey L. Molotch, "The City as a Growth Machine," *American Journal of Sociology* 82 (September 1976): 309–31.
11. John R. Logan and Harvey L. Molotch, *Urban Fortunes: The Political Economy of Place* (Berkeley: University of California Press, 1987).
12. Charles Rutheiser, *Imagineering Atlanta: The Politics of Place in the City of Dreams* (London: Verso, 1996), 20.
13. Howard L. Preston, *Automobile Age Atlanta: The Making of a Southern Metropolis* (Athens: University of Georgia Press, 1979), 56.
14. Ronald H. Bayor, *Race and the Shaping of Twentieth-Century Atlanta* (Chapel Hill: University of North Carolina Press, 1996), 188.
15. Preston, *Automobile Age Atlanta,* 61.

16. Stone, *Regime Politics,* 16.
17. Bayor, *Race and the Shaping of Twentieth-Century Atlanta,* 23. (This decision applied the Supreme Court's 1944 decision on Texas in *Smith v. Allwright* to Georgia.)
18. Stone, *Regime Politics,* 19–21.
19. Stone, *Regime Politics,* 32.
20. Edward Weiner, *Urban Transportation Planning in the United States: An Historical Overview* (rev. and exp. ed.) (Westport, Conn.: Praeger, 1999), 27–29.
21. Stone, *Regime Politics,* 82.
22. Bayor, *Race and the Shaping of Twentieth-Century Atlanta,* 61.
23. Stone, *Regime Politics,* 59 ff.
24. Stone, *Regime Politics,* 100.
25. Stone, *Regime Politics,* 192.
26. *AJC,* September 13, 1999.
27. Regional Business Coalition of Metro Atlanta, 1998.
28. For classifications, see Weiner, *Urban Transportation Planning in the United States,* 169.
29. *AJC,* September 14, 2000.
30. September 14 and December 19, 1997.
31. Rebecca Poynor Burns, "Is Traffic Killing Atlanta?" *Atlanta,* January 1998, 60–66.
32. Brian Trelstad, "Georgia Regional Transportation Authority: A Case Study of an Innovative Regional Planning Institution," *Berkeley Planning Journal* 14 (2000): 23–45.
33. *AJC,* December 28, 1998.
34. *AJC,* December 28, 1998.
35. *AJC,* February 8, 1999.
36. *AJC,* December 14, 1999.
37. *AJC,* May 3, 2000.
38. *AJC,* February 8, 2002.
39. *AJC,* December 5, 2001.
40. *AJC,* March 4, 2002.
41. *AJC,* December 11, 2000.
42. David Rusk, *Inside Game/Outside Game: Winning Strategies for Saving Urban America* (Washington, D.C.: Brookings Institution Press, 1999), 153–77.
43. *AJC,* October 23, 2000.
44. *AJC,* July 11, 2002.
45. *AJC,* July 11, 2002.
46. *Community Review* (Decatur, Ga.), April 22, 1999.
47. Stone, *Regime Politics.*
48. Arnold Fleischmann, "Atlanta: Urban Coalitions in a Suburban Sea," in *Big City Politics in Transition,* ed. H. V. Savitch and John Clayton Thomas (Newbury Park, Calif.: Sage), 87–114.
49. *AJC,* January 11, 2002.
50. Rusk, *Inside Game/Outside Game,* 277–315.
51. Rusk, *Inside Game/Outside Game,* 296.

Index

Italicized pages refer to tables and illustrations.

About the Contributors

Hugh Bartling is an assistant professor of political science at the University of Central Florida. He teaches courses on public policy, environmentalism, urban studies, and political theory. He has published articles and book chapters on a number of subjects, including New Urbanism, cinema and the city, and critical approaches to the study of urbanism.

H. William Batt is a political scientist who has made a living as a university professor, staff policy analyst (on taxes) for the New York State Legislature, and a consultant to governments and nonprofit organizations. His current work focuses on public budgeting and finance consistent with sustainable development, such as using fiscal policies to foster sound policies on transportation, land use, and environmental matters.

Michele Byers is an assistant professor at Saint Mary's University in Halifax, Nova Scotia, where she teaches sociology, media studies, cultural studies, and women's studies. She wrote her doctoral thesis on *Buffy the Vampire Slayer* and performance. Currently, she is working on a variety of projects in such areas as Degrassi and the construction of Canadian identity, third-wave feminism, and the popular culture of disaster.

Milton Curry is an associate professor of architecture and theory in the Department of Architecture at Cornell University. Curry's scholarship explores the relationships among architecture, culture, and cultural identity. His interdisciplinary construct of culture broadly engages economic theory and urban planning paradigms and examines the role of architectural space in shaping identities and how that role differs from those of literature, cultural studies, and history. Curry teaches architectural and urban design studios and theory seminars, using anthropological, theoretical, and critical texts to study the human relationship to cities, and is preparing a book manuscript on the multivalent conditions of urbanism and racial theory. He is the cofounder/editor of the refereed journal *Appendx*, a venue for interdisciplinary scholarship in cultural theory and criticism.

Wende Vyborney Feller teaches in the Executive MBA program at St. Mary's College in Moraga, California. Since earning her doctorate in speech-communication from the University of Minnesota, she has provided communication consulting as well as teaching at a number of colleges. She lives, with husband and cats, in a traditional small town in the San Francisco Bay Area and is working on a project on perceptions of California's Central Valley.

Ronald Hayduk teaches political science at the Borough of Manhattan Community College of the City University of New York. He is a coeditor and contributing author of *Democracy's Moment: Reforming the American Political System in the Twenty-First Century* (Rowman & Littlefield, 2002) and coeditor and contributing author of *From ACT UP to the WTO: Urban Protest and Community Building in the Era of Globalization* (Verso, 2002). Hayduk has also contributed essays included in *Leftist Movements in the 20th Century,* edited by John Berg (Rowman and Littlefield, 2002); *In Defense of the Alien,* edited by Lydio Tomasi (Center for Migration Studies, 2000); the Aspen Roundtable website (www.aspenroundtable.org, 2000); *Mobilization: The International Journal of Research and Theory about Social Movements, Protest, and Collective Behavior* (San Diego State University, 1998); and public affairs magazines.

Mark Lapping is a professor of public policy at the Muskie School at the University of Southern Maine in Portland. Previously he served as founding dean of the Bloustein School of Planning and Public Policy at Rutgers University and founding director of the School of Rural Planning and Development at the University of Guelph in Ontario. He is the author/editor of eight books, many articles, and monographs and consults throughout North America and Europe.

Matthew J. Lindstrom teaches political science at Siena College in Loudonville, New York, and serves as director of the Program for Sustainable Land Use. He is coauthor of *The National Environmental Policy Act: Judicial Misconstruction, Legislative Indifference, and Executive Neglect* (Texas A&M

University Press, 2001). He has contributed essays to *Redefining Suburban Studies: Searching for a New Paradigm,* edited by Daniel Rubey and Barbara Kelly (Westport, CT: Greenwood Press, forthcoming), and to *Environmental Policy: Cases in Managerial Role-Playing,* edited by Robert P. Watson, Dwight Conrad Kiel, and Steven Robar, in addition to several journal articles.

Göktuğ Morçöl is an associate professor at Kennesaw State University. He is a coeditor of *New Sciences for Public Administration and Policy* (Chatelaine Press, 2000) and the author of *A New Mind for Policy Analysis: Toward a Post-Newtonian and Postpositivist Epistemology and Methodology* (Praeger, 2002). His research interests are complexity theory applications in public policy and administration and regional governance.

Josh Protas is a public historian who grew up in the shadow of the Phoenix Mountain Preserves, a place where he enjoyed hiking frequently. He now lives in Tucson, Arizona, with his wife, Abigail; son Eli; and dog Matilda. He serves as the executive director of the Historic Stone Avenue Temple.

Amanda Rees is a visiting assistant professor in the Department of Geography and Recreation at the University of Wyoming. Her present research interests include an analysis of historical and contemporary British and American utopian built space. She is presently researching two contemporary architectural and planning movements: the Urban Village movement in the United Kingdom and New Urbanism in the United States. She is also interested in the relationships between culture, landscape, and region in the American West and is presently editing *The Great Plains,* part of the American Regional Cultures series.

Patricia E. Salkin is associate dean and director of the Government Law Center of Albany Law School, where she also holds the title of professor of government law. She has written and lectured extensively on the subjects of smart growth and state statutory land use reform, regionalism in land use planning, and intermunicipal cooperation in land use planning and zoning. She is the author of the three-volume treatise *New York Zoning Law & Practice* (West Group) and editor of *Trends in Land Use Law from A to Z: Adult Uses to Zoning* (American Bar Association, 2001).

Lydia Savage is an assistant professor of geography and anthropology at the University of Southern Maine. She has authored numerous publications concerning the relationship between economics and geography and has received a U.S.M. Faculty Senate Award for Excellence in Teaching.

Bethany Stich is currently working on her Ph.D. in public administration at the Center for Public Administration and Policy at Virginia Polytechnic and State University. She received her Master of Public Administration from Kennesaw State University. Professionally, she has worked for the Georgia Department of Transportation in environmental compliance.

Ulf Zimmermann teaches public administration and an occasional seminar on sprawl in the MPA Program of the Department of Political Science and International Affairs at Kennesaw State University in Atlanta. He has a Ph.D. from the University of Texas at Austin and has written on various cities.